UNDERSTANDING & USING
CHALLENGING
EDUCATIONAL THEORIES

Sara Miller McCune founded SAGE Publishing in 1965 to support the dissemination of usable knowledge and educate a global community. SAGE publishes more than 1000 journals and over 800 new books each year, spanning a wide range of subject areas. Our growing selection of library products includes archives, data, case studies and video. SAGE remains majority owned by our founder and after her lifetime will become owned by a charitable trust that secures the company's continued independence.

Los Angeles | London | New Delhi | Singapore | Washington DC | Melbourne

2ND EDITION

UNDERSTANDING & USING
CHALLENGING
EDUCATIONAL THEORIES

KARL AUBREY &
ALISON RILEY

SAGE

Los Angeles | London | New Delhi
Singapore | Washington DC | Melbourne

Los Angeles | London | New Delhi
Singapore | Washington DC | Melbourne

SAGE Publications Ltd
1 Oliver's Yard
55 City Road
London EC1Y 1SP

SAGE Publications Inc.
2455 Teller Road
Thousand Oaks, California 91320

SAGE Publications India Pvt Ltd
B 1/I 1 Mohan Cooperative Industrial Area
Mathura Road
New Delhi 110 044

SAGE Publications Asia-Pacific Pte Ltd
3 Church Street
#10-04 Samsung Hub
Singapore 049483

Editor: James Clark
Senior assistant editor: Diana Alves
Production editor: Nicola Carrier
Copyeditor: Diana Chambers
Proofreader: Thomas Bedford
Indexer: Gary Kirby
Marketing manager: Dilhara Attygalle
Cover design: Naomi Robinson
Typeset by: C&M Digitals (P) Ltd, Chennai, India

Library of Congress Control Number: 2020933930

British Library Cataloguing in Publication data

A catalogue record for this book is available from
the British Library

ISBN 978-1-5297-0349-8
ISBN 978-1-5297-0348-1 (pbk)

CONTENTS

ABOUT THE AUTHORS

Karl Aubrey is a Visiting Tutor on the Professional Studies in Education programmes at Bishop Grosseteste University. Prior to this, Karl was the Programme Leader for a range of initial teacher education and professional development programmes at a large city further education college. Between 2003 and 2005 he was seconded to the DfES Standards Unit as a learning and teaching practitioner in the East Midlands. Karl has contributed to the *Oxford Dictionary of Education*. His doctoral thesis explored the reforms in further education teacher education from 2000 to 2010, from the viewpoint of teacher educators. Karl's research interests include inclusion, education policy, pedagogy and work-based learning.

Alison Riley is the Programme Leader for the BA (Hons) Early Childhood Studies degree at Bishop Grosseteste University. She has also worked on a number of educational-related programmes at the university, including initial teaching training courses. Prior to joining Bishop Grosseteste University, Alison spent sixteen years working in primary education as a classroom teacher, deputy head teacher and finally head teacher of a large junior school. Alison has been involved in a number of collaborative projects and has recently been involved in an EU-funded project researching 'Creativity in Early Science and Mathematics Education'. Alison has recently commenced doctoral studies in which she is researching the journey of students entering higher education with alternative qualifications.

ACKNOWLEDGEMENTS

SAGE would like to thank the following people whose comments helped to shape the first and second editions of this book:

Shirley Allen, Middlesex University;

Catherine Ashdown, Canterbury Christ Church University;

Lynn Boyle, University of Dundee;

Tarisai Chikomba, Anglia Ruskin University;

Stephen Dixon, Newman University;

Alex Kosogorin, Nottingham Trent University;

Janet Lord, Manchester Metropolitan University;

Karan Vickers-Hulse, University of the West of England.

NEW TO THIS EDITION

This second edition brings three new chapters, which follow the same format as the first edition, on the works of the following key educational thinkers: Ivan Illich (Chapter 6), Loris Malaguzzi (Chapter 9) and Michael Apple (Chapter 12). The Introduction has been expanded to offer an overview of the particular themes of challenging educational thought, and each chapter has a glossary of the key words that are pertinent to that theorist's work. All chapters have been reviewed and revised, with new references and expansions to existing sections taking discussions and critical commentary further.

INTRODUCTION

WHY A BOOK ABOUT THEORISTS WHO CHALLENGE EDUCATIONAL THINKING AND PRACTICE?

This is a companion volume to our *Understanding and Using Educational Theories*, 2nd edition (2019) and, as such, aims to complement the theories already covered. Similar to our previous volume, the purpose of this book is to introduce students to theories and enable them to link theory with practice. The difference is that this book contains what could be perceived as *challenging* theories. This is our second edition of *Understanding and Using Challenging Educational Theories*; the first edition was published in 2017. We have used the word 'challenging' in an eclectic sense. For example, characters like Bourdieu, Foucault, Giroux, Bernstein and Mezirow could be considered challenging because of the supposed complexities of their ideas. Maslow, Rogers and Malaguzzi are quite established learner-centred educational thinkers, but this volume aims to explore the wider aspects of the thinkers and explore other features of their work in addition to their well-known concepts. Neill, Holt, Illich and hooks are perhaps challenging in the sense of their radical approach to teaching and schooling (or, indeed, non-schooling). Stenhouse, Apple, Goodlad, Darling-Hammond and Noddings offer alternative ideas on the curriculum, schooling, teacher professionalism and moral education.

We contend, as we did in the last book, that current education policy and resultant practices are being ideologically driven with the object of competing in the global marketplace. Consequently, the principal purpose of education, to foster personal growth and fulfilment, is being neglected. This book adds to the breadth and depth of evidence from these contemporary theorists who counter the increasingly prescriptive and competence-based notion of education championed by educational policy-makers. As such, the book offers readers the opportunity to adopt a critically analytical approach to their understanding of education generally, schooling, teaching and culture that encompasses the learning process, both for adults and children.

We reiterate the point that this book is not intended as a comprehensive appraisal of each of the theorists' work; rather, it acts as more of an introduction into the way of their thinking and possible applications of their ideas. However, we argue that these theories, based upon empirical research, augment those of the previous book and allow where possible readers to challenge current policy and practice. The book provides a valuable foundation for students who wish to explore the theories in more depth; it also makes links between the different ideas of the educational thinkers. Finally, it is hoped that the book will provide food for thought about creating meaningful learning opportunities in practice.

We continued to find deciding which theorists to include problematic. Again, we sought opinions from colleagues and students, including postgraduate students, and finally considered that the conditions for inclusion would be that first, all thinkers should have a degree of 'challenge' in their ideas as we have explained, and second, we thought they should be reasonably contemporary. Finally, we wanted an international and cultural blend, and with diverse areas of focus. Therefore, we have included theorists from mainland Europe, Britain, North America, and Central and South America. Once more, grudgingly, we have omitted the older social reformers and the classical educational thinkers.

THEMES OF 'CHALLENGING' EDUCATIONAL THOUGHT: EDUCATION AS A PROCESS THAT EMBRACES SOCIAL JUSTICE

In our companion volume *Understanding and Using Educational Theories*, 2nd edition (2019), we were, for the most part, able to attempt to classify the ideas from the theorists into three broad psychological schools of thought about education. These schools of thought were behaviourism, constructivism and humanism. All three had, and still have, an enormous impact on advancing the theory of learning. The theories considered in this volume, however, add another distinct dimension to the theory of learning, as well as including aspects of constructivism, and particularly humanism. It will become evident that many of the ideas expressed here are, to some extent, incompatible with traditional and current educational practice; some of the ideas may be considered quite radical and even subversive in nature. These ideas can be termed radical, progressive or experimental. For the purpose of this book, it is contended that these terms are transposable in their use. Regardless of the term used and the particular themes they advocate, the thinkers included in the chapters of this edition all championed a student-centred approach to education, reinforced by a strong sense of democracy and social justice. For these theorists, education was an engaging, emancipatory, questioning and transformative process.

We will very briefly outline and match the theories with the particular themes of challenging educational thought later in the introduction, and of course in more detail in each of the chapters. It is fitting that we consider the influences that could have spurred their thinking, and then explore the themes involved at this early stage to give the reader context and a flavour of what follows. It is interesting, yet not greatly surprising, that the works of the majority of the thinkers we have included were researching and writing at a time of major changes in the world. The second half of the last century brought about seismic changes in the world order, which saw an upsurge in people crying out for a more just society. Europe was relinquishing its colonial responsibilities at a rapid pace and the Cold War focused people's minds regarding the threat of a catastrophic nuclear conflict until the fall of the Berlin Wall in 1991. The United States of America during this period witnessed the rise of the civil rights movement, calls for gender equality and mass protests against the Vietnam War. In the United Kingdom, it was not really surprising that the pinnacle of 'British state-sanctioned progressivism contained in the Plowden Report [1967] coincided with the decriminalisation of homosexuality and [the end of] capital punishment, [and] the legalisation of abortion' (Howlett, 2013: 4). These changes were in keeping with the social tolerance and openness of 1960s' Britain, and in particular Harold Wilson's Labour government (Howlett, 2013). Many of the ideas in this volume can be aligned with political thought – either a broad political alliance which challenged traditional educational thinking and policy, or by being unambiguously left wing.

As a word of caution, the themes included in the following pages are somewhat nebulous. There are instances where themes cross boundaries and even occasions where one thinker will encompass more than one theme within their work. Worthy of note here, though, is that many of these themes and the ideas involved can be linked back to John Dewey's notion of democratic education. With these limitations in mind, we offer our own thematic groupings:

- *Aspiration, self-actualisation, and the idea of multiple intelligences.* This theme, for the most part, follows a humanistic approach. Self-actualisation is very much a learner-centred concept, which was key to Maslow's work. It focused on learner autonomy and stressed the notions of creativity and dignity. The idea of self-actualisation and the importance of learners achieving their aspirations was also advocated by Rogers. In challenging traditional pedagogy, Rogers promoted the role of the teacher as the facilitator, encouraging pupils to develop the qualities of self-direction, empathy and acceptance. The conventional perception that intelligence was a single academic entity that could be measured by an IQ test was contested by Howard Gardner. He argued that there were a number of intelligences: linguistic, logical-mathematical, musical, bodily kinaesthetic, spatial, interpersonal and intrapersonal. The ideas in this theme questioned established classroom practice and enabled educators to reconsider the concept of intelligence.

- *Freedom in childhood and schooling, and freedom as practice.* The term 'freedom' is used frequently by progressive educational thinkers. There are, however, two aspects that are particularly relevant to this book: first, freedom related to the child; second, education as the practice of freedom. The first of these concerns the notion, espoused by A.S. Neill, of the free and self-regulating child, which was practised (and still is) at his Summerhill School. The concept of education as the practice of freedom promoted by bell hooks calls for educators to create a democratic environment by using what she calls 'engaged pedagogy', where teachers and students work in partnership, and where student dissent is welcomed in creating an equally liberating learning experience.

- *Unschooling and deschooling.* These two themes are quite far-reaching as they both come from the premise that schools are not the best places for children to learn. John Holt uses the term 'unschooling' to describe and promote the notion of home-schooling, where traditional teaching methods are discounted and, rather than follow a set curriculum, learning is focused on children's individual needs, where they learn at their own pace. Ivan Illich's idea of deschooling is similar but more radical in its purpose and resolve, in that it advocates that children should not be legally bound to attend school. Illich was particularly critical of school rituals that placed children in age-specific groups following a nationally sponsored curriculum, legitimised the primacy of the teacher and required children to attend full time. Both these notions also have an alignment with the thoughts of A.S. Neill, in that all three shared a vision of an alternative form of schooling; Neill, however, managed to set up his own progressive school at Summerhill.

- *Social class, reproduction and the relationship between power and knowledge.* The concepts here relate to the philosophical position that argues that social class affects differing educational outcomes. Bourdieu, for example, contested that the lower classes accepted social reproduction as they considered themselves subordinate to the upper classes, because they lacked the cultural capital of the dominant culture. In so doing, inequality is reproduced. This was similar to Bernstein's work, which aligns the inequalities of social class with his concepts of elaborate language codes – evident in middle-class children – and restrictive language codes – evident in working-class children. Both these thinkers' views are associated with Foucault's work concerning discourse, and the relationship between knowledge and power, to manipulate social control through educational policies, systems and practice.

- *Education renewal rather than reform, and renewed curricula.* This theme includes an eclectic range of thoughts, but collectively they advocate a complete renewal of educational thinking, instead of piecemeal reform processes. Central to this is the curriculum. This is exemplified in the work of John Goodlad who focused on creating a democratic education through his work on non-grading, teacher education and curriculum enquiry. These ideas are similar to Darling-Hammond, as well as

Apple's radical work on ideology and the curriculum. Nel Noddings wished to develop the curriculum which took account of the individual and personal needs of the learners. Perhaps the most significant curriculum scholar to challenge the traditional ideas behind curriculum design was Lawrence Stenhouse, who promoted the process curriculum rather than the objectives curriculum model. Bernstein also was very influential in relating social class inequalities to what he termed the classification and framing of the curriculum.

- *The notions of care, love and community involvement in educational practice.* It could be argued that this theme is closely connected to the first listed here, particularly the thoughts of Maslow and Rogers. Although this point is acknowledged, we contend that this particular theme is separate from the humanistic school of thought because of the wider social implications involved. From a feminist point of view, Noddings championed the notion of the caring teacher and how the ethics of such caring could help children develop a moral attitude. This in turn she thought could enable education to be the catalyst for the development of a caring society. Similarly, bell hooks considered that care and love should be important factors in the relationships between students and teachers. Key to this idea is the fostering of tolerance, human spirit, forgiveness and kindness. She also emphasised the importance of building trusting learning communities – communities that recognised and faced up to what people have in common, as well as what created differences. Malaguzzi and Illich stressed the importance of including the wider community in the educational systems to encompass the nurturing and cultural aspects of the learning process.

- *Critical and transformative pedagogy.* These two terms, for the most part, are comparable in their meaning. For those who advance critical pedagogy such as Henry Giroux and Michael Apple, it means that students should be able to comprehend the social composition and the source of the knowledge they come across. This is achieved by facilitating students to uncover the inequalities that exist, but are hidden, in educational systems and curricula. The purpose of critical pedagogy is to empower students by creating a democratic learning experience that advances social justice through active critical discourse. This is similar to bell hook's idea of engaged pedagogy. Jack Mezirow's concept of transformative, or emancipatory, pedagogy comes mainly from work and research in the adult education sector. This stressed the importance of personal experience and critical reflection on learners' own inherited beliefs to bring about changes in the way they think and engage with the learning process.

WHO WOULD FIND THIS BOOK RELEVANT?

We hope this book has a use and appeal for a variety of readers with an interest in education and learning, whether formal or informal. Our aim is that it will be of assistance in bridging the gaps between theory and practice, and in enhancing readers' own professional development. We also have a goal that it will enable students to advance their skills in critical analysis, synthesis and evaluation in their research and assignment submissions, regarding perhaps those thinkers they may have already been aware of, but need additional ideas and further reading on the subject. Furthermore, our desire is that it will be of benefit to both undergraduate, and, more than the first book, postgraduate students (many postgraduates wished they had been introduced to some of these *challenging* ideas). Once more our aspiration is that this book will be valuable for those who are concerned with all sectors of education from early years, to formal stages of schooling, to further, higher, adult and offender education, as well as informal education such as youth work. Again, this will include students on work-based degrees and their progression routes, as well as those undergraduates undertaking teacher education for all sectors of education – schools, further and higher education, and youth work. It is our hope that teachers and practitioners, whether studying or not for formal programmes, may find this volume of interest.

ORGANISATION AND STRUCTURE OF CHAPTERS

Chapters in the book are sequenced in an approximate chronological order, starting with Abraham Maslow and finishing with Linda Darling-Hammond. We have adopted this arrangement so that readers can follow how educational thinking has evolved over time, and in relation to the characters' focuses of concern. Furthermore, the sequence makes it possible for the reader to make links, not only between the theorists included here, but between other significant thinkers they may wish to explore further. We have avoided organising this book in a manner that places the thinkers into theoretical categories and themes, as we feel this is too simplistic and does not reflect the complexity and the multidirectional nature of many of their ideas; we consider that in their own way they are *challenging*.

Each chapter considers a particular theorist and follows a common arrangement of sections. First, the learning outcomes indicate what readers should be able to do having read the chapter; this is followed by a list of key words that are pertinent to the theorist's work. The Introduction aims to set the scene by outlining the significance and impact of the theorist's work, before briefly considering their biography. The next section explores the theories in greater detail and then links these theories with other educational thinkers. This is then followed by a critical examination of their ideas, based upon evidence from other theorists and other academic sources. The subsequent section offers suggestions for ways in which that particular theorist's ideas could be applied in the reader's practice. Then, ahead of the summary, readers are invited to reflect upon the chapter and complete a task which ventures to consolidate theory with their current or future practice. Following the summary, a glossary of the chapter's key words is included. Each chapter ends with suggestions for further reading which readers can follow for further in-depth study, as well as a list of references that have been cited in the chapter.

As we have noted, the opening chapter starts with Abraham Maslow's concept of the humanistic approach to education. Chapter 2 then goes on to Rogers's idea of learner-centred teaching. Chapter 3 focuses on Neill's freedom to learn in the quite radical environment of Summerhill School. Chapter 4 explores Goodlad's concept of schools and teaching from his North American point of view. Chapter 5 considers Bernstein's ideas on social class, pedagogy and the curriculum. Chapter 6 concerns Illich's theory of a deschooling society, while Chapter 7 looks at Bourdieu's theory of society from an educational viewpoint. Chapter 8 outlines Foucault's notion of power and control in education, whereas Chapter 9 examines the work of Malaguzzi and the Reggio Emilia approach to learning. Chapter 10 contemplates the notion of moral education in Noddings's thinking, and in Chapter 11 we look at Stenhouse's thoughts on linking the curriculum with theory, research and practice. Chapter 12 looks at the work of Michael Apple on ideology, knowledge, power and the curriculum, while Chapter 13 is an opportunity to consider the more radical aspects of critical pedagogy through an examination of the thoughts of Giroux. Chapter 14 investigates Gardner's ideas on multiple intelligences and in Chapter 15 we learn about Holt's idea of unschooling or home-schooling. Chapter 16 examines bell hooks's work on education as a practice of freedom. The ideas of Mezirow's transformational learning are reviewed in Chapter 17. Finally, Darling-Hammond's ideas for reforming schools and teachers are considered in Chapter 18.

USING THE BOOK

We have followed the previous book in suggesting how to use this book. There are a number of ways in which this book can be read. Perhaps you could read it as a whole entity where you start at the Introduction and finish at the end, which would offer you a sequential and chronological order of the theories as they evolve. However, it is suggested that it would be more beneficial if you chose the chapters and theorists that interest you, so you can begin to know or refresh your understanding of their ideas, to consider the criticisms of them and how they link to others, and how to apply their ideas in practice. Furthermore, you could track the links with other like-minded theorists, as well as use the References and Further Reading to delve deeper. We again also suggest that readers use the reflective tasks to consider and reflect on their ideas and practice, which hopefully will develop future practice and understanding. Regardless of the way you use this book, it is our deepest hope that it will help with your understanding of the ideas of these theorists, and add to your criticality for your practice and assignments.

REFERENCES

Aubrey, K. and Riley, A. (2017) *Understanding and Using Challenging Educational Theories.* London: SAGE.

Aubrey, K. and Riley, A. (2019) *Understanding and Using Educational Theories* (2nd edn). London: SAGE.

Howlett, J. (2013) *Progressive Education: A Critical Introduction.* London: Bloomsbury.

1
ABRAHAM MASLOW

THE THIRD FORCE IN PSYCHOLOGY

LEARNING OUTCOMES

After reading this chapter, you should be able to:

- understand the life and work of Abraham Maslow;
- define humanist theory in relation to human psychology;
- differentiate between basic needs and growth needs in humans, and recognise their importance in relation to healthy development;
- critique the work of Maslow;
- identify how Maslow's work can be applied to learning in adults and children.

KEY WORDS

Hierarchy of needs; self-actualisation; motivation; third force; humanism; deficiency need; growth need; transcendence.

INTRODUCTION

Abraham Maslow is perhaps one of the best-known educational theorists in the field of humanist psychology. Despite initially studying in the field of behaviourist psychology and having renowned behaviourist Harry Harlow as a mentor, Maslow quickly turned his attention to contributing to a new school of thought – **humanism** – believing this to be a more positive way of viewing people.

Maslow is best known for his **hierarchy of needs**, a diagrammatic representation of the physiological and psychological needs which humans must pass through on the path to **self-actualisation**. Maslow theorised that all humans aspired to be the best they could be, stating that 'What a man can be, he must be. This we call self-actualization' (Maslow, 1954 [1987]: 93). Maslow presented his ideas in the form of a pyramid, with physiological needs forming the base, followed by safety and security, love and belonging, and esteem needs. These he categorised as lower order needs, or **deficiency needs**, and he theorised that these must be met before a person could aspire to the **growth needs** at the top of the pyramid. By its very nature, the pyramid became less stable the further one ascended, thereby illustrating the importance of setting a firm foundation.

While Maslow was later criticised for the methods employed in developing his theory, particularly when defining what it meant to be self-actualised (see the 'Critiquing the theory' section in this chapter), it cannot be denied that he played an important role in encouraging a view of the whole person, taking account of all the factors required to develop a psychologically and physiologically healthy individual. O'Connor and Yballe (2007) observe that Maslow sought to build an appreciative understanding of human beings at their best and was instrumental in taking a positivist stance towards psychology at a time when the focus was traditionally based around what was wrong with the human psyche.

Leontiev (2008) sees Maslow as a visionary, and suggests that rather than being afraid of the mistakes he made, Maslow used these as a basis for continually developing and refining his theories. Leontiev (2008) suggests that this is why Maslow's work endures in the psychologies of today. Hoffman (2004) suggests that Maslow saw himself as a psychological pioneer, 'exploring new territories of human experience' (2004: 442). In his later years, Maslow turned his attention to management theory, supporting managers in the workplace to help motivate the workforce to increase productivity.

Maslow himself led a simple life. He maintained an interest in humanity up until his untimely death in 1970, sadly leaving behind a number of unfinished projects, but also a legacy which has endured to the present day.

ABRAHAM MASLOW, THE PERSON

It is unsurprising that Maslow spent a lifetime theorising on the conditions under which human beings thrived best, given his own difficult childhood experiences.

The eldest of seven children, Maslow was the son of Russian immigrants, Samuel and Rose Maslow. Maslow's parents were uneducated but hardworking people, who sought a better life economically for their children (Hoffman, 1992). However, Maslow's upbringing was not a happy one. Born in Brooklyn in 1908, Maslow had a poor relationship with his parents, he was at odds with his father for much of his childhood, and was documented to have loathed his mother, a relationship that was never reconciled. To further add to his unhappy and lonely childhood, Maslow's parents were Jewish immigrants and he found himself the target of antisemitic hatred, being the sole Jewish boy in his community; this increased his feelings of isolation and loneliness:

> I was a little Jewish boy in the non-Jewish neighborhood. It was a little like being the first Negro enrolled in an all-white school. I was isolated and unhappy. I grew up in libraries and among books, without friends. (Maslow, cited in Hall, 1968: 37)

Maslow, then, sought solace in the local library where he immersed himself in books, thus beginning a lifelong love of learning.

Maslow attended the Brooklyn Boys High School where he became an active member of several academic clubs, in addition to editing the school's Latin magazine and the school's physics paper for a year. Hoffman observes that, like many youngsters coming from a background of hardship, Maslow's early education experiences 'inexorably shaped his world view' (1992: 440) and saw him seeking an intellectual route that would ultimately lead to 'overcoming religious and ethnic prejudices to create a world based on economic justice and universal education' (Hoffman, 1992: 440).

Despite his animosity towards them, Maslow initially sought a route that would satisfy his parents, especially his father. Therefore, on leaving school, Maslow went on to study law at City College, New York. However, he struggled with his studies and after only three semesters transferred to Cornell University, before transferring back to City College and then proceeding to graduate school at the University of Wisconsin. During this time Maslow also married his first cousin, Bertha Goodman, against his parents' wishes. Maslow saw his marriage as giving him 'a feeling of love and belongingness' (Bayer and Mottarella, 2005: 814). This period also saw Maslow find an academic path which suited him better than law, and as he began to pursue the study of psychology, he also started to achieve much greater academic success. During his time at the University of Wisconsin, Maslow gained three degrees in psychology: a bachelor's degree in 1930, followed by a master's in 1931 and a doctorate in 1934.

Maslow was initially drawn to behaviourism, a strand of psychology that was prevalent at the time through the work of renowned psychologists such as Watson and Skinner. However, on transferring to the University of Wisconsin, he became influenced by the work of Alfred Adler and Harry Harlow, who later became Maslow's doctoral adviser, which led him to an interest in a more practical, socially orientated approach to psychology (Hoffman, 1992). Maslow began teaching at Brooklyn College in 1931, a role he continued in until 1951, when he became Chair of the Psychology

Department at Brandeis University, a position he held until 1969. During his time at Brooklyn College, Maslow carried out a pioneering study on women's sexuality, which built on his doctoral research examining dominance and sexual behaviour in monkeys' social orders (Hoffman, 2004). This was an early indication of Maslow's interest in human behaviour, since he posited that working on sex was the easiest way to help humanity, and argued that if he could improve sexual life by even 1 per cent, then he could improve the whole species (Hoffman, 2004).

Maslow's period at Brooklyn College also led him to encounter a number of influential and eminent European intellectuals who were immigrating to the United States, the most notable being Gestalt psychologist Max Westheimer and anthropologist Ruth Benedict. It was his observations of these 'two favourite mentors' (Hoffman, 1992) that led him to his ground-breaking studies of self-actualising people. This work was also influenced by the Second World War, since while Maslow himself was ineligible for the military draft, he was horrified by what he saw through the media, and was convinced that a better understanding of what motivated people would help to bring peace to the world. In a 1992 interview with Edward Hoffman, Maslow states:

> It was at this moment that I realised that the rest of my life must be devoted to discovering a psychology for the peace table. That moment changed my whole life. (Hoffman, 1992)

Throughout the 1940s, Maslow developed and refined his hierarchy of inborn needs, attempting to understand and explain human **motivation**. However, despite first proposing his theory of needs hierarchy in the 1943 paper 'A theory of human motivation', his findings were not formally published until 1954 when his landmark book *Motivation and Personality* was released, documenting fifteen years of theorising about human nature. Maslow's work at this time was ground-breaking since it offered a view of psychology that focused on the positive side of human nature rather than the negatives:

> The science of psychology has been far more successful on the negative than on the positive side ... it has revealed much to us about man's shortcomings, his illness, his sins but little about his potentialities, his virtues, his achievable aspirations, or his psychological health. (Maslow, 1954 [1987]: 354)

It was during the 1960s that Maslow's work gathered pace. He was elected as President of the American Association for Humanist Psychology in 1961 and published his second book on human needs, *Towards a Psychology of Being*, in 1962. Maslow found himself receiving accolades from colleagues and former students and was in demand from managers and entrepreneurs who saw the potential in his work for motivating the workforce.

Unfortunately, Maslow's work was interrupted in 1967 following a major heart attack, and despite having suffered with heart problems for most of his adult life, he suddenly found himself constrained by a lengthy period of convalescence. Maslow became increasingly frustrated by his slow recovery and had to put on hold future plans for research, lectures and travel; it was at this time that he began to think about his own mortality and 'began to ponder his career accomplishments and his unrealised goals' (Hoffman, 1992). Following his heart attack, Maslow relocated to the San Francisco Bay area with Bertha in the hope that the milder climate would help with his health problems. Although his health troubles persisted, Maslow continued to write, teach and consult. He died from a fatal heart attack in 1970 at the age of 62, leaving behind a lifelong legacy devoted to maximising human potential.

THE HIERARCHY OF NEEDS AND SELF-ACTUALISATION

Maslow is most well known for his hierarchy of human needs and his theory of self-actualisation which, according to Koltko-Rivera (2006), was one of his most enduring contributions to psychology. However, in order to fully understand the context of this work, it is useful to consider the influences behind this theory.

Maslow, along with other eminent humanist psychologists, including Carl Rogers, is credited with developing what was referred to as the '**third force**' in psychology. In looking for an alternative theory to the prevalent psychologies of the time – behaviourism and psychoanalysis – humanist theory was born with a focus on the positive side of human nature. Maslow saw behaviourism as the first force in psychology, with the emphasis on human behaviour being influenced and controlled by the manipulation of the external environment. Alongside this, he referred to psychoanalysis as the second force where human behaviour was controlled almost totally by internal, unconscious forces (De Marco and Tilson, 1998). Maslow rejected the idea that behaviour could be controlled by either external or internal forces; he felt stifled by the very nature of behaviourism and believed that 'humans were more than billiard balls on the pool table of life' (O'Connor and Yballe, 2007: 741). Instead, Maslow was keen to develop a theory that combined aspects of both behaviourism and psychoanalysis, but embraced an appreciation of human beings at their best, looking at the farthest reaches of human nature.

Humanist theory, then, has a focus on the healthy individual, rejecting in particular Freudian psychology, common at the time, which Maslow believed placed far too much emphasis on the unhealthy side of the human condition (Weinberg, 2011). Maslow set out a vision and purpose for his new psychology, stating that 'Freud supplied to us the sick half of psychology, and we must now fill it out with the healthy half' (Maslow, 1962: 7), thus commencing a life's work establishing the physiological and psychological human needs required for a person to function fully and productively. It is through this study that Maslow's hierarchy of needs evolved.

In developing his theory, Maslow focused his attention on psychologically healthy individuals; this marked a change from previous studies in which the focus was most frequently on damaged individuals (Weinberg, 2011). It also broke away from traditional thinking as Maslow sought to determine which factors brought about a state of good psychological health. Maslow was concerned with the factors that motivated people and identified two kinds of motivation: *deficiency motivation*, which demanded the need to reduce physiological tensions such as hunger or thirst, and *growth motivation*, which was concerned with the satisfaction of needs such as the need to be loved and belong. Maslow noticed that needs tended to fall into specific patterns, which he arranged into a hierarchy (see Figure 1.1); these needs he believed were inborn into everyone regardless of culture and were genetic in origin (DeMarco and Tilson, 1998). At the base of the hierarchy Maslow placed physiological needs such as sleep, rest, food, drink and shelter; this was then followed by safety and security needs such as feeling safe from harm, being secure in home and life, financial security and routine. Maslow proposed that once lower-level basic needs are met, then the human psyche naturally looks to satisfying newer and higher needs, stating that:

> At once other (and "higher") needs emerge and these, rather than physiological hungers, dominate the organism. And when these in turn are satisfied, again new (and still "higher") needs emerge and so on. This is what we mean by saying that the basic human needs are organized into a hierarchy of relative prepotency. (1943: 375)

Maslow identified that as people progress up the pyramid, the need for belongingness, love and esteem becomes more prevalent, and while these are still referred to as deficiency needs, they become more about personal growth, with individuals seeking acceptance and affection, as well as respect and personal esteem. Maslow identified good self-esteem as being

> soundly based on real capacity, achievement and respect from others ... satisfaction of self-esteem needs leads to feelings of self-confidence, worth, capability and adequacy of being useful and necessary in the world. (1943: 382)

While Maslow believed that most individuals are aspiring towards this feeling of good self-esteem and high self-worth, he also acknowledged that as an individual ascends the pyramid, the relative strength of each need is reduced (Snowman and Biehler, 2006), and at any point in the hierarchy an individual might stop striving towards a higher need if a lower-level need is activated.

Maslow theorised that these steps on the pyramid were important stages in a person achieving their growth needs and becoming self-actualised, which, for Maslow, was the pinnacle of the pyramid and, ideally, the ultimate goal of every individual. While Maslow placed self-actualisation at the top of the pyramid, he did not, however, consider it to be an endpoint; rather, he viewed it as an ongoing process with growth choices requiring risk and courage (O'Connor and Yballe, 2007). Maslow is well documented as stating that for most people the goal of self-actualisation will never be achieved simply because progress is all too often disrupted by a failure to

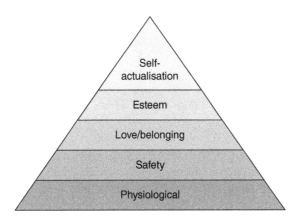

Figure 1.1   Maslow's Hierarchy of Needs (Maslow, 1943)

fully meet lower-level needs. Maslow suggested that only 1 in 100, or between 1 and 2 per cent of the population, become fully self-actualised, and this may partly be the result of society's tendency to reward motivation based on esteem, love and social needs – in which case, Maslow questioned where the motivation to become fully actualised was.

For individuals who are fully actualised, Maslow created clear, defining criteria, stating:

> Self-actualising people have a wonderful capacity to appreciate again and again, freshly and naively, the basic goods of life, with awe, pleasure, wonder, and even ecstasy, however stale those experiences have become to others. Thus, for such a person any sunset may be as beautiful as the first one, and flowers may be of breath taking loveliness, even after he has seen a million flowers. The thousandth baby he sees is just as miraculous a product as the first one he saw. He remains as convinced of his luck in marriage thirty years after his marriage and is as surprised by his wife's beauty when she is sixty as he was forty years before. For such people, even the casual workaday, moment-to-moment business of living can be thrilling, exciting and ecstatic. (1959: 43)

In essence, then, the self-actualised individual is not just fulfilled, having achieved everything he is capable of, but has also a feeling of euphoria, joy and wonder in every aspect of his life. While Maslow initially believed that self-actualisation would automatically follow all other needs, he revised this theory after identifying individuals who did not follow this pattern. In this respect, Maslow later typified self-actualisers as those who hold certain values such as truth, goodness, beauty, justice, autonomy and humour (Feist and Feist, 2001). It is such values that enable self-actualised people to stand apart from those who only meet their esteem needs.

Maslow continued to refine his hierarchy of needs, and while his original theory suggested that each tier of the pyramid must be successfully met before progressing to the next, Maslow later amended this, proposing that the hierarchy was 'not nearly so rigid as we may first have implied' (1954 [1987]: 77). Maslow attributed this to the fact that individuals themselves may place less importance on some needs than on others – for example, for some the importance of high self-esteem may be more important than the need for love and belonging. Furthermore, individual circum-stances might also influence the importance which an individual might place on a need.

In addition to revising the emphasis on each layer of the pyramid in the 1960s and 1970s, Maslow expanded the hierarchy futher by adding more growth needs. These he identified as cognitive needs, which he viewed as knowledge and under-standing, curiosity and exploration needs, and aesthetic needs, which he saw as an appreciation of beauty, balance and form. Maslow also began to question how far self-actualisation was suitable as a motivational capstone (Koltko-Rivera, 2006) and instead began to focus on the prominence of peak experiences, including mystical, aesthetical and emotional experiences. These he referred to as **transcendence** needs which he situated above self-actualisation, and which he saw as values that transcend the personal self. In his text, *The Farther Reaches of Human Nature*, Maslow defines transcendence as

> the very highest and most inclusive or holistic levels of human consciousness, behaving and relating, as ends rather than means, to oneself, to significant others, to human beings in general, to other species, to nature, and to the cosmos. (1971: 269)

Maslow referred to this shift in emphasis to a more transpersonal psychology as the fourth force in psychology which stemmed from influences from Eastern philosophies, emphasising meditation as a means of developing a higher level of consciousness, capturing phenomena such as epiphanies, peaks, revelations and transformative moments. However, Maslow abhorred the hippy culture of the time and was keen not to be associated with the mysticism prevalent in some areas of 1960s American culture (Hoffman, 2008). Instead, Maslow's later work saw a focus on personal mission, choice and self-investment (Leontiev, 2008), since he 'ultimately felt far more comfortable studying entrepreneurs and business organisations than mystics, sages and exalted states of consciousness' (Hoffman, 2008: 442).

↻ LINKS WITH OTHER THEORISTS

Maslow was a humanist in the truest sense; as such, links can be made with other theorists in the field of humanism such as Carl Rogers and Alfred Adler. Like Maslow, Rogers developed his own theory of self-actualisation; however, rather than basing his theories on personal views, Rogers used empirical evidence from his own clinical observations to develop his theory. Unlike Maslow, Rogers (1951) considered the obstacles to self-actualisation and looked at the characteristics of the fully functioning person when developing his own definition of self-actualisation. Rogers also looked at supporting the individual to help them achieve self-actualisation, whereas Maslow believed that this would happen automatically once all other needs had been met. Both Maslow and Rogers did, however, believe that gaining acceptance was far more important than gaining self-actualisation.

Maslow was heavily influenced by the work of Alfred Adler who, like Maslow, had also dismissed the work of Freud. Initially one of Freud's first disciples, Adler became one of the first dissidents of psychoanalysis, creating his own psychoanalytical school which he called 'individual psychology' to distinguish it from Freud's school (Chiriac, 2003). Adler was keen that when viewing humans, it should be done from a holistic perspective, rather than through bits of their personalities such as the id and ego. He also suggested that the physical and social environment were important factors in the development of the individual. Adler postulated that the driving force behind all human behaviour was the strive for perfection, which he saw as the desire to fulfil one's potential; it is not difficult to see the similarity here with Maslow's theory of self-actualisation. However, whereas Maslow saw this as being an individual endeavour, Adler believed that a driving force behind achieving one's potential was through social interest, and thereby achieving a sense of solidarity with humanity and the local community. This is in opposition to Maslow who saw the self-actualiser as one who could resist social conformity.

As we saw earlier in the chapter, Maslow's later work was seen to influence practice in business organisations, with managers looking to Maslow's theory to help motivate their workforce, with MIT management professor Douglas McGregor (1960) drawing from Maslow's work on human potential and the hierarchy of needs in his management text, *The Human Side of Enterprise*. Furthermore, links can be seen between Maslow's work and that of Frederick Herzberg (1964), who developed his own two-factor motivation theory related to satisfaction in the workplace, also referred to as Herzberg's motivation-hygiene theory. Herzberg sought to identify the factors in the workers' environment that caused satisfaction and dissatisfaction, suggesting that by eliminating the factors that caused dissatisfaction, an increase in work motivation would be achieved. Herzberg identified a set of hygiene factors, or maintenance factors, that were required before workers experienced job satisfaction. Herzberg's hygiene factors, including achievement, recognition, responsibility and advancement, run in parallel to Maslow's growth needs. It could be argued that Maslow's work was then the stimulus for Herzberg's theory.

CRITIQUING THE THEORY

Maslow was heavily criticised for the elitist elements in his theories, particularly in relation to those people he considered to be self-actualisers, which some believe to be unrepresentative of real individuals, living in real society with real jobs

(Pearson, 1999). Indeed, it could be argued that Maslow's work on self-actualisation was somewhat subjective, since his choice of subjects when defining the criteria for self-actualisation was very much based on his own personal observations and choice. It could be argued, therefore, that he had already selected his criteria and was looking to find subjects that formed a best fit to the observations he had already made.

The methodology used by Maslow when defining the characteristics of the self-actualised individuals was called into question since this relied largely on biographical analysis, and his sample size for making these generalisations was small in number, consisting of only eighteen individuals whom Maslow himself decided were self-actualised people. Drawing from people of esteem, such as Abraham Lincoln and Albert Einstein, and including his own mentors, Ruth Benedict and Max Westheimer, Maslow has been criticised for selecting only the most highly educated, and pre-dominantly white, males to develop his theory. As such, it is difficult to see where people from lower social classes or different ethnic groups fit into his theory.

A further criticism of Maslow's theory lies in the hierarchical nature of the needs, since if we interpret the hierarchy literally, then it would follow that only once the deficiency needs have been met can people strive towards high self-esteem and self-actualisation. However, if this were the case, it could be argued that artists such as Van Gogh, for example, may never have reached the heights of their creative endeavours, since the very fact that they lived in poverty for most of their lives should, according to Maslow, have stifled their creative ability (Tay and Diener, 2011). Similarly, it is quite possible that a person living in poverty may well feel tired and hungry, yet may still feel love and belonging.

O'Connor and Yballe (2007) suggest, however, that Maslow may well have been misrepresented and misunderstood, and they question whether the positive message that Maslow was trying to promote was undermined by too much emphasis on the invalid research methods employed. They suggest that Maslow did not intend to suggest that people move through the hierarchy in a series of stages, and in fact may well move between levels at different periods of their life.

APPLYING MASLOW IN PRACTICE

Maslow's work is eminently applicable in the classroom and, not surprisingly, it can frequently be seen reflected in a variety of teaching and classroom management practices in use today. Maslow himself did not set out to influence classroom practice, so it is testament to his work that his theory has been adopted in educational settings, albeit unconsciously in many cases.

As we have seen, Maslow's work centred on human motivation and the conditions required to maximise the human experience, including the desire to learn. At its simplest level, then, the role of the educator must be to ensure that everything possible is done to ensure that learners' physiological needs have been addressed, since 'even the most inspirational educator will not be able to reach a student whose lower-level needs are not being met' (DeMarco and Tilson, 1998: 93) and it cannot be assumed that a learner entering the classroom has already had these needs met.

In recent years in England, we have seen an increased focus on the holistic needs of the child, particularly for those children at the primary level of education. This was almost certainly prompted by the introduction of the *Every Child Matters* agenda (DfES, 2003), a green paper following the investigation into the abuse and subsequent death of Victoria Climbié. While the objectives of the paper were predominantly to ensure that child protection processes in England and Wales were strengthened, a further focus on five specific outcomes (be healthy, stay safe, achieve economic well-being, enjoy and achieve, and make a positive contribution) reflected strongly the deficiency needs as theorised by Maslow. All settings that held responsibility for children aged from zero to nineteen years were tasked with the challenge of meeting the holistic needs of their pupils through a range of initiatives that were designed to ensure that the basic needs of children were met, thereby ensuring that the foundations for learning were set. Such initiatives saw, for example, the introduction of breakfast clubs into schools, an increased focus on healthy and nutritional hot school meals, and extended school provision, to name but a few. While subsequent UK governments have failed to acknowledge the *Every Child Matters* agenda in its original form, the legacy of these initiatives has prevailed with a continued emphasis on the needs of the child being seen through more recent government policies, such as Pupil Premium and the introduction of the School Fruit and Vegetable Scheme (SFVS) which targeted pupils in the 4–6 years age range (NHS, 2015), and the provision of hot school meals for Key Stage 1 pupils in schools in England, both of which have essentially targeted vulnerable pupils and those from disadvantaged backgrounds.

While not directly linked to Maslow's work, it can be seen therefore that there is an increasing awareness that learning can be seriously compromised if deficiency needs are not met. However, it is perhaps more pertinent to look at needs further up the pyramid to consider how practitioners can more effectively influence student motivation through their own actions. Assuming that all psychological needs have been met, the next two tiers on Maslow's hierarchy are concerned with matters related to safety and belongingness and love. We need look no further than the physical layout of the learning environment and policies related to visitors in school to consider how these might promote the safety of the learner. Health and safety practices around the use of classroom policies can certainly contribute to both the child and family feeling confident in the physical safety of the child.

In early years settings, provision includes ensuring that each child has a key person in the setting who is responsible for their individual needs. The most recent Early Years Foundation Stage (EYFS) framework, applicable in England, makes clear that each child must be assigned a key person. Their role is to ensure that each child's care is tailored to meet their individual needs ... to help the child become familiar with the setting, offer a settled relationship for the child and build a relationship with the parents. (DfE, 2017: 22–3)

While the 'key person' concept is more reflective of the theories of Bowlby (1969), Ainsworth (1964) and, more recently, Elfer et al. (2003), there are also clear parallels with the safety and belonging needs theorised by Maslow. Indeed, the EYFS framework also makes clear the importance of developing a safe, suitable and appropriate environment, as well as attending to a child's health needs.

The importance of a child feeling welcome and a part of the classroom remains throughout the period of statutory education. Maslow (1987) theorised that belonging was an essential and prerequisite human need which needed to be met before one could ever achieve a sense of self-worth. Therefore, the role of the classroom practitioner should be to ensure that individuals develop a feeling of belonging – for example, through ensuring that children's views are heard, listening and responding positively to individuals, and being seen to act on their suggestions and opinions. On a wider scale, the development of school councils has been a positive move forward in allowing pupil voices to be heard, and in encouraging students to take a more active role in the development of the school community.

According to Maslow's theory, students are more likely to aspire to the growth needs at the top of the pyramid if their deficiency needs have been met; in contrast, a student who does not feel that their teacher cares about them or what they do is more likely to give up trying, feeling their efforts will not be appreciated (Snowman and Biehler, 2006). This emphasises the important role of the practitioner in ensuring that students feel supported in their endeavours; as suggested by DeMarco and Tilson (1998), students need to be told 'you've done a good job', otherwise their needs become frustrated and the student begins to feel inferior. At the same time it is essential that the practitioner creates a learning experience which sets an appropriate challenge for the learner, but which allows each to succeed at their own level. In this way the practitioner is assisting the learner in developing a feeling of self-worth and accomplishment.

A student who has developed a high level of esteem is, according to Maslow's theory, most likely to achieve self-actualisation or to maximise their potential, although, as we saw earlier, Maslow believed only a small number of the population will ever fully reach the top of the pyramid. It is also highly unlikely that self-actualisation will be seen within the educational setting since, in Maslow's theory, this is defined as the full use and exploitation of one's talents, capacities and potentialities (Maslow, 1954 [1987]), and in this respect it could be argued that the educational journey is preparation for self-actualisation, and only once the student has left formal education can their true potential be realised. If this is indeed the case, then the role of the educator becomes even more important in setting the developmental foundations for self-actualisation to be fully realised.

REFLECTIVE TASK

When defining self-actualisation, Maslow looked to the individual characteristics of people, including human centredness, sense of personal autonomy, dignity, spontaneity, creativity and solitude.

Do you think these values still hold true in the fast-paced world of today, when success is often measured by material resources, or do you think that Maslow's work is outdated?

SUMMARY

Maslow can be credited with putting human beings at the centre of psychology. At a time when the focus was on what was wrong with the human psyche, Maslow developed a theory that looked at the positive side of human nature. In so doing, he established a hierarchy of needs which is instantly applicable to any given situation, and which practitioners can use as a guide to developing practice and ensuring that individuals are given the best possible conditions for success to occur.

For Maslow, the key to his work was in establishing what it meant to be self-actualised, and while he identified that all humans had basic needs that were innate, such as hunger and thirst, he also acknowledged that self-actualisation was much harder to achieve. In defining what it meant to be self-actualised, Maslow chose people who he himself believed to be self-actualised and it is for this that his work received the most criticism, since its very nature showed a degree of subjectivity which made it difficult to generalise his concepts.

Nevertheless, despite this criticism, Maslow continued to develop his theories; he accepted that his methods had flaws and sought to find further ways of establishing his ideas, particularly around what motivates people. This led him to apply his works to management situations where he advised managers on how to motivate their workforce.

Maslow left a legacy that is still as applicable today as it was when he was alive. He applied a common-sense approach to psychology in a format that could be practically applied in most formal situations. Any theory that seeks to establish the most favourable conditions to promote the best in people must surely be one worthy of note.

GLOSSARY OF TERMS

Deficiency needs   Sometimes referred to as lower order needs, the deficiency needs formed the lower tiers of Maslow's hierarchy of needs and included physiological, safety, and love and belonging needs. According to Maslow, deficiency needs grew out of deprivation and when unmet were a motivating force.

Growth needs   Unlike deficiency needs, growth needs do not emerge from a lack of something, but rather from the individual's desire to grow as a person. Maslow referred to this as self-actualisation, which he situated at the very top of the pyramid. This, according to Maslow's early work, was the highest point that could be reached, although he later added to the growth needs so that cognitive and aesthetic needs were included, while above self-actualisation Maslow placed transcendence.

Hierarchy of needs   The hierarchy of needs is a five-tier model representing the needs that Maslow identified as being key to motivating human behaviour. Typically depicted as a pyramid, Maslow placed the deficiency needs at the bottom, while the growth needs were situated at the top of the pyramid. Maslow theorised that growth needs could only be met once the deficiency needs had been satisfied.

Humanism   Humanism is a theoretical framework that emphasises the whole person and the unique experiences and personalities of the individual. Maslow was a key figure in the development of the humanist theory which he developed in response to his perception of the limitations in the behaviourist and psychodynamic theories of the time.

Motivation   For Maslow, motivation arose out of the individual's desire to satisfy their growth needs. Maslow believed that growth needs created an internal pressure which impacted on human behaviour.

Self-actualisation   In his original theory, Maslow saw self-actualisation as the highest point an individual could achieve. This included realising one's potential, being personally fulfilled, and seeking personal growth and peak experience. Maslow saw this as 'becoming capable of everything one is capable of becoming' (Maslow, 1987: 64).

Third force   Maslow saw humanism as the third force in psychology since it arose as a result of some of the criticisms of behaviourism and psychodynamic psychology prevalent at the time. Third force psychology specifically focuses on the inner needs of the individual, including happiness, fulfilment and the search for an identity. Humanist theorists believed that these issues had been neglected by behaviourists and those who followed the teaching of Freud.

Transcendence   Maslow added transcendence to the top of the hierarchy in 1969, observing that this was a motivational step which reached beyond self-actualisation. Maslow believed this to be the highest and most inclusive level of human consciousness, with the individual living at the state of Being. This was assumed to be most likely for those individuals with a strong and free identity.

 # FURTHER READING

Goble, F.G. (2004) *The Third Force: The Psychology of Abraham Maslow*. Anna Maria, FL: Maurice Bassett Publishing.

A condensation of Maslow's ideas from his books and publications, presented in a user-friendly format.

King, P.W. (2009) *Climbing Maslow's Pyramid: Choosing Your Own Path through Life*. Leicester: Matador.
An examination of how individuals can use their life experiences to change the person they are, using aspects from Maslow's hierarchy of needs.

Maddi, S.R. and Costa, P.T. (2009) *Humanism in Personology: Allport, Maslow and Murray*. Piscataway, NJ: Transaction Publishers.
A summary of the works and their applicability to the development of personality.

McGuire, K.J. (2011) *Maslow's Hierarchy of Needs: An Introduction*. Norderstedt: Books on Demand.
Maslow's hierarchy of needs as applied to the workplace; an evaluation of how Maslow's work can motivate the workforce.

REFERENCES

Ainsworth, M.D. (1964) 'Patterns of attachment behavior shown by the infant in interaction with his mother'. *Merrill-Palmer Quarterly of Behavior and Development*, 10: 51–8.

Bayer, M. and Mottarella, K.E. (2005) 'Maslow, Abraham (1908–1970)'. In: Salkind, N.J. (ed.) *Encyclopaedia of Human Development*. London: SAGE.

Bowlby, J. (1969) *Attachment and Loss*. New York: Basic Books.

Chiriac, J. (2003) *Freud versus Adler. AROPA*. Available online at: www.freudfile.org/freud_adler.pdf

De Marco, M.L. and Tilson, E.R. (1998) 'Maslow in the classroom and the clinic'. *American Society of Radiologic Technologists*, 70: 91–4.

Department for Education (DfE) (2017) *Early Years Foundation Stage*. London: Crown copyright.

Department for Education and Skills (DfES) (2003) *Every Child Matters*. Green Paper. London: Crown copyright.

Elfer, P., Goldschmied, E. and Selleck, D. (2003) *Key Persons in the Nursery: Building Relationships for Quality Provision*. London: David Fulton.

Feist, J. and Feist, G.J. (2001) *Theories of Personality* (5th edn). Dubuque, IA: McGraw-Hill.

Hall, M.H. (1968) 'A conversation with Abraham Maslow'. *Psychology Today*, July: 35–7, 54–7.

Herzberg, F. (1964) 'The motivation-hygiene concept and problems of manpower'. *Personnel Administrator*, 27: 3–7.

Hoffman. E. (1992) *Overcoming Evil: An Interview with Abraham Maslow, Founder of Humanistic Psychology*. Available online at: www.psychologytoday.com/articles/199201/abraham-maslow

Hoffman, E. (2004) 'Abraham Maslow's life and unfinished legacy'. *Japanese Journal of Administrative Science*, 17: 133–8.

Hoffman, E. (2008) 'Abraham Maslow: A biographer's reflections'. *Journal of Humanist Psychology*, 48: 439–43.

Koltko-Rivera, M.E. (2006) 'Rediscovering the later version of Maslow's hierarchy of needs: Self-transcendence and opportunities for theory, research and unification'. *Review of General Psychology*, 10: 4, 302–17.

Leontiev, D. (2008) 'Maslow yesterday, today and tomorrow'. *Journal of Humanist Psychology*, 48: 451–3.

Maslow, A.H. (1943) 'A theory of human motivation'. *Psychological Review*, 50: 370–96.

Maslow, A.H. (1954 [1987]) *Motivation and Personality*. New York: Harper & Row.

Maslow, A.H. (1959) 'Cognition of being in the peak experiences'. *The Journal of Genetic Psychology*, 94: 43–66.

Maslow, A.H. (1962) *Towards a Psychology of Being*. New York: Harper & Row.

Maslow, A.H. (1971) *The Farther Reaches of Human Nature*. New York: The Viking Press.

McGregor, D. (1960) *The Human Side of Enterprise*. New York: McGraw Hill.

National Health Service (NHS) (2015) *School Fruit and Vegetable Scheme*. Available online at: www.nhs.uk/Livewell/5ADAY/Documents/SFVS%20Factfile%20Newsletter%20May%202015.pdf

O'Connor, D. and Yballe, L. (2007) 'Maslow revisited: Constructing a road map of human behaviour'. *Journal of Management Education*, 31: 733–58.

Pearson, E.M. (1999) 'Humanism and individualism: Maslow and his critics'. *Adult Education Quarterly*, 50: 41–55.

Rogers, C. (1951) *Client-centered Therapy: Its Current Practice, Implications and Theory*. London: Constable.

Snowman, J. and Biehler, R. (2006) *Psychology Applied to Teaching*. Boston, MA: Houghton Mifflin.

Tay, L. and Diener, E. (2011) 'Needs and subjective well-being around the world'. *Journal of Personality and Social Psychology*, 101: 354–65.

Weinberg, D.R. (2011) 'Montessori, Maslow and self-actualization'. *Montessori Life*, 23: 16–21.

2
CARL ROGERS

LEARNER-CENTRED TEACHING AND THE FULLY FUNCTIONING PERSON

LEARNING OUTCOMES

After reading this chapter, you should be able to:

- appreciate how Rogers's upbringing led to his development of psychoanalytical theories of development;
- recognise the impact of Rogers's work on the psychotherapy movement in America;
- understand Rogers's theory of self-actualisation when applied in educational settings.

KEY WORDS

Client-centred therapy; self-actualisation; facilitator; self-direction; unconditional positive regard; conditional positive regard; ideal self; congruence.

INTRODUCTION

Renowned psychologist Carl Rogers is best known for his work in the field of **client-centred psychology** and counselling. However, his influence has been far-reaching in sectors outside of clinical psychology, including in the areas of education and health (Smith, 2004), making him one of the most influential psychologists of the twentieth century.

Rogers had a diverse education, which saw him studying in the fields of agriculture, religion and education, before he finally settled on clinical and educational psychology as his area of specialism. It could be argued that this journey into the field of psychology exposed him to a range of influential ideals and philosophies, which ultimately led him to developing his own theory of client-centred therapy. Rogers was able to draw on the work of Otto Rank and John Dewey (through W.H. Kilpatrick) and, through linking together elements of their work, he took their notions of the human as a whole being capable of possibilities and applied his own therapeutic insight. From this, Rogers developed his own theory, which advocated the idea that the client usually knows better than the theorist in how to proceed with their treatment. At a time when psychologists such as Freud were trying to 'cure' the human psyche, this was seen as a revolutionary approach to therapy.

Rogers had a career that spanned over fifty years, beginning in child psychology as director of the Society for the Prevention of Cruelty to Children; he then undertook numerous roles working predominantly in the academic field. Rogers was able to use his roles in academia to undertake scientific research, an approach that Kirschenbaum (1979) suggests was still underutilised in the field of psychotherapy, possibly due to therapy still being in its infancy. It is perhaps for this reason that Rogers's work really resonated with other professionals.

Rogers published numerous articles and books in which he recorded his findings from the research undertaken; however, he is perhaps best known for his text *On Becoming a Person* (1961), in which he first set out his theory that people have the resources for self-healing and growth, which formed the basis for his client-centred therapy, later to become person-centred therapy. Rogers's theory was widely accepted in the field of therapy and was subsequently applied to other person-facing professions such as education and nursing. Smith (2004) suggests that Rogers was both an accomplished communicator and committed practitioner who was able to draw from his own experiences. It is perhaps for these reasons that his work was so widely accepted and enduring, along with the fact that his work had relevance to a number of professional fields.

CARL ROGERS, THE PERSON

Carl Ransom Rogers was born in 1902 in Oak Park, Illinois. He was one of six children born to Walter and Julia Rogers, a staunchly religious and uncompromising couple who could trace their lineage far back into US history (Thorne, 1992). Rogers's father, a college graduate of the University of Wisconsin, had already established himself as a businessman in the engineering field when Rogers was born, and his mother too had a college education and came from a family who 'had made notable contributions to the community and to the development of the new country over more than 300 years' (Thorne, 1992: 1). Thorne suggests, then, that Rogers was not a European emigrant like many of his contemporaries, but a 'genuine product of Midwestern America' (1992: 1).

Rogers was brought up in a Christian household, where the family were strict observers of the faith; as such, the emphasis was on family life, with close-knit family ties and strict adherence to a moral code. Rogers grew up, then, having little social life outside the immediate family, and even within this his social life did not extend to such frivolities as theatre visits, dancing or card games. Likewise, the drinking of alcohol was strictly prohibited. Rogers had a somewhat lonely childhood, perceived by his family as a 'sickly child who was prone to be over-sensitive' (Thorne, 1992: 2). He spent his formative years seeking solace in books, which Thorne believed served as the starting point to his scholarly endeavours.

Given his Christian upbringing, it is perhaps unsurprising that Rogers eventually opted to study theology at university, becoming convinced that his calling was to be a Christian minister. However, his journey to this calling was not straightforward, nor was it enduring. In fact, when he first became a student at the University of Wisconsin in 1919, it was to study the field of scientific agriculture, the result of time spent on the family farm where his father encouraged him and his brothers to take on responsibility for various ventures. It was at Wisconsin that Rogers became familiar with scientific methodology and learned about what it entailed to set up valid experiments (Thorne, 1992). Indeed, it seemed that the satisfaction he gained from this was in some way seen as a substitute for the human intimacy he so yearned for.

While Rogers's early ambition was to manage his own farm eventually using the most scientific methods possible, Thorne (1992) acknowledges that his experience of university was a period of profound personal change and development, which ultimately saw him changing his major from agriculture to religion. The turning point came when he joined a Sunday morning group for agriculture students and, influenced by the leader, Professor George Humphrey, Rogers began to see a world outside the family circle. This led to a reaffirmation of the Christian values he had grown up with and convinced him of a calling to the ministry.

Rogers's renewed interest in religion saw him move away from his evangelical upbringing into one that focused on the possibility of personal freedom. This was further affirmed during a visit to Beijing for the World Student Christian Federation Conference where Boeree (1998) observed that Rogers broadened his thinking to the extent that he began to doubt some of his basic religious views. We can see that Rogers had a somewhat ambiguous relationship with religion, and his ambition to enter the ministry was shaken once again following his attendance of a student-led seminar at the Union Theological Seminary, entitled 'Why am I entering the Ministry?' Rogers was later to comment that such a class should not be taken unless you want to change your career, and observed that most of the participants who attended 'thought their way right out of religious work' (Boeree, 1998).

Boeree (1998) observed that religion's loss was psychology's gain, as Rogers switched to the clinical educational psychology programme at Columbia University where he received his PhD in 1931. During his time at Columbia, Rogers undertook clinical work at the Rochester Society for the Prevention of Cruelty to Children, where he became influenced by the work of Otto Rank and John Dewey, through the work of W.H. Kilpatrick. Reflecting on their techniques and theories, Rogers was able to apply his own techniques to clinical psychology through his own clinical practice (this will be expanded on further in the next section of this chapter).

Following on from his tenure at Columbia, Rogers was offered a full professorship at Ohio State in 1940; here he found a certain amount of freedom, which he attributed to the fact that he had not had to work his way up through the university faculty, entering the academic world at professorial level (Thorne, 1992). While at Ohio, Rogers was able to undertake some lecturing but was also afforded the opportunity to write numerous articles, serve on committees and, perhaps most importantly, establish a 'practicum in counselling and psychotherapy' (Thorne, 1998: 11). He also published his first book, *Counseling and Psychotherapy* (1942), followed in 1951 by his renowned work, *Client-Centered Therapy* (1951), in which he outlined his basic theory (Boeree, 1998).

Rogers returned to the University of Wisconsin in 1957; however, this was not a successful move since he had returned at a time of great conflict in the Psychology Department (Boeree, 1998), and while he was able to carry out one of his major research projects there, he soon became disillusioned with higher education. Rogers did, however, publish his most influential work, *On Becoming a Person* (1961), while at Wisconsin, which 'catapulted him into the limelight and brought him more fame and influence than he could ever have hoped for' (Thorne, 1998: 11). It was the success of this book that gave Rogers the confidence to move out of established institutions, and accept a research position at La Jolla, California. Rogers remained there, giving speeches, providing therapy and writing, up until his death in 1987.

THE THEORY

Rogers could be viewed as a humanist theorist, having much in common with Maslow when considering the conditions needed by humans to grow and develop. However, Thorne observes that Rogers himself 'was highly suspicious of theories' (1992: 24), preferring to view himself as a pioneer, rejecting the idea of trying to apply theories to a situation, and instead working individually with his clients to identify what worked best for them.

Rogers is most well known for his work on client-centred therapy, in which he expounded the belief that therapy works best when the client is at the centre. The foundations of his belief are reflected in the fact that he used the term 'client' rather than 'patient', preferring not to think of the person as having a condition to be cured. Whereas contemporaries of Rogers, such as Freud, sought to establish what was wrong with the human psyche, Rogers based his work on the belief that people were essentially good and healthy. The therapist, according to Rogers, should be empathetic and non-judgemental, and should support the client in overcoming any personal challenges in their quest to reach **self-actualisation**.

Boeree (1998) suggests that Rogers's theory is both simple and elegant, being built on one single 'force of life', which he called *the actualising tendency.* DeRobertis explains that Rogers saw the actualising tendency as 'the innate tendency of the organism to develop all of its biological and psychological capacities in ways that serve to maintain or enhance itself' (2006: 179). For Rogers, the organism sought to increase its autonomy through lessening the influence of external forces, a tendency he believed to be present from birth. As the child develops through infancy, they seek more and more control over their environment, which is the early development of the 'self'; Rogers saw this as 'the capacity of the individual, in a growth promoting environment, to move towards self-understanding and **self-direction'** (1986: 128).

For Rogers, not only did the organism seek to maintain itself through its interactions within the environment, but it also sought to 'move towards the constructive accomplishment of its potential' (Thorne, 1992: 26). It is not enough to survive; to achieve satisfaction the organism must feel that it has maximised its own potential. Rogers recognised that this was influenced by the environment that the organism grew up in; an unfavourable environment would undoubtedly stunt the growth of the actualising tendency (Thorne, 1998).

Rogers suggested that people have two fundamental psychological needs: positive self-regard and self-actualisation. In order to achieve positive self-regard, Rogers believed that the human organism required love, affection and respect from others. However, he also identified two types of response to behaviour, which he classified as **unconditional positive regard** and **conditional positive regard**. In the case of unconditional positive regard, the developing organism receives positive affirmation from others regardless of how far their behaviour meets the expectations of those making the judgement, whereas in the case of conditional positive regard, praise and approval is only exhibited where the behaviour of the organism is compatible with the expectations of those making the judgement. For the developing child, the main caregiver is the most influential in supporting the development of positive self-regard, and through the early interactions and responses to certain behaviours Rogers observed:

> The parent who is able (1) genuinely to accept ... feelings of satisfaction experienced by the child, and (2) to fully accept the child who experiences them, and (3) at the same time to accept his or her own feelings that such behaviour is unacceptable in the family,

creates a situation for the child very different from the usual one. The child in this relationship experiences no threat to his concept of himself as a loved person. He can
experience fully and accept ... himself. (1951: 502)

To put this simply, the caregiver who provides unconditional positive regard and
demonstrates consistent interactions with the developing child is setting the foundations for the development of good positive self-regard, since the child will come to
view themselves as good and worthy of love (Rogers, 1951). On the other hand, the
child who experiences conditional positive regard and inconsistent parental interactions, whereby behaviour is often disapproved of, is likely to develop negative
self-worth, feeling they are not worthy of love. Rogers saw this as a threat to the
development of the self, since the child in seeking parental approval will moderate
and change their behaviour. Rogers suggested that where an organism denies and
distorts their own experience in favour of introjected values, then 'self-concept
becomes increasingly alienated from the organism' (1951: 505).

Rogers believed that a child who experiences positive self-regard is most likely
to develop the *real self* – that is, the person they were meant to become. However,
he also recognised that society was frequently out of sync with the actualising tendency (Boeree, 1998), in which case it was necessary for the organism to make
compromises. Rogers referred to this as the development of the **ideal self**, something he categorised as being not real, 'something that is always out of our reach,
the standard we can't meet' (Boeree, 1998). Rogers referred to the gap between the
real self and the ideal self as incongruity, and believed that the wider the gap the
greater the incongruity, which could lead to problems in later life, as the organism
became out of sync with itself.

Rogers had a firm commitment to the development of the healthy individual, which
he referred to as the *fully functioning person*. Rogers recognised that only a few could
aspire to this, since it required the individual to have experienced the most ideal environment for developing self-actualisation. Rogers saw the psychologically healthy
person as one who has 'been fortunate enough to live in contexts that have facilitated
the emergence of self-concepts which allow them to be in touch for at least part of
the time with their deepest experiences and feelings' (Thorne, 1992: 32). Nevertheless,
for those who had been fortunate enough to become a fully functioning person, he
identified five specific attributes, these being:

- *openness to experience* – an ability to listen to one's self and others, as well as an
  ability to experience what is happening without feeling threatened;
- *existential living* – to live fully in the present, being attentive to each moment as
  it is lived and trusting each experience rather than feeling fearful of it;
- *organismic trusting* – regarding experiences of what feels right as the most valid
  sources of information, to trust their own judgement rather than deferring to
  others;

- *experiential freedom* – to accept responsibility for determining actions and consequences;
- *creativity* – the sense of being a free agent, adjusting or adapting to changing conditions to produce creative ideas or to initiate imaginative projects.

(adapted from Thorne, 1998: 34)

Rogers believed that the fully functioning person was not trapped by the conventions of society. However, they are still able to take their place fully in that society, being neither ostracised nor seen as an eccentric or radical extremist (Thorne, 1992).

Rogers's theoretical observations came predominantly from his work with individuals in his client-centred therapy. Initially referred to as non-directive therapy, Rogers based his work on the notion that the client should direct the progress of the sessions, with the therapist taking on the role of **facilitator**. He later changed the name to client-centred therapy following his observations that the client still looked to the therapist as a guide. In this respect he believed that the client themselves should seek to identify what was wrong and determine their own conclusion (Boeree, 1998). Rogers identified three specific qualities which the therapist should demonstrate: **congruence**, empathy and respect.

While Rogers's enduring work was in the field of therapy, we will see in the following sections that many of his ideas can be applied to the field of education, particularly when considering the importance of creating the most favourable environments for self-actualisation to develop, which each individual should be aspiring towards.

LINKS WITH OTHER THEORISTS

Rogers was initally influenced by the work of Otto Rank, observing that a personal encounter with Rank revolutionised the way he thought about psychotherapy (Kramer, 1995). Formerly a pupil of Sigmund Freud, Rank disassociated himself from Freud's theory, which focused on a patient's past experience, and developed his own therapeutic process which specifically emphasised the interactions between therapist and patient. Rank also introduced action-oriented and reflective therapies into practice, including dramatic role play and psychodrama. Rogers developed Rank's patient-centred philosophy to establish his own client-centred therapy, although while Rank utilised artistic creativity to support his patients, Rogers developed his work around the therapeutic relationship of authenticity, empathy and **unconditional positive regard**.

Rogers's work can be linked to that of Abraham Maslow in that they both sought to study the positive side of human nature, looking for the good in people as opposed to trying to put right what was wrong. Like Maslow, Rogers believed that in order to be fully satisfied, a person must become self-actualised, or, in Rogers's terms, a fully functioning person. Maslow developed his theory around a set of needs to be met built on a hierarchy, in which self-actualisation was positioned at the pinnacle. For self-actualisation to occur, all needs on the pyramid must first be met. For Rogers, the self-actualising tendency was the key motive of the organism and was what drives the individual. In his writings, Rogers openly admits that the actualising tendency was not unique to his own theoretical viewpoint and notes the work of Maslow in his own reflections (Thorne, 1992).

In looking at Rogers's humanistic view on child development, parallels can be seen with his work and that of Karen Horney (DeRobertis, 2006). DeRobertis suggests that both Rogers and Horney made observations about child development through a reconstruction of their patients' childhoods. For both Horney and Rogers, the development of self is key to their theories of development, and while they differed in their conceptions of 'self', they both agreed that it was fundamental to the social and emotional development of the child.

When considering Rogers's views on education, parallels emerge with the work of John Dewey, particularly in respect of his focus on experience as a basis for learning. Rogers was influenced by Dewey's progressive view of education, which advocated the importance of a student-centred approach to learning. Both Rogers and Dewey were critical of an education system that stifled creativity and prevented the teacher from developing learning experiences that were informed by the pupil, believing that the child knew what he needed to learn and would direct his own learning accordingly. This, too, is in accordance with the work of John Holt who believed that formal education was stifling creativity and engendering a fear of failure into children. Rogers wrote: 'our educational system is suffering from many elements of a crippling sort ... the tangled web of law and bureaucratic regulations that so often dehumanizes the classroom' (1983: 17). Moreover, like Holt, Rogers suggested that while teachers would prefer to facilitate a more experiental and meaningful learning experience, they were 'locked into a traditional and conventional approach that makes significant learning improbable' (Rogers, 1983: 21).

CRITIQUING THE THEORY

Rogers's insistence that individuals should seek to find their own answers to their problems has attracted much criticism in recent years (Thorne, 1992). Thorne suggests that at a time when people are looking for swift answers to their problems, Rogers's focus on the person-centred approach has been somewhat usurped in favour of more cost-effective techniques that lead to quicker results. Additionally, it could be argued that it is irresponsible to ask a person to find their own way forward when dealing with some of the more challenging issues related to the human condition and could reflect a somewhat naive view of the human psyche.

Despite his own Christian upbringing and his early religious studies, Rogers was heavily criticised by Paul Vitz, a Christian professor of psychology (Vitz, 1977, in

Thorne, 1992). Vitz argued that Rogers made no allowances for human nature, seeing only the good and not the bad in people. In this respect, Rogers's work deviated from the Christian ethos, which is based around the philosophy of redemption. Rogers's belief that humans are fundamentally good meant that there was no place for good and evil in the world, which was a significant challenge to the Christian belief.

It is perhaps Rogers's optimistic view of human nature which has attracted the most criticism of his work, particularly since he applied this not just to his client-centred therapy, but also to other aspects of his work, such as education. Rogers had an idealistic view of the education system, which saw him promoting the idea of the teacher acting as facilitator, and the learner initiating their own learning (Rogers, 1951). In this model, he believed that self-assessment and self-criticism were the most important forms of feedback, and any external assessment was inconsequential. In such a model, Rogers is assuming that the individual has the capacity for such self-assessment, and that a curriculum would be flexible enough for learner-initiated work. In reality, this is an ideal that is unlikely to be realised due to curriculum constraints and the measurement of success through formal assessment processes.

APPLYING ROGERS'S THEORY TO EDUCATION

As we have already seens Rogers's work was carried out in the field of clinical psychology. However, Rogers himself was a gifted teacher (Smith, 2004), and in his text *Freedom to Learn* (1969), he documented how he applied the role of facilitator, as seen in his client-centred therapy, to his role in the classroom. In *Freedom to Learn*, Rogers focused on the attitudes of the teacher rather than on methods or techniques to be applied (Patterson, 1977). He believed that successful teaching was based on the relationship between student and teacher, stating that 'the facilitation of significant learning rests upon certain attitudinal qualities which exist in the personal relationships between facilitator and learners' (Rogers, 1969: 19).

Rogers raised a number of philosophical, social and psychological questions that he believed education should be responding to, suggesting that education should be seen as a vehicle for preventing potential crises. In this respect, for Rogers education was not merely about knowledge exchange or cognitive and intellectual development, but focused increasingly on the areas of personal development and interpersonal relationships (Patterson, 1977). In this, he was applying his notion of the importance of personal growth and the development of the whole person or the fully functioning person.

Rogers identified two distinct types of learning: rote learning, typified by facts to be learned and memorised, which he considered to be meaningless, alongside the more beneficial learning which came from the everyday experiences that students had. Rogers believed that the traditional classroom teaching methods, in which a formal curriculum was followed, applying methods that required the learner to be a passive recipient of knowledge, lacked any personal meaning to the student, neither responding to feelings nor the whole person; he referred to this as 'being educated from the neck up' (Patterson, 1977: 18). On the other hand, learning that came from a person's first-hand experience – experiential learning – had meaning and personal relevance (Patterson, 1977). Such learning, he said, was more easily retained.

Rogers recognised that although the education system promoted the type of learning that fostered the passive learner, he also recognised that, for the most part, teachers would prefer the style of teaching that actively promoted experiential learning. Rather than just theorising this, Rogers made suggestions as to how this type of learning might be realised. Rogers believed that in order for learning to be centred on the experiences of the learner, the traditional roles of teachers and students needed to be re-evaluated. Using his own teaching experiences as a model, he explored the notion of teacher as facilitator, theorising that 'we cannot teach another person directly; we can only facilitate his learning' (1951: 389). He also believed that traditional learning conditions could prove potentially threatening to the individual and suggested that the organism becomes rigid under threat, thereby restricting learning. For Rogers:

> The educational situation which most effectively promotes significant learning is one in which 1) threat to the self of the learner is reduced to minimum, and 2) differentiated perception of the field of experience is facilitated. (1951: 123)

Alongside the teacher facilitating learning, Rogers also expressed the notion that the learner should set their own objectives, believing that this is the most effective way of motivating the learner and reducing threat. By its very nature, if a student is setting their own agenda, then learning will proceed at a pace. Rogers believed that humans have a natural propensity to learn, and where the student can see the value of the subject matter to their own personal growth, then learning would be a natural progression. However, we can see here a tension, since if Rogers is suggesting that learning cannot be taught, then this begs the question as to whether there is indeed a role for the teacher. Rogers himself mused: 'it seems to me that anything that can be taught to another is relatively inconsequential and has little or no significant influence on behaviour' (Kirschenbaum and Henderson, 1989: 302), and in his own personal reflections he suggests that even where teaching appears to succeed, it leads to the individual distrusting his own experience and stifling significant learning (Patterson, 1977).

Rogers's ideals create a significant challenge for teachers, and these would not be easy to apply in the current education system which relies so heavily on the outcome of tests and assessments. Indeed, Rogers himself identified that the education system should do away with examinations since they measure only inconsequential learning, and likewise grades and credits should be outlawed for the same reason (Rogers, 1951). It is unlikely that such radical measures would ever be considered, particularly given a government agenda which emphasises the importance of more traditional means of measuring success. It is perhaps unthinkable, then, that teachers might adopt the style of teaching that Rogers advocated.

Nevertheless, we should not discount some of the ideas that Rogers presented regarding the relationship between student and teacher, and there is merit here in respect of the mutual respect which should be formed. Rogers raises the concept of a community of learners, where students share rather than hoard information, and where the development of skills outside of the cognitive domain should be encouraged (Patterson, 1977). In this model, cooperation and not competition is encouraged, and, in this way, positive self-concept is developed, leading to a positive regard and respect for others. It is hard not to show a commitment to the establishment of such an ethos even within a standards-driven culture.

Rogers believed that teacher education and administration should change, with teacher education encouraging the adoption of facilitation over teaching and administration accepting this as a possibility. In this way, the climate for self-directed learning might begin to exist (Patterson, 1977). Collins et al. (2002) suggested that the three basic qualities, which Rogers identified in effective counselling as being key to warm 'person-centred' relationships, could equally be applied to learning, the suggestion being that the three qualities of acceptance, genuineness and empathy are in common with the reflective teacher who should demonstrate 'an open-mindedness and a wholehearted commitment to the learner' (2002: 21). Teachers should reflect on the powerful discourse between learner and teacher, and should create a learning environment conducive to the development of 'self' even within the constraints of a curriculum-led system.

REFLECTIVE TASK

When I try to teach, as I do sometimes, I am appalled by the results, which seems a little more than inconsequential, because sometimes the teaching appears to succeed. When this happens I find that the results are damaging. It seems to cause the individual to distrust his own experience, and to stifle significant learning. Hence, I have come to feel that outcomes of teaching are either unimportant or hurtful. (Rogers 1961: 276)

Why was Rogers concerned that 'the teaching appears to succeed'? What is this statement saying about the relationship between teacher and learner?

SUMMARY

Thorne (1992) observes that person-centred scholars and therapists no longer have the same standing in the field of academic psychology that they once had, appearing as 'naïve enthusiasts from a former age' (1992: 64). It is then testament to Rogers's work that his writings have endured, and certainly in the world of clinical psychology his work remains a significant force, with a 1982 survey of American psychologists revealing him to be the most influential figure in twentieth-century psychotherapy (Kirschenbaum and Henderson, 1989: xiii). Thorne suggested that he had become 'an idealised figure symbolising a "purity" of approach and a hopefulness about both people and therapy' (1992: 64).

For others outside of the arena of clinical psychology, Rogers encouraged a new way of thinking, opening up questions about the relationship between groups of people. Rogers firmly advocated that his core conditions for therapy – congruence, acceptance and empathy – could be applied to other situations where relationships were being formed, such as between student and teacher, and sought to change some of the more traditional roles of individuals. Ultimately, Rogers believed that all human beings were seeking self-actualisation, and therefore it was the role of the practitioner to support them in becoming the fully functioning person they aspired to be.

Rogers had a genuine interest in the human psyche and his life's work was to promote those conditions that allowed for human growth, be that through the counselling he developed, or in his writings on education and health in which he encouraged the development of an increasingly person-centred approach. Rogers increased the popularity of humanistic theory, particularly in the field of psychology, and did much to encourage thinking around the whole person, focusing on goals and aspirations, rather than merely treating symptoms.

GLOSSARY OF TERMS

Client-centred therapy A non-directive approach to treatment which Rogers developed during the 1940s and 1950s. Rogers used the term 'client' rather than 'patient' to indicate that it was the individual who was in control of their own destiny with the power to overcome difficulties. The role of the therapist was to provide assistance through guidance rather than administering a cure.

Conditional positive regard The use of rewards and praise when a child behaves in a manner which the parents deem acceptable, which could be construed as the child not feeling loved because of who they are, but rather on condition of demonstrating a specific behaviour that meets the parents' approval. If the child only ever experiences conditional positive regard, this could lead to them constantly seeking approval from others.

Congruence Congruence exists when a person's ideal self is in harmony with their actual self. Rogers believed that a total state of congruence rarely existed, but the closer the two were in similarity, the more likely a person was to become self-actualised. The development of congruence was more likely to be realised in a person who experiences unconditional positive regard.

Facilitator   Facilitator refers to the role that Rogers believed a teacher should take in an education setting. Adapting his client-centred therapy model, Rogers developed a concept of 'student-centred teaching' in which the term 'teaching' was substituted as 'facilitation', and which promoted the notion that learners should be able to relax and learn in an environment free from threat. The facilitator, then, should promote an ethos of mutual respect and trust, in which they enable real one-to-one encounters. Empathy and understanding are key in the facilitation model.

Ideal self   The ideal self is an idealised version of the self, which derives from life experiences, societal demands and attributes admired in role models, and reflects a person's goals and ambitions. The ideal self will change throughout a person's life, so the ideal self as a fully functioning adult will be different from that of the teenage self.

Self-actualisation   Rogers saw self-actualisation as fulfilling one's potential and achieving the highest level of human beingness as is possible. Rogers believed that self-actualisation could be achieved once the ideal self and self-image were in congruence. However, he acknowledged that success was dependent on environmental factors with self-actualisation only being fully realised in the right environmental conditions.

Self-direction   In client-centred therapy Rogers saw the individual as moving away from the need to please others towards self-direction in which they are motivated by the excitement of the process rather than the end result, and in which they learn to value themselves and their own feelings. In children, self-direction emerges when the child gains control of their own environment and shows autonomy in their actions.

Unconditional positive regard   Rogers used the term 'unconditional positive regard' to describe a situation whereby a person gains acceptance and support as they are, regardless of what they say or do. Rogers believed that children who received unconditional positive regard from their parents were more likely to gain feelings of self-worth as they grew older.

FURTHER READING

Cohen, D. (2000) *Carl Rogers: A Critical Biography*. London: Robinson.
A 'warts-and-all' account of the life and works of Carl Rogers, including some of his own challenges set against the background of his work.

Farber, B.A., Brink, D.C. and Raskin, P.M. (1996) *The Psychotherapy of Carl Rogers: Cases and Commentary*. New York: The Guilford Press.
An opportunity to look at some of Rogers's work with complete transcripts of ten cases alongside commentary from other notable psychotherapists.

Kirschenbaum, H. (2007) *The Life and Works of Carl Rogers* (2nd edn). Ross-on-Wye: PCCS Books.

The second edition of Kirschenbaum's biography of Carl Rogers includes the period prior to his death, which was one of the most important stages of his career. The book gives a personal and professional account of the life and works of Carl Rogers.

REFERENCES

Boeree, C.G. (1998) *Carl Rogers*. Available online at: http://webspace.ship.edu/cgboer/Rogers.html

Collins, J., Harkin, J. and Nind, M. (2002) *Manifesto for Learning*. London: Continuum.

DeRobertis, E.M. (2006) 'Deriving a humanistic theory of child development from the works of Carl R. Rogers and Karen Horney'. *The Humanist Psychologist*, 34 (2): 177–99.

Kirschenbaum, H. (1979) *On Becoming Carl Rogers*. New York: Delacorte Press.

Kirschenbaum, H. and Henderson, V.L. (eds) (1989) *The Carl Rogers Reader*. New York: Houghton Mifflin.

Kramer, R. (1995) 'The birth of client-centred therapy: Carl Rogers, Otto Rank and "the beyond"'. *Journal of Humanist Psychology*, 35 (4): 54–110.

Patterson, C.H. (1977) 'Carl Rogers and humanistic education'. In: Patterson, C.H. (ed.) *Foundations for a Theory of Instruction and Educational Psychology*. New York: Harper & Row.

Rogers, C.R. (1942) *Counseling and Psychotherapy*. New York: Houghton Mifflin.

Rogers, C.R. (1951) *Client-Centered Therapy: Its Current Practice, Implications and Theory*. London: Constable.

Rogers, C.R. (1961) *On Becoming a Person: A Therapist's View of Psychotherapy*. New York: Houghton Mifflin.

Rogers, C.R. (1969) *Freedom to Learn: A View of What Education Might Become*. Columbus, OH: Merrill.

Rogers, C.R. (1983) *Freedom to Learn for the 80's*. Columbus, OH: Merrill.

Rogers, C.R. (1986) 'Rogers, Kohut and Erikson'. *Person-Centred Review*, 1: 125–40.

Smith, M.K. (2004) *Carl Rogers, Core Conditions and Education*. Available online at: http://infed.org/mobi/carl-rogers-core-conditions-and-education

Thorne, B. (1992) *Carl Rogers*. London: SAGE.

3
A.S. NEILL

FREEDOM TO LEARN

LEARNING OUTCOMES

After reading this chapter, you should be able to:

- appreciate Neill's background and his contribution to education and child development;
- understand and identify his educational philosophies;
- be aware of the origins of his theories and how his ideas influenced others within education;
- critically evaluate Neill's works and theories;
- recognise how his ideas could be used in practice.

KEY WORDS

Summerhill School; free child; self-regulation; self-government; repression; psychoanalysis.

INTRODUCTION

Alexander Sutherland Neill (1883–1973) was arguably the most progressive, and possibly the most controversial, educator of the twentieth century, whose philosophy centred upon democratic free schooling and a child-centred approach to learning and teaching. He was also the founder of 'that dreadful school', Summerhill (Croall, 1983). His philosophy was no doubt a response to his own strict Scottish Calvinist childhood and education. He felt that children should not be exposed to a set of values and morals dictated to them by adults, nor should children be frightened or threatened by the imposition of traditional forms of school discipline. Neill's ideas on education were radical to say the least and have drawn attention from a worldwide audience, including teachers and parents, who have been appalled, elated or enthused by his many writings and talks.

Neill is synonymous with **Summerhill School**, which he established in 1921 and is renowned throughout the world. Here, Neill's radical philosophy of democratic, child-centred learning was put into practice. Summerhill is still very much a functioning school today and is still based upon Neill's ideas. It has received considerable criticism since its inception, especially from some sections of the press who consider it a 'school without rules' and a place of 'all play and no work' (Howlett, 2013: 163). However, Neill endeavoured to create an environment where children could find happiness. He believed they could only find true happiness if they were free from external **repression** from adults in authority; such repression he felt created unhappiness and hostility. Neill's ideas were influenced by Freud, who argued that since hostility could not be articulated to the adult by the child, the hostility became owned by the child, which then turned into self-loathing and ultimately into anti-social behaviour. A number of children who displayed such anti-social behaviour ended up at Summerhill where they were 'cured, Neill maintains, by the application for the first time in their lives of freedom' (Hobson, 2001: 2).

It is without doubt that Neill's ideas on education are of great consequence even today, but are at the same time controversial. The concept of Summerhill has been imitated throughout the world. Neill's writing spread over a considerable number of years and spanned an era of massive social change where established and traditional methods of learning and teaching were being challenged. The notion of the **free child** who is essentially wise, and who if left by themselves without adult imposition can grow with confidence and happiness, continues to interest parents and teachers alike.

Neill was a thinker who was captivated by radical viewpoints and whose many writings still attract attention. Bailey states that Neill's beloved creation 'Summerhill School remains noteworthy in part because of the relative extremity of its philosophy and practices' (2013: 151). Furthermore, in establishing Summerhill School, Neill had created 'the oldest children's democracy in the world' (Vaughan, 2006: vii). Aspects of Neill's philosophy, along with the criticisms it has endured and the application of his ideas, will be explored later in this chapter.

NEILL, THE PERSON

Neill was born in the town of Forfar, Scotland. His father was a teacher in the nearby village of Kingsmuir at the school where Neill himself was taught. Howlett (2013) suggests that it was Neill's unhappy childhood experience at school, where the response to any form of misbehaviour by pupils was the use of corporal punishment without any regard for the emotional welfare of the child, which sowed the seeds of his own educational philosophy. After leaving school, he had a number of jobs before he was taken on as an apprentice school teacher in 1899. He eventually achieved matriculation to Edinburgh University studying the arts and graduated in 1905 after reading English literature. Following graduation, he taught in government schools in Scotland for twelve years (Hobson, 2001). In 1917, Neill enlisted in the British Army, but he was neither a competent nor an enthusiastic soldier. He found the class divisions within military life abhorrent. He also loathed the requirement for the lower ranks to comply without question to orders from their superiors. This, together with his earlier experience of authority, as a school pupil and as a teacher, had reinforced his aversion to coercion (Croall, 1983).

Following the war, and with a growing dislike of the traditional forms of education, Neill's career direction changed, which enabled him to follow the interests of his embryonic philosophy. First, he taught at King Alfred School in London, which was a new experimental establishment, and then in 1921 he became, for a short duration, assistant editor for the radical New Education Fellowship. He then took up a position at a progressive school in Dresden, Germany, where he stayed until 1923 when the school was moved to Vienna, Austria. Neill returned to England in 1924 and set up his own progressive school in Lyme Regis with the aid of Frau Neustatter, a co-worker from the schools in Dresden and Vienna. The new school was Summerhill and Neill became the head teacher. Neill and Frau Neustatter were married in 1927 and in the same year the school's location was moved to Leiston in Suffolk, where it remains to this day (Hobson, 2001).

From the earliest days at Summerhill, Neill began putting his notions of pupil freedom into practice by stripping away the trappings of teacher authority. Even though the pupil enrolment was low, the school became well known mainly because of Neill's prolific writing: he wrote some twenty books. In 1953, Neill published *The Free Child*, which was an account of his daughter Zoë's first six years of life. In this book he contested that parents should 'step back and limit themselves to providing physical requirements such as food, bedtimes, and clothing' (Bailey, 2013: 75). Neill's seminal work *Summerhill* (1960), which collates much of his noteworthy ideas and their application, is especially sought after as required reading by undergraduate and postgraduate students in relevant fields such as education, psychology and sociology (Howlett, 2013; MacBlain, 2014). However, because he wrote so many books, and in a style that was often one-dimensional, it is difficult to condense and codify exactly his educational philosophy, as Croall, who wrote an influential text on Neill and Summerhill, states:

> I found Neill's best books a delight to read. Fresh, humorous, provocative, they were often inspiring in their profound common sense. Yet Neill could also be infuriatingly simple-minded or evocative when tackling certain issues. I had constantly to bear in mind the fact that, though in many respects he was a brilliant publicist for his own ideas, he was also a propagandist, intent on convincing an often puzzled or hostile world of the value and practicality of his revolutionary ideas about children. (1983: 3)

Yet his books continued to sell globally, which not only generated widespread interest in his ideas, but also brought many visitors to Summerhill who were keen to imitate his ideas in their own countries. His 1960 work *Summerhill* sold two million copies. Most of his works explored and promoted his revolutionary ideas of child development. However, *Neill! Neill! Orange Peel! A Personal View of Ninety Years* (1973) is also an account of his early influences regarding the notions of **self-regulation** and **self-government**. These notions were the cornerstone of Neill's philosophy of a democratic and pupil-centred education, which he considered was of vital importance in providing a happy childhood for those children in his care at Summerhill, a philosophy which, essentially, is present in Summerhill to this day. When Neill died in 1973, the school was run by his second wife Ena until her retirement in 1985. Their daughter Zoë then took over the reins, which at the time of writing is still the situation. Neill's philosophy is both inspirational and controversial in its extremes, yet it has certainly stood the test of time.

NEILL'S PHILOSOPHY

Neill's philosophy has had little impact on educational policy or much bearing upon initial teacher education practices because his ideas were considered to be too rebellious (Croall, 1983). However, Neill's thoughts about education drew an immense degree of interest from educators and parents who were interested in his revolutionary democratic approach to child development. In his 1960 work *Summerhill: A Radical Approach to Child Rearing*, Neill set out the principles of his philosophy, which can be summarised as follows:

- A faith in the goodness of the child.
- The aim of education is to work joyfully and to find happiness.
- Education is about both intellectual and emotional development.
- Education needs to match the psychic needs of the individual child.
- Discipline and punishment is harmful to child development.
- Freedom does not mean licence – respect needs to be a two-way process.
- Learning and development needs to be free from guilt.

These aspects will be interwoven in this section, which will cover aspects of Neill's principles and philosophies such as freedom and repression, guilt, sex, religion, democracy and the curriculum.

First, it should be acknowledged that the basis for Neill's ideas of child development and education emanated from Freud and **psychoanalysis**. Freud considered that children's inhibitions, anxieties and problems originate from sexual repression and the resultant feelings of guilt. He also argued that the *unconscious* is more crucial to child development than the *conscious* – children are more likely to be happier if they are free to act on their own instincts rather than be subject to the censures and punishments imposed by adults (MacBlain, 2014). For Neill, an important aspect of Freud's thinking was the notion of freedom in their development and their education: the free child and the free school. For children to be truly happy, they need to feel they have negligible repression, and only then can they feel free. At Summerhill, he endeavoured to create an all-round education that provided such freedom, unlike a conventional school which 'makes the mistake of exalting the intellect over the emotions with the result that children may know a lot of facts but lack inner contentment and fulfilment' (Hobson, 2001: 2).

Neill strongly contended that freedom was related to his belief in the inherent goodness of children, that 'a child is innately wise and realistic' (Neill, 1960: 20). He could not countenance the idea of original sin where a child is born with inborn wickedness. However, 'if left to himself without adult suggestion of any kind, he will develop as far as he is capable of doing' (Hobson, 2001: 2). He also stressed how important it was that children experience freedom at an early age, and how freedom is linked to love from the parents: 'No amount of freedom at school can completely counteract the influence of a bad home. Character acquired in the first months or years of life can be modified by freedom, but it can never be completely changed' (Neill, 1953: 36). Furthermore, he argues that 'there is only one truth about children, that if they are loved and free they become good and honest' (Neill, 1953: 86–7). On the other hand and by way of caution: 'by continually correcting children we must make them feel inferior; we injure their natural dignity' (Neill, 1953: 107). Neill's opinion on the effect of free schools reflects not only his philosophy but also the aim of Summerhill:

> If all schools were free and all lessons were optional, I fancy that children would find their own level, and indifferent scholars who, under discipline, scrape through college or university and become unimaginative teachers and doctors and lawyers. (1953: 34)

Freedom for Neill gave children courage and tolerance, and enabled them to meet difficult challenges with confidence. Freedom also helped create the self-regulated child, where the child's conduct is governed by the child themselves and not from adult imposition. Conversely, a 'moulded child has no self; he is only a replica of his parents' (Neill, 1967: 9). There is a danger, recognised by Neill, that outright freedom of action could lead to a chaotic and unjust environment; freedom then at Summerhill 'means doing what you like so long as you do not interfere with the freedom of others' (1967: 19). He thought there was a fine dividing line between freedom and licence, which was balanced by the practice of mutual respect between teachers and pupils. Neill's view of freedom originated from the appreciation that a child was adept at self-regulation. Repression by adults, Neill felt, hindered and indeed harmed the natural development of children.

Unfree children, Neill contested, were greatly hampered by guilt, which he thought served the manifestations of authority. Guilt, he argued, was an obstruction to independent thought and actions as well as creativity. Feelings of guilt 'start a cycle which oscillates constantly between rebellion, repentance, submission, and new rebellion' (Neill, 1960: xiii). Guilt is related to conscience and the fear that non-compliance with the conventional moral standards will result in punishment. Punishment for a child, especially at the time of Neill's writings, could be in the form of physical harm such as beatings, or emotional harm such as the withholding of love from a parent or being ignored. Neill had a great deal of experience in what he called 'curing' children who had been damaged by adults who induced guilt and fear into their young lives. He considered that only hate could thrive in an environment of guilt and the fear of punishment.

Sex, and indeed religion, played a major part in contributing to a child's fear and sense of guilt. Neill emphasised his thoughts in the following extract:

> To a frightened child sex *is* everything! Yes, the child uses sex as the chief peg on which to hang his fears. For he has been told that sex is wicked. The child with night terrors is often the child who is afraid of his sex thoughts. The devil may come and take him to hell, for is he not a sinful boy who deserves punishment? The bogeyman, the ghost, the goblin are only the devil in disguise. Fear comes from a guilty conscience. It is the ignorance of the parents that gives the child his guilty conscience. (1960: 121–2)

Neill also found that many of the more difficult and challenging children he had worked with had, like himself, undergone a strict religious upbringing. It was, he felt, this strict background and the moralistic teachings of religion that gave sex an inflated status that increased the guilt and fear in children, and he considered that this was because many religions acknowledged the notion of original sin. Although Summerhill did not have religious education as part of the curriculum, Neill thought Jesus would have favoured the manner in which children were treated: 'In Summerhill, we give children love and approval' (Neill, 1960: 373).

Neill's philosophy of democracy and freedom was applied in Summerhill, which was, and still is, a self-governing school, democratic in structure and organisation. All matters associated with communal and social life, including the awarding of punishments for social wrongdoings, were decided by vote at the weekly school meetings. Teachers and pupils had one vote each, including Neill, and the majority of votes carried the day. It created a democracy where children and their opinions were listened to, prized and valued (Howlett, 2013). When it came to dealing with a wrongdoer at these weekly meetings, Neill thought children were more judicious and astute than adults in comparable circumstances (Croall, 1983).

Democracy in the form of pupil choice played a large and controversial part in Neill's philosophy and is linked very closely to the curriculum at Summerhill.

There was no compulsion for children to attend lessons, some newly arrived pupils at Summerhill spent weeks and even months playing before attending lessons, and even then only those which they wanted to. As we have seen, Neill felt that children were capable of developing, both intellectually and emotionally, without guidance from adults. He argued that children would eventually find out what interests them without imposition and they were the best judge, a notion based on the idea that children are born inherently good.

The usual academic subjects were on offer at Summerhill but were not unduly promoted. Instead, great emphasis was placed on aesthetic subjects that promoted creativity such as art, craft, drama and dance. Neill thought that these subjects helped foster children's emotional welfare; they also offered an opportunity for non-academic pupils to shine (Hobson, 2001). Play, especially outside and undirected by adults, was also encouraged. Neill considered play vital for children's all-round development, where they could live out their fantasies. However, Neill had certain misgivings about team sports. His main worry was that those who were particularly gifted in sport would be considered heroes:

> I take it that the underlying motive for encouraging team games is the wish to cultivate team spirit ... In Summerhill the team spirit arises out of a self-government in community living. Hence no child is ever a hero or heroine with us. Games prowess means nothing and brilliance in lessons also means nothing. Free children do not worship. (1967: 31)

The growing concern over exam results and the inclination to label children as academic or not from an early age were an anathema to Neill. Following his death, the introduction of the national curriculum (in England and Wales) in the 1980s meant that schools were disinclined to follow Summerhill's progressive approach to the curriculum, particularly with the increased authority given to the school inspection organisation Ofsted. However, Summerhill's successful legal rebuff following a damning Ofsted report in 1999 does offer some hope for Neill's philosophy being carried forward well into the future (Brighouse, 2006). David Carr offers a clear summary of Neill's philosophy of education for freedom as being

> directed towards the production of confident, self-assured and responsible young people capable of critical reflection that is above all needed for mature engagement with the democratic processes of an open or liberal society ... It is recognised that this can only be achieved in the sort of positive climate of reciprocal trust and respect in which young people are free from the manipulatory pressures of social, political or other indoctrination and to express their views without fear or anxiety. (2003: 226–7)

The practice of participatory and democratic education similar to Neill's philosophy, and which is evident in Summerhill, is also reflected in the Sudbury Valley School model set up by the progressive educational thinker Philip Greenberg in Massachusetts, USA. In this model, akin to Summerhill, the pupils are free to determine what and how they will learn. 'This freedom for children to decide for themselves is viewed as being a fundamental human right' (Warwick, 2012). The Sudbury Valley School model has been replicated by many other schools in the USA and also internationally in countries such as Japan, Belgium, Germany and Israel, thereby promoting and expanding many of the progressive and democratic practices originally expounded by Neill (Warwick, 2012).

↻ LINKS WITH OTHER THEORISTS

Most of those educational thinkers associated with Neill, as can be imagined, have progressive philosophies regarding child development. It should be recognised that Neill came from a background in psychology and psychoanalysis, he strongly believed that child psychology should be at the core of educational thinking (Neill, 1973). As we have already seen, Neill was influenced by Freud in how he 'linked education to an unconscious problem of learning for love' (Britzman, 2011: 20–1). Neill's belief that there was no such thing as original sin was also shaped by Rousseau's naturalism. Also, like Rousseau, Neill did not discard the necessity for rules and discipline, but he thought that 'discipline should be self-imposed and rules self-generated' (Carr, 2000: 144). Whereas Rousseau was concerned with the mind, Neill was concerned with both the mind and body. There are strong connections with early educational thinkers such as Steiner who stressed the importance of play without adult intervention, as well as Froebel who encouraged notions of children exploring and learning through nature.

Neill approved of some of Montessori's notions, specifically that children should be free to play without the imposition of adults, although other ideas he considered to be abhorrent. He thought that Montessori lacked emotion and that her methods were too scientific and controlling. Furthermore, Neill was very uneasy with Montessori's religious principles, which underpinned much of her work (Croall, 1983). Pestalozzi also has some very close links to Neill's view of a free education. He contested that children should be encouraged to pursue their own particular interests and make their own discoveries, and emphasised the role that nature played in these discoveries. For Pestalozzi and Neill, allowing children such freedom was important in their development and progress into the adult world. Moreover, Pestalozzi also felt that education placed too much emphasis on intellectual matters and paid too little attention to practical and emotional issues (Howlett, 2013). John Dewey's philosophy is similarly linked with Neill's ideas. Dewey's Laboratory School in Chicago explored the best conditions for childhood development and he emphasised that children should be encouraged to foster skills and activities centred on their own interests instead of being directed by teachers (Croall, 1983).

Neill's ideas on self-regulation and self-governance were influenced by Wilhelm Reich and Homer Lane. Indeed, it was a visit to Homer Lane's Little Commonwealth School for young offenders, in Dorset, which inspired Neill's work at Summerhill.

At Homer Lane's school he found that once quite hardened youngsters were given freedom in a community of self-government, where the adults were on the side of the children, many steadily progressed into balanced and respected citizens (Neill, 1960). In his influential 1969 book *How Children Fail*, John Holt noted that schools could be places of fear and negate any inherent aspiration to learn, and, like Neill, he criticised overt motivation such as awards and hero worship because it might underline a child's fear of failure (Williams, 2004). Holt, like Neill, argued that 'children can be trusted to learn about their world with far less adult interference than is commonly believed' (Meighan, 2007: 5). For the most part, Neill's ideas also mirror Ivan Illich's notion of the deschooling society as they both considered that the traditional school system was overly restrictive in not allowing children the freedom of choice on what to learn. However, Illich argued that schools such as Summerhill romanticised the concept of childhood rather than prepared the learners for the real world (Illich, 1971).

Carl Rogers, an American psychologist and advocate for humanistic methods in education, who we discussed in Chapter 2, also argued that children intuitively knew what they wanted and suggested that teachers should facilitate these desires. Neill's idea that guilt hampered children's personal development and constrained their capacity to be creative due to a fear of failure is comparable with Carol Dweck's entity theory. Links are also evident with the progressive Brazilian educational philosopher Paulo Freire, particularly in relation to matters of oppression and freedom. Freire also argued that children who were raised in controlling and repressive families are themselves in later life liable to submit to dominance from authority and also have a propensity to dominate others (Spring, 1994). Many progressive teachers and thinkers have endeavoured to follow Neill's philosophy, although his ideas have also attracted considerable criticism.

CRITIQUING THE THEORY

Neill's philosophy, and undeniably his practice, at Summerhill have invited both praise and criticism, which have been poles apart in their nature. Much of the condemnation Neill received came from exaggerated responses from the conservative press because of their perception of Summerhill as 'all play and no work', and as such may, to some extent, be discarded. Nevertheless, there are a number of aspects of Neill's work which do appear susceptible to censure, particularly as he pushed the limits of even the most progressive educational thinkers, who themselves had attracted criticism for their pupil-centred views (Hobson, 2001; Howlett, 2013). Specific aspects of Neill's work can be questioned, such as 'Do children actually know what is best for them socially and educationally?'; 'Should education be centred on practical rather than intellectual matters?'; 'Will children be able to use their given freedom without a fundamental intellectual background when making significant decisions about their future?' (Hobson, 2001). Such aspects of educational voluntariness are challenged by Bailey (2013); he argues that it is hard to imagine how a child's interest can be cultivated in a subject if they have not been introduced to that subject. He further explains that

> Without some sort of structured curriculum, delivered by a competent teacher, it is difficult to imagine how children will be in a position to make an informed judgement about their passions and interests because their introduction is based on happenstance and lack, or fad and fashion. (2013: 142–3)

Arguably, the most fundamental criticism could be that his educational thinking was not underpinned by any methodical or logical philosophy, or significant concept of knowledge. Neill's thinking mainly originated from his 'experiences and observations, supplemented with some study of psychological (especially psychoanalytic) theory' (Hobson, 2001: 3). Although it could be said that experience is a significant factor in forming an educational philosophy, the lack of a substantial theoretical base does weaken its credibility. This paucity of theory is evident in his very readable books, which focus on the practicalities of child development and include many unsubstantiated and embellished claims. At times he is apt to generalise and simply state aspects of his thinking rather than explore in-depth the philosophical rationale of his declarations. This is particularly the case in relation to the difference between *freedom* and *licence*, which are complex and important issues that have significant impact for the application of his ideas (Hobson, 2001). Further critical comments are in relation to the teaching methods at Summerhill. It is interesting to note that Neill is often regarded as one of the more progressive educators of the twentieth century. Yet, it seems that he paid scant regard to educational processes: 'Summerhill was actually criticised by the Inspectorate of the day for its deployment of highly conventional formal and didactic teaching techniques' (Carr, 2000: 140).

Another area for criticism is whether children when unrestrained from the guidance of adults and the norms of civilisation would choose violence and spitefulness. It is interesting to note that Neill acknowledged that a number of children who arrived at Summerhill presented such behaviour, but this behaviour he contested was caused by the discipline imposed upon them by their parents or their earlier experience of education. According to Neill, 'savagery and barbarism in humanity was caused by an abundance of civilization and not seemingly by its lack!' (Howlett, 2013: 174). It is perhaps that Neill's view of civilisation and indeed education has become outdated. During Neill's early career, industry – mainly heavy industry – was at the forefront of the economy and the vast majority of the population worked and earned a wage and some self-respect, but not much more. Recently, there have been vast changes in technology and a growth in the creative industries which offer greater opportunities, and these have in turn altered the way in which education is preparing young people for the world of work and life. More is known about how the brain develops, which has helped to improve methods of learning and teaching, and enhanced the life chances for all children regardless of background (Brighouse, 2006). Equally, Neill's views on religious and moral education could also appear old-fashioned; today, such subjects are introduced through debate, and with consideration for cultural differences (Hobson, 2001).

APPLYING NEILL'S IDEAS IN PRACTICE

In spite of the numerous and substantial criticisms of Neill's philosophy, there are a number of his ideas which can, even in today's highly regulated classrooms, be applied in practice. It may appear that the approaches used at Summerhill would have very little place in schools. This is particularly the case perhaps when Neill himself states: 'I am criticised because I do nothing to help teachers practically ... I am not interested in organisation or exams or methods of teaching' (1973: 162). Yet his under-pinning beliefs and philosophies of tolerance, his understanding and genuine love of children have, and continue to enlighten the practice of many teachers in both the private and state sectors (Brighouse, 2006). In accordance with Neill's philosophy this section will explore features such as respect, pupil voice, creativity and teaching approaches which could be employed in practice.

A major aspect for Neill was the notion of respect for children. Whether teachers realise that they are directly implementing Neill's core concepts or not, respect for a child's individual distinctiveness is greater today than in the more didactic and submissive classroom of the past. Teachers endeavour to discover as much as possible about the children they are responsible for, and take into account and value the ever-changing differences in 'culture and racial identities of their mobile multilingual, multi-faith, increasingly inclusive pupil population arriving from all parts of the world' (Brighouse, 2006: 3). For Neill, respect not only involved getting to know the child, but doing so without judgement and without attempting to shape the child (Neill, 1973). A core feature of respect is that of listening to children's interests and concerns. Currently, pupil voice is highly valued in forms such as school councils, and many schools utilise pupils to evaluate lessons and even to voice their opinion on the employment of new members of staff. Views are also sought from children by the use of anonymous questionnaires to evaluate areas of concern about school life and to gather ideas for areas of possible school improvements. Some schools involve children in making judgements about accusations of bullying. All these practices are akin to Neill's notion of self-governance (Brighouse, 2006).

Even though Neill would have scoffed at employing formal learning and teaching activities, there are a number of suggestions, now acclaimed as pupil-centred practice, which would have been close to Neill's thinking. Although these practices are now commonplace, they are worth reinforcing here if only to propose that perhaps Neill's ideas were far ahead of his time. Listening and displaying enthusiasm for children's ideas, even if they seem offbeat, builds trust and lessens the fear of derision. By adopting a conversational and informal style when replying to children's questions, adults help to create a much safer setting. Also, allowing children plenty of time to give responses to questions reduces their anxieties. Underpinning all these points, and aligned with Neill's thinking, is the need for adults to get to know the individual children by discovering the things they think are important and which interest them, and use these interests to plan and inform learning activities (Williams, 2004).

Key to the learning experience at Summerhill was the focus on creativity. This was underpinned by Neill's thinking that the more children develop creative and contrary approaches to learning, the more they will disregard negative thoughts of failure so often associated with the more traditional subject-based teaching and learning. As Gilbert argues, we should not only use 'creative-strategies, we need to encourage them to have the sort of levels of hope that will keep them optimistic in the face of apparent failure' (2002: 166). Providing occasions for creative thinking gives children the confidence to respond to questions without fear of censure and gives everybody an opportunity to achieve. This includes planning time in lessons for pupil responses and to use these to inform lessons, and the use of open-ended questions to stimulate discussion and debate (Neill, 1973). Neill was fond of drama to encourage creativity: at Summerhill a form of dramatic art called spontaneous acting was very popular with most pupils. He felt that the performing of already written plays lacked the opportunity for creativity and was merely imitation, whereas performing plays written and produced by the children fostered resourcefulness and imagination. Imagination and creation were also encouraged through dance: 'the joy of dancing is the joy of invention. When invention is left out, dancing becomes mechanical and dull' (Neill, 1960: 74).

Play involving the visual arts and practical creative activities allows children the freedom to explore aspects of personal interests and also experience success. Furthermore, symbolic play where children take on the role of adults (according to Neill, children at Summerhill enjoyed playing gangsters), gives children opportunities to explore their own feelings and experiment with language. It also supports socialisation, cooperative learning and imagination (Cohen et al., 2004). It is also possible to enthuse children's imagination within their written work – for example, here is one of Neill's methods of doing this: 'I once said to a class. This is the first line of an essay or story: "'Bloody hell' cried the bishop," Carry on' (Neill, 1967: 65). Although it is suggested that you do not actually use this particular example, for obvious reasons, the essence of Neill's strategy does offer a way of stimulating children's imagination in their written work.

Similar to much of the learning in schools today, learning at Summerhill was activity-based. According to Kyriacou: 'active learning refers to any activities where pupils are given a marked degree of autonomy and control over the organisation, conduct and direction of the learning activity' (1991: 42). Neill probably would have preferred total autonomy for the children. However, it is unrealistic to advocate such freedom in schools with such constraints as the national curriculum and the pressures of examinations. Nevertheless, active learning, which often includes problem solving and research, could be either an individual or a collaborative project. The advantages of active learning approaches are that they are enjoyable, less stressful than teacher-led approaches, and the collaborative projects foster imaginative outcomes (Kyriacou, 1991).

The fundamental aspects of Neill's ideas, where children opt out of attending lessons and make decisions about what subjects are taught, will probably never be on the agenda for other schools, especially state schools. Yet there is now an acknowledgement of the needs of the whole child and not just the intellectual child. Schools are increasingly providing support for children's emotional and physical needs in the form of pre- and after-school clubs (Brighouse, 2006: 3). Children's intellectual interests are also now taken into account through personalised learning and intervention group work and differentiated practice, although Neill would probably not have been totally in favour of such impositions.

It is perhaps fitting to end this application section with the observations of Neill's daughter Zoë regarding the broader meaning of freedom:

> Summerhill gives freedom to teachers too. We put a lot of faith in children to grow up without much interference from adults. We also put a lot of faith in the teachers we employ because we do not use any of the instruments of control that schools normally employ to keep track on what their teachers are doing. Teachers [at Summerhill] are pretty creative with their teaching time once they have got used to this. (Neill Readhead, 2006: 101).

REFLECTIVE TASK

One of Neill's key principles was that education should match the cognitive needs and interests of the individual child (Neill, 1960). List the practices that are in place in your setting, classroom or in placement settings to ensure this is achieved. Then list any other practices that could be adopted to enhance matching children's needs and interests even further.

SUMMARY

There is little doubt that Neill has had a major impact on the thinking behind child development and education. His ideas on the free and self-regulating child have drawn extremes of both criticism and praise. Although few would align with Neill's notions on total child freedom, present-day thinking on learning and child development is underpinned by a greater wish for honesty and inclusion than in the past. His idea of the free child, which he endeavoured to put into practice, originated from his understanding that a child is skilled at self-regulation. Furthermore, he considered repression by adults impeded children's natural and personal development. Perhaps his greatest influence was not his prolific writing on education, 'but the unconditional love of children which he both exemplified and demanded' (Howlett, 2013: 175). Neill will always be linked with Summerhill School, which is still going strong over forty years after his death. Summerhill still follows his philosophy and attracts pupils from all over the world. For Neill, it was the environment of Summerhill that made an impact on the children rather than him as an individual.

Neill's ideas can be associated with Freud, but also with a number of other educational thinkers. Neill's ideas resonate with some of the early thinkers such as Rousseau regarding the thought that there was no such thing as original sin. There are also connections with Steiner and, for the most part Montessori, about the importance of letting children play without adult intrusion, and with Froebel who encouraged children to explore and learn through nature. Neill's notions of children following their own interests, rather than a set curriculum, are similar to the ideas of Pestalozzi and Dewey. There are close links with the progressive and radical thinkers such as Reich and Homer Lane, as well as Holt, Illich and Freire, all of whom questioned the concept of traditional schooling. Additionally, Dweck's entity theory, and the fear of failure, can be associated with Neill who felt that guilt hindered children's development. Criticism of Neill's work has focused on a number of areas, including the radical approach of allowing children to choose what lessons to attend and the option of non-attendance. This, along with children's democratic involvement in the running of the school, is questioned by some critics who ask whether children are in a position to make valued and informed judgements. There has also been censure that Neill's philosophy is based upon experience alone, without any regard to theory or wider empirical evidence.

Former pupils and colleagues who worked with Neill felt it was his 'humanity and understanding that produced the results' (Croall, 1983: 407). It is fitting to close this chapter with a quote from Neill's *Summerhill* which encapsulates his philosophy:

> If Summerhill has any message at all it is: Thou shalt not opt out. Fight world sickness, not with drugs like moral teachings and punishments but with natural means – approval, tenderness, tolerance … love. (1960: 13)

GLOSSARY OF TERMS

Free child   For Neill, the concept of the free child is one who is fundamentally wise, and who if left alone and without adult encumbrance can develop with confidence and happiness. Neill (1953: 86–7) argued that 'if a child is loved and free, they become good and honest'. The free child is synonymous with the concept of self-regulation and the self-regulating child.

Psychoanalysis   Another term that comes from the work of Sigmund Freud, psychoanalysis is a set of methods that looks to delve into the motivations behind human behaviour. Neill endeavoured to use psychoanalysis (although he was not qualified to do so) with some pupils who demonstrated what he considered to be anti-social behaviours, or those he thought were troubled children. This was his attempt to 'cure' the children of their perceived difficulties.

Repression   This term, for Neill, was an important element of Freud's thinking and was fundamental in the idea of freedom in a child's educational development. It is also important in the notion of a free child and a free school, because for children to lead a natural and joyful life, they need to be as free as possible from control or repression from adults. Neill also thought that the reason that some children exhibit worries, inhibitions and embarrassments was sexual repression and the consequential feelings of guilt. The idea, espoused by parents, that sex is evil and sinful is seen as responsible for children feeling guilt and creating anxiety.

Self-government   This term originates from Neill's premise that all children are naturally good and wise, and in no need of the impositions of adults with their rules and regulations. Children, Neill considered, could govern themselves in a democratic manner, which they did with the help of staff at Summerhill; staff and children had equal votes on deciding day-to-day decisions at weekly meetings. Self-governance stimulated a degree of team spirit among the pupils because they were empowered to make judgements about their lives within the school community.

Self-regulation   Neill's idea of freedom came from his understanding that a child was skilled at self-regulation. A self-regulated child's behaviour and conduct will be managed by the child themselves, and not by any imposition from an adult. On the other hand, a child who is overly governed by their parents is not considered to have any self; rather, they become an imitation of their parents (Neill, 1967). Self-regulation is advanced by allowing the child to grow in the most free and healthy manner possible without any involvement from adults or parents which could cause any inhibitions that might hamper their natural development.

Summerhill School   The school founded by Neill in 1921 and internationally recognised as a place where Neill's progressive educational philosophy was put into practice. The philosophy underpinning the school is that of democracy, child-centred learning and the development of the free child. Students are free to choose the lessons they attend or whether to attend at all. Entry for examinations is not obligatory, nor is following the national curriculum. The school is in Leiston, Suffolk, and the current head teacher is Neill's daughter, Zoë Neill Readhead.

FURTHER READING

Hemmings, R. (1972) *Fifty Years of Freedom: A Study of the Development of the Ideas of A.S. Neill.* London: Allen & Unwin.
This book traces the development of Summerhill and Neill's ideas aligned to the political and social context of the period as well as making connections with other progressive thinkers.

Neill, A.S. (1966) *Freedom Not License!* New York: Hart.
Neill's offer of advice on child rearing to American parents.

Stronach, I. (2006) 'Inspection and justice: HMI and Summerhill School'. In: Vaughan, M. (ed.) *Summerhill and A.S. Neill*. Maidenhead: Open University Press.
Stronach outlines the story of the famous Ofsted inspection of Summerhill and the following legal battle with the Department for Education and Employment.

REFERENCES

Bailey, R. (2013) *A.S. Neill*. London: Bloomsbury.
Brighouse, T. (2006) 'Introduction'. In: Vaughan, M. (ed.) *Summerhill and A.S. Neill*. Maidenhead: Open University Press.
Britzman, D. (2011) *Freud and Education*. London: Routledge.
Carr, D. (2000) *Professionalism and Ethics in Teaching*. Abingdon: Routledge.
Carr, D. (2003) *Making Sense of Education: An Introduction to the Philosophy and Theory of Education and Teaching*. London: RoutledgeFalmer.
Cohen, L., Manion, L. and Morrison, K. (2004) *A Guide to Teaching Practice* (5th edn). London: RoutledgeFalmer.
Croall, J. (1983) *Neill of Summerhill: The Permanent Rebel*. London: Routledge & Kegan Paul.
Gilbert, I. (2002) *Essential Motivation in the Classroom*. London: RoutledgeFalmer.
Hobson, P. (2001) 'A.S. Neill, 1883–1973'. In: Palmer, J. (ed.) *Fifty Modern Thinkers on Education: From Piaget to the Present*. London: Routledge.
Holt, J. (1969) *How Children Fail*. Harmondsworth: Penguin.
Howlett, J. (2013) *Progressive Education: A Critical Introduction*. London: Bloomsbury.
Illich, I. (1971) *Deschooling Society*. London: Marion Boyars Publishers.
Kyriacou, C. (1991) *Essential Teaching Skills*. Oxford: Blackwell.
MacBlain, S. (2014) *How Children Learn*. London: SAGE.
Meighan, R. (2007) *John Holt*. London: Bloomsbury.
Neill, A.S. (1953) *The Free Child*. London: Herbert Jenkins.
Neill, A.S. (1960) *Summerhill: A Radical Approach to Child Rearing*. New York: Hart.
Neill, A.S. (1967) *Talking of Summerhill*. London: Gollancz.
Neill, A.S. (1973) *Neill! Neill! Orange Peel! A Personal View of Ninety Years*. London: Weidenfeld & Nicolson.
Neill Readhead, Z. (2006) 'Summerhill Today'. In: Vaughan, M. (ed.) *Summerhill and A.S. Neill*. Maidenhead: Open University Press.
Spring, J. (1994) *Wheels in the Head: Education Philosophies of Authority, Freedom, and Culture from Socrates to Paulo Freire*. Maidenhead: McGraw-Hill.
Vaughan, M. (ed.) (2006) *Summerhill and A.S. Neill*. Maidenhead: Open University Press.
Warwick, P. (2012) 'Alternative Education'. In: Arthur, J. and Peterson, A. (eds) *The Routledge Companion to Education*. London: Routledge.
Williams, J. (2004) *Great Minds: Education's Most Influential Philosophers*. London: A *Times Education Supplement* Essential Guide.

4

JOHN GOODLAD

THE RENEWAL OF TEACHING AND LEARNING, SCHOOLS AND TEACHER EDUCATION

LEARNING OUTCOMES

After reading this chapter, you should be able to:

- appreciate the life and ideas of John Goodlad;
- identify and understand Goodlad's thoughts on non-grading, curriculum enquiry, schooling, teacher education and educational renewal;
- critically evaluate Goodlad's ideas;
- appreciate the links between his work and other educational thinkers;
- appraise how Goodlad's concepts are related to education and practice.

KEY WORDS

Non-grading (standards and standardised testing); curriculum enquiry; teacher education; educational renewal (not reform); morals, ethics and democracy in education.

INTRODUCTION

John Goodlad, the leading North American progressive educational thinker, scholar and researcher, died in 2014 aged ninety-four. For more than sixty years his work had an important influence on schooling, education and **teacher education**, particularly in the United States (Soder, 2014). He was a tireless campaigner for a more humanistic approach to education. The focuses of his work in education were many, but he had a profound impact on the discourse surrounding the role and function of schools. Goodlad's overarching aspiration was that schools should facilitate children to become free and full contributors in a democratic world by encouraging them to embrace learning and appreciate their civic responsibilities (Goodlad, 2004). This humanistic ideal was not only central to his work, but also underpins his optimism and sense of fair play in the education process. **Morals, ethics and democracy** are core aspects of the teaching process. For Goodlad, 'teaching the young has a moral dimension ... because education – a deliberate effort to develop values and sensibilities as well as skills – is a moral endeavour' (Goodlad et al., 1990: xii).

Goodlad's empirical research and writings can be identified as falling into the following major individual themes: **non-grading**, **curriculum enquiry**, schooling, teacher education and **educational renewal** (rather than reform). These themes evolved over the span of his long career and are very much interconnected. Shen, writing in 2001, clearly asserts the breadth and depth of Goodlad's work:

> As an educator, Goodlad is unique in the sense that he is a researcher, an activist and a philosopher. He conducts empirical studies on schooling and education, engages in putting his innovative ideas into practice, and reflects philosophically upon the social phenomenon called 'education'. The combination of being an empirical researcher, a philosophical thinker and an activist of educational renewal is uncommon in education. (2001: 123)

Goodlad wrote numerous books, many of which have been translated into other languages such as Japanese, Italian, French, Chinese, Hebrew and Spanish. His most seminal work, *A Place Called School: Prospects for the Future* (1984), was a landmark text that explored the effectiveness of public schooling in the United States. The data for the book were collected from 27,000 teachers, parents and pupils in schools across the United States. The book was given the Outstanding Book of the Year Award from the American Educational Research Association and the Distinguished Book of the Year Award from Kappa Delta Pi (Harmon, 2014). His other major works include: *The Dynamics of Educational Change: Toward Responsive Schools* (1975), *What Schools Are For* (1979), *Teachers for Our Nation's Schools* (1990), *Educational Renewal: Better Teachers, Better Schools* (1994), *In Praise of Education* (1997), *Romances with Schools: A Life in Education* (2004) and, with his associates, *Curriculum Inquiry: The Study of Curriculum Practice* (1979). To fully appreciate

Goodlad's works, we need to have an insight into his background, and an overview of his long career as a teacher and academic.

GOODLAD, THE PERSON

John Goodlad grew up in Vancouver, British Columbia, Canada during the time of the Great Depression. At school, in spite of his advanced reading ability, his parents were advised that he should repeat a year. His father, however, insisted that he progressed to the next level without hindrance, which he did and he even skipped forward a year later on in his schooling. The Great Depression and the requirement that pupils should repeat levels in their schooling were two factors that would have a lasting effect on his career. His first teaching post was in a rural one-room, multi-graded school – Woodward's Hill School in a rural setting in British Columbia. He quickly became exasperated by the set curriculum and inflexible grading processes. He began to adopt pioneering teaching methods using inventive resources. He did this to help engage pupils so that they could enjoy the learning process, because many of his pupils had to repeat grades as they failed the required tests for promotion to the next grade (Goodlad, 2004; Amrein-Beardsley, 2012).

His second teaching post was at the British Columbia Industrial School for ('delinquent') Boys – a 'reform' school. The word 'reform', as we shall see, features significantly in Goodlad's works. The school was near the town of Port Coquitlam and was known, for succinctness, as 'BISCOQ – pronounced *bisco* ... a fortresslike prison' (Goodlad, 2004: 156). His experience at his multi-graded first school stood him in good stead for BISCOQ. Many of his charges had already repeated a minimum of two grades and he could not be certain of the students' actual grade classifications. This notion of students not being promoted from one grade to another and having to repeat grades he found a fruitless and personally damaging process. At BISCOQ, he found this led to an 'ethos of defeat' for the boys and many of the staff (Goodlad, 2004: 178). His experiences at BISCOQ stimulated the focus for his PhD thesis, a study of the effects of promotion and non-promotion.

Goodlad's education leading to, and including, his master's degree was completed in Canada. He attained his doctorate at the University of Chicago in 1949; from there, he held a number of academic and leadership roles in higher education. He was a professor at Emory University, the University of Chicago, the University of California at Los Angeles (UCLA) and the University of Washington. The many leadership positions he held include Director of the University Elementary School (UES) (this was as part of the Englewood Project, an experiment in non-graded schooling at elementary level), and Dean of the Graduate School of Education, both at UCLA; Director of the Centre for Teacher Education at the University of Chicago; Director of the Centre for Educational Renewal at the University of Washington; and the President of the Institute for Educational Inquiry in Seattle. He was also the President of both the American

Educational Research Association and the American Association of Colleges for Teacher Education (Shen, 2001; Soder, 2014).

GOODLAD'S IDEAS

Goodlad's thoughts on non-grading, curriculum enquiry, schooling, teacher education and his overriding quest for educational renewal will be explored at this point. Also considered here will be his mission to create a moral, ethical and democratic form of education. Non-grading is an aspect of Goodlad's work that interested him professionally since his first teaching days at Woodward's Hill School and BISCOQ; this interest was to be maintained throughout his career as a researcher. For Goodlad, the grading process was harmful, both academically and morally:

> If kids don't pass some arbitrary standard of what a grade means, you punish them twice. They've already experienced failure, an enormously debilitating experience, and then you tell them they have to do it all over again. (Goodlad, in Goldberg, 2000: 83)

Goodlad was an avid campaigner for non-graded elementary schools. He was also instrumental in setting up and leading UCLA's University Elementary School (UES), which practised the principle of non-grading. His research from his PhD and postdoctoral work enabled him to build a convincing argument for championing non-grading for moral, psychological, economic and pedagogical reasons (Shen, 2001). He also challenged the growing trend of the use of national standardised testing. Furthermore, the term 'standards' he felt was being used by the government and business as a key tool for the promotion of school reform. Goodlad argued that:

> The central issue had to do, of course, with aligning standards, tests, and classroom teaching. Who can be held accountable when the tests are prepared to measure the standards but teachers do not teach to the standards because they are ill prepared or because they disagree with them, and the test items are thus selected from content unfamiliar to the students? (2002: 18)

Instead, he called for self-imposed standards which most teachers strive to set for their children as well as for themselves. The delay in receiving national standardised test results, he thought, hampered teachers with their daily lesson planning, and he argued that teachers were well aware of the progress their pupils were making without national standardised testing. Goodlad emphasised that although teachers welcomed help, they strongly felt aggrieved by the 'totalitarian intrusion into decisions for which they will be held responsible and the side effects that invariably accompany such reform mandates' (2002: 18).

His involvement in curriculum enquiry was far-reaching, with the ultimate aim of improving students' lives so they could discover their own meanings of the world.

Curriculum enquiry, for Goodlad, was the study of all the facets of curriculum practice, such as 'context, assumptions, conduct, problems, and outcomes' (Goodlad and associates, 1979: 17). His notion of curriculum enquiry involved three aspects:

> The first is *substantive* and has to do with goals, subject matter, materials, and the like – the commonplaces of any curriculum. Inquiry into their nature and worth. The second is *political-social*. Inquiry involves the study of all those human processes through which some interests come to prevail over others ... The third is *technical-professional*. Curriculum inquiry examines those processes ... through which curricula are improved, installed, or replaced. (Goodlad and associates, 1979: 17)

Goodlad, then, argued that the curriculum was a complex and multifaceted entity that merited in-depth enquiry for it to be developed. He was frustrated by those who thought that curricula could be built by authors of curriculum textbooks or even by teachers in their schools. For Goodlad (1984), the curriculum was a living thing; it could not be built, as it already exists. He contended that the curriculum was constantly changing in all schools. The reasons for these changes were many and include students continually reconstructing how they saw themselves; students differing from one year to the next; and the evolution of technology and its uses in schools. These changes are usually small, but for Goodlad they merited enquiry so that teachers could be informed in their pursuit of improving the students' learning experience (Stake, 1987). As such, we feel that Goodlad would have agreed with Stenhouse's view that any 'curriculum study should be grounded in the study of classrooms' (Stenhouse, 1975: 75).

Goodlad was dismayed by the notion that schools should concentrate explicitly on the influence that teachers have on pupil learning. He thought that schooling should also embrace and interact with families and the community to enhance the learning experience (Amrein-Beardsley, 2012). Schools, for Goodlad, should be extending their role to include less restricted hours of opening, and encouraging all age groups in the community to be involved so 'the school becomes the centre for community education, recreation, and education-related human services' (Goodlad, 1984: 350). He also argued that when schooling was seen as contributory to the economy, 'the scope of education provided will continue to narrow, to the detriment of childhood' (Goodlad, 2000: 89). In a similar vein, he felt that schooling should not be solely focused on preparing children for employment. He contested that a young person with a broad and grounded education would be readily equipped to assimilate the skills of a particular work role when needed (Goodlad, 2000).

His research into schooling was extensive and included aspects of the classroom environment, the history of schools and early years schooling. Overall, from his research activities he perceived that the 'function of schools today appears to be more to sort the young for their place in society than to educate them for productive, responsible, satisfying participation in it' (Goodlad, 2002: 22). Moreover, this research into schooling in the USA revealed the use of rote learning, prescriptive methods for teaching practice, and set and standardised tests that were fixated on low-level cognitive skills. The research also found a lack of investment for both promoting aspiring classroom teaching and for advancing teacher education (Darling-Hammond, 1997; Goodlad, 1984). Goodlad addressed the questions of the aims, functions and goals of schools. In particular, the goals of schools are quite interesting in that they encapsulate Goodlad's personal philosophy of the purpose of schooling. His idea was that the goals of schools form four separate, yet interwoven, categories:

1. *Academic*, embracing all intellectual skills and domains of knowledge.
2. *Vocational*, geared to developing readiness for productive work and economic responsibility.
3. *Social and civic*, relating to preparing for socialisation into complex society.
4. *Personal*, emphasising the development of individual responsibility, talents and free expression.

(Shen, 2001: 124)

Another major theme of Goodlad's work was teacher education. He railed against the 'increasing technification of teacher education' and called for the inclusion of the 'moral dimensions of teaching and moral mission of schooling' (Shen, 2001: 125). Goodlad thought that teacher education focused too much on

> psychological considerations which emphasise such things as human development and teaching methods at the expense of the sociological and cultural phenomena as well as the functioning of the school. (Wideen, 1987: 8)

Teacher education departments in universities should also be closely linked with schools, a model similar to that practised at UES. His thoughts, and those of his associates, on teacher education are explored in *Places Where Teachers Are Taught* (1990) (Shen, 2001). Goodlad was quite scathing of the teacher education programmes in the USA. He found them lacking in innovative practice, as well as being disconcertingly similar to each other and generally inadequate (Goodlad, 1984). He also highlighted a number of major points that needed addressing to improve teacher education provision. These included the lack of synergy between subject departments and schools of education, and the need for more research-informed practice and more engagement in the research process. He also argued that greater care and consideration was needed when assigning student teachers with classroom teachers to ensure that the students were not being encouraged to perpetuate outdated practices (Goodlad, 1984).

Educational renewal is central to Goodlad's thinking and the focus of his research on schools and teacher education. He stressed the need for the school to be at the heart of renewal and the head teacher to be the lead in such renewal. Goodlad contested that for renewal to occur, there must be some combination of internal responsiveness and external stimulation; for renewal to continue, there must be some continual, productive state of tension between these two essential sets of forces. (Shen, 2001: 125)

He uses the term 'renewal' rather than educational 'reform'. For Goodlad, the term 'reform' is a disgrace as he felt it reflected all that was wrong with the American system of public schooling, as it was 'a linear model of inputs and outputs, prescribed by well-meaning outsiders, whose initiatives show just how out of touch they are' (Coffield and Williamson, 2012: 70).

Goodlad became exasperated with those who readily used the term 'reform'. He recalled his days at BISCOQ, which was also known as a reform school, where the perceptions from the public and many of the staff were that the boys were bad. It was also assumed that the staff at BISCOQ would do something with these boys to make them law-abiding citizens and that they would comply with the staff's directions, but this seldom happened. Indeed, many pupils filled cells in the adult prison system after leaving BISCOQ. He argued that this was a shocking model to use for schools and education generally (Goodlad, 1999, 2004). Furthermore, he considered that reform was 'a nasty concept that suggests bad people and bad conditions that must be reformed in somebody else's image' (2000: 83).

Goodlad thought such reforms were driven by political and market forces, and did not provide a genuine learning experience for all children. He called for a Bill of Educational Rights and an Educational Constitution that would ensure a process of educational renewal. Goodlad contested that these two measures would assure that the children receive the education that they deserved. It would also ensure that education would embrace the 'freedoms, responsibilities, and justice embedded in its democratic principles' (Goodlad, 2004: 330). Conversely, he argued that the current system of schooling was more fitting 'to the packaging, distribution and standardisation of milk products than the development of thoughtful, responsible, caring members of a social and political democracy' (2004: 280). He thought that all educational reform was politically driven and as such it

> puts policy and practice out of balance. Adults with quite ordinary academic records invent the past in exhorting schools to be hard and tough, as schools supposedly were for them. 'Educating the whole child' is frequently viewed as a dangerous notion of woolly-headed progressive educators ... [and] when the next era of reform comes around, the targets of blame are once more the students, their teachers, teacher educators, and the schools. (2002: 17–18)

Goodlad stressed that questions regarding public schooling were indeed moral questions, and that teaching was a moral ethical undertaking. He stated that teaching practice is itself an ethical and difficult function. Good teaching should encompass these complex moral and ethical issues rather than the evidence from test results, performativity and technical indicators (Goodlad et al., 1990). For example, Goodlad disputed the call from business circles for the use of tougher standardised testing, because higher test scores did not predict the more ethical and moral attributes of those being tested and graded. Test scores fail to produce the desired virtues: 'not problem-solving skills, not good work habits, not honesty, not dependability, not loyalty, and not the dispositions and virtues embedded in our expectations for schooling' (Goodlad, 2002: 19). These issues in teaching involve matters of caring for pupils and the community, a regard for social justice, a high level of competence in teachers' subject knowledge, and the engagement in collegiate inquiry. Goodlad and his contemporaries felt strongly that teachers need these attributes to enable them to act ethically:

> A non-intellectual and/or non-reflective classroom environment is hardly conducive to a thoughtful engagement with information and knowledge beyond rote learning. Teachers who lack competence in their disciplines and/or who teach outside their areas of competence, as well as those who conspire in such practices disgrace the very concept of pedagogy and are engaged in clearly unethical activities. (Sirotnik, 1990: 311)

The democratic, moral and ethical aspects of Goodlad's ideas, together with his thoughts on non-grading, curriculum enquiry, schooling, teacher education and educational renewal have close associations with a number of other educational thinkers.

⟳ LINKS WITH OTHER THEORISTS

As Goodlad's work is so far-ranging, it would be feasible to make connections between his ideas and numerous other educational thinkers. Primarily, though, it is with other North American progressive educators, particularly those with a strong sense of social justice, where the closest links can be made. There is clear evidence of John Dewey's work in the notions developed by Goodlad in a number of ways. Both thought that education should be about developing children to become caring human beings in the broadest sense (Goodlad, 1984). Also, that education should not be focused and driven solely for economic reasons; rather, it requires a broader more social and critical aim, which

> enables people to think for themselves and debate with others, to respect them and to engage with political life of their societies and not merely their own local communities, is a necessary requirement of a healthy democracy. (Coffield and Williamson, 2012: 22)

There is also a close association with the manner in which both Dewey and Goodlad put into practice their thoughts and philosophies. Dewey's Laboratory School at the University of Chicago for observing children and developing teaching and learning methods served as a centre for exemplary practice. This is similar to the role and function of UES, which was started and led by Goodlad at UCLA (Goodlad, 1984).

Furthermore, UES has since been renamed UCLA Lab School (Harmon, 2014). Similarly, there are ties between Goodlad and a number of other North American progressive educational thinkers, most notably Nel Noddings, Michael Apple and Linda Darling-Hammond.

Noddings was also drawn to curriculum enquiry and the adverse effects of political imposition on schooling. However, it was her commitment to encouraging teachers to adopt an ethical and caring approach to their teaching that was most in tune with Goodlad's ideas. Noddings argued that 'caring is a moral attitude' and urged teachers to embrace this approach in their practice (Flinders, 2001: 214). Resembling Goodlad's notion of educational renewal and the imposition of education policy from politicians, Apple (1988) contested that those people with close links to the realities of schools such as pupils, parents and teachers should have a greater say in the process of education. Apple's work also involved the relationship between culture and power in education, as well as the increasingly economically driven character of the school curriculum. Like Goodlad, he argued that schools should adopt democratic practices that reflect the democratic principles in society as a whole (Torre, 2001). Similar to Goodlad, Ivan Illich challenged the notion that schools assemble and grade young people in age-specific groups, an idea that Illich considered was founded on the institutionalisation processes and rituals of schools where separating children into different age groups submits children to the control of the teacher (Illich, 1971). Also, Illich's idea of commodification resonates with Goodlad's thoughts that schooling and the curriculum are being packaged like commercial products. For the most part, it would appear that there are a number of associations between Goodlad and Darling-Hammond: both worked tirelessly on matters of research, fairness, schooling and teacher education, and her formation of Professional Development Schools has similarities with UES. However, there are two major differences: 1) their different standpoints on assessment; 2) more significantly, between Goodlad's notion of renewal and Darling-Hammond's work in educational reform as a policy-maker.

The English educator Basil Bernstein was likewise interested in matters of the curriculum. He was also, more poignantly, interested in the democratic notion that all young people experience a rich education. Bernstein called for a democratic set of three rights for students, and that schools guarantee these rights. These are the rights of enhancement, inclusion and participation (Bernstein, 2000). Another English educational thinker with close connections with Goodlad was Lawrence Stenhouse. Stenhouse was embedded in curriculum research and he also thought those closely connected with school practice should have a greater say in the development and content of the curriculum. Stenhouse's views were that the curriculum was overly influenced by the dominant class and culture in society, and his Humanities Curriculum Project (HCP) endeavoured to explore this concept. Like Goodlad, Stenhouse also encouraged, through the HCP, close partnership working between teachers in schools and academics in university schools of education (Stenhouse, 1975). There are other educational thinkers who could be associated with Goodlad. Most of these thinkers would loosely belong to a progressive genre of educators and, as such, this would be the foundation of some of the criticisms his work attracted.

⊛ CRITIQUING GOODLAD'S IDEAS

First, criticism of Goodlad's work relates to the impracticability of some of his ideas because of the political and market-driven approach to education in the United States and in other developed countries. Second, parts of his work are somewhat contradictory. Third, his concept of renewal being driven from school head teachers and teachers is considered an unrealistic option.

Similar to Dewey, conceivably one of the most influential thinkers in education even today, Goodlad's ideas of renewal and school democracy were considered too revolutionary for the United States government, educational policy-makers and even most parents. The drive to create an economy-focused and skills-based education system by many countries appears to be the current pattern where, unfortunately, the needs of the market override the humanistic aspects of a democratic progressive education system. Despite the innovative ideas that, Goodlad pursued, which included the setting up of UES, it has proved that implementing renewal and sustaining its concept is a remarkably difficult undertaking. Even those teachers who began to use democratic and ethically based classroom practice eventually returned to traditional methods of teaching (Gibbons and Norman, 1987). His notion of non-graded schools grounded on pupils' interests, particularly in a skills-based and economically driven education system, is an example of the impracticability of some of his ideas (Amrein-Beardsley, 2012).

Goodlad's inclusive ideas on schools – involving and encouraging all the community, regardless of age, to take part in the learning process – is rather at odds with his 'age-four-to-sixteen model [of schooling which was] better suited to the developmental characteristics of the young' (Goodlad, 2004: 323). He contended that the presence of students between sixteen and eighteen years of age had a detrimental effect on the younger children. For example, he offers the view that exposure to and use of alcohol and drugs increased markedly in the culture of the sixteen-and-over age groups, and therefore questions whether 'they are best suited to remain as role models for their younger schoolmates?' (Goodlad, 2004: 323).

The idea of head teachers and teachers being the instigators of educational renewal is a worthy concept and he argues his case very passionately. However, within the increasingly demanding environment evident in schools, it is a challenging and unrealistic prospect. As he admitted himself, renewal 'requires motivation, dedication, systematic and systemic evolution, and *time*, and it is not possible in the current educational system' (Goodlad et al., 1990: 25). Furthermore, it is possibly naive to expect that all teachers and head teachers will possess the revolutionary zeal to implement and sustain the renewal that was envisaged by Goodlad. It is accepted that many will take up this call for renewal and endeavour to make decisions themselves for change while others will be content to comply and carry out directions imposed from above (Coffield and Williamson, 2012). In a similar way, it is idealistic to consider that the successes of exemplary schools such as UES can be replicated more widely. Nevertheless, it is argued that such idealism and optimism should be an inspiration to policy-makers and educators when they consider the way in which they think about and apply Goodlad's ideas.

GOODLAD'S IDEAS IN RELATION TO EDUCATION AND PRACTICE

Some of Goodlad's work relates to education in its broadest sense, which encompasses such conceptual notions as the function of schools, democracy and social justice. While other areas of his work are related to practice, it is recognised that his ideas are quite progressive and could be tricky to apply within the current constraints in formal educational settings. However, it is argued that the spirit underpinning his ideas is student-centred, meaningful and positive, and as such they are worth pursuing where possible. This part of the chapter will offer ideas relating to Goodlad's work in the broader aspects of education, schools and communities, teacher education and teaching.

Goodlad's vision of educational renewal was based upon the foundations of an ethical, moral and democratic set of principles. The key actors in this renewal were to be an alliance of school educators and other interested members of the community. This would be a school and community endeavour, because it was these people who knew the area, school and the cultural context of the locality, with head teachers taking the leading role. The reason why he felt this was significant was because he thought the politically driven concept of educational reform was 'the perpetuation of myths ... [implemented by outside] policy makers, who are currently bogged down in determining matters of teaching, learning, and assessment for which they are unqualified' (Goodlad, 1999: 38).

Coffield and Williamson (2012) agree with the sentiments behind Goodlad's concept of educational renewal rather than reform. However, they argue that, particularly in the context of the UK education system, the head teacher of the school (or college principal or university vice-chancellor) is not in the best position to advance the cause of renewal and make it work. Leaders of schools, colleges and universities are hindered in carrying out this renewal leadership role:

> Their time is absorbed in responding to the latest round of government initiatives and changes in funding, the ensuring of survival and growth in their institutions, and the day-to-day running of huge, complex social organisations. (Coffield and Williamson, 2012: 70)

Nevertheless, Coffield and Williamson offer a way in which renewal can be implemented in practice that is still within the spirit of Goodlad's concept. For them, the impetus for renewal needs to come from teachers and tutors who are excited about a more democratic educational system, curriculum and classroom practices. This can be further enhanced by schools' senior leaders encouraging high expectations of learners and teachers alike, and also avoiding being drawn into administrative encumbrances wherever possible (Chubb and Moe, 1997). Coffield and Williamson, like Goodlad, championed the cause of building alliances with the community and employers, and between other teachers in the larger community (Coffield and Williamson, 2012). These alliances, for Goodlad, could also include other schools. Such alliances encouraged innovative ideas on school organisation, the curriculum and cooperative teaching methods; they could also act as a conduit for challenging the traditional conventions of schooling (Goodlad, 1984).

Practical ideas for realising his ideas of the age-four-to-sixteen model of schooling were founded on his thoughts on what best matched the developmental needs of the young. His ideas are of interest as they begin to set out the sequential and developmental content of a renewed educational system – possibly a brief outline for a renewed curriculum. The proposal was:

> for there to be three small four-year units, each with differentiated educational functions ... the early unit devoted to romantic exploration of children's close-at-hand world, extended through stories of other times and places; the middle unit of greater precision, connecting with the larger and human and natural environment; and the third emphasising generalisation and application. (Goodlad, 2004: 323)

For schools to be truly effective within his concept of educational renewal, they needed to be 'richly textured environments guided by caring, competent, and professional teachers' (Goodlad, 1998: 2). He argued that children thrive intellectually when they are born into invigorating sensory surroundings. This development is enhanced if the children enrol in schools in prosperous communities, with a wealth of teaching resources, and which attract and keep teachers of note. Such schools are schools of choice and often oversubscribed (Goodlad, 1998). However, in his vision for renewal this correlation between affluence and an enhanced intellectual development need not occur; all schools could benefit all children. Included in Goodlad's vision was the age-four-to-sixteen model, with the three small four-year units of development, which has been described. There would no longer be the need in schools for choice, or for specialist schools, because arts, sports and sciences would be included in the education for all pupils (Goodlad, 1999).

Goodlad set out his vision of the ideal school based upon his empirical research carried out and published in his seminal 1984 text *A Place Called School: Prospects for the Future*. His ideal school was clearly articulated in an interview:

> The ideal school is small. The only valid argument for enlarging schools is to provide a broader curriculum, which runs out very quickly with increasing size. This [increasing size should be limited to] ... 400 youngsters in elementary school, 600 in middle school, and 800 in secondary school. (Goodlad, 1999: 38)

To support his vision of the ideal school, he also advocated that schools should embrace the concept of professional development centres to provide teachers with leadership skills. These centres would also enable teachers to be closely involved with other public service professionals in areas such as health and welfare (Goodlad, 1999). Another aspect which he encountered in his research into schooling was the difference in the classroom environments between the early years and secondary schools. Mostly, he found the early years' classroom contained stimulating, informative and colourful displays and artefacts, whereas, in contrast, the secondary classrooms were drab, cramped for space and devoid of wall displays. Goodlad felt that a stimulating classroom environment was just as important for students as they progressed through the latter grades of schooling (Goodlad, 1984).

Goodlad was an enthusiastic advocate for a mode of teacher education that was less prescribed and technically orientated. He strove to promote a more intellectually and morally based form of teacher preparation and continuing teacher professional development. With this in mind, his practical ideas for improving teacher education centred on closer relationships between faculties of teacher education (or schools of education) in universities and schools themselves, a notion that was prompted by his experiences as the director of UES. He was particularly interested in creating schools that could be designated as centres of innovation and best practice. Goodlad explains his concept of who would be involved and the role and function of such schools:

> To them [centres of innovation and best practice], outstanding career and head teachers are to be drawn. Beginning teachers are to be interned *only* in these schools. University faculty members orientated to research and development in school organisation, curriculum, and teaching are to be provided with space in these schools and here carry out their scholarly inquiries, sharing their expertise with the school faculty. The head teachers and a few highly gifted teachers will serve as clinical faculty in the schools of education ... Research, school improvement, in-service education of experienced teachers, and preservice teacher education will proceed hand in hand. (Goodlad, 1984: 316)

For Goodlad, an effective teacher education programme 'lies not in classroom competence, but the development of a professional commitment within which each competence is based' (Goodlad and Soder, 1990: 244). He argued that a crucial task for teacher educators was to transform the required professional commitment into workable approaches for those learning to teach. This task, he felt, included five core factors: first, motivation to want to teach; second, creating an ethos of professional behaviour; third, building and negotiating proficiencies with parents; fourth, acquiring a spirit of acceptance of criticism through reflective practice; and fifth, developing professional partnerships within, and outside, the profession (Goodlad and Soder, 1990).

The primary duty of teachers is to establish and maintain an environment that will foster learning for all their pupils. A central part of this, both morally and pedagogically, is that teachers need to believe that each of their charges is able to learn. It is the teacher's role to plan, make choices in creating a learning environment and reflect on the effectiveness of those choices. Goodlad contended that there were fundamental conditions that teachers needed to demonstrate for pupils' learning to occur. These included 'motivation and encouragement, knowledge of subject matter, opportunity to learn, time, space, appropriate curricula materials, clear instruction, and methods of measuring student learning progress' (Goodlad and Soder, 1990: 261). Interestingly, he goes further by arguing that if just one of these conditions is absent or lacking, 'learning is compromised, and the teacher is not fulfilling his or her moral responsibility' (Goodlad and Soder, 1990: 261).

Goodlad observed some excellent teaching during his research into classroom practice. For example, he came across a teacher who expended less energy than other teachers in controlling students. This teacher was observed to be fair and demonstrated a caring persona, and set tasks for the students that were challenging but not too difficult. Goodlad also noticed that in this class the pupils had more respect for each other, and worked cooperatively with each other and the teacher (Goodlad, 1984). This observation also indicated some of the benefits of teachers creating cooperative and collaborative classroom environments, where pupils learn to change effortlessly between talking with their fellows and the teacher (Moore, 2000).

Goodlad argued that teachers should have the freedom to choose topics that matched the interests of pupils; furthermore, that they should use all the teaching methods, activities and resources available to encourage their charges to be creative. He felt that it was better for pupils to learn fewer topics and to know them thoroughly than to cover lists of topics just for regurgitation. For Goodlad, the quest 'is for understanding and for the processes basic to acquiring this understanding' (Goodlad, 1984: 339). What was paramount for Goodlad in his thoughts on teaching was that teachers should work collaboratively, and in doing so exercise their democratic status as professionals (Coffield and Williamson, 2012).

Goodlad's research and his work is located within the context of US education; nevertheless, it is contested that his notions of moral and democratic education, together with his ideas of non-grading, curriculum enquiry, schooling, teacher education and educational renewal certainly have relevance for educators in other countries.

REFLECTIVE TASK

Goodlad stated that school goals should have four interlinking categories: academic, vocational, social and civic, and personal. Thinking about your own practice setting, list the opportunities that are *currently* provided for learners for the social and civic, and the personal categories. Then, having read and reflected on Goodlad's ideas in this chapter, list any further opportunities that could be offered to students for these same two categories.

SUMMARY

John Goodlad's long and distinguished career as an educator and academic has influenced the way that educators think about schooling and education in the United States and internationally. His sense of fairness and the quest for a democratic, ethical and moral system of education is evident throughout his works. His main themes of interest, however, were non-grading, curriculum enquiry, schooling, teacher education and the overarching concept of educational renewal. These themes were explored in his numerous articles and books. Apart from being an educator and academic, he was also the leader of a number of higher education institutes and innovative projects such as UES. These leadership roles enabled him to apply his ideas and to encourage others to adopt humanistic practices.

Both Goodlad and Dewey shared a belief in the concept of a democratic education. They created exemplar schools to observe and develop teaching and learning practice. Other North American progressive educators have similar ideas to Goodlad. Noddings's thoughts on a caring and ethical approach to teaching are aligned with Goodlad's ideas. There are also parallels between Apple's thoughts on culture and power in education, economy and the curriculum, and democracy. Similarly, Illich's radical views have a certain resonance with Goodlad's ideas of standards and testing, the role of the teacher and the increasing commodification of education, in particular the packaging of the curriculum. Darling-Hammond's and Goodlad's ideas are similar on a number of counts; however, her involvement in educational reform would be at odds with Goodlad's renewal. There are two British educators with close connections with Goodlad: first, Bernstein and his democratic rights for students; second, Stenhouse, regarding curriculum research and the call for greater links between schools and universities.

Goodlad's work has attracted criticism because of the impracticability and unsustainability of some of his ideas, particularly in the political and economy-driven approach to educational policy-making. There are also some contradictions in his work. Furthermore, the notion that head teachers lead and nurture the changes he advanced in schools is unrealistic in terms of time and their current roles and responsibilities. Yet there are a number of areas where Goodlad's ideas can be put into practice. Some of these include schools involving the whole community in their activities in more innovative ways; thinking more about the social and civic and personal aspects of schooling; and providing for closer links between university schools of education and individual schools for professional development and research opportunities. Goodlad's work provides a refreshing, optimistic and caring foundation for practice and reflection.

GLOSSARY OF TERMS

Curriculum enquiry   Goodlad was critical of the ordered and obligatory product-based curriculum. He argued that curriculum enquiry should be founded on the complexities involved in the learning and teaching that occurs in the classroom. For Goodlad, the curriculum was a living entity and curriculum enquiry was beyond the scope of writers of curriculum textbooks. Curriculum enquiry, for Goodlad, consisted of three aspects: *substance* (goals, subject matter and resources); *political–social* (human processes and ordering of interests); *technical–professional* (curricula improvement and development processes).

Educational renewal   Coffield and Williamson (2012: 70) stated that Goodlad had found the 'phrase "school reform" an abomination'. Goodlad's strong condemnation of the phrase originates from his early career as a multi-graded school teacher, as well as at BISCOQ – the 'reform school'. He thought the term 'reform' offered a narrow and deficit meaning, in which pupils, teachers and schools were in need of improving. What was required was a radical renewal, rather than reform, where education embraced social justice and the principles of democracy for both pupils and teachers alike.

Morals, ethics and democracy in education   This, for Goodlad, underpinned his whole philosophy of education. He argued that thoughtful and effective teaching was about caring for learners and the community around schools. Teachers and indeed schools should prioritise the multifaceted ethical and moral issues over instrumental and performative teaching and the reliance on standards and standardised test results. He also thought that teacher reflection was key in creating a moral, ethical and democratic learning environment.

Non-grading   From his time at Woodward's Hill School and BISCOQ, Goodlad felt that the grading system, and later the use of standards and standardised testing, were harmful to learners' academic and moral development. He championed the cause of non-graded elementary schools that were modelled on his innovative University Elementary School. Furthermore, he challenged the increasing use of standards and standardised testing, as he felt they did not produce the desired virtues of nurturing the whole child.

Teacher education   Goodlad considered that teacher education programmes in the United States were too prescriptive and technically orientated. What was required, he argued, were programmes that encompassed a more moral position in relation to teachers' roles in schools. There was, he contested, too much emphasis on teaching methods, child development and psychological matters, rather than the important issues of the social and cultural influences on schooling and the function of the teacher.

 # FURTHER READING

Goodlad, J. and associates (1974) *Looking Behind the Classroom Door*. Worthington, OH: Charles A. Jones Publishing.

A report on a far-reaching observational study of the organisation, curriculum and pedagogy of numerous elementary schools in the United States.

Goodlad, J., Mantle-Bromley, C. and Goodlad, S. (2004) *Education for Everyone: Agenda for Education in Democracy*. Indianapolis, IN: Jossey-Bass.
The forefathers of the United States looked upon education as providing an understanding and a practical preparation of democracy. This book argues for a universal system of education to make schools safe and democratic environments.

Oakes, J. and Goodlad, J. (2005) *Keeping Track: How Schools Structure Inequality* (2nd edn). New Haven, CT: Yale University Press.
An exploration of how grouping students according to ability levels mirrors the class and racial inequalities in the United States.

Sirotnik, K. (1999) 'On inquiry and education'. In: Sirotnik, K. and Soder, R. (eds) *The Beat of a Different Drummer: Essays on Educational Renewal in Honor of John, I. Goodlad*. New York: Peter Lang Publishing.
A review of Goodlad's positive contribution in advancing schooling as an important factor for human and social well-being.

REFERENCES

Amrein-Beardsley, A. (2012) *Inside the Academy*. Video with Dr John Goodlad. Available online at: http://insidetheacademy.asu.edu/john-goodlad

Bernstein, B. (2000) *Pedagogy, Symbolic Control, and Identity: Theory, Research, and Critique* (revised edn). London: Taylor & Francis.

Chubb, J. and Moe, T. (1997) 'Politics, markets, and the organisation of schools'. In: Halsey, A., Lauder, H., Brown, P. and Stuart Wells, A. (eds) *Education: Culture, Economy, Society*. Oxford: Oxford University Press.

Coffield, F. and Williamson, B. (2012) *From Exam Factories to Communities of Discovery: The Democratic Route*. London: Institute of Education, University of London.

Darling-Hammond, L. (1997) 'Restructuring schools for student success'. In: Halsey, A., Lauder, H., Brown, P. and Stuart Wells, A. (eds) *Education: Culture, Economy, Society*. Oxford: Oxford University Press.

Flinders, D. (2001) 'Nel Noddings, 1929–'. In: Palmer, J. (ed.) *Fifty Modern Thinkers on Education: From Piaget to the Present*. London: Routledge.

Gibbons, M. and Norman, P. (1987) 'An integrated model for sustained staff development'. In: Wideen, M. and Andrews, I. (eds) *Staff Development for School Improvement: A Focus on the Teacher*. London: Falmer Press.

Goldberg, M. (2000) 'Leadership for change – interview with John Goodlad'. *Phi Delta Kappan*, 82 (1): 82–5.

Goodlad, J. (1975) *The Dynamics of Educational Change: Toward Responsive Schools*. New York: McGraw-Hill.

Goodlad, J. (1979) *What Schools Are For*. Bloomington, IN: Phi Delta Kappa.

Goodlad, J. (1984) *A Place Called School: Prospects for the Future*. New York: McGraw-Hill.

Goodlad, J. (1994) *Educational Renewal: Better Teachers, Better Schools*. San Francisco, CA: Jossey-Bass.

Goodlad, J. (1997) *In Praise of Education*. New York: Teachers College Press.

Goodlad, J. (1998) 'Schools for all seasons'. *Phi Delta Kappan*, 79 (9): 670–1.

Goodlad, J. (1999) 'Interview: Educational renewal'. *Phi Delta Kappan*, 36 (1): 35–8.

Goodlad, J. (2000) 'Education and democracy'. *Phi Delta Kappan*, 82 (1): 86–9.

Goodlad, J. (2002) 'Kudzu, Rabbits, and School Reform'. *Phi Delta Kappan*, 84 (1): 16–21.

Goodlad, J. (2004) *Romances with Schools: A Life in Education*. New York: McGraw-Hill.

Goodlad, J. and associates (1979) *Curriculum Inquiry: The Study of Curriculum Practice*. New York: McGraw-Hill.

Goodlad, J. and associates (1990) *Places Where Teachers Are Taught*. San Francisco, CA: Jossey-Bass.

Goodlad, J. and Soder, R. (1990) *Teachers for Our Nation's Schools*. San Francisco, CA: Jossey-Bass.

Goodlad, J., Soder, R. and Sirotnik, K. (eds) (1990) *The Moral Dimensions of Teaching*. San Francisco, CA: Jossey-Bass.

Harmon, J. (2014) *In Memoriam: John Goodlad, Former Dean of the UCLA Education School*. Los Angeles, CA: UCLA.

Illich, I. (1971) *Deschooling Society*. London: Marion Boyars Publishers.

Moore, A. (2000) *Teaching and Learning: Pedagogy, Curriculum and Pedagogy*. London: RoutledgeFalmer.

Shen, J. (2001) 'John I. Goodlad, 1920–'. In: Palmer, J. (ed.) *Fifty Modern Thinkers on Education: From Piaget to the Present*. London: Routledge.

Sirotnik, K. (1990) 'Society, schooling, teaching, and preparing to teach'. In: Goodlad, J., Soder, R. and Sirotnik, K. (eds) *The Moral Dimensions of Teaching*. San Francisco, CA: Jossey-Bass.

Soder, R. (2014) *John Goodlad – Obituary*. Available online at: www.uwyo.edu/wsup/_files/docs/johngoodladobituary.doc

Stake, R. (1987) 'An evolutionary view of programming staff development'. In: Wideen, M. and Andrews, I. (eds) *Staff Development for School Improvement: A Focus on the Teacher*. London: Falmer Press.

Stenhouse, L. (1975) *An Introduction to Curriculum Research and Development*. Oxford: Heinemann Educational.

Torre, C. (2001) 'Michael W. Apple, 1942–'. In: Palmer, J. (ed.) *Fifty Modern Thinkers on Education: From Piaget to the Present*. London: Routledge.

Wideen, M. (1987) 'Perspectives on staff development'. In: Wideen, M. and Andrews, I. (eds) *Staff Development for School Improvement: A Focus on the Teacher*. London: Falmer Press.

5

BASIL BERNSTEIN

LANGUAGE CODES, SOCIAL CLASS, PEDAGOGY AND THE CURRICULUM

LEARNING OUTCOMES

After reading this chapter, you should be able to:

- appreciate how Bernstein's background led to his work on language and social class in relation to education;
- identify and understand Bernstein's notions of language codes, classification and framing, and pedagogy;
- recognise the links between Bernstein's ideas and those of other educational and sociological thinkers;
- critically appraise his works;
- identify which facets of Bernstein's works could be applied to the classroom.

KEY WORDS

Restricted and elaborate language codes; classification and framing; collection and integrated types of curriculum; visible and invisible pedagogies; democratic pedagogy; message systems.

INTRODUCTION

Basil Bernstein, who died in 2000, was the most renowned British social theorist in the field of the sociology of education; his work was of intellectual substance and significance, and his ideas will be of consequence in the future (Moore, 2006). It was through his many papers that social scientists in the 1960s and 1970s became conscious of the possibilities of sociolinguistics. He demonstrated a stimulating insight into the associations between social and cultural groupings, and the manner in which culture was assumed (Giglioli, 1972). Bernstein became an active member of a growing group of sociologists of the time whose principal aim was to explore and expose the effects of social class and regionalism in British schooling. Within this group of sociologists, 'Bernstein was, by far, the most persuasive, generative and articulate of his generation' (Goodson, 2001: 163). His work was known to, and often cited by, linguists, sociologists and educators throughout the world, as well as being the focus of interest and contention (Atkinson, 1985).

Throughout his academic life, Bernstein strove to analyse one of society's great afflictions, that of the recurrence of disadvantage in the educational system. He viewed schools as being active purveyors of privilege and disadvantage – his aim was to make schools fairer environments for all, regardless of class background. He examined how language, family and the complex systems and processes of education influenced social and educational inequalities (Goodson, 2001; Sadovnik et al., 2013). He found that many children with average levels of intelligence finished their compulsory education labelled as failures. The prevailing thought from many was that 'society has given them the opportunity, and they have failed to respond to it'. This perception, in Bernstein's view, was hurtful and wrong; he wanted to know why these young people were identified as failures and then to rectify the causes (Halliday, 1973: ix).

Bernstein's work spanned three evolving and interrelated major themes. The first theme in his earlier work was mainly concerned with language codes; the second theme focused on **classification and framing** and the construction of the curriculum; the third theme explored pedagogic practice (Goodson, 2001). All three of these themes were, for Bernstein, connected with issues of social class. It is arguably the first theme of language and social class that Bernstein is most noted for. He contended that social class and family socialisation produce characteristic types of speech. For him, working-class students learn and use **'restricted' language codes**, while middle-class children learn and use **'elaborated' language codes**. Thomas uses frank and explicit language to show the difference between the two codes, which is possibly fitting to consider at this early stage of the chapter:

> There is the elaborated or 'posh' register used by the world of officialdom, and importantly, by school; and there is a restricted code used by friends and family for most of the encounters of everyday life. The restricted code is used where there is a kind of implicit understanding between speakers; it's short and sweet, pointing hearers to a mass of shared but unspoken meaning. (Thomas, 2013: 85)

As such, Bernstein thought that schools, as a rule, tend to devalue students who use restricted language codes, but reward students who use the elaborated codes of the middle class (McLaren, 2003).

These evolving themes are reflected in the chronological sequencing of his major texts. These books are really a collection of individual papers that were loosely concerned with the development and reinforcement of his ideas. The titles and subtitles of each are a true indication of the progression of his thinking. These are: *Class, Codes and Control: Theoretical Studies towards a Sociology of Language*, Vol. 1 (1971); *Class, Codes and Control: Theoretical Studies towards a Sociology of Language*, Vol. 2 (1973); *Class, Codes and Control: Theoretical Studies towards a Theory of Educational Transmission*, Vol. 3 (1975); *Class, Codes and Control: The Structuring of Pedagogic Discourse*, Vol. 4 (1990); and *Pedagogy, Symbolic Control, and Identity: Theory, Research, and Critique* (2000). The latter text is sometimes referred to, unofficially, by many as Volume 5, even though it is the only one of this series without *Class, Codes and Control* in the title (Bernstein and Solomon, 1999). To achieve a better understanding of how his thinking developed, we need to explore his early life and experiences as a teacher and how his academic career as an educational sociologist developed.

BERNSTEIN, THE PERSON

Born in 1925 to a Jewish family, Bernstein had experienced the hardships of working-class education in the 1930s. He left school at fourteen and joined the Royal Air Force at an early age, spending the latter years of the Second World War as a bomb-aimer in Sunderland flying boats (a type of seaplane) above the West African coast (Inglis, 2001). Following the war, Bernstein accepted a post as resident worker at the Bernhard Baron Settlement in Stepney, in the East End of London. He remained in this post for three years. While at the settlement he took part in the running of boys' clubs, with ages ranging from nine to eighteen. The settlement was a religious institution based upon Reform Judaism, whereas the community it served was Orthodox. This in turn introduced Bernstein to the interrelationships between social class and religion. Furthermore, during this time he was also involved with family casework, which had a profound influence on his life: 'It focused and made explicit an interest I always seemed to have had in the structure and process of cultural transmission' (Bernstein, 1971: 2).

Following his time at the settlement, Bernstein read Sociology at the London School of Economics (LSE). In his characteristically honest reflection he admits: 'I did not obtain what is called a "good" degree: my work was too undisciplined and I had agonising difficulties in expressing what I was trying to grasp' (Bernstein, 1971: 5–6). However, he was at the LSE along with a number of sociologists who were researching the impact of social inequality in fields such as health, welfare and education (Goodson, 2001); Bernstein chose education. After the LSE he enrolled on a postgraduate certificate in education (PGCE) at Westminster College of Education, which he completed in 1954, and he was then appointed as a grade 'A' teacher at the City Day College, London, where he stayed until 1960 (Bernstein, 1971).

His role at the City Day College involved teaching students released for the day from their particular industry. The students that Bernstein taught had been failed by the formal, compulsory school system. He has written about these experiences of working with students from different trade and industrial backgrounds. He struggled with the significant lack of interest shown by his students in arithmetic, English and liberal studies in contrast to their captivation with practical topics (Inglis, 2001). This rift between theory and practice 'must have been especially fascinating in his class on car mechanics: Bernstein had been a life-long non-driver, so theory must have led to practice here' (Goodson, 2001: 163). His practical experience of teaching these students exposed Bernstein to the impact of social class differences. Furthermore, this experience also enabled him to explore the fields of linguistics and the 'problematic status of educational contents (curriculum) [which] provided further grist to Bernstein's mill' (Atkinson, 1985: 12).

His attraction to language and its association with social class led to a two-year study at the Department of Phonetics at University College London in the early 1960s (Goodson, 2001). Bernstein started his doctoral studies, also at University College London, in 1960 where he obtained his doctorate in linguistics. After completing his PhD, he moved to the Social Research Unit at the London Institute of Education, where he stayed for his whole academic career, eventually becoming the Karl Mannheim Chair of Sociology (Goodson, 2001). During his career, Bernstein's contribution to the theory of linguistics and its link with social class and education was profound.

�he BERNSTEIN AND HIS KEY THEMES

In this section, Bernstein's key themes of language codes, classification, framing and the curriculum, and pedagogic practice will be considered. These key themes do overlap and all are underpinned by Bernstein's concern with social class and the power, or lack of power, associated with class. Sadovnik clarifies, and gives purpose, to Bernstein's work to

link the microprocesses (language, transmission, and pedagogy) to macroforms – to how cultural and educational codes and the content and processes of education are related to social class and power relations. (Sadovnik, 2001: 5)

To highlight the significance of the restricted and elaborated codes in relation to the educational possibilities and limitations they may have for the speakers, it is fitting that we start with Bernstein's definition of the codes:

They can be defined, on a linguistic level, in terms of the probability of predicting for any one speaker which syntactic elements will be used to organize meaning. In the case of

an elaborated code, the speaker will select from a relatively extensive range of alternatives and therefore the probability of predicting the pattern of organizing elements is
considerably reduced. In the case of the restricted code the number of these alternatives
is often severely limited and the probability of predicting pattern is greatly increased.
(1971: 77)

In short, the elaborated code has a greater range of vocabulary and reasoning power
in comparison with the restricted code. He also linked these codes with two other
distinctive forms of language, 'formal language' (elaborated code) and 'public language' (restricted code). In general, 'a middle-class child could speak in both
languages, while working-class children were restricted in codes of public language'
(Goodson, 2001: 164).

For Bernstein, then, these language distinctions indicate the different levels of
attainment which could be achieved by working-class and middle-class children. He
argued that language is a crucial element of social structure which can advantage, or
disadvantage, children in their schooling. 'According to this position, language does
not simply reflect the world but actively organizes the world into categories of experience' (Bartlett et al., 2001: 183). As such, different language codes mirror specific
forms of social experience peculiar to their cultural environments. Therefore, when
children arrive in school from different social and cultural backgrounds, their use of
language may not correspond with the language expected in schools, which favours
the dominant elaborated language code. Hence, children who use a restricted code
may encounter isolation in school because of their language, whereas those who use
the elaborated language code connected with "standard English' are more in tune with
the linguistic environment of schooling' (Bartlett et al., 2001: 183).

What is important to consider about the restricted code, from Bernstein's point of
view, is that schools require children to use an elaborated language code which is
without context, clear and universally understood. He argues that it is not that some
children lack the aptitude to use this language required in school; rather, he contends,
that when the 'task is set for them in school they understand the task as being one in
which a restricted code is sufficient, and this is clearly in conflict with what is expected in
school' (Scott, 2008: 75). This difference between what the learners bring with them
in the form of experience and culture, and what the school expected, was of great
interest to Bernstein throughout his career. Furthermore, Bernstein (1971) asserted that
the way that 'society selects, classifies, distributes, transmits and evaluates the education knowledge it considers to be public, reflects both the distribution of power and
the principles of social control' (cited in Goodson, 2005: 52). As such, he sought to
answer the question: 'how are forms of experience, identity and relation evoked,
maintained and changed by the formal transmission of educational knowledge and
sensitivities?' (Bernstein, 1971: 202). For Bernstein, such formal educational knowledge
could be analysed through three '**message systems**': curriculum, pedagogy and
evaluation. He defines each of these message systems and introduces his notions of
classification and framing:

> Curriculum defines what counts as valid knowledge, pedagogy defines what counts as valid transmission of knowledge, and evaluation defines what counts as a valid realization of this knowledge on the part of the taught. The term 'education knowledge code' ... refers to the underlying principles which shape curriculum, pedagogy and evaluation ... the form this code takes depends upon social principles which regulate the classification and framing of knowledge made public in educational institutions. (1971: 203)

Classification denotes the boundaries between curriculum types, where a strong classification signifies a curriculum that is clearly segregated into traditional subject knowledge. A weak classification signifies an integrated curriculum with very loose borders. These two types of curricula are respectively termed as '**collection and integrated**'. Framing, on the other hand, refers to the transmission of what matters as educational knowledge through pedagogic practice in schools. Framing involves the amount of control that teachers and students have over the choice and organisation of educational knowledge and the pace of teaching. A strong framing restricts the choices, whereas a weak framing means a wider choice and flexibility (Goodson, 2001). Bernstein explains these two notions further: 'Classification, here, does not refer to *what* is classified, but the *relationships* between the contents [and] [f]rame refers to the form of the *context* in which knowledge is transmitted and received' (Bernstein, 1971: 205). Bernstein argued that the stronger the classification and the framing, the more the educational relationship between learner and teacher has a tendency to become hierarchical and traditional and the student is perceived as an ill-informed entity with little standing or entitlements (Gewirtz and Cribb, 2009).

Bringing classification and framing together with the two curriculum types, the following brief outline is offered to give these notions context. The collection curriculum type is strongly classified, and has differentiated and separate boundaries. Students have to satisfy certain admission needs, enrol for examinations and select a number of different subjects, modules and credits; therefore, students begin to construct their own educational knowledge by creating their own sets of modules and subjects. Hence, it is suggested that the framing is also strong, and teachers and students have less choice in how and what is taught, and the pace at which it is taught. Conversely, in the integrated curriculum type the subjects and the content are interrelated and the isolating borders are weak (Atkinson, 1985). The integrated curriculum has similarities with the cross-curricular mode adopted by primary schools in England, as for 'primary teachers the boundaries between knowledge and disciplines are blurred rather than defined' (Robertson, 2000: 191). The framing is also, apart from the increasing restrictions required by the national curriculum, relatively weak.

The links between Bernstein's themes of the curriculum and pedagogic practice are clear, and they still have the underlying theme of the advantages and disadvantages of social class. In his later writings, Bernstein explored the disparities in curricula and teaching in different regions of England. Generally, he found that schools in working-class districts tended to have authoritarian and teacher-centred pedagogic practices as well as, in secondary schools, having more vocationally based curricula. On the other hand, in schools in middle-class areas there was more evidence of student-centred teaching. The curricula in these middle-class schools included more liberal, humanistic and arts subjects; students were also coached in preparation for further and higher education. Furthermore, he found that upper-class students attended private schools, experienced an authoritarian form of teaching, and at secondary level a classical and humanistic curriculum which also helped students prepare for further studies (Sadovnik et al., 2013).

Bernstein, in his 1990 work *Class, Codes and Control: The Structuring of Pedagogic Discourse*, Vol. 4, outlined two generic types of pedagogic practice: **visible pedagogies** (normally found in traditional education) and **invisible pedagogies** (normally found in progressive education). Visible pedagogies stress the importance of performance, where the student learns to set criteria, and are found in working-class schools. Furthermore, with visible pedagogies, each student achieves a graded outcome, thus creating hierarchical differences between students. Bernstein demonstrates that invisible child-centred approaches comprise of tacit 'power relations which make it difficult for students who do not already know the "rules of the game" to learn what the teacher expects of them' (Halsey et al., 1997: 494). Consequently, it is only those students who have similar cultural backgrounds and perceptions as the teachers, and the school, who are likely to succeed (Halsey et al., 1997). Invisible pedagogies are more subtle in nature (and initially invisible to the student) and do not focus on a 'gradable' performance, but rather concentrate on the competence of the acquirer attaining cognitive, linguistic, affective and motivational processes (Bernstein, 1990: 71). Furthermore, the use of invisible pedagogies enables teachers to give students facilitative and nuanced feedback by using implicit language, whereas visible pedagogies use a more directive and explicit form of feedback (Sortkaer, 2019). Bernstein maintained that invisible pedagogies were more likely to be found in middle-class schools, while the visible pedagogies were more likely to be evident in working-class schools. He contended that such class differences related to pedagogic practices are the consequence of different purposes for different social groups. Therefore, because such differences are possibly caused by sociological influences, they may be significant in 'understanding the differences in academic achievement between groups' (Sadovnik et al., 2013: 298).

The final aspect of his pedagogic practices is Bernstein's call for **democratic pedagogy**. He felt that education must be focused on guaranteeing the 'empowerment of every individual, on developing a real sense of involvement and control of the social context of one's life' (Kelly, 2004: 89). To achieve this, Bernstein, in his last major work *Pedagogy, Symbolic Control, and Identity: Theory, Research, and Critique* (2000), wrote about the democratic need to safeguard three interconnected rights for students in educational institutes. These rights are: enhancement, inclusion and participation. Bernstein sees the first right as 'experiencing boundaries, be they social, intellectual or personal ... it is the right to the means of critical understanding and new possibilities'. The second right is 'the right to be included socially, intellectually and personally'. The third right 'is the right to participate in construction, maintenance and transformation of order' (Bernstein, 2000: xx). Each of these three rights has corresponding social conditions for involvement and levels of operating, which are:

Rights	Conditions	Levels
Enhancement	Confidence	Individual
Inclusion	Communities	Social
Participation	Civil discourse	Political

(adapted from Bernstein, 2000: xxi)

It is fitting to end this section with an insight into what, in his later work, underpinned Bernstein's thinking. He lamented the manner in which market-led education policies manifested themselves as being focused on competencies for the labour market (Lauder et al., 2006). He felt that knowledge for the market had been normalised and had strayed from the humanistic nature of knowledge, instead morphing into what he termed 'official' knowledge. For Bernstein, knowledge had become now official, a commodity where knowledge flows 'like money to wherever it can create advantage and profit. Indeed, knowledge is not like money, it *is* money' (Bernstein, 2006: 122). Within the same theme, Bernstein railed against what he considered the indiscriminative pedagogisation of society, promoted by governments with the aim of encouraging people to become more entrepreneurial so they become more competitive and employable on the international market (Ball, 2008).

Bernstein's key themes of language, curriculum and democratic pedagogy are shared with sociological and educational thinkers, particularly those with radical and sociocultural viewpoints.

↻ LINKS WITH OTHER THEORISTS

There is little doubt that Bernstein was heavily influenced by the French sociologist Emile Durkheim (1858–1917). He was particularly inspired by Durkheim's analysis of the evolution of education in France, which began with the 'discourse, social structure and social relations of the medieval university ... which provided the dynamics of the development of the university' (Bernstein, 2006: 119). Durkheim also demonstrated how the structure of societies could be broken down into classifications and frames to uncover the distribution of power and the norms of social control. Bernstein also felt that Durkheim's work provided an impressive understanding of social relationships, social orders and the structuring of experience (Bernstein, 1971). There are also clear associations between John Dewey, who promoted the notion of democracy in schools, and Bernstein's democratic pedagogies and his idea of the three democratic rights in education: enhancement, inclusion and participation (Bernstein, 2000).

According to Ball (2001), Bernstein's ideas on linguistics originated from the continental sociology of the time: 'it is now difficult to read Bernstein and not see resonances with Bourdieu and Foucault' (Ball, 2001: 41). Like Bernstein, Bourdieu viewed social class and culture as playing a large part in deciding educational success or failure. In particular, Bourdieu felt that the failure of working-class children in education was directly associated with a systematic bias in schools that is primarily concerned with the dominant class culture. Bourdieu felt that 'in schools working class culture is either not recognized and simply negated or is denigrated as an inferior form of culture, a kind of anti-knowledge' (Bartlett et al., 2001: 186). This is also similar to Michael Apple's notion of official knowledge, where the education policy is produced by people of the dominant culture who wish to reproduce the inequalities in society. This is evidenced and validated in the language used in the curriculum and in textbooks (Apple, 1979). Although Bernstein was somewhat critical of the analytical depth to Foucault's work, he welcomed and acknowledged Foucault's ideas on power and knowledge, and particularly discourse, which links closely with language codes (Bernstein, 1990).

Bernstein's view that schools control the content and teaching of the curriculum, and as such manipulate knowledge in a way that suits the dominant class and culture, is similar to what Stenhouse was endeavouring to solve with his Humanities Curriculum Project (HCP – see Chapter 11). The HCP was concerned with enabling students to have access to knowledge so they could use it in innovative ways to solve problems, because, Stenhouse argued, the traditional (content) curriculum produced 'acceptance rather than speculation' (Stenhouse, 1975: 49). William Labov, an American linguist, like Bernstein discovered that social class and success in learning could be detected by the identification of language structures and codes. Although Labov and Bernstein used different approaches in their research, their findings demonstrate 'that language brought to and used in the classroom has a significant effect on what is learned and known to be learned' (Leighton, 2012: 62). However, Labov was to become one of Bernstein's critics; it was Bernstein's approaches to his work and the generalisation of his findings that attracted most criticism.

CRITIQUING THE THEORY

Throughout his career, Bernstein was very open about the possible shortcomings of his work, and in his last book he suggested the reasons for, and examples of, the criticism of his work, which

> has caused strong controversy and has sometimes become the object of crude oversimplification, miscomprehension, as well as political and ideological misuse. The case of language codes, elaborated and restricted, constitutes a notorious example of all of the above. (2000: 197)

It was indeed his work on elaborated and restricted language codes that caused a bitter debate in the 1960s and 1970s. Even though Bernstein suggested that it was the language and not the children who were, or were not, capable of abstract thought and reasoning, his viewpoint was seen by many as a deficit model. For his critics, this deficit model blamed the working-class children instead of the linguistically biased educational system (Moore, 2000). His main critic regarding language codes was Harold Rosen, a colleague of Bernstein's. Rosen disputed the insinuation that working-class language was in any way subordinate to the standard English used in schools, and further censured Bernstein that it was unsafe and misguided to say that it was. This criticism was reinforced by Labov whose own research found that working-class language was more animated, reasoned and effective than middle-class language, which he considered to be hesitant and overburdened by detail (Moore, 2000).

He was also criticised by the political parties of the day in the UK. The left wing saw his work on language codes as a condemnation and stereotyping of the working classes. On the other hand, the right wing thought that he had given some justification to the curious idea that 'high culture' was not for the working class (Bernstein, 1971: 18). It appears that he took the criticism of his language codes to heart when his work was denounced by linguists and educators alike at a classroom level. These criticisms indicated that his work on language codes had lowered the expectations that teachers had of some of their children, and that the notion of the elaborated code had reinforced the teachers' middle-class perception of appropriate language. The code definitions themselves, Bernstein acknowledges, 'are said to have given rise to mechanical grammar and vocabulary drills' (Bernstein, 1971: 19). His work on language codes was controversial and many of his critics regarded his ideas as a deficit theory. However, Bernstein argued that restricted codes were not deficient, 'but rather functionally related to the social division of labour, where context dependent language is necessary in the context of production' (Sadovnik, 2001: 2).

Bernstein's writing was also unconventional in style, structure and content. Halsey (2000), writing Bernstein's obituary, thought that:

> The prose is extremely difficult because being an autodidact and not a traditionally learned man, and being an innovator rather than one who seeks to maintain an established conversation, Basil developed his own, if I may borrow one of his own inventions, 'elaborate code' ... He never hesitated to write down an incomplete argument.

Comments regarding his writing were plentiful; Atkinson thought a lot of readers 'find his ideas difficult, obscure and elusive ... leaving the reader to grapple with some rather abstruse and slippery notions' (Atkinson, 1985: 6). With typical honesty, Bernstein responds to such criticism of his writing in his first book by stating towards the beginning, 'the papers are obscure, lack precision and probably abound with ambiguities' (Bernstein, 1971: 19). In spite of these criticisms, there are a number of aspects of Bernstein's work, such as the drive for equality and democracy, which, even within the constraints of a national curriculum, can be used in practice.

APPLYING BERNSTEIN'S IDEAS IN PRACTICE

Applying some of Bernstein's theoretical ideas in practice could appear at first glance to be quite problematic. But perhaps somewhat surprisingly his ideas generate feasible opportunities for democratic practices in schools and universities. Before we consider these opportunities, it is fitting that we reflect on a philosophical question and response regarding whether we change the school or the child posed by Lawrence Stenhouse:

> To what extent is it the result of a gap between everyday culture and the culture of worthwhile learning which is greater in the case of working class than middle class children? Should we change the school or should we change the working class child?
>
> A bit of both I fancy, but I confess that I find it difficult to strike a balance. (1975: 31)

Stenhouse's response to his own question is interesting in that it implies a dilemma and a degree of uneasiness. It is intended to leave Stenhouse's response open to the reader's own way of thinking. What this section will do, however, is explore some progressive and radical ideas that reflect Bernstein's thoughts – thoughts from his early work on language code theory and then on to his ideas of curriculum, pedagogy and discourse, which culminated in a 'systematic theory that provides an analytic description of the way in which the educational system is related to the social division of labour' (Sadovnik, 2001: 6).

Bernstein maintained that academic knowledge used in schools, particularly secondary schools, was different from everyday knowledge, because both forms of knowledge are rooted in different systems of meanings. Academic knowledge is arranged through subject discipline curricula which are strongly classified, and have clearly defined borders and their own language, all of which segregate them from other disciplines. The way in which each academic discipline is arranged affects the manner in which it is interpreted for teaching. Therefore, it is important that teachers enable students to be able to recognise the different types of knowledge and their borders, so that they differentiate between subjects such as biology, physics and geography, for example. Teachers should ensure that the borders between academic subjects are made visible to the students. This is not only so that they are introduced to the forms of language that are specific to each subject, but more importantly so that they use that knowledge to make links between subjects and broaden their range of understanding. This can be best achieved by first, during induction for studying a new subject, making students aware of the forms of language and knowledge types; and then, during subsequent sessions, ensuring that students know how the different subjects interlink (Wheelahan, 2009). In practice, this has been, and still is, used with joint, or combined awards, in the sciences, for example.

Bernstein would likely propose that for the most part the student–teacher relationship in universities could be described as having a weak frame. The pedagogical relationship in higher education can offer both students and teachers an avenue with which they can open up. Some teachers who use a weak frame employ 'a wide range of human-being feelings, reflections and emotions, self-disclosure, hopes challenges and aspirations – to come into their exchanges' (Barnett, 2007: 133). On the other hand, some teachers in higher education preserve a tight relationship with their students, keeping within the limits of the set curriculum. As such, these teachers do not allow the students to see them as a whole person; they view their task simply in rational and academic terms. There is no doubting that teachers who use a weak frame are engaging in a risky undertaking. Yet it is argued that the weak frame relationship will enhance the degree of criticality required by students at university. Such criticality is enabled by the willingness on behalf of the student, with the encouragement of the teacher, to access new experiences and new understandings which, for many, requires courage and curiosity. Therefore, teachers in universities who adopt a weak frame relationship are much more likely to foster a critical spirit in their students than those teachers who adhere to the intellectual domain of the formal curriculum (Barnett, 2007).

In primary schools, there is a greater scope for school staff to enhance children's vocabulary with the use of one-to-one teaching or small intervention groups led by teachers, teaching assistants, parents and carers, and by members of the community. Children are listened to while they read a selected text and then they discuss what they have read with an adult or with other children. This is done with a view to extending their vocabulary and to increase their confidence in tackling what they may find to be difficult words and sentences. This in turn is supported by the use of word and grammar walls and the use of role play where children can model language acquired. Such activities are also aligned with the 'Narrowing the Gap' research findings by the National Foundation for Educational Research, which sought ways of breaching the gap in outcomes for vulnerable children (Waldman, 2009).

The involvement of parents and carers in schools, in the form of partnerships with teachers, is vital in closing the gap for disadvantaged children (McIntyre, 2003). Children's learning can be enriched if they have the assistance of parents' or carers' perceptions about their home lives – for example, what the children enjoy doing, their interests, attainments and ambitions. Parents and carers, rather than teachers, have more chances and usually more reasons to know their children. This is especially the case in secondary schools where teachers might only see their students once or twice a week. It is suggested that more use could be made of the parents' and carers' knowledge of their children not only in being involved in classroom learning activities, but also by greater sharing of information (McIntyre, 2003). Stenhouse (1975) likewise recommends that those who work in university teacher training and education departments could also be a resource that schools and teachers could utilise in classrooms to support children's language development.

Exploring the impact of policy and practice in further education in line with Bernstein's notion of democratic pedagogy, Coffield et al. (2008) have analysed the individual stories of students who enter colleges. They found that students arrived at college 'with complex and multi-faceted needs that are not just educational, but social economic and personal; many have been scarred by their learning experiences in the school system' (Coffield et al., 2008: 67). From these student stories Coffield et al. have compiled a list of implications for policy and practice, which could be relevant and adopted across most sectors of education:

- Policy needs to refocus on supporting and sustaining the tutor–learner relationship.
- Success at lower levels depends upon a flexible, patient and informal approach that starts where the learners are, is tailored to their needs, and can gradually build their confidence through small group learning and one-to-one support.
- More needs to be done to support learner progression by, for example, providing step bridging courses.
- Provision for the most disadvantaged groups needs to be properly resourced.
- A truly effective lifelong learning strategy needs to pay greater attention to failures within the school system, to problems of transition and to the impact of poverty and deprivation on educational attainment.

(adapted from Coffield et al., 2008: 66)

It is appropriate at the end of this section on application that we briefly focus on Bernstein's own teaching. In a journal article written following Bernstein's death, a colleague, Julia Brannen, reflected on the nature of his teaching and learning:

Basil's ability to engage in the discussion of ideas and their formulation and, in the moment of their realisation, to make it such fun! If this was a process of teaching and learning, which it clearly was, then the great art of the teacher and the magic of the learning that went on lay in the fact that neither of us noticed it nor even cared! (2001: 2)

REFLECTIVE TASK

Bernstein (2000) outlined the following three democratic rights for students that needed to be safeguarded:

enhancement;

inclusion;

participation.

Reflect upon your own experience from school or university and list, under each, your opportunities to access these rights.

SUMMARY

Basil Bernstein was a sociologist and educationalist whose ideas of linguistics, social class and education still have much to offer academics and practitioners today. Although his ideas evolved during his academic career, their overall purpose was to discover the effects on social class in British schools and the associated repetitions of disadvantage inherent in the educational system. His works can be loosely categorised in three interrelated themes: language codes and social class; classification, framing and the construction of the curriculum; and the exploration of knowledge systems and pedagogies. The ethos of his work was shaped by his experiences as a youth worker and teacher in the East End of London. He had a distinguished academic career which was spent mainly, and latterly, at the London Institute of Education where he became the Karl Mannheim Chair of Sociology.

He was influenced by Emile Durkheim's analysis of the evolution of French education and his notion of showing how the structures of societies were separated into classifications and frames to demonstrate the division of power and norms of social control. Bernstein's ideas on democratic pedagogies are closely linked with John Dewey. His work on linguistics, as it is associated with different social classes and cultures, mirrors Bourdieu's notion of social reproduction and Foucault's work on discourse. Another whose work is closely related to Bernstein, particularly regarding pedagogies and the curriculum and social class, is Lawrence Stenhouse and his research and findings from his Humanities Curriculum Project, which is explored in Chapter 11 of this book. There are also similarities with Apple's notion of official knowledge, where the education policy is produced by people of the dominant culture who wish to reproduce the inequalities in society, and where knowledge becomes official and a commodity. This is evidenced and validated in the language used in the curriculum and in textbooks (Apple, 1979).

Bernstein was the focus of considerable criticism regarding his elaborated and restricted language codes, and how these related to the perceived disadvantage of working-class children. He also attracted censure because of his complex, ambiguous and unconventional writing style. Regardless of these criticisms and the theoretical nature of his ideas, there are opportunities for application of his work in all sectors of education. These opportunities include the breaking down of borders between subject disciplines and the fostering of student–teacher relationships. Practical ideas of small group work and one-to-one teaching and learning to close the gap, and the use of parents and carers in classrooms and in the sharing of information for children, are also linked to Bernstein's ideas. A final goal which would meet Bernstein's notion of democratic pedagogy would be to consider implementing policies that would improve the learning chances for disadvantaged groups.

GLOSSARY OF TERMS

Classification and framing   The concept of classification is key to Bernstein's work on pedagogy. Classification indicates the borders between the contents and subjects, and the organisation of knowledge. A strong classification signifies a highly differentiated curriculum. However, a weak classification involves a curriculum where the boundaries between the subjects are blurred. Framing refers to the transmission of knowledge through the teaching and learning process; it is about the amount of choice both teachers and students have in this process. A strong framing is indicated by a limited level of choices available to teachers and students, while a weak framing allows for greater freedom.

Collection and integrated types of curriculum   Bernstein outlined two types of curriculum which are very much aligned with classification and framing. First, the collection type of curriculum is strongly classified, and has defined and separated subjects. There is also a strong framing with the collection curriculum; teachers and students have few options in the manner and the rate at which knowledge is taught. Second, the integrated curriculum is less defined and has less prescribed separation between subjects, and is similar to the cross-curricular model evident in English primary schools. Framing in the integrated curriculum, apart from the restrictions imposed by the national, is relatively weak.

Democratic pedagogy   Bernstein promoted a democratic form of pedagogy. He argued that students should have their voice heard and that students should be enabled to feel a sense of control in their learning process and in their own social world. He advanced the idea of the democratic aim of securing the following three interdependent rights for students: enhancement, inclusion and participation.

Message systems   Bernstein thought that formal educational knowledge could be analysed through scrutinising what he called message systems. An analysis of the underlying beliefs of these message systems could reveal the levels of control evident in the classification and framing of knowledge. There are three message systems: curriculum, pedagogy and evaluation. The curriculum outlines what is regarded as valid knowledge; pedagogy relates to what is thought of as valid transmission; and evaluation relates to the understanding and valid achievement of knowledge from the student's viewpoint (Bernstein, 1971).

Restricted and elaborate language codes   Bernstein's idea of restricted and elaborate language codes is underpinned by his concerns with social class and social justice. The elaborate code, relating to middle-class and formal language, has a greater range of vocabulary and reasoning power, whereas the restricted code, relating to working-class and public language, lacks sophistication. These distinctions between the two language codes, according to Bernstein, signified the different levels of achievement that could be attained by middle-class and working-class students.

Visible and invisible pedagogies   Bernstein highlighted two broad forms of pedagogy. Visible pedagogies are usually found in traditional educational settings where performance and teaching to criteria are at the forefront of practice. Visible pedagogies are usually found in working-class schools. Conversely, although invisible pedagogies are more understated and nuanced, they are also initially invisible to the learners. Invisible pedagogies focus on motivational factors, the development of linguistics and cognitive processes, and are found in more progressive schools.

 # FURTHER READING

Bernstein, B. (1997) 'Class and pedagogies: Visible and invisible'. In: Halsey, A., Lauder, H., Brown, P. and Stuart Wells, A. (eds) *Education: Culture, Economy, Society*. Oxford: Oxford University Press.
A definitive account of visible and invisible pedagogies and the notion of social control, including how they relate to transitions between the different stages of education.

Coffield, F. and Williamson, B. (2011) *From Exam Factories to Communities of Discovery: The Democratic Route*. London: Bedford Way Papers.
A review of Bernstein's democratic pedagogies and democratic rights in education.

Davison, J. (2012) 'Social class and education'. In: Arthur, J. and Peterson, A. (eds) *The Routledge Companion to Education*. London: Routledge.
An informative piece that demonstrates how social class and attainment levels in education in the UK are closely linked.

Goodson, I. (2005) *Learning, Curriculum and Life Politics: The Selected Works of Ivor F. Goodson*. London: Routledge.
Some interesting insights into Bernstein the person and his work by Ivor Goodson, a close associate and fellow educationalist.

REFERENCES

Apple, M. (1979) *Ideology and Curriculum*. London: Routledge & Kegan Paul.
Atkinson, P. (1985) *Language, Structure and Reproduction: An Introduction to the Sociology of Basil Bernstein*. London: Methuen.
Ball, S. (2001) 'On first reading ...' In: Power, S., Aggleton, P., Brannen, J., Brown, A., Chisholm, L. and Mace, J. (eds) *A Tribute to Basil Bernstein 1924–2000*. London: Institute of Education, University of London.
Ball, S. (2008) *The Education Debate*. Bristol: Polity Press.
Barnett, R. (2007) *A Will to Learn: Being a Student in an Age of Uncertainty*. Maidenhead: Open University Press.
Bartlett, S., Burton, D. and Peim, N. (2001) *Introduction to Education Studies*. London: Paul Chapman.
Bernstein, B. (1971) *Class, Codes and Control: Theoretical Studies towards a Sociology of Language*, Vol. 1. London: Routledge & Kegan Paul.

Bernstein, B. (ed.) (1973) *Class, Codes and Control: Theoretical Studies towards a Sociology of Language*, Vol. 2. London: Routledge & Kegan Paul.

Bernstein, B. (1975) *Class, Codes and Control: Theoretical Studies towards a Theory of Educational Transmission*, Vol. 3. London: Routledge.

Bernstein, B. (1990) *Class, Codes and Control: The Structuring of Pedagogic Discourse*, Vol. 4. London: Routledge.

Bernstein, B. (2000) *Pedagogy, Symbolic Control, and Identity: Theory, Research, and Critique* (revised edn). London: Taylor & Francis.

Bernstein, B. (2006) 'Thoughts on the trivium and quadrivium: The divorce of knowledge from the knower'. In: Lauder, H., Brown, P., Dillabough, J.-A. and Halsey, A. (eds) *Education, Globalization and Social Change*. Oxford: Oxford University Press.

Bernstein, B. and Solomon, J. (1999) '"Pedagogy, identity and the construction of a theory of symbolic control": Basil Bernstein questioned by Joseph Solomon'. *British Journal of Sociology of Education*, 20 (2): 265–79.

Brannen, J. (2001) 'Basil Bernstein 1924–2000'. *International Journal of Social Research Methodology*, 4 (1): 1–3.

Coffield, F., Edward, S., Finlay, I., Hodgson, A., Spours, K. and Steer, R. (2008) *Improving Learning, Skills and Inclusion: The Impact of Policy on Post-Compulsory Education*. London: Routledge.

Gewirtz, S. and Cribb, A. (2009) *Understanding Education: A Sociological Perspective*. Cambridge: Polity Press.

Giglioli, P. (ed.) (1972) *Language and Social Context*. Harmondsworth: Penguin.

Goodson, I. (2001) 'Basil Bernstein, 1925–2000'. In: Palmer, J. (ed.) *Fifty Modern Thinkers on Education: From Piaget to the Present*. Abingdon: Routledge.

Goodson, I. (2005) *Learning, Curriculum and Life Politics: The Selected Works of Ivor F. Goodson*. London: Routledge.

Halliday, M. (1973) 'Foreword'. In: Bernstein, B. (ed.) *Class, Codes and Control: Theoretical Studies towards a Sociology of Language*, Vol. 2. London: Routledge & Kegan Paul.

Halsey, A.H. (2000) Basil Bernstein's obituary in *The Guardian*, 27 September. Available online at: www.guardian.co.uk/obituaries

Halsey, A.H., Lauder, H., Brown, P. and Stuart Wells, A. (eds) (1997) *Education: Culture, Economy, and Society*. Oxford: Oxford University Press.

Inglis, F. (2001) 'Elaborating Bernstein: The great sociologist and his pedagogic devices'. In: Power, S., Aggleton, P., Brannen, J., Brown, A., Chisholm, L. and Mace, J. (eds) *A Tribute to Basil Bernstein 1924–2000*. London: Institute of Education, University of London.

Kelly, A. (2004) *The Curriculum: Theory and Practice* (5th edn). London: SAGE.

Lauder, H., Brown, P., Dillabough, J.-A. and Halsey, A. (eds) (2006) *Education, Globalization and Social Change*. Oxford: Oxford University Press.

Leighton, R. (2012) 'Sociology of education'. In: Arthur, J. and Peterson, A. (eds) *The Routledge Companion to Education*. London: Routledge.

McIntyre, D. (2003) 'Has classroom teaching served its day?' In: Nind, M., Rix, J., Sheehy, K. and Simmons, K. (eds) *Inclusive Education: Diverse Perspectives*. London: David Fulton.

McLaren, P. (2003) 'Critical pedagogy: A look at the major concepts'. In: Darder, A., Baltodano, M. and Torres, R. (eds) *The Critical Pedagogy Reader*. London: RoutledgeFalmer.

Moore, A. (2000) *Teaching and Learning: Pedagogy, Curriculum and Culture*. London: RoutledgeFalmer.

Moore, R. (2006) 'The structure of pedagogic discourse'. In: Lauder, H., Brown, P., Dillabough, J.-A. and Halsey, A. (eds) *Education, Globalization and Social Change*. Oxford: Oxford University Press.

Robertson, S. (2000) *A Class Act: Changing Teachers Work, the State, and Globalisation*. London: Falmer Press.

Sadovnik, A. (2001) 'Basil Bernstein (1924–2000)'. *Prospects: The Quarterly Review of Comparative Education* (Paris, UNESCO: International Bureau of Education), 31 (4): 687–703. Available online at: www.ibe.unesco.org/sites/default/files/bernstein.pdf (accessed 1 October 2019).

Sadovnik, A., Cookson, P. and Semel, S. (eds) (2013) *Exploring Education: An Introduction to the Foundations of Education* (4th edn). London: Routledge.

Scott, D. (2008) *Critical Essays on Major Curriculum Theorists*. London: Routledge.

Sortkaer, B. (2019) 'Feedback for everybody? Exploring the relationship between students' perceptions of feedback and students' socioeconomic status'. *British Educational Research Journal*, 45 (4): 717–35.

Stenhouse, L. (1975) *An Introduction to Curriculum Research and Development*. London: Heinemann.

Thomas, G. (2013) *Education: A Very Short Introduction*. Oxford: Oxford University Press.

Waldman, J. (2009) *Narrowing the Gap in Outcomes for Vulnerable Groups – the Messages that Matter ... To Narrow the Gaps*. Slough: National Foundation for Educational Research.

Wheelahan, L. (2009) 'The limits of competency-based training and the implications for work'. In: Field, J., Gallacher, J. and Ingram, R. (eds) *Researching Transitions in Lifelong Learning*. London: Routledge.

6
IVAN ILLICH

DESCHOOLING SOCIETY: CHALLENGING THE CONCEPT OF SCHOOL

LEARNING OUTCOMES

After reading this chapter, you should be able to:

- appreciate Ivan Illich's background and his role as a social critic;
- understand his radical notions, particularly in relation to the deschooling of society;
- recognise the associations between his work and those of other educational thinkers;
- critically appraise Illich's work;
- evaluate his philosophy from a real-world educational viewpoint.

KEY WORDS

Deschooling; institutionalisation; conviviality; lifelong learning; learning webs; commodification; skill centres.

INTRODUCTION

Ivan Illich, who died in 2002, was an Austro-Croatian–Mexican-American radical social critic and theorist (Daniels, 2003). During his career he was a Catholic priest, lecturer and professor, centre director, writer and university administrator. Most of his working life was spent in the USA and Latin America. Education was one of a range of issues that occupied his thinking. Overall, his prominence came from his railing against virtually all forms of institutions, including schools, healthcare, energy and transport, which he thought were destructive and corrupting forces within industrial society. Illich was perhaps ahead of his time regarding some of his ideas. He was one of those few thinkers to be concerned with ecological problems, and his ideas sought to embrace technology in a constructive way. At the time of his writing, few people had even heard about computers, yet he thought about developing computers as a medium to create **learning webs**. 'He had seen social networking and its promise 30 years ahead of its actual appearance' (Thomas, 2013: 113). Illich's ideas resonated with the protest movement of the era with the backdrop of the Vietnam War and the awakening of a social conscience against oppression and the dominance of the multinational institutions – against the 'system'. Yet his ideas went deeper than most like-minded thinkers of the time because of his much wider intellectual background. His anarchist tendencies and his background as a historian and anthropologist, together with his experience as a priest working with the most disadvantaged people, allowed him to give depth and grounding to his voice as a critical commentator. His appraisal of the dominant educational system, which included his promotion of collective learning, gained considerable interest at the time. These ideas, though, 'were perhaps too radical even for the radicals' (Finger and Asun, 2001: 7).

From an educational point of view, he is mostly recognised for the revolutionary ideas he championed during the 1960s and 1970s, especially the ideas he explored and advocated in his seminal 1971 book *Deschooling Society* (Gabbard and Stuchul, 2001). He believed that schools were bad for students, particularly those in poverty. Students were being

> 'schooled' to confuse teaching with learning, grade advancement with education, a diploma with competence, and fluency with ability to say something new. His imagination is 'schooled' to accept service in place of value. (Illich, 1971: 1)

Although as a practitioner, like his friend and collaborator Paulo Freire, he was an adult educator, Illich made a very convincing case for the disestablishment of schools because he felt that the entitlement to learn was restricted by compulsory school attendance (Illich, 1971). Moreover, Matheson (2008) considers that Illich felt that school is the inverse of education and the main purpose of school is to afford supervised care of the students, such supervised care being provided by 'the *teacher-as-custodian*' (Illich, 1971: 30). *Deschooling Society* reached far beyond the matter of schools as an entity. Illich did not oppose the presence of schools as such if they were seen as advantaged institutions and did not dominate people's options. The book was based on his notion 'of freedom from envy, from addictive dependence, and from what he then called "the institutionalization of values"' (Cayley, 2007: 10). What Illich sought was the disestablishment of education. By disestablishment he meant that taxpayers' money should not be used to fund schools; in so doing, schools would be seen as a luxury, consequently providing the legal foundation for stopping the discrimination against people for their deficiency of learning (Gabbard and Stuchul, 2001). Because the disestablishment of churches (under the US Constitution) had a beneficial consequence for Christianity, he thought it would have a similar positive effect on education (Cayley, 2007). During one of his rare interviews, he made his thoughts clear by stating: 'I've nothing against schools! I'm against *compulsory schooling*' (Cayley, 2007: 68).

Illich was a prolific writer, and his books and articles have been published in a number of languages, including Spanish, French and Japanese. His most notable book relating to education, as previously noted, was *Deschooling Society* (1971). His other most important texts encompassed a wide range of topics relating to social criticism. These include *Tools for Conviviality* (1973); *Energy and Equity* (1974); *Medical Nemesis: The Expropriation of Health* (1975); *Gender* (1982); *In the Vineyard of the Text* (1993); and, with Barry Sanders, *The Alphabetization of the Popular Mind* (1989). To gain a fuller insight into Illich's philosophy, particularly in relation to education and schooling, we need to understand his varied and interesting upbringing and his academic careers.

IVAN ILLICH, THE PERSON

Ivan Illich was born in 1926 in Vienna to affluent parents; his civil engineer father was a Catholic and his mother was of Jewish descent. He and his two younger twin brothers enjoyed a contented and well-cared for childhood. His early years were spent in Vienna, Dalmatia and France, but from the 1930s his principal home was in his grandfather's house in Vienna, where his intellectual development was nurtured by a number of private tutors. With the help of these tutors, he became fluent in a number of languages. During his early years, he also benefited from conversations with prominent visitors to his home who were friends of his family, such as Rudolf Steiner and the family doctor, Sigmund Freud. In 1941, the family was expelled by the occupying Nazis because of his mother's Jewish ancestry. After this, Illich spent a time living a somewhat nomadic life travelling the world with little money or belongings. By the time he reached twenty-four, he was ordained as a Catholic priest and obtained a master's degree in philosophy and theology from the Gregorian University, Rome. Soon after, he completed a PhD in History at the University of Salzburg, where he was able to cultivate his interest in the interpretation of historical texts; he always wanted to be understood as a historian rather than any other title allotted to him (Cayley, 2007). His education in the Church came at a point of political tension between the traditional and scholastic elements of the Church on one side and the left-thinking faction on the other. This no doubt had an impact on his thinking and practice as a priest (Finger and Asun, 2001). He was a model contender for high office in the Vatican, yet he chose instead, because of Church politics, to exile himself from Rome and carry out postdoctoral studies in the USA at Princeton University researching Albert the Great's work in alchemy (Gabbard and Stuchul, 2001).

On the day of his arrival in New York, he learned about the 'Puerto Rican problem', a discovery that resulted in him abandoning the idea of studying at Princeton. The Puerto Rican problem was the perceived difficulty of assimilating the immigrants into the 'American-style Catholicism – an idea that Illich regarded as chauvinistic and completely at odds with Christian love' (Gabbard and Stuchul, 2001: 183). Illich obtained permission from the Archbishop of New York, Cardinal Spellman, to be assigned as a priest in a Puerto Rican parish in Washington Heights, New York, a traditional Irish community facing the arrival of many Puerto Rican immigrants. As soon as he took up this post, Illich adopted an entirely different approach to the usual practice of assimilating the immigrants into the American-style of Catholicism. He became fluent in Spanish very quickly, first from an intense programme of study, then by developing his fluency through personal contact and interaction with the Puerto Rican immigrants. He then engrossed himself with the Puerto Rican culture, mainly by making friendships and by engaging enthusiastically in their cultural activities. He also spent his holidays travelling in Puerto Rico, where he came to appreciate the unique character of the Puerto Ricans as Catholics.

Illich's accomplishments with the Puerto Rican immigrants in New York were recognised, and at the age of twenty-nine he became the youngest monsignor in the history of the American Church. He was appointed as vice-rector of the Catholic University at Ponce, Puerto Rico, in 1955 (Gabbard and Stuchul, 2001). Once in position, he opened the Institute of International Communications (IIC) not only to teach the aspiring American Catholic priests and missionaries the Spanish language, but also to educate them in Puerto Rican and Latin American culture. It was during this period on the island that he experienced his first interaction with non-Church administrations, when he became a board member of Puerto Rico's educational establishment. It was an experience that would motivate him to fully comprehend exactly what the purpose of schools was. 'He came to the conclusion that compulsory education in Puerto Rico constituted "structured injustice"' (Cayley, 2007: 7). As a result of his experience of sitting on the board of education, Illich made it his task to criticise the school system at every opportunity (Cayley, 2007). He realised that children were forced to engage in schooling that the state could not afford. For Illich, the cruellest feature of this was that students began to blame themselves for failing to achieve and to fulfil their aspirations, even though they had fulfilled their time in compulsory schooling (Cayley, 2007).

Despite his successes, after five years Illich was compelled to leave Puerto Rico due to his resistance to the Bishop of Ponce's prohibiting Catholics to vote for the Governor because of his promotion of state-sponsored birth control. Illich returned to the USA and with the sponsorship of Cardinal Spellman, he set up the Centre for Intercultural Formation (CIF), first at Fordham University in New York. The CIF was established in 1961 as Illich's 'centre for 'de-Yankeefication'. It would later become known as the Centre of International Documentation (CIDOC). He then set up CIDOC in Cuernavaca, Mexico, where he attempted to undermine President Kennedy's Alliance for Progress, which Illich thought was being used to spread US imperialist ideas at the expense of the cultures of South America. Another reason for CIDOC, for Illich, was that he could challenge the papal edict which commanded the American Catholic Church to send 10 per cent of its clergy to Latin America (Gabbard and Stuchul, 2001). Illich's work at CIDOC was very effective in providing a comprehensive evaluation of poverty in the developing nations which aroused criticism from both the Catholic Church and the CIA alike. Such criticism was understandable because most of Illich's denunciations from CIDOC were targeted at the Catholic Church and US charitable endeavours to fight poverty in the developing world. 'For Illich, such attempts reeked of cultural and ideological imperialism and were designed, ultimately, to impose particular Western structures and viewpoints upon developing nations' (Howlett, 2013: 254). As a result, he was instructed to leave CIDOC, which he eventually did in 1976 (Cayley, 2007; Smith, 2011).

Illich left the priesthood in 1969, yet he remained a committed Christian for the rest of his life, although he never cited his faith to underpin his opinions. Cayley argues that Illich is impossible to categorise in the usual way; perhaps he may be termed an anarchist, 'but only insofar as he believes the refusal of power to be the heart of the Christian Gospel' ... [as such he shows how] 'revolutionary a faith Christianity is' (2007: 54).

Illich's ideas were appreciated by progressive educators for a relatively brief period, during his leadership of CIDOC. It was, after all, during his time at CIDOC that he met and debated with other free radical educational thinkers of the time, such as Paulo Freire, John Holt and Everett Reimer, which helped cultivate Illich's revolutionary ideas, especially that of **deschooling**.

ILLICH AND HIS IDEA OF DESCHOOLING

Illich's 1971 *Deschooling Society* is a collection of seven essays which he gathered from conversations with other progressive educators during his time at CIDOC. The essays first explore his thoughts and criticisms of the notion of school as an institution; second, they offer approaches to education which he argues are more democratic and less oppressive in their nature. The second of these will be considered in the application of his ideas in a later section of this chapter. This section, however, will consider the first of these aspects, starting with an overview of his major points of argument to give context to what follows. It then considers why he thinks the deschooling of society is necessary, the unravelling of 'school' as a phenomenon, and the institutional rituals and myths embedded in schools.

Finger and Asun (2001) offer a useful overview of Illich's position and they contend that Illich's argument is fundamentally of an anti-organisational nature. They highlight the following abridged four areas within this argument:

> First, there is the critique of the *process of institutionalisation*, here Illich criticises the way modern society creates more and more institutions ... This process undermines people – it diminishes their confidence in themselves, and in their capacity to solve problems. This process also kills what he calls 'conviviality'; that is, it kills convivial relationships.
>
> Second, there is the critique of *experts* and *expertise*; indeed, the agents of such institutionalisation are experts, the technocrats and professionals. Experts and an expert culture always call for more experts. Experts also have the tendency to cartelise themselves by creating 'institutional barricades.'
>
> Third, there is a critique of *commodification*. [Where education has an economic value dependent on scarcity of supply]
>
> Finally, there is the *principle of counterproductivity*, ... By counterproductivity Illich means a mechanism which turns a fundamentally good process (of institutionalisation and organisation) into a profoundly negative or 'counterproductive' one ... For example, Illich is not against schools and hospitals as such, but once a certain threshold of institutionalisation is reached, schools make people more stupid, while hospitals make them more sick. (2001: 10–11)

So, these are the general underpinning criticisms of organisations, and particularly **institutionalisation**, from which Illich approaches his thesis in *Deschooling Society* (1971). Illich argued that schools are failing institutions and that such failure is because of poverty rather than any problems inherent in the pupils. This was a very farsighted notion that took away the fault of failure from the child and placed the fault at the feet of the school as an institution. His main premise was that looking for any in-house school reform to overcome this failure would be futile since most of what goes on in school was not educational. For Illich, real learning more often than not happened in a casual manner and for a reason; schools, on the other hand, seldom allow casual learning or offer real reasons for learning (Thomas, 2013).

In Illich's *Deschooling Society* (1971) he begins by presenting a thought-provoking appraisal of the concept of school. His assertion that society as a whole needs deschooling is based upon his proposition that, regardless of wealth, there is a dependency on schools and hospitals to guide the way people see the world and describe for them what is legitimate and what is not. The poor have forever been impotent because of the escalating dependence on institutions for care, which only deepens their level of vulnerability. Schools, particularly by their institutional organisation, contest the focus of privilege on those designated in need of help. For example, even in those schools of perceived equivalent levels of quality, a poor child can very rarely gain the ground of a child from a middle-class family. The middle-class child benefits from an assortment of advantages from travel, discussions and access to books. Poor children who depend on school alone for progression and development will fail to catch up with their middle-class contemporaries (Illich, 1971). This injustice Illich considered was made crueller for the learner because of obligatory schooling, which he felt not only divided society, but graded 'the nations of the world according to an international caste system ... closely related to per capita gross national product' (Illich, 1971: 9). Illich's more liberal idea of education, on the other hand, involved a much more positive benefit for the learner's personal aspirations rather than the institutionalised school system which advocates the economic productivity through education (Bartlett et al., 2001). A major theme of his thinking was his vision of a convivial society. This is very much a facet of his liberal idea of education; the notion of **conviviality** is a term he uses as a contradiction to industrial productivity. He perceives conviviality to be an ideal and crucial aspect of liberal education; it allows learning to take place which is independent and imaginative, and involves dialogue with people and their environment. This is in contrast to institutionalised education which requires pupils to passively defer to the demands from the teacher in a planned and artificial learning environment (Illich, 1973).

Illich defines '"school" as the age-specific, teacher-related process requiring full-time attendance at an obligatory curriculum' (1971: 25–6). These aspects draw a considerable amount of criticism from Illich as the reason why schools fail society. He starts his criticism of these aspects by challenging why schools assemble people by age. For him, age-related schooling is based on three unfounded principles: that school is the place where children belong, that they learn in school and that they can only be taught in school. Yet Illich argues that the concept of childhood, like schools, is a relatively modern phenomenon. Furthermore, he contests that these age-specific principles are based on institutional wisdom which maintains that only by separating people into different groups of childhood would they get children to yield to the control and dominance of the teacher (Illich, 1971). Another institutional wisdom that Illich disputes is that learning is the product of teaching. Most learning, he argues, comes from casual peer groups, media and observations that take place outside the planned obligatory curriculum-based education experienced in school, without the intrusion of the teacher (Illich, 1971). Regarding the aspect of full-time attendance, Illich considered that since school demanded the full attention and energies of the pupils, it entitled teachers to three separate forms of authority: *teacher-cum-custodian, teacher-as-moralist* and *teacher-as-therapist*. The teacher-cum-custodian becomes the pupils' navigator and guide to ensure compliance with the school's rituals, organisation and rules. The teacher-as-moralist, as a proxy for both God and parent, inculcates the children regarding what is deemed to be right and wrong both inside and outside school. The teacher-as-therapist is permitted to probe into the private affairs of the pupil. When these three roles of authority are combined, it means that the child is influenced by the teacher to defer to a tame and pacified notion of truth and what is just. All these aspects Illich argues reinforce and underpin the hidden curriculum of schooling which 'adds prejudice and guilt to the discrimination which a society practices against some of its members and compounds the privilege of others' (1971: 33).

Schooling, for Illich, came to be seen more and more as the ritual of a society compelled towards seeking continuous growth and development. As such, schooling generates a number of myths relating to the notion 'knowledge as a value – not as a good, but as a value – and which conceives of it therefore in commercial terms' (Cayley, 2007: 67). He advances four such myths. First, the *myth of institutional values* is where parents and pupils associate learning and personal development with the intricate planning involved with any large institution. Second, the *myth of measurement of values* relates to the idea that all learning can be assessed through a standard curriculum, where the results can be compared and contrasted on a global economic scale, although Illich argues that 'personal growth is not a measurable entity' (1971: 40). Third, the *myth of packaging values* where a school sells a curriculum – a bundle of goods made according to the same process and having the same structure as any other merchandise (Illich, 1971). This package of values makes it a profitable enterprise – the **commodification** of education. Finally, the *myth of self-perpetuating progress*. Schools tend to drive pupils to higher and higher levels of competitive progress, yet an undertaking to unlimited measurable improvement corrupts any chance of natural and creative development (Illich, 1971). Illich, then, claims that organised and planned schooling entails the obligation of values which is embedded within the planned curriculum. Furthermore, he contests the acceptance that teaching is a fundamental aspect in the learning process, which creates a discriminatory way of social control through the provision of knowledge (Kelly, 2004).

There are a number of other progressive educational thinkers whose ideas resonate with Illich. These include those who wish to disestablish schools and also those who challenge the traditional concepts of education.

⟳ LINKS WITH OTHER THEORISTS

Illich never alluded to his Christianity in support of his ideas because he thought that any drive for social change was beyond the range of the Church. For that reason, he wrote as a radical humanist making a point of using secular language to advance his arguments (Gabbard and Stuchul, 2001). Nevertheless, it is argued that he was deeply influenced by the teachings of Jesus of Nazareth. Illich, like Jesus, was an egalitarian who defied political and social conventions (Seraphine, 2001).

Illich had very close associations with other free progressive educational thinkers of the time, many of whom he met and collaborated with during his time at CIDOC. These included fellow 'deschoolers' Everett Reimer and John Holt, as well as the radical Brazilian adult educator Paulo Freire. He was particularly inspired by Reimer who published a similar book to his *Deschooling Society*, entitled *School is Dead: An Essay on Alternatives in Education* (1971) which was a further, and possibly more detailed, case for the disestablishment of schools. Holt, an advocate for home-schooling, whose books include *How Children Fail* (1964) and *How Children Learn* (1967) echo much of Illich's ideas on schooling. However, he was also interested in Illich's wider notion of deinstitutionalisation, particularly in the differences between coercive institutions (founded on obligation) and convivial institutions (founded on choice) (Meighan, 2007). There is a very close association with Freire: both are contested to have been guided by the social justice aspects of Christianity and both had a vision that education should be democratic and empowering for the learners. Both also criticised the bureaucratic frameworks of the conventional school which they felt produced disaffected learners. They thought 'educational projects should promote creativity and autonomy and were ardent humanists who put high value on freedom' (Schugurensky, 2014: 132). While Illich wanted to decimate educational systems rather than democratise them, Freire intended to democratise the system as part of a bigger plan to democratise society as a whole (Schugurensky, 2014). Along with Illich's *Deschooling Society* (1970), Freire's *Pedagogy of the Oppressed* (1970 [1996]), together with A.S. Neill's *Summerhill* (1960), became the most extensively read and discussed educational books of the time (Finger and Asun, 2001).

A.S. Neill's ideas also mirror, to a certain degree, those of Illich. Both observed that the traditional school system was restrictive and hampered individual freedom of choice for the learner. Neill soon realised at the start of the twentieth century that the purpose of schools was to produce people to work in the factories, rather than to develop the aspirations of the individual child. His free school at Summerhill certainly gave the pupils choice and freedom with licence. But Illich thought that such schools romanticised the notion of childhood instead of preparing them for the world, and free schools such as Summerhill ultimately existed as a means of supporting the concept of traditional schooling (Illich, 1971; Lister, 1976). The works of Pierre Bourdieu, which highlighted the inequalities in social and cultural capital on the less advantaged in society, resonate with Illich's criticism that the traditional school debilitates the poor and marginalises pupils. Michel Foucault, like Illich, challenged established beliefs relating to truth and the nature of power, arguing that the establishment used these beliefs to influence social control. Also, Foucault's work on surveillance and his concept of the panopticon has close correlations with Illich's notion of the teacher-cum-custodian. Similar to a number of learner-centred and progressive educational thinkers, there is a recognition, and association, with the visionary ideas of the philosopher and humanist educator John Dewey and his advocacy for democratic education. Dewey challenged the traditional educational system in schools and argued for schools to be active democratic communities that would prepare pupils to participate in the larger democratic society (Illich, 1971). Other democratic, social and politically aware educational thinkers are aligned with Illich's ideas, such as Henry Giroux and Michael Apple, both of whom were critical regarding the dominant neoliberal system of conventional education.

🧠 CRITIQUING HIS IDEAS

Comparable with many radical educational thinkers, Illich attracted considerable criticism. Halsey et al. (1997) raise a salient and principal contention that Illich's deschooling was an idealistic concept with little evidence of links between theory and policy, nor much of an indication of how to translate the ideas into practice. This paucity of detail in the application of his ideas is evident when trying to discover what the required preconditions were for people to be able to engage in learning webs. For example, to partake in these learning webs and study a chosen subject people will need to be literate, set up communications with fellow learners, and have access to a computer and the ability to use it. Yet, Illich is very vague on how this would be achieved or which institution would be available to help the learner to achieve these preconditions. Possibly, he meant that families would be responsible for helping learners through the provision of, and by facilitating the necessary training to access, the learning webs. This, however, would not allow for the varying levels of economic capital in society and would therefore disadvantage the lower income groups, something which he railed against (Schugurensky, 2014). There is, furthermore, a lack of detail relating to the role of qualified teachers. Lister argues that one of the significant criticisms of deschooling is 'that it has little or nothing to say to teachers about how they could contribute to educational reform, or about how they might evolve a strategy of operation from the crucial base they possess' (1976: 10).

To some extent, Illich could be accused of being a hypocrite; he denounced traditional education, yet he still spent a great deal of his career as a university lecturer (Daniels, 2003). Furthermore, Illich's contention that deschooling as an entity can be transferred from developing to developed nations is not a plausible, or realistic, proposition. Most of his work was undertaken in Latin America where the working classes held robust nationalist opinions based on a non-industrialist economy. Therefore, Howlett (2013) argues that his ideas cannot be relocated to another location which has different social and political environments. Illich attracted a considerable amount of feminist censure from his 1982 work *Gender* which represented a robust anti-feminist analysis; it was his most maligned publication (Cayley, 2007). It should also be noted that Illich's writing is mainly male-dominant language, such as the use of 'he' and 'his' in its composition. In spite of these criticisms and his revolutionary idea of deschooling, Illich offers a refreshing alternative analysis to education as a whole. This analysis contains thoughtful and unconventional ideas for consideration, particularly regarding matters of inclusivity and social justice.

ILLICH'S IDEAS IN RELATION TO EDUCATION AND SCHOOLING

The actual application of Illich's ideas in classrooms would be very challenging – and probably impossible – for most teachers to achieve in today's compulsory, age-specific and curriculum-driven educational system. This section will present and appraise his resolutions on education by first exploring his overall philosophy for enabling the disestablishment of school; second, by considering the resources and networks Illich offers that are available to learners; third, by examining the practical approaches by which he argues these resources could be made available to learners; finally, there is a brief conclusion that offers some broad possibilities for his ideas to come to fruition.

Finger and Asun (2001: 13) present an informative overview of Illich's philosophy for his alternative idea of education:

- *learning*, as opposed to schooling;
- *conviviality*, as opposed to manipulation;
- *responsibilisation*, as opposed to deresponsibilisation;
- *participation*, as opposed to control.

Participation and taking responsibility are vital in what Illich calls a convivial society. His idea of a convivial society, it is argued, is key to the underlying spirit of his educational thought particularly for practitioners. Apart from conviviality being opposed to manipulation, Illich was seeking an opposite form of social intercourse between people as that which is evident in an industrial society, and between teachers and learners in schools. He wanted a convivial rather than a confrontational intercourse, where learners had freedom, individual choice and the responsibility to study what they wished (Illich, 1971), thus creating a convivial society consisting of learning webs where people would have access to their own specific learning tools. People's participation in their learning, he argued, should be a holistic process:

> I believe that only actual participation constitutes socially valuable learning, a participation by the learner in every stage of the learning process, including not only free choice of what is to be learned and how it is to be learned but also a free determination by each learner of his own reason for living and learning – the part that his knowledge is to play in his life. (1976: 44)

Furthermore, Illich's idea that age should not be a barrier for those wishing to learn a new skill advanced the now familiar notion of **lifelong learning** (Lister, 1976), although it is contested that lifelong learning for Illich would not have included the associations it has today with neoliberalism. He thought that people should be given 'edu-credit cards' when they are born to empower them to gain new knowledge and the skills that were most in demand, when they wanted, without the unwelcomed influences of school. Illich was, before his time, an advocate of computers in the learning process, especially in the functioning of learning webs. He believed that their use could have the potential to create excitement and surprise in the classroom or, if used unimaginatively, they would just 'follow Skinner ... [and] compete with the classical teacher and sell economy packages of measurable behavioural modifications' (Illich, 1976: 37).

Aligned to Illich's notion that society is duty-bound to follow the custom of pursuing continuous growth and development is the assertion that governments continue to persist with this ritual. For example, the participation in education leaving age was increased from sixteen years to eighteen years in 2015. There has also been an expansion of the higher education sector. Thomas (2013) suggests that governments should examine instead and question what happens to those 40 per cent who finish their secondary education with hardly any accomplishments. Thomas expresses his agreement with Illich's ideas:

> Why do we force them to attend school when they don't want to attend and when there is so little evidence for the success of our certificate-orientated education system? Why not, from the age of fourteen onwards, offer Illich's edu-credit cards, which students would be able to use as they wish: apprenticeship, or staying on at school, or having the option of education later on – in their late teens, twenties, thirties, or beyond? Apart from anything else, it would be good to see schools normalized by the presence of a range of students of all ages. (Thomas, 2013: 117)

For Illich, the most fundamental alternative to school would be a network of services that would enable every individual to access a way of communicating and imparting their existing learning requirements with others with similar concerns and expertise (Illich, 1971). These learning requirements, he argued, could be furnished by **skill centres** that would be evaluated by the learners regardless of the people they use or the curricula they provide. These skill centres may also be in the workplace with the employer's staff 'supplying instruction as well as jobs to those who choose to use their educational credits [edu-credit cards] in this way' (Illich, 1971: 15).

Illich considered the best way of replacing school would be to use a network of services that offered an opportunity to every person to connect via their specific learning need with other like-minded learners with a similar focus for study (Illich, 1971). These networks, or learning webs, should not start with the question '"What should someone learn?" but with "What kinds of things and people might learners want to be in contact with in order to learn?"' (Illich, 1971: 78). He identified four different ways to facilitate learners in approaching any educational means available to assist them in achieving their learning aims:

1. Reference to Services to Educational Objectives, which facilitate access to things or processes used for formal learning. Some of these things can be reserved for this purpose, stored in libraries, rental agencies, laboratories, and showrooms like museums and theatres.

2. Skill Exchanges, which permit persons to list their skills, the conditions under which they are willing to serve as models for others who want to learn these skills, and the addresses at which they can be contacted.
3. Peer-matching, a communications network that permits persons to describe the learning activity in which they wish to engage, in the hope of finding a partner for the inquiry.
4. Reference Services to Educators-at-Large who can be listed in a directory.

(Illich, 1971: 78–9)

For Illich, the use of computers was key for people to access these four learning webs or learning networks. His ideas regarding how these could work in practice require further exploration at this stage.

Reference to Services to Educational Objectives: Illich considered that much of the workings of industry, commerce and agriculture are kept secret from ordinary people. He advocates that access to these workings, together with their artefacts, should be opened up to the non-specialist either as apprenticeships or during learners' own time. Illich also promotes the use of educational games, which he sees as 'a special form of liberating education ... and – to a large extent – can be organized by the players themselves' (Illich, 1971: 81).

Skill Exchanges: These involve the use of a skills model which, for most skills, is the sole human resource needed in the learning process. Illich contests that the reason why skills models are scarce in the conventional educational system is that it has become an institutional prerequisite that those who wish to impart their skills need a certificate to teach. He argues that 'people who can demonstrate skills will become plentiful as soon as we learn to recognise them outside the teaching profession' (Illich, 1971: 88). He also envisaged the skill exchanges being accommodated in skill centres which would be open to the public and set up in industrial areas. These skill centres would focus on the skills that prepare learners to enter apprenticeships relating to the specific industries of that area.

Peer-matching: Illich thought an advantageous and convivial educational system would allow every learner to choose their subject of interest and select a peer to help them learn and develop that subject. This, in turn, would provide opportunities for learners to connect and discuss matters of mutual interest. Many schools, though, use peer-matching to develop shared interests to very good effect; however, such schools are constrained by the age-specific, full-time attendance of a set curriculum.

Reference Services to Educators-at-Large (Professional Educators): Illich does not categorically state that professional educators, such as certified teachers and administrators, have no place in his deschooling society. Nevertheless, he is quite negative regarding the role they would play because many people 'attracted to teaching are profoundly authoritarian' and as such would not fit into his convivial notion of education (Illich, 1971: 99). However, he does see a role for these professional educators as long as they discard their assertion of superiority. This role includes using their experience to manage the learning networks and skill exchanges, helping students and parents access these processes, and in guiding and supporting students through their learning journeys (Illich, 1971).

Finally, Thomas (2013) offers some broad possibilities of how aspects of Illich's notion of a deschooling society, albeit less radical, could be envisioned. Children should be allowed to start school later rather than earlier in their lives, and nursery education and early years initiatives such as Sure Start should be extended. This would reduce the pressure on young children in having to adapt and comply with the restrictions of a set curriculum. According to Illich, the time spent in school is not important compared with learning outside of school. Therefore, perhaps it is time to cut the numbers of children in schools at any one time, which would in turn reduce class sizes. Thomas (2013) argues that this could be achieved by giving children a choice of which modules they wished to pursue; it would also allow for greater flexibility in school attendance. Children should be empowered to draw up schedules of what learning, in the broadest sense, they would be doing instead of attending school, such as project work in the local library.

REFLECTIVE TASK

Illich promotes the notion of conviviality rather than confrontation and manipulation by giving learners freedom of choice and responsibility to study what interests them. Reflecting on your experiences as a student, and perhaps your practice, to what extent was conviviality evident? Then, from this reflection, list the strategies that could be adopted to cultivate conviviality in classroom/learning practice in the future.

SUMMARY

Illich was a radical social critic, one-time Catholic priest, educator and writer who spent most of his working life in the USA and Latin America. Much of his thinking was influenced by his background and his early peripatetic life. He is best remembered for his condemnation of the institutionalisation of schools, healthcare, energy and transport. His focus and censure on schools and traditional education were outlined in his ground-breaking text *Deschooling Society* (1971). In this work, he made a very persuasive argument for the disestablishment of schools because he contested they served to enhance economic productivity, rather than the individual aspirations of the pupils. He also felt that the structured organisation disadvantaged poor children. Illich was particularly critical of the rituals of schools which placed pupils in age-specific groups, advocated the primacy of the teacher and the following of an obligatory curriculum and required full-time attendance. Instead, he promoted a more progressive, liberal and flexible approach to education which centred on the learning needs and interests of the pupils. He suggested the creation of webs to allow pupils to access their learning needs and pay for these with edu-credits. Illich also called for a more convivial, rather than confrontational, approach to learning and teaching.

Illich's anti-establishment ideas, together with his championing of social justice, can be associated with a number of other progressive educational thinkers. Although he never referred to Christianity in support of his ideas, it is suggested that he was proudly influenced by Jesus. Similarly, Illich has very close connections through Christianity with Paulo Freire, particularly with regard to the democratisation of education. Freire was also a collaborator with Illich, along with John Holt and Everett Reimer during his time at CIDOC. There are also links with A.S. Neill as they both considered that the structure of traditional schools restricted learners' choices and aspirations. Pierre Bourdieu's notions of social and cultural capital and how this can benefit middle-class children also resonates with Illich. So does Michel Foucault's thinking, which challenged the norms of the establishment, particularly his work on power and surveillance which is associated with Illich's idea of the teacher-cum-custodian. John Dewey's writing on democratic education also contested traditional schooling. Similarly, the views of critical educators Henry Giroux and Michael Apple echo Illich's ideas.

Illich's ideas drew a considerable amount of criticism, particularly because his notion of deschooling was unrealistic in practice and lacked any supporting evidence. He could very well be reproached for being a hypocrite for censuring traditional education, especially as he spent the majority of his working life as a university lecturer. He also attracted disapproval for basing his ideas on his experiences in the developing nations of Latin America and suggesting that these could be transferred to developed nations. Furthermore, he is criticised for his male-dominated language and for some of his anti-feminist writings. Although his ideas would be very difficult to apply in current over-regulated educational settings, they are still very thought-provoking and grounded in the desire for social justice for individual learners. As such, they deserve an appreciation even if it is as an awareness of an alternative approach to schooling as we know it.

GLOSSARY OF TERMS

Commodification   This term relates to education being a lucrative commodity. This is achieved by schools and universities packaging and monopolising the values of learning and certification, in so doing making it a desirable product for the learner and a profitable enterprise.

Conviviality   For Illich, conviviality related to the independent, creative and harmonious social dialogue in the learning process. This notion is opposite to the controlling nature of institutionalised education where pupils passively comply with the demands from the teacher and the obligatory curriculum.

Deschooling   By the word deschooling, Illich did not wish to ban schools as such. A better term he thought would be to disestablish schooling, whereby children would not be legally bound to attend school.

Institutionalisation   The growing institutionalisation of the provision of education, health services, transport and energy Illich thought had an inverse impact on what they were originally intended for. Schools, for example, tend to serve their own purpose by protecting the professional expertise of the teachers and maintaining the established order, rather than providing for the aspirations of individual pupils.

Learning webs   Illich considered that a meaningful education process should give those who wish to seek to learn the means of doing so through the use of learning webs. These would provide access to learning resources, and the sharing of knowledge and skills at any time in their lives. Learners would use their edu-credits to pay for the learning. The use of computers would be to the fore in making these connections for access to particular learning topics. Illich's learning webs could be facilitated in the following ways: reference services to educational objects; skill exchanges; peer-matching; and reference to service-to-service educators-at-large.

Lifelong learning   Lifelong learning for Illich was an inclusive and flexible concept that offered people the opportunity to expand their knowledge and skills which were most in demand at any time of their life without the constraints of formal education. This, it is argued, is dissimilar to the neoliberal meaning of lifelong learning used today.

Skill centres   Skill centres would be the main alternative to schools and would provide a network of services that would empower individuals to communicate with others with similar concerns and expertise (Illich, 1971).

 # FURTHER READING

Illich, I. and Verne, E. (1976) *Imprisoned in the Global Classroom*. London: Writers and Readers. A text that explores and challenges the notion of a permanent education.

Marsh, J. (2011) *Class Dismissed: Why We Cannot Teach or Learn Our Way Out of Inequality*. New York: Monthly Review Press.
Marsh argues that education will not resolve poverty and unfairness. Society needs to reduce poverty and unfairness first, then, and only then, will educational improve.

Ravitch, D. (2010) *Left Back: A Century of Failed School Reforms*. New York: Simon & Schuster. An appeal for a fresh approach in thinking about what education involves; criticising the accepted notion that exam scores and standards are key to a 'good' education.

REFERENCES

Bartlett, S., Burton, D. and Peim, N. (2001) *Introduction to Education Studies*. London: Paul Chapman.

Cayley, D. (2007) *Ivan Illich in Conversation*. Toronto: House of Anansi Press.

Daniels, A. (2003) Notebook: Ivan Illich 1926–2002. *New Criterion Journal*, 21 (5): 78–80.

Finger, M. and Asun, J. (2001) *Adult Education at the Crossroads: Our Way Out*. London: Zed Books.

Freire, P. (1970 [1996]) *Pedagogy of the Oppressed*. London: Penguin.

Gabbard, D.A. and Stuchul, D.L. (2001) 'Ivan Illich, 1926–'. In: Palmer, J. (ed.) *Fifty Modern Thinkers on Education: From Piaget to the Present*. Abingdon: Routledge.

Halsey, A., Lauder, H., Brown, P. and Stuart Wells, A. (eds) (1997) *Education: Culture, Economy, Society*. Oxford: Oxford University Press.

Holt, J. (1964) *How Children Fail*. London: Penguin Books.

Holt, J. (1967) *How Children Learn*. London: Penguin Books.

Howlett, J. (2013) *Progressive Education: A Critical Introduction*. London: Bloomsbury.

Illich, I. (1971) *Deschooling Society*. London: Marion Boyars Publishers.

Illich, I. (1973) *Tools for Conviviality*. London: Calder & Boyars.

Illich, I. (1974) *Energy and Equity*. New York: Harper & Row.

Illich, I. (1975) *Medical Nemesis: The Expropriation of Health*. New York: Pantheon.

Illich, I. (1976) *After Deschooling, What?* London: Writers and Readers Publishing Cooperative.

Illich, I. (1982) *Gender*. London: Calder & Boyars.

Illich, I. (1993) *In the Vineyard of the Text*. Chicago: University of Chicago Press.

Illich, I. and Sanders, B. (1989) *The Alphabetization of the Popular Mind*. London: Penguin.

Kelly, A.V. (2004) *The Curriculum: Theory and Practice* (5th edn). London: SAGE.

Lister, I. (1976) 'Introduction'. In: Illich, I. *After Deschooling, What?* London: Writers and Readers Publishing Cooperative.

Matheson, D. (ed.) (2008) *An Introduction to the Study of Education* (3rd edn). London: Routledge.

Meighan, R. (2007) *John Holt*. London: Bloomsbury.

Neill, A.S. (1960) *Summerhill: A Radical Approach to Child Rearing*. New York: Hart.

Reimer, E. (1971) *School is Dead: An Essay on Alternatives in Education*. London: Penguin Books.

Schugurensky, D. (2014) *Paulo Frere*. London: Bloomsbury.

Seraphine, C. (2001) 'Jesus of Nazareth'. In: Palmer, J. (ed.) *Fifty Major Thinkers on Education: From Confucius to Dewey*. Abingdon: Routledge.

Smith, M. (2011) *Ivan Illich: Deschooling, Conviviality and the Possibilities for Informal Education and Lifelong Learning. The Encyclopaedia of Informal Education*. Available online at: www.infed.org/thinkers/et-illc.htm

Thomas, G. (2013) *Education: A Very Short History*. Oxford: Oxford University Press.

7

PIERRE BOURDIEU

THEORY OF SOCIETY

LEARNING OUTCOMES

After reading this chapter, you should be able to:

- appreciate the life and works of Pierre Bourdieu;
- understand the contribution made by Bourdieu in the field of sociology;
- recognise the concept of cultural reproduction and how this is applied to the education system;
- critically evaluate Bourdieu's theories in the current education climate.

KEY WORDS

Habitus; social capital; cultural capital; economic capital; symbolic capital; cultural reproduction; field; symbolic violence.

INTRODUCTION

Pierre Bourdieu was a French social philosopher who is renowned for his work which saw him engaged in the fight against social oppression and injustice. Bourdieu developed a methodology from the fields of sociology, anthropology, philosophy and literary theory in his attempts to uncover those mechanisms that resulted in the separation and inequalities that existed among different social groups (*New World Encyclopedia*, 2013). For Bourdieu, his aim was to create a fairer, more equitable society for all.

Born into a peasant family, Bourdieu was an outstanding student who excelled academically and was able to attend some of the most prestigious schools in France. However, while Bourdieu showed a natural aptitude towards his studies, he was acutely aware of the social differences between himself and his peers, which is undoubtedly one of the reasons why he chose sociology, particularly social inequality, as an area of study. Bourdieu was interested in the objective structure of social class, and studied how class relations conditioned everyday culture and social interactions (Dillon, 2014).

Bourdieu is perhaps best known for his work on capital to conceptualise inequality and social stratification, and while this work reflects that of Karl Marx, Marx himself was predominantly interested in **economic capital** as the source of inequality in society. For Bourdieu, the issue was more complex than this, leading him to identify economic, social and **cultural capital**, all of which he believed illustrated inequalities within society. Bourdieu believed that social class was distributed according to the ownership and use of the different types of capital held by the individual, and those lacking the economic and **social capital** of the dominant class were seen as the most deprived in society.

Further key terms popularised by Bourdieu were '**habitus**', '**field**' and '**symbolic violence**', which are further reflections on the position an individual takes in society. For Bourdieu, habitus related to the 'structured and structuring mental structure through which individuals acquire their views and behaviour as a second nature' (Johannesson and Popkewitz, 2001: 230). Habitus, then, is created from social processes, in which behaviour learned in one context can be transferred to another. Since it is those in upper-class society who would set the accepted rules and norms, this creates a further tension between the classes, in which those from the lower classes are already at a disadvantage due to poor understanding of the rules of expected behaviour.

Bourdieu was a prolific writer and some of his most well-known texts include: *The Inheritors* (1964 [1979]) (co-written with Jean-Claude Passeron), *Distinction* (1979 [1984]), *Homo Academicus* (1988) and *The State Nobility* (1989); he also wrote over 300 articles. Bourdieu referred to his work as reflexive sociology (Johannesson and Popkewitz, 2001), a phrase that refers to his desire not just to reflect on individuals in society, but to look at both the objective and subjective status of those individuals within a social and discursive framework (Johannesson and Popkewitz, 2001). For Bourdieu, the aim was to see the world in an entirely different way and to facilitate social change, thereby promoting a more equitable society.

PIERRE BOURDIEU, THE PERSON

Pierre Bourdieu was born on 1 August 1930, in Denguin, a rural area in south-western France. An only child, Bourdieu came from a typical rural peasant family (Grenfell, 2008), his father was a peasant sharecropper turned postman who had failed to complete his education, and while his mother had completed her education to the age of sixteen, the family had moderate economic means. Bourdieu was educated at the local elementary school, before boarding at the *lycée* in Pau. While at the *lycée*, Bourdieu gained his first insight into the impact of cultural difference on attitudes, since as a rural boarder he was made to wear a grey smock while his classmates wore the latest attire; he was also made fun of because of his accent. Bourdieu began to see education as a double-edged sword, one that highlighted idiosyncrasies, while at the same time offering a means by which to escape, and which Grenfell (2008) suggests may well be the reason why Bourdieu ultimately chose education and culture as the principal focus for his research.

Despite the challenges Bourdieu experienced at the *lycée*, he showed academic talent (Grenfell, 2008), and was encouraged by one of his high school teachers to 'pursue an elite academic curriculum in Paris' (Ollion, 2012). Bourdieu passed the entrance examination to the elite Lycée Louis-le-Grand in Paris and then went on to attend the École Normale Supérieure, also in Paris, which was at the time at the apex of French academic life and was seen as the 'incubator of the French intelligentsia' (Grenfell, 2008: 12). Bourdieu had then set out on an academic career for himself, which was very much in contrast to his humble beginnings, and which set him alongside past graduates of the École, including Jean-Paul Sartre and Simone de Beauvoir.

Bourdieu graduated from the École with a degree in Philosophy, having studied Epistemology and the History of Science, which Ollion (2012) observes set him against the dominant discourse of existentialism, popularised by Sartre. However, his focus on philosophy shifted towards an interest in the social sciences following his involvement in the Algerian War, into which he was drafted in 1955. His time in Algiers saw him involved in administrative duties at the height of what was a cruel and bloody war of independence. His experiences both challenged and inspired Bourdieu (Grenfell, 2008), and resulted in him becoming more heavily involved in enquiry of a more empirical nature, involving ethnographical and statistical studies of colonial transformation (Ollion, 2012).

Bourdieu returned to France in 1960, where he documented his experiences of the Algerian war in some of his principal publications, including *Sociologie de l'Algerie* (1958),

Travail et Travailleurs en Algerie (Bourdieu et al., 1963) and *Le Déracinement: La Crise de l'Agriculture Traditionnelle en Algérie* (Bourdieu and Sayad, 1964). Once back in France, he also continued the transition to sociology, being offered a job as assistant to the French intellectual Raymond Aron. This was followed by his appointment as Director of Studies at the École Pratique des Hautes Études, which later became the School for Advanced Studies in the Social Sciences. While in position as Director, Bourdieu also founded his own research centre in 1968, followed by the launch of a journal, *Actes de la Recherche en Sciences Sociales*, in 1975. In this journal, Bourdieu sought to blend analysis, raw data, field documents and pictorial illustrations to make social science more accessible and explicable, the motto for the journal being 'to display and demonstrate' (Crossman, n.d.). Alongside this, Bourdieu also assembled a research team with which he began to look more closely at symbolic power and social inequalities in their broadest manifestations (Ollion, 2012).

Ollion (2012) observes that throughout the 1980s and beyond, Bourdieu began to tackle 'an increasingly diverse set of empirical topics' and also began to develop the conceptual framework for which he is perhaps best known, which includes his theory of habitus, capital and fields. During this time he was also elected to the Collège de France in 1982, which, according to Grenfell, 'marked a period of prolific output with major book publications' (2008: 14), reflecting his growing interest in new topics, including cultural life, academia and state training schools, methodological and philosophical statements, and language. During this time, he also expanded his research interests to include the state, gender domination, the social foundations of the economy and the experiences of social suffering in contemporary society (Ollion, 2012). Bourdieu also joined political committees set up by François Mitterrand's socialist government in order to review the structure and curriculum of the French education system. Interestingly, Bourdieu seemed somewhat at odds with the socialist government at the time, since in his publication *La Misère du Monde* [*The Weight of the World*] (1993), he recorded the personal accounts of social suffering brought about by the neoliberal policies of the socialist government.

Prior to his untimely death in 2002, Bourdieu began to increase his public profile through appearances on television and radio, a surprising move since prior to this period he had eschewed public life (Grenfell, 2008). This period saw him increase his involvement in the global mobilisation against neoliberalism (Ollion, 2012), and he used meetings at social assemblies, strikes and pressure groups to further this cause. As a result, Bourdieu became a leading figure, and gained international status in the fields of the social sciences and the humanities.

Over the course of his life Bourdieu published thirty books and over 300 articles, which spanned a wide range of disciplines, including philosophy, literary theory, sociology and anthropology. Most notable was his development of methodologies, in which he combined theory and empirical data in an attempt to dissolve some of the most troublesome problems in theory and research in order to increase accessibility of his subject matter to a wider audience.

CAPITAL, HABITUS AND FIELD

As we have seen from the previous section, Bourdieu's work was complex, covering a wide range of themes and ideas. It would be impossible to cover all of these in one short chapter, so for the purpose of this book the focus will be on Bourdieu's work on capital, habitus and fields, which are most closely aligned with education.

It should be noted that Bourdieu himself rejected the use of the term 'theories' and did not refer to himself as a theorist despite the fact that his theoretical terminology, such as capital, fields, habitus and distinction, are used widely in a number of disciplines (Webb et al., 2002). For Bourdieu, it was more important that his theories were able to be applied as tools to understand real situations. Bourdieu states:

> these tools are only visible through the results they yield, and they are not built as such. The ground for these tools ... lies in research, in the practical problems and puzzles encountered and generated in the effort to construct a phenomenally diverse set of objects in such a way that they can be treated, thought of, comparatively. (Bourdieu and Wacquant, 1992: 160)

Nevertheless, given the wide-ranging applicability of the theoretical notions of capital, habitus, fields and distinction, this would seem to be an appropriate place to start when considering his 'theories'.

A key focus for Bourdieu was social inequality (Dillon, 2014), asserting that everyday culture and social interaction was, to a great extent, dictated by social class and class relations. Bourdieu also believed that social order was maintained through a complex hierarchy by which those in the higher classes were able to retain their position through their social and cultural capital (Sullivan, 2002; Gauntlett, 2011). Bourdieu identified that within any social space there were many different classes and class subcomponents, which would be distinguished by the different types of capital they held. For Bourdieu, capital and power amounted to the same thing, and he saw that there was a vast chasm between those who were best provided with economic and cultural capital and those who were the most deprived (Bourdieu, 1979 [1984]).

Dillon (2014) observes that economic capital is a fairly straightforward concept to understand, measurable by way of money in the bank, home ownership, investments, and so on, and suggests that it is easy to see how the volume of economic capital can be measured between different groups and individuals. Bourdieu, however, believed that even within homogeneous groups, subcultures can be seen, creating competition within groups, which he referred to as class fractions. This, too, applied to the cultural capital which a person held, a concept that Dillon (2014) suggests is more difficult to define and measure, but which Bourdieu saw as being equally important as economic capital.

Bourdieu used his observations of French society when defining cultural capital, referring to it as a 'familiarity with prestigious aesthetic culture' (Ritzer, 2002: 3); such 'high culture' encompassed the high arts, literary culture and linguistic ability, and Bourdieu believed these to be the trappings of the upper classes, used by people as cultural signifiers. In his book *Distinction* (1979 [1984]), Bourdieu outlines the way in which people seek to identify themselves with those above them on the social ladder, while at the same time demonstrating their differences from those below (Gauntlett, 2011). Cultural capital is then very much linked to social class, with each class having its own specific cultural capital, be that, for example, through listening to classical or hip-hop music, and through this an individual will gain *cultural competence* – the ease with which an individual carries himself within the cultural capital of the group they are in. However, according to Bourdieu, within society it is inevitable that some cultures and competences will be more highly valued than others, and for Bourdieu this is the higher class culture that he referred to as the *legitimate culture*.

Bourdieu identified three forms of cultural capital: embodied, objectified and institutionalised. Embodied culture he saw as an accent or dialogue, while objectified culture related to the material goods people possessed such as cars or property. Institutionalised culture Bourdieu referred to as the qualification and credentials a person held, which he suggested symbolised cultural competence and authority. Bourdieu did not suggest that the dispositions of the higher classes had more value in themselves; rather, it is the strategies employed by the upper classes to exclude other classes through their privileged positions that creates such distinctions between cultural capital. It is a perception, then, reinforced by the upper classes through their privileged positions, that their cultural capital is the dominant capital, often reinforced by economic capital, since those with greater economic capital can afford the trappings of the dominant culture, thereby buying cultural capital. This too leads to **cultural reproduction**, in which the status quo for social class is maintained, since parents will expose their children to the right cultural capital and, as we shall see later, this is frequently reproduced through the education system.

Inevitably, the cultural capital possessed by an individual will have a direct correlation with their social capital, this being the social connections, social networks and alliances that an individual has access to (Dillon, 2014). In essence, this refers to 'who you know, rather than what you know' and those who possess the dominant cultural capital will most likely move in the circles that allow them to retain that capital; this is another example of social reproduction and one that further reflects Bourdieu's observation of social inequality. For those who are outside the legitimate culture, it becomes increasingly difficult to gain the appropriate cultural and social capital to access the benefits apportioned to the dominant culture.

Bourdieu saw the relationship between the different forms of culture as a form of **symbolic capital** whereby different forms of culture can be mobilised in certain social situations and which he described as 'a reputation for competence and an image of respectability and honorability' (1984: 291). According to Ihlen (2018), symbolic capital has its basis in power and the fabric of society, which he argues make it the overarching and most coveted form of capital. When considering how symbolic capital could lead to social reproduction, Bourdieu identified a form of symbolic violence which he suggested was the way in which people themselves are responsible for reproducing their own subordination through internalising and accepting the ideas that lead to their subordination (Connolly and Healy, 2004). Bourdieu argued that this was a form of violence because it led to constraint and subordination. However, since such actions are carried out indirectly, without force or coercion, this was viewed as a symbolic act.

Sullivan (2002) suggests that a further way in which social reproduction is reinforced is through the attitudes and values first learned through the home, an idea that reflects another central theme of Bourdieu, that of *habitus*, defined as

> A system of durable, transposable dispositions, structured structures predisposed to function as structuring structures, that is, as principles which generate and organise practices and representations that can be objectively adapted to their outcomes without presupposing a conscious aiming at ends or an express mastery of the operations necessary to attain them. (Bourdieu, 1990: 53)

Habitus is, therefore, an internalised set of schema and dispositions, first learned through early socialisations and, according to Sullivan (2002), is what gives the individual competence in certain social settings. For Bourdieu (1977: 506), it is 'the manners and tastes resulting from good breeding'. In unpacking these dispositions, Sullivan (2002: 150) refers to definitions provided by Bourdieu, including a 'tendency', 'propensity' or 'inclination', but here again we see a strong illustration of a class divide in which children of the dominant culture learn from an early age how to behave accordingly in certain social situations, thereby setting them apart from their lower class peers. Bourdieu saw habitus as a further means by which individuals internalise forms of perception and appreciation, and thus saw habitus as a means by which symbolic violence can be played out in a practical sense since, as in the case of cultural capital, the set of dominant values and attitudes would then be those held by the dominant class.

Finally, another central theme of Bourdieu's work is that of *cultural fields*, or, put simply, the context in which cultural life and production is situated. Webb et al. (2002: 21) define cultural fields as 'a series of institutions, rules, rituals, conventions, categories, designations, appointments and titles which constitute an objective hierarchy, and which produce and authorise certain discourses and activities'. A cultural field might include an educational setting, a museum or a theatre. The challenge here is defining the rules and rituals for a particular field, and here again we can see how the dominant culture might be influential in the instigation of this, which also reinforces the dominance of that culture. Nevertheless, Bourdieu saw cultural fields as being fluid and dynamic, and anticipated that these would be subject to change dependent upon the group influence and the point of reference. The cultural field is important, then, in terms of contextualising a subject, thereby increasing the depth of understanding.

We can see that through the combined lenses of capital, habitus and fields Bourdieu demonstrated the impact of class on an individual's social mobility, and later in this chapter parallels will be drawn with the education system and how this might reinforce social reproduction. It should be pointed out, however, that this is a mere snapshot of Bourdieu's work and the further reading listed at the end of this chapter is highly recommended.

↻ LINKS WITH OTHER THEORISTS

Bourdieu's work has parallels with Marxism, particularly in respect of some of the terminology he uses such as capital and class; however, Wolfreys (2000) states that Bourdieu steadfastly refused to associate himself with Marxism, dismissing it as a 'religious alternative'. Despite this, there are aspects of Bourdieu's work that certainly support a Marxist philosophy, particularly when we consider his views on cultural reproduction and the role of education in perpetuating cultural domination. Bourdieu concurs with the Marxist philosophy that proposes the idea that the dominant class 'ensures its hold over the means of ideological production, not simply because of the fact of its control, but because it is able to legitimise its privileged status by disguising it as the result of meritocratic triumph through sheer talent' (Wolfreys, 2000).

Both Marx and Bourdieu dealt with the concept of class in their work; however, for Marx, the main focus was that of class struggle as a catalyst for social change with economic capital being the main driver for distinguishing between the classes. Bourdieu, however, identified three fundamental types of capital: social, cultural and economic, with the two former able to convert to the latter.

As a social reformer, Bourdieu was heavily influenced by founders of sociology, including Max Weber and Emile Durkheim, along with the theories of phenomenologists Maurice Merleau-Ponty and Edmund Husserl. Brubaker (1985) suggests that Bourdieu owes the substance of his theory outlined in *Distinction* to Max Weber, particularly in respect of his theory of symbolic power and the relationship with economic and political power. Likewise, Brubaker (1985) suggests that Bourdieu took much of his ideas of *collective representation* and *primitive classifications* from the work of Durkheim.

Bourdieu was a contemporary of Michael Foucault and similarities can be seen across their work as they both engaged in social anthropology. Both Bourdieu and Foucault believed that human beings are historically structured agents, and both agreed that by living in the world human beings are structuring the world back (Jensen, 2014). However, Jensen (2014) also observes that there were inherent differences in their work, since while Foucault believed that thinking was determined as the result of historical processes, for Bourdieu it was social context that influenced thought. Bourdieu believed that practical knowledge was informed by habitus – that is, the knowledge gained from first-hand experiences related to the environment in which the individual is brought up. This, too, has parallels with Foucault's work since he also believed that it was through relationships with others that rules and boundaries were formed and language developed.

Parallels can also be drawn between the work of Bourdieu and the British sociologist Basil Bernstein. Like Bourdieu, writing from a sociolinguistic perspective, Bernstein identified the significance of class difference, particularly in the educational experience of young people, arguing that working-class pupils were disadvantaged in language-based subjects since they were unable to access the elaborated language codes used by educators. For Bernstein, habitus was specifically related to sociolinguistic capacities, and he saw his work as complementary to Bourdieu's, observing that while Bourdieu's view of habitus addresses 'the structure of reproduction', his was concerned with the 'process of reproduction' (Bernstein 1977: 14) (see Chapter 5).

CRITIQUING THE THEORY

Interestingly, when critiquing Bourdieu we need only look at his own experience to show where flaws might exist when considering how cultural capital and habitus might impact on the educational experience of children. According to Bourdieu's theory, those children who do not have the right cultural capital will be disadvantaged in an education system which is influenced predominantly by those from the dominant class. However, while Bourdieu himself would have lacked the cultural capital required to succeed in education, coming from a peasant family, he was clearly an exception to his own rule, succeeding as he did with an academic career. Nevertheless, Webb et al. (2002) observe that Bourdieu had always been conscious of how different he was from his colleagues and suggest that as an academic and sociologist, he was always more interested in observing the actions of others than reflecting on his own experience. Bourdieu accepts that there will be exceptions to the rule; however, he sees this as strengthening the position of the dominant culture, since it legitimises a flawed system by giving the appearance of a meritocracy (Sullivan, 2002).

Of course, the first-hand experiences Bourdieu was observing took place within the French education system, which in essence was a tiered system of education with elite *lycées* that focused on academic excellence, alongside the more vocational colleges and elementary schools. Webb et al. (2002) observe that the education system in France was heavily centralised with an emphasis on standardising the curriculum, rather than accounting for the needs of different social groups. It could, then, be argued that this lacks applicability to the current situation of education in England which has seen a drive to promote a system which caters for, and actively promotes, widening participation in education. Research undertaken by Halsey et al. (1980) showed that expansion of secondary education in 1970s Britain designed to encourage social mobility was doing far more than 'reproducing' cultural capital; they were creating it, too ... They were not merely maintaining a 'cycle of privilege' in which cultural capital is acquired by those from educated homes. They were at least offering an opportunity to acquire cultural capital to those homes that had not secured it in the past.

Thus, we can see that far from perpetuating a class system, as Bourdieu suggests, education can indeed be seen as a vehicle for social change, and a trend which began in secondary education can now be seen continuing in the field of tertiary education, with increasing numbers of students now entering the higher education system.

⚙ CULTURAL CAPITAL AND THE EDUCATION SYSTEM

Webb et al. (2002) acknowledge that Bourdieu's views on the education system will have certainly been influenced by the closed, elitist and openly competitive French education system he studied. However, they also suggest that his ideas have resonance with other Western education systems that are more open and democratic. The field of education for Bourdieu is closely tied to his theory of cultural reproduction in as much as it perpetuates a link between original class membership and ultimate class membership (Sullivan, 2002).

It could be argued that success in the field of education has a correlation with the possession of cultural capital and higher class habitus, thereby advantaging those in the dominant culture. As we have seen previously, cultural capital is how far a person has a familiarity with the dominant culture of society, and in respect of the education system this would relate to how far the individual can access and use the language of education. For those lacking in the cultural capital of the dominant education system, the use of educational language can create a barrier that will directly impact their ability to fully engage with the system, an issue that is intensified the further up the education ladder one climbs. Bourdieu states that:

> By doing away with giving explicitly to everyone what it implicitly demands of everyone, the education system demands of everyone alike that they have what it does not give. This consists mainly of linguistic and cultural competence and that relationship of familiarity with culture which can only be produced by family upbringing when it transmits the dominant culture. (1977: 494)

For Bourdieu, then, the education system is not a fair one, since those who have already had access to the dominant culture in the home environment will already have an advantage over those who do not. In this respect, Bourdieu argues that the education system has inefficient pedagogic transmissions (Sullivan, 2002), in which teaching automatically favours those in the dominant culture since the teachers themselves are in possession of cultural capital. In this case, those lacking in linguistic and cultural capability will simply not understand what it is their teachers are telling them, leading to disengagement with the school system, poor attainment and ultimately a failure to continue with education beyond compulsory schooling.

While the education system could then be an agent of social change, presenting young people with the tools with which to combat social inequality, Bourdieu argues that what actually happens is that 'schools tend to reproduce existing social relationships and inequalities' (Webb et al., 2002: 113). He also notes that children from working-class families are more likely to drop out of education, a factor which he relates to the habitus of the working-class family, suggesting that preconceptions of their chances in the education system might lead to a self-fulfilling prophecy:

> the negative predispositions towards the school which result in the self-elimination of most children from the most culturally unfavoured classes and sections of a class ... must be understood as an anticipation, based upon the unconscious estimation of the objective probabilities of success possessed by the whole category, of the sanctions objectively reserved by the school for those classes or sections of a class deprived of cultural capital. (Bourdieu, 1977: 495)

It would seem, then, that failure of lower class students in the field of education is inevitable, since the school system automatically targets those in possession of cultural capital. For Bourdieu, this serves to reproduce and legitimise social inequalities, maintaining the status quo and ensuring that the upper classes maintain their position in society (Sullivan, 2002). Webb et al. (2002) suggest that the ruling classes maintain their domination through ensuring that those members of less powerful groups have limited access to educational resources, thereby supposing that education is fundamental to gaining economic, social and cultural capital.

This would seem to paint a rather bleak picture of the education system, reflecting a system of control rather than one that presents opportunities for those who most need it. It could be argued that changes to the education system in England, over the past thirty years, have redressed the balance in terms of accessibility of the education system, creating a fairer system of education. Government education policies have reiterated the importance of a fair education for all (e.g., *2010 to 2015 Government Policy: Education of Disadvantaged Children* (Department for Education, 2010); *Supporting the Attainment of Disadvantaged Pupils* (Department for Education, 2015); *Educational Excellence Everywhere* (Department for Education, 2016)), with an emphasis on those schools in the most deprived areas of the country providing a parity of provision. Likewise, in the higher education sector the drive to widen participation to include those who would not traditionally have entered higher education was outlined in the 1997 Dearing Report. In this report, Dearing set out a vision which included widening participation to include those students who would not normally access a university education, including those with alternative qualifications to the standard A levels, mature students, students with disabilities, working-class students and those from minority ethnic groups. Individuals from these groups would certainly seem in direct contrast to Bourdieu's definition of those in possession of the dominant cultural capital required to attend university. Furthermore, a remit of the newly formed Office for Students (OfS) is to widen access to universities through the development of access and participation plans, which are designed to improve equality of opportunity for underrepresented groups through improving access to university. Finally, a renewed emphasis on cultural capital has been seen more recently in the field of early years education in which within the revised Education Inspection Framework all early years' settings will be judged on how far the curriculum provides children with cultural capital. Ofsted defines this as 'the essential knowledge that children need to prepare them for future success' (2019: 9) and reflects a government agenda designed to reduce social inequalities and increase life chances for the most socially disadvantaged.

However, while such steps would appear to be encouraging a fairer system of education, in which the cultural capital of an individual would not adversely impact on their access to the education system, it must be questioned just how fair this is in reality. Webb et al. (2002) express the view that the child from the upper-class family will still be able to afford the best possible resources, so for a child who is struggling with their education, tutors can be employed, and access to elite schools will be made possible where classes are much smaller and the most up-to-date technology used. Regardless of the good intentions of the education policies, practically speaking these things are just not possible in systems of mass education. Likewise, the language used in schools is embedded in the culture of those delivering it, making it challenging for both teacher and student to make the necessary adjustments required to make this universally accessible.

In the field of higher education, it could be argued that the illusion of fairness and accessibility is even more complex than in compulsory education. While the widening participation agenda and subsequent government policies have certainly expanded access to higher education, how open this is to all is an area of some discussion. When considering higher education choice in respect of Bourdieu's work, it is conceivable that subconsciously an individual might choose an institution that best reflects their own cultural capital and in which habitus does not become a barrier to success. Therefore, some young people will automatically discount applying to some of the more prestigious Russell Group universities due to the perception that they will not fit in, thereby reinforcing the theory of social reproduction. While selecting a higher education institution on the basis of how comfortable they feel with it would seem acceptable on the face of it, this may not provide graduates with the best chance of economic success, since research also suggests that 'graduates from Oxford and Cambridge enjoy starting salaries approximately £7,600 (42%) higher per year, on average, than graduates from post-1992 universities' (de Vries, 2014: 5).

Baker and Brown (2007: 388) observed that even when students did choose a more prestigious institution, they still maintained 'a realistic if sometimes allegorically framed grasp of the material differences in status and cultural capital between themselves as applicants and the prestige of the institutions to which they had applied', in which case, choice of higher education becomes a form of social reproduction with students from lower class backgrounds often opting for the less prestigious post-1992 universities since these better reflected their own cultural capital.

REFLECTIVE TASK

Potentially, education can be a powerful catalyst for social change, yet we can see from Bourdieu's work that all too often it becomes a tool for social reproduction, where those in the dominant culture get access to the best and most prestigious education systems. How far do you agree that this is the case in the education system in your country, and how far does this reflect your own experience of education?

SUMMARY

Despite the fact that Bourdieu's work was positioned in French society, there is much about his observations on social inequality that resonates across a range of different cultures and societies, making his work eminently applicable today. Bourdieu was interested in the way that inequality gets reproduced, creating a vicious cycle in which those with the greatest cultural capital retain their position in society by means of symbolic violence, defined by Bourdieu and Wacquant (1992: 167) 'as the violence which is exercised upon a social agent with his or her complicity'. For Bourdieu, the lower classes allowed social reproduction to happen because they believed themselves to be inferior to the upper classes, lacking as they did the cultural capital of the dominant culture. Bourdieu asserts that people play the game of culture (Dillon, 2014), suggesting that despite recognising the power struggle that exists between different social classes, people are unwilling to change, accepting instead their place in society. This would seem a somewhat disheartening conclusion, and while he acknowledges that the social order can be changed, he suggests that this is a long, slow process (Dillon, 2014).

The Guardian (2002), in their obituary following Bourdieu's death, referred to him as being, for many, the leading intellectual of present-day France, and it is a testament to his position as a leader in the field of sociology that his work has been translated into over two dozen languages. Bourdieu's work has influenced a number of fields in the social sciences, and has straddled sociology, education, anthropology and cultural studies, reflecting the wide appeal of his work.

In the final years of his life, Bourdieu increased his standing in the political field, turning his attention from the development of methodological frameworks and instead making numerous television appearances, writing in the press and delivering speeches. However, fundamentally the message remained the same: that of sympathy for the oppressed, anger for their life conditions and a scepticism for conventional wisdom (Ritzer, 2002).

GLOSSARY OF TERMS

Cultural capital   For Bourdieu, cultural capital referred to a familiarity with the dominant culture in a society, which could be seen as 'high culture'. Bourdieu believed that families were responsible for passing cultural capital on to their children – for example, through taking them on trips to the theatre, through the music they exposed them to and in discussing literature over family meals. For Bourdieu, the more cultural capital a person had, the more powerful they were.

Cultural reproduction   Cultural reproduction is the means by which the dominant class replicate and legitimate aspects of their culture within an unequal society. Through cultural reproduction, the dominant class is able to retain power and ensures that the cultural forms of the dominant class, such as language, dress and art, prevail over any alternative forms of culture.

Economic capital   In simple terms, economic capital refers to the measurable economic resources held by an individual – for example, money and property.

Field   Bourdieu referred to the field as the setting in which individuals are located, and which reflected their own specific social standing. Through identifying fields, Bourdieu reaffirms the notion that social worlds are highly differentiated, with each carrying their own specific positions and practices, and having a set of rules, knowledge and forms of capital.

Habitus   Habitus refers to the ingrained habits, skills and dispositions which an individual possesses. Bourdieu identified close links between habitus and cultural capital since it also reflected a person's tastes for cultural objects, such as art, music and theatre, which were a direct result of their access to cultural capital. For Bourdieu, habitus was important because it allowed a person to successfully navigate social situations.

Social capital   In comparison to cultural capital, which is collective in nature, social capital refers to the resources (actual or virtual) held by the individual. Bourdieu did not see social capital as being accessible to all those in a collective, but identified it as something that the individual might gain through achieving a position of power and status, and through the development of goodwill.

Symbolic capital   Symbolic capital has its roots in other forms of capital and defines how a person might capitalise on different types of capital depending on the situation in which they find themselves. For example, a person working in an educational setting will imply a different form of capital from those working in a business industry. For Bourdieu, symbolic capital reflected power and the fabric of society.

Symbolic violence   Symbolic violence refers to the power that the dominant class exerts over the subordinate classes, which for Bourdieu served to legitimise and naturalise the status quo. Bourdieu argued that symbolic violence is stored within habitus and is a means by which people's acceptance of their own domination can be understood.

FURTHER READING

Bourdieu, P. (1979 [1984]) *Distinction*. Abingdon: Routledge.
One of Bourdieu's best-known works in which he illuminates the social pretensions of the French middle class.

Bourdieu, P., Passeron, J.C., Nice, R. and Burton Bottomore, T. (1990) *Reproduction in Education, Society and Culture*. London: SAGE.
An analysis of education in which the authors show how education carries an essentially arbitrary cultural scheme based on power, in which reproduction of culture through education plays a key part in social reproduction.

Fowler, B. (1997) *Pierre Bourdieu and Cultural Theory: Critical Investigations*. London: SAGE.
A comprehensive and systematic study of Bourdieu's theory of culture and habitus. The book examines the role of cultural capital as set out by Bourdieu and outlines some of the key critical debates that inform his work.

Grenfell, M. and James, D. (1998) *Bourdieu and Education: Acts of Practical Theory*. London: Falmer Press.
An examination of some of Bourdieu's theoretical assumptions and how these relate to education, with some practical suggestions for those wishing to use Bourdieu's work when undertaking research in the field of education.

Savage, M. (2015) *Social Class in the 21st Century*. London: Pelican Books.
An introduction to Bourdieu's work through an examination of social class in modern-day society.

REFERENCES

Baker, S. and Brown, B. (2007) 'Images of excellence: Constructions of institutional prestige and reflections in the university choice process'. *British Journal of Sociology of Education*, 28 (3): 377–91.
Bernstein, B. (1977) *Class, Codes and Control: Towards a Theory of Educational Transmission*, Vol. 3. London: Routledge.
Bourdieu, P. (1958) *Sociologie de l'Algerie*. Paris: PUF.
Bourdieu, P. (1977) 'Cultural reproduction and social reproduction'. In: Karabel, J. and Halsey, A.H. (eds) *Power and Ideology in Education*. Oxford: Oxford University Press.

Bourdieu, P. (1979 [1984]) *Distinction*. Abingdon: Routledge.

Bourdieu, P. (1988) *Homo Academicus*. Stanford, CA: Stanford University Press.

Bourdieu, P. (1989) *The State Nobility: Elite Schools in the Field of Power*. Stanford, CA: Stanford University Press.

Bourdieu, P. (1990) *In Other Words*. Cambridge: Polity Press.

Bourdieu, P. (1993) *La Misère du Monde [The Weight of the World]*. Paris: Seuil.

Bourdieu, P. and Passeron, J.-C. (1964 [1979]) *The Inheritors: French Students and Their Relation to Culture*. Chicago, IL: University of Chicago Press.

Bourdieu, P. and Sayad, A. (1964) *Le Déracinement: La Crise de l'Agriculture Traditionnelle en Algérie*. Editions de Minuit Chateau-Gontier: Print of el'Indépendante.

Bourdieu, P. and Wacquant, L. (1992) *An Invitation to Reflexive Sociology*. Cambridge: Polity Press.

Bourdieu, P., Darbel, A., Rivet, J.-P. and Seibel, C. (1963) *Travail et Travailleurs en Algerie*. Haye: Mouton.

Brubaker, R. (1985) 'Rethinking classical theory: The sociological theory of Pierre Bourdieu'. *Theory and Society*, 14: 745–75.

Connelly, P. and Healy, J. (2004) 'Symbolic violence, locality and social class: The educational and career aspirations of 10–11-year-old boys in Belfast'. *Pedagogy, Culture and Society*, 12 (1): 15–34.

Crossman, A. (n.d.) *Pierre Bourdieu: A Biography in Brief*. Available online at: http://sociology.about.com/od/Profiles/p/Pierre-Bourdieu.htm

de Vries, R. (2014) *Earning by Degrees: Differences in the Career Outcomes of UK Graduates*. The Sutton Trust. Available online at: www.suttontrust.com/wp-content/uploads/2014/12/Earnings-by-Degrees-REPORT.pdf

Dearing, R. (1997) *National Committee of Inquiry into Higher Education*. Available online at: https://bei.leeds.ac.uk/Partners/NCIHE

Department for Education (2010) *2010–2015 Government Policy: Education of Disadvantaged Children*. London: DfE.

Department for Education (2015) *Supporting the Attainment of Disadvantaged Pupils*. London: DfE.

Department for Education (2016) *Education Excellence Everywhere*. London: DfE.

Dillon, M. (2014) *Introduction to Sociological Theory: Theorists, Concepts and Their Applicability to the Twenty-first Century*. Chichester: Blackwell Publishing.

Gauntlett, D. (2011) *Three Approaches to Social Capital*. Available online at: www.makingisconnecting.org

Grenfell, M. (2008) *Pierre Bourdieu: Key Concepts*. Durham: Acumen.

Halsey, A.H., Heath, A.F. and Ridge, J.M. (1980) *Origins and Destinations*. Oxford: Clarendon Press.

Ihlen, Ø. (2018) 'Symbolic capital'. In: Heath, R.L. and Johanesen, W. (eds) *The International Encyclopedia of Strategic Communication*. Malden, MA: Wiley-Blackwell. Available online at: https://onlinelibrary.wiley.com/doi/book/10.1002/9781119010722

Jensen, M.L. (2014) 'Structure, agency and power: A comparison of Bourdieu and Foucault'. *AU: Central Debates in Anthropology*. Available online at: www.academia.edu/10258956/Structure_Agency_and_Power_A_Comparison_of_Bourdieu_and_Foucault

Johannesson, I.A. and Popkewitz, T. (2001) 'Pierre Bourdieu, 1930–' In: Palmer, J. (ed.) *Fifty Modern Thinkers on Education: From Piaget to the Present*. London: Routledge.

New World Encyclopedia (2013) *Pierre Bourdieu*. Available online at: www.newworldencyclopedia.org/entry/Pierre_Bourdieu

Office for Standards in Education (Ofsted) (2019) *The Education Inspection Framework*. London: Crown copyright.

Ollion, E. (2012) *Pierre Bourdieu*. Available online at: www.oxfordbibliographies.com/view/document/obo-9780199756384/obo-9780199756384-0083.xml

Ritzer, G. (2002) *Encyclopedia of Social Theory*. Thousand Oaks, CA: SAGE.

Sullivan, A. (2002) 'Bourdieu and education: How useful is Bourdieu for educators?' *The Netherlands Journal of Social Science*, 38 (2): 144–66.

The Guardian (2002) *Obituary: Pierre Bourdieu*. Available online at: www.theguardian.com/news/2002/jan/28/guardianobituaries.books

Webb, J., Schirato, T. and Danaher, G. (2002) *Understanding Bourdieu*. London: SAGE.

Wolfreys, J. (2000) 'In perspective: Pierre Bourdieu'. *International Socialism Journal*. Available online at: http://pubs.socialistreviewindex.org.uk/isj87/wolfreys.htm

8
MICHEL FOUCAULT

POWER, SURVEILLANCE, DISCIPLINE AND CONTROL IN EDUCATION

LEARNING OUTCOMES

After reading this chapter, you should be able to:

- appreciate the life and works of Michel Foucault;
- identify and understand Foucault's concepts of discourse, hierarchical observation, normalisation of judgements, the examination and panopticism;
- appraise how Foucault's philosophy is related to education;
- critically evaluate Foucault's philosophy from an educational point of view.

KEY WORDS

Poststructuralism; discourse; power/knowledge; discipline; docile bodies; surveillance; hierarchical observation; normalising judgement; the examination; panopticon.

INTRODUCTION

Michel Foucault is considered by many to be one of the most influential French philosophers since the Second World War. Known primarily as a social historian, his main ideas revolve around the reciprocally empowering connection between knowledge and power, and the employment of these two in influencing social control (Schwan and Shapiro, 2011). The range and complexity of Foucault's philosophy spans a number of branches of learning, which include sociology, history, literary theory and education (McNay, 1994). Thomas explains 'the refreshing and enlightening aspect of Foucault's work is its homelessness; its theoretical and methodological anarchy' (2007: 31). As such, it is difficult to classify his work, or compartmentalise him into a particular academic or philosophical category as he changed the focus of his interests so often. The purpose of philosophy for Foucault was to challenge the conventional 'ways we think, live and relate to other people and to ourselves in order to show how that-which-is could be otherwise' (Oksala, 2007: 10). It is this challenging of the taken-for-granted way of thinking that has fascinated educators, particularly as they try to understand the numerous politically driven policy initiatives, and the increased culture of performativity and **surveillance** (Murphy, 2013).

Foucault offers educators a radical concept of how children develop and learn, which centres on how we communicate with each other. He argues that the manner in which we communicate is governed by a set of regimes which are not primarily formed within our personal consciousness. For Foucault, the way in which we communicate develops from the historical perspectives in which we mature; they are not set but change as time passes. These perspectives are reflected in the language we use to make sense of the world. This concept, according to MacBlain (2014), has important consequences for how we converse and how we understand ideas which were previously considered to be firmly established as knowledge. As such, MacBlain (2014) suggests that educators should challenge the understanding that child development and learning are static in nature and never change. This in turn implies that educators should also query the approach to comprehending how children learn and how they are taught (MacBlain, 2014). Communication and the use of language are central to Foucault's philosophy as part of his notion of **discourse**, which will be considered later in the chapter.

Oksala (2007) suggests that Foucault's works (first published in French) have usually been grouped into three distinguishing stages. First, in the 1960s were his historical studies, which he termed his 'archaeology phase' and include *Madness and Civilization: A History of Insanity* (1961), *The Birth of the Clinic: An Archaeology of Medical Perception* (1963), *The Order of Things* (1966), and finally in this first stage, *The Archaeology of Knowledge* (1969). The second stage in the 1970s he termed the 'genealogical phase', which focused on the study of power. It is this stage that attracted most attention and that is most relevant to education. His major works during this stage were *The History of Sexuality: The Will to Knowledge*, Vol. 1 (1976) and *Discipline and Punish: The Birth of the Prison* (1979). In the third stage, Foucault was concerned with works of the ancient ethical scholars. In this final stage, he produced the last two volumes of *The History of Sexuality: The Use of Pleasure*, Vol. 2 (1984a) and *The Care of the Self*, Vol. 3 (1984b) (Oksala, 2007). When evaluating the different stages of Foucault's writing, Ball believes that the last phase of his 'work is difficult, confusing and fascinating in a number of ways ... [but then continues], although we might want to say that about all of his work' (2013: 142).

The importance of Foucault's work to education is that he presents conceptual and original approaches to examining education within the evolving field of human sciences by 'focussing on the power/knowledge relations and conditions under which subjects are constituted objects of knowledge' (Peters, 2001: 174). His work with power and knowledge relationships explored and evaluated the extent to which power and control were employed by different establishments and institutions (Cole, 2008), all of which provides fresh insight for viewing the field of education, and how we talk about education, in relation to policy and its implementation in places of learning. To acquire a deeper understanding of the aspects that underpinned his philosophical ideas, we need to explore Foucault's upbringing and his career as a scholar.

FOUCAULT, THE PERSON AND THE SCHOLAR 🔍

Foucault was born in Poitiers, France, in 1926 and died of an AIDS-associated illness in 1984 when he was fifty-seven years old. Despite his relatively short life, he was recognised as one of the leading intellectuals in Europe and the Western world (Peters, 2001). During his formative years he must have been affected by a number of experiences, one of which was the advent of the Second World War. Following the German invasion of France in 1940, Poitiers first became part of the unoccupied area of Vichy France. Then, in the latter stages of the war, the city came under the direct control of the German Third Reich – a time of suspicion and anxiety for the population. Foucault grew up in comparative comfort; his father, Paul, was a successful surgeon. However, his father exerted firm control over his family and he expected his eldest son to follow in his footsteps and pursue a career in medicine – an idea that Michel rebelled against. This rebellious streak was also evident during Foucault's adult life where his refusal to acknowledge accepted norms and establishment authority was renowned (Oliver, 2010).

Foucault attended local state schools and gained his *baccalaureate* at a Roman Catholic school. From there, he gained his *licence de philosophie* at the prestigious École Normale Supérieure. Then, in 1950 he achieved his *licence de psychology* and also worked as a practitioner in a psychiatric in-patient institute, an experience he utilised to research his interest in mental illness. He became increasingly influential as a philosopher and historian, and took up his first chair as Professor of Philosophy at the University of Clermont-Ferrand. From there, he went on to the newly founded experimental University of Vincennes, and finally on to the esteemed Collège de France where he became Professor of the History of Thought (Peters, 2001). During his academic career Foucault held a number of international university teaching posts which, it is argued, helped to develop his ever-shifting philosophy. These international posts were numerous, including Sweden, Germany, Poland, Brazil, Tunisia, Japan and Canada, and in his later years he made numerous visits to the United States (Oksala, 2007).

During his academic career, Foucault was also a political and human rights activist who challenged the established order. As a new graduate he briefly, like many French intellectuals of the time, joined the Communist Party and became increasingly engaged as an activist who supported the marginalised and oppressed of society. The late 1960s and early 1970s were a time of massive social protest, including demonstrations against the war in Vietnam and the university student riots in Paris, and both these causes were actively supported by Foucault. In 1970, with his partner Daniel Defert, a fellow professor, he established the Group d'Information sur les Prisons (GIP), which was set up to publicise the degrading conditions of French prisons. GIP gained quick success and demonstrated how Foucault was able to sway the French government regarding the formation of prison policy (Oliver, 2010). This experience also stimulated his interest in the power used by authorities and their use of incarceration and surveillance to ensure compliance, and led to the publication of *Discipline and Punish: The Birth of the Prison* (1979).

Before we explore Foucault's concepts and philosophy, particularly how these relate to education, it is fitting to reflect that he considered his ideas and his works to be closely connected with events in his own life (Oksala, 2007). To take this personal association with his work further, Ball states: 'He regarded his intellectual endeavours as a way of working on himself; he was always work in progress, always unfinished, restless and angry' (2013: 7).

FOUCAULT AND HIS IDEAS

Some of Foucault's works can be quite complex and convoluted to decipher, but the meanings, once uncovered, are profound. Ball found 'reading Foucault was a struggle and a shock but also a revelation' (2013: 2). With this in mind, and before we address his ideas which directly relate to education, this section will first explore some of the terms and key ideas associated with Foucault. These terms and key ideas are: **poststructuralism**, **power/knowledge** and discourse. This section will then consider those aspects of Foucault's ideas, mainly from *Discipline and Punish: The Birth of the Prison* (1979), such as **discipline**, **docile bodies**, **hierarchical observation**, **normalising judgement**, **the examination** and **panopticism** – all of which have resonance with education.

It is difficult to categorise Foucault's philosophy because of his disparate thoughts and the shifting of his ideas over time. For some, he was at different times a Marxist and/or postmodernist. Nevertheless, it is commonly agreed that much of his philosophy emanates from poststructuralism, although Foucault would discount any attempt to be labelled as a poststructuralist (Oksala, 2007). The word 'poststructuralism' is a contested and complicated term which has originated from European scepticism (Peters and Besley, 2012). Poststructuralist thinkers, such as Foucault, particularly challenged the established ways of thinking and the acceptance of knowledge that were formed during the Age of Enlightenment, which began at the time of the French Revolution. Poststructuralists contested 'the taken-for-granted "truths" about the world; grand narratives or comprehensive systems that simplistically explain historical or social realities' (Rawlings, 2019: 702–3). These poststructuralist ways of thinking encompassed a wide range of ideas and mind-sets:

> concerning reason, justice, equality, progress and rationality and a series of political events ... [and for Foucault were] based on an interrogation of how and what things are, and as a particular self-referential attitude to one's time. (Danaher et al., 2000: xi)

Furthermore, poststructuralism can also be understood as a theoretical counter to the use of scientific approaches in the human sciences (Peters and Besley, 2012). The poststructuralist viewpoint is vital to understanding Foucault's notion of power/knowledge where the conventional idea of knowledge is powerful as 'it makes us its subjects, because we make sense of ourselves by referring back to various bodies of knowledge' (Danaher et al., 2000). However, power, for Foucault, is not only 'prohibitive it is productive ... [it] is sometimes an opportunity to be successful or loved. It is not always harmful' (Ball, 2013: 30).

The meanings which are created by the notion of the power/knowledge relationship, Foucault argues, are rooted in different political and social institutions; these meanings are communicated by way of what he calls 'discourses' (MacLure, 2003). Discourse usually indicates the style of language used by different institutions or professions which reflects their particular beliefs and principles (Danaher et al., 2000). For example, the type of discourse used in an educational sense frequently encompasses notions of assessment, achievement, standards and qualifications (Oliver, 2010). Discourse can be firmly aligned with the use of power: 'discourses are about what can be said and thought, but also about who can speak, when, and with what authority' (Ball, 2010: 2). There are some modes of discourse, especially those used by the more powerful and established professions like law and medicine, which are typified by complicated terminology. This allows those of the same profession to talk with each other with ease and understanding. They do this by means of 'discursive practices which makes it almost "impossible to be outside of them; to be outside of them is, by definition, to be mad, to beyond comprehension and therefore reason" (Ball, 2013: 20–1). However, it has the effect of excluding those outside the profession from participating in the communication, which in turn allows the professional to have power over those who are outsiders (Oliver, 2010). In short, Foucault's notion of power/knowledge associations

> allows for the relationship to be established, within any discourse, between knowledge (say, relating to the curriculum, policy, and so on) and power (who creates, controls, receives specific knowledges). (Weiner et al., 1997: 622)

These key ideas of Foucault are interwoven throughout his writing and are relevant in gaining a holistic understanding of his philosophy in connection with education. It is *Discipline and Punish: The Birth of the Prison* (1979) which 'charts how the eighteenth century saw a transition from public execution to penal retention as a technique of social control' (Fisher et al., 2010: 109). This book is particularly associated with schools because it examines notions of discipline and power, and of 'educational processes as being concerned with the construction of an obedient and governable subject' (Fisher et al., 2010: 109). Foucault organises the book about the history of prisons into four chronological phases. Part 1 is entitled 'Torture', Part II 'Punishment', Part III 'Discipline' and Part IV 'Prison', which has three sections: complete and austere institutions, illegalities and delinquency, and the carceral. By the sequential unfolding of the history of prisons:

> The story Foucault tells is the move from excessive public, physical punishments to private, invisible discipline of our psychological sense of selfhood, as a middle-class tactic to control popular (mass) socialization and alternative political and economic outlooks. (Schwan and Shapiro, 2011: 12)

Because of its association with education, it is Part III, Discipline, which will be explored further in this section. For Foucault, 'Discipline "makes" individuals; it is the specific technique of a power that regards individuals both as objects and as instruments of its exercise' (2006: 124). Discipline has three elements: 'docile bodies', 'the means of correct training' (which is further subdivided into 'hierarchical observation', 'normalising judgement' and 'the examination') and 'panopticism' (Foucault, 1979).

'Discipline' in *Discipline and Punish: The Birth of the Prison* (1979) is closely associated with Foucault's notion of power/knowledge. He emphasised that discipline is not only enforced from above, but imposed by people themselves so that they could prosper in the 'new social and economic conditions that were emerging in Europe during the eighteenth and nineteenth centuries' (Danaher et al., 2000: 51). A core concern of discipline for Foucault was creating healthy docile bodies who could be controlled. As such, he argued that the human body was entering a process of the

> 'mechanics of power' ... [which] defined how one may have a hold over others' bodies, not only so that they may do what one wishes, but so that they may operate as one wishes, with the techniques, the speed and the efficiency that one determines. Thus discipline produces subjected and practised bodies, 'docile' bodies. (1979: 138)

This idea of docile bodies is aligned with schools where the day is governed by the timetable. Students and, to some extent, teachers conform to the needs of time and move between different classrooms, as well as changing from one subject area to another (Danaher et al., 2000).

Within 'the means of correct training' element of *Discipline and Punish: The Birth of the Prison* (1979) Foucault explains how people were restricted and constrained through the use of three surveillance methods of discipline to guarantee that 'individuals were sorted, regulated, normalised and made to behave in particular ways' (Allan, 2013a: 24). The first of these was hierarchical observation. Observation, he stated, was the ideal disciplinary method 'which would make it possible for a single gaze to see everything constantly' (Foucault, 1979: 173). Hierarchical observation then

> encompassed a form of supervision of supervisors, with everyone accountable to authority from above. The effectiveness of the supervision was guaranteed ... and since it was impossible to know when one was being watched, it was necessary to behave as if that was the case. (Allan, 2013a: 25)

This form of observation is evident in the design of schools where the 'buildings took on some of the characteristics of the factory ... [which] facilitated supervision, hierarchy and reward' (Fisher et al., 2010: 109).

The second notion within this element was normalising judgement, which Foucault argued was employed to rationalise methods of oppression. Humans can be assessed for the degree in which they differ from set standards. Then, 'disciplinary techniques can be used to homogenise and normalise, and, of course, exclusion can be justified as a means to these ends' (Allan, 2013a: 25). As such, normalising judgement is closely associated with the idea of discourse through the categorisation of certain behaviours as 'normal', or by identifying a student as a 'troublemaker' as a way of shaping the way they think about themselves. Therefore, this induces students not only to partake in scrutinising their own behaviours, but they also become engaged in the practice of normalisation. In doing this, they begin to develop an acknowledgement of what forms of behaviour are acceptable or not acceptable. Through this normalisation, students in schools could come to understand, and agree, that particular behaviours could lead themselves or other students to be labelled 'troublemaker' without even challenging the label (Hope, 2013).

The third notion, the examination, Foucault explains is 'a normalizing gaze, a surveillance that makes it possible to qualify, to classify and to punish' (Foucault, 1979: 184).

> The creation of hierarchy through observation and judgement about deviations from the norm becomes fused in the examination, in the dual sense of looking (to examine) and grading (by subjecting individuals to tests). The examination is discipline's ritual ceremony that establishes the 'truth' about the subject, a knowledge that will both give individuals a subjective identity through their ranked result and objectify them as things to be manoeuvred or exercised further. (Schwan and Shapiro, 2011: 121)

The examination allows for individuals to be moulded in certain ways by society. It also enables society to have knowledge about individuals, which not only has the effect of creating homogeneous and powerful groups, but in addition creates people who would also engage in self-monitoring (Scott, 2008).

The final element, and much cited principle, of the Discipline section is panopticism, a principle that applies a process of surveillance that was founded on an architectural prison structure – 'the **panopticon**' – designed by the eighteenth-century English philosopher and radical thinker Jeremy Bentham. The panopticon functions by prison officials being able to continuously observe the prison inmates in their tiered and back-lit cells from a central position in the prison building. However, the prisoners would be not be aware that they were being watched. Thus, 'control' would be 'internalised' in the mind of the individual. The prisoner therefore 'is seen, but he does not see; he is the object of information, never a subject in communication' (Foucault, 1979: 200). The aim of the panopticon is 'to induce in the inmate a state of conscious and permanent visibility that assures the automatic functioning of power' (Foucault, 1979: 201). The designs of even recently constructed schools and colleges have physical similarities with the panoptic principle, with their large and easily observable open spaces (Fisher et al., 2010). Furthermore, modern schools also adopt simulated surveillance systems with the use of imitation CCTV cameras to encourage students to behave as if the cameras were authentic (Hope, 2013). However, in the panopticon principle, when it is associated with the state, surveillance is not reinforced by the threat of physical violence and intimidation but by the power of discursive practices. These '"discursive practices" are frequently a reinforcement of [the] dominant ideology' (Barry, 2002: 186).

Many of Foucault's ideas were shaped by early and contemporary philosophers. His own thoughts have since been adopted by thinkers from a variety of fields, not least in education. Many of these thinkers are those who wish to explore and challenge the taken-for-granted idea of knowledge and power.

⟳ LINKS WITH OTHER THEORISTS

Many of Foucault's ideas can be traced to the thoughts of the German philosopher Immanuel Kant (1724–1804) 'who challenged us to ask not what the world is made of but rather why we view it in the way we do' (MacBlain, 2014: 5). Kant was absorbed with critiquing the idea of what was seen as accepted knowledge during the Age of Enlightenment. What Foucault took from Kant's thinking about the Enlightenment was not a concept or theory but the idea of critique. Foucault challenged the thinking that knowledge is set for eternity; for him, knowledge may alter from one historical period to the next (Bartlett et al., 2001). This notion of critique is evident throughout Foucault's writing; he even completed a thesis on Kant's works as part of his doctorate (Oliver, 2010).

It was another German philosopher, Friedrich Nietzsche, whose thoughts inspired Foucault to structure his work as a history and to see individuals as subjects (Peters, 2001). Nietzsche suggested that knowledge and truth are created by, and between, establishments and professional disciplines, and are offered as if they are timeless and complete, similar to Foucault's notion of dominant discourse (Barry, 2002).

Although Foucault was briefly a member of the Communist Party, he did not consider himself a Marxist, yet he often cites Marx in his writing, particularly in *Discipline and Punish: The Birth of the Prison* (1979). Foucault uses Marx to substantiate his writing and not in a disproving manner (Schwan and Shapiro, 2011). There is also a clear connection between the Italian Marxist thinker Antonio Gramsci and Foucault, particularly regarding power and knowledge in the way in which the state operated. Gramsci discussed how state institutions 'work to "win" popular consent for their authority through a variety of processes which disguise their position of dominance' (Barry, 2002: xii). Furthermore, Foucault's multifaceted notion of power is linked with Gramsci's concept of 'hegemony' as a combination of 'coercion and consent to any organisation of society' (Schwan and Shapiro, 2011: 43). There are also similarities between Foucault and Ivan Illich: both contested the established principles about truth and the nature of power; they both maintained that the establishment used these principles to induce social control. Foucault's work on surveillance and the panopticon also has parallels with Illich's notion of the teacher-cum-custodian.

Foucault's notion that power centres on certain sections of society, and that power is driven by his idea of dominant discourse, is similar to the English educational thinker Basil Bernstein's linguistic codes. A contemporary of Foucault, Bernstein offered two codes of language: a restricted code and an elaborate code. The elaborate code, which was used by the middle classes, had the capacity for reasoning and had a wider vocabulary which gave learners an advantage in their schooling. On the other hand, the restricted language code used by the working-class students was a hindrance to their learning (Moore, 2000). Foucault's challenge to the way society thought about knowledge was reflected also, to differing degrees, by his fellow philosophers in France, including Pierre Bourdieu. Jean-François Lyotard also questioned the way in which knowledge is understood and how this process changes as time passes (MacBlain, 2014). Jacques Derrida challenged us to think differently in the way in which we read and interpret the written word (MacBlain, 2014). The thoughts of Foucault and his contemporaries attracted considerable criticism.

CRITIQUING THE IDEAS

Today, Foucault is considered one of the great philosophers whose ideas have formed the ways in which we think and understand. However, when his and the other contemporary French philosophers' works were first published, they drew a great deal of condemnation. This was because their ideas were considered as 'posing threats and challenges to established fields and disciplines such as history, political economy, philosophy, sociology, literature, geography and psychology' (Danaher et al., 2000). Foucault and his colleagues were engrossed in the French academic debates of the time within the prestigious Paris universities. Foucault, and poststructuralist colleagues generally, were criticised for limiting themselves 'to questions of literature and philosophy. The implications for society and politics are left for others to draw' (Kumar, 1997: 102). Each was conversant with the others' theoretical opinions and as such they developed a 'writing style that signalled their own position with a few casual words' (Schwan and Shapiro, 2011: 5). Foucault's writing in particular could be 'elliptical and obscure ... he is always trying out ideas and going off on tangents' (Ball, 2013: 12).

Foucault's convoluted and poetic style of writing has been seen by some of his critics as a mask intended to perplex readers and cover the historical errors he made. Oksala (2007) states that there were a number of faults in his periodisation, particularly in relation to the confinement of the mad and the medicalisation of madness. Criticism also came from different intellectual fields: 'historians have rejected Foucault's work for being too philosophical, philosophers for the lack of rigour and sociologists for its literary or poetic quality' (McNay, 1994: 1). Perhaps the reason for such criticism is that his ideas can be employed in so many different fields of study even though they do not offer a definitive theory. Furthermore, Foucault's engagement in political action appears not to have been based upon any obvious theoretical standpoint. On the other hand, his position as a philosopher was considered to be naive and politically hollow because it lacked specific political evaluations (Oksala, 2007).

He received widespread condemnation from feminist and cultural thinkers because 'of gender blindness and ethnocentrism' (McNay, 1994: 10). Even though there is a scarcity of gender issues in his writing, many of his ideas, such as discourse and power, have appealed to some feminist thinkers (Ball, 2013). Hope (2013) infers that Foucault could have paid more attention to the technologies of surveillance that were available during the 1960s and 1970s instead of the eighteenth and nineteenth centuries. This deficit of attention to the current technologies of the time, Hope argues, has weakened Foucault's analysis regarding surveillance. Furthermore, the rise in technologies since the 1960s and 1970s with the increasing use of CCTV, databases, social media and mobile communications should lead to a reappraisal of the panopticon principle (Hope, 2013). Notwithstanding these criticisms, Foucault's ideas have a profound relevance for education.

FOUCAULT'S IDEAS IN RELATION TO EDUCATION

The application of Foucault's ideas to education can be difficult for the practitioner working in classrooms. This is not surprising when his ideas are mainly conceptual and located within the intellectual milieu of continental philosophical circles which must seem detached from the realities of teaching practice (Murphy, 2013). However, the aim of Foucault's work was that as human beings we should 'work towards transformation, and, to a small degree, be agents of it ... [and] to change the way we perceive the people we judge' (Oksala, 2007: 24). These sentiments are core to caring and student-centred teaching, and many of Foucault's ideas have much to offer the education practitioner and researcher. This section will first explore his thoughts as they are specifically linked with education. Second, it will outline where his ideas can be related to practice.

Ball describes the state education system in England towards the end of the nineteenth century as 'ramshackle, ugly and smelly' (2013: 39). However, it was the start of the state control of education which would shape and prepare children to be the docile bodies required to serve society and contribute to the nation's workforce. In line with Foucault's hierarchical observation, schools were being built to create an architectural 'space in ways that allow for total supervision' (Schwan and Shapiro, 2011: 115). It was not only buildings that allowed such classified observations; school inspectors observed teachers, who in turn observed students. Normalising of judgement and the examination were also evident:

> The judgements of the inspectors were also embedded in the classificatory practices of the classroom as new types of learner, 'bright' boys and their 'failing' counterparts, were identified within the newly evolving techniques of pedagogy and assessment. (Ball, 2013: 42)

School students and staff were being drawn into processes of discipline that normalise and standardise through observation and modification. This was done by breaking multifaceted aspects of the school down into small components, so each part can be seen. Ball explains:

> Schools are broken down into houses, the school day into a timetable and a curriculum (a serial space of serial knowledges) and into specialist locations; pupil movements are broken down within and into lessons, they are allocated to seats, organized onto tables or in rows, labelled, tested, measured and calculated by the techniques of examination. (2013: 46)

These processes of discipline are evident in schools and other educational settings today. They are processes that are sustained and advanced by 'reforms' in education policy. Policy plays a significant role because it 'is about power to determine what gets done, or not done. These are profoundly political issues' (Bell and Stevenson, 2006: 23). Bell and Stevenson also stress the importance of taking into account 'the wider socio-political environment in shaping the discourse in which policy debate is conducted' (2006: 23).

When the coalition government in the UK came to power in 2010, they felt that there was a need to return to a more traditional approach to education in England, which included deregulation, and the discourse from government certainly reflected that. This deregulation took the form of giving schools more autonomy in how they spent their funds; it also sought to expand freedom of choice by increasing the number of academies and free schools. But schools were also required to improve examination results and comply with ever more stringent Ofsted inspections. Foucault was attracted to the idea of the power that emerges from changes in government and the resultant discourse that emerges. Both the coalition government and, from May 2015, the Conservative government espoused the discourse of deregulation and freedom of choice in schools. This, however, it is argued, relates more to Foucault's idea of self-regulation rather than deregulation, where the 'individual watches over his or her own behaviours, one that increases control while preserving the illusion of freedom' (Allan, 2013b: 219).

The education reforms in England since 2010 have centred on, as we have seen, the expansion of academies and free schools, a review of the curriculum, assessment (with an increasing level of importance given to examinations over coursework) and qualifications. The new government also sought to revamp initial teacher education as they considered that not enough training took place in classrooms. The major skill set required for teachers was predominantly concerned with 'good behaviour management and the maintenance of effective classroom discipline' (Chitty, 2014: 96). The link between Foucault's notions of discipline and control was also evident in the coalition's 'Troops to Teachers' initiative led by the then Education Secretary Michael Gove. This is a scheme to create a new and efficient teaching cadre from service personnel who are about to leave the Armed Forces, even though they may not have the standard qualifications to enter teacher training (Chitty, 2014).

A number of Foucault's ideas can be related to work in the classroom. However, Foucault argues that what teachers are teaching is not really about knowledge, rather it is about the preferred and dominant discourses that are imprinted within routine classroom practices (Whitty, 1985). There are also some ideas that challenge the dominant discourse relating to what is perceived as good teaching. Moore uses the term 'discourse' in the sense that Foucault does; he briefly outlines on the cover of his book *The Good Teacher: Dominant Discourses in Teaching and Teacher Education* (2004) what he feels are the three dominant discourses of good teaching, which are:

- The competent craftsperson, currently favoured by central governments.
- The reflective practitioner, which continues to get widespread support among teacher trainers and educators.
- The charismatic subject, whose popular appeal is evidenced in filmic and other media representations of teaching.

He explores the idea that the two discourses of the competent teacher and the reflective practitioner are the 'dominant "official" discourses in teacher education, but have the capacity – if not the intention – both to weaken one another and to marginalise alternative teacher-education discourses' (Moore, 2004: 7). This then can create a dilemma for practitioners. However, for Foucault this dilemma presents teachers with an opportunity to question perceived notions of knowledge and truth about what is a good teacher and make their own individual judgements.

The concept of reflective practice, from Foucault's point of view, is also problematic. Reflective practice has been heralded as a way of solving problems with the aim of improving future practice. The process of reflective practice involves the practitioner sharing problems or writing journals that contain personal feelings related to practice, as such:

> This writing then is similar to autobiographical writing in the sense that one writes the self in connection with the presence of a virtual other. In this case, the virtual other takes the role of the master or the priest to compel us to speak (reflect on) the truth about ourselves and to interpret and assess this truth in relation to the norm ... By confessing the true self to virtual others, a modification of behaviour is expected. (Fejes, 2013: 64)

It should be emphasised here that this represents Foucault's notion of reflective practice as being a process of self-monitoring, and is offered as an academic challenge with the aim of providing a critically analytic viewpoint. The role of reflective practice with its goal of personal development can be, and is, very actively emancipatory (Fejes, 2013).

As a university lecturer, Foucault was suspicious of the value of teaching his students what they should think. He much preferred to urge the students to work things through themselves, which is similar to Socratic dialogue, where

> Instead of students being 'told' that something was true, they were invited to consider the logical consequences of certain forms of evidence. Students were thus invited to observe the empirical world, to record their observations, and then to draw systematic conclusions. (Oliver, 2010: 37)

During the late 1960s there was a movement, supported and practised by Foucault, to make education more student-centred. Students were given more liberty in their studies, and teachers and students enjoyed more equitable relationships. This new movement also saw a rise in more diverse forms of assessment. The traditional examinations where students could be individually ranked and classified were being slowly replaced by group assignments and project work. These new forms of assessment made it difficult to contrast between students and, as such, there was a trend to keep clear of the system of categorising and ranking student outcomes. Foucault was a key influence in the advancement of student-centred teaching, and particularly assessment. The advances in student-centred education have 'helped make possible the transmission to the mass system of university education we know today' (Oliver, 2010: 37).

Foucault's philosophy has been instrumental in providing practical and theoretical depth to educational research. Silverman points out that Foucault had recognised that the effectiveness of observation had been core to prison development, and how interviewing had been key to the Catholic confessional (Silverman, 2006). Where Foucault's ideas have particularly influenced educational research is in the field of discourse analysis, which explores the nature and structure of data gathered from speech, text and images in association with power and hierarchies (Punch, 2009). The foundation of discourse analysis is that the data 'should never be taken "at face value" but, instead, should be investigated to reveal the hidden messages' (Denscombe, 2007: 308). This sceptical approach to research is closely connected to Foucault's ideas regarding education as a whole. His philosophy questions the ways of thinking rather than offering specific methods to apply. However, it is argued that educators should take a questioning approach to practice in their attempts at providing a transformational learning experience for students and for themselves.

REFLECTIVE TASK

In *Discipline and Punish: The Birth of the Prison* (1979), Foucault explains the notion of the examination as 'a normalizing gaze, a surveillance that makes it possible to qualify, to classify and to punish' (Foucault, 1979: 184).

From your own experience of education:

1.   List the mechanisms that support the notion of the examination.
2.   Consider ways in which these mechanisms could be transformed to alleviate any undue pressure on those being examined.

SUMMARY

Foucault's profound and radical philosophy remains influential for educators and educational researchers. His ideas were contentious because they challenged long-held beliefs about truth, knowledge and the nature of power. Furthermore, he emphasised the ways in which knowledge and power were used to influence social control. His most important text for educators is *Discipline and Punish: The Birth of the Prison* (1979). From a practitioner and educational researcher's point of view, there are two major aspects that are highly significant. First, his ideas regarding discourse, which usually involve matters such as assessment, achievement, standards and qualifications. Second, his notion of surveillance, which includes the physical ways in which we observe and are observed, but also the ways in which we self-monitor and self-regulate ourselves.

Foucault's philosophy emerged from his personal experiences and his involvement with other influential French philosophers of the time. He was actively involved in the protest movement during the 1960s and 1970s, a time of great social unrest. It is difficult to categorise Foucault as a follower of any particular movement. However, he is considered by many as being associated with poststructuralism because he contested conventional ways of thinking and the taken-for-granted forms of knowledge. Foucault's ideas were guided by Kant, Nietzsche and, to some extent, by Marx. There are strong links with Gramsci regarding power and knowledge. Furthermore, Basil Bernstein's work with language codes has resonance with Foucault's notion of discourse; there are also close associations with his fellow French philosophers, Lyotard, Bourdieu and Derrida. Illich, like Foucault, also challenged the established principles about truth and the nature of power.

Foucault attracted considerable criticism for a number of reasons. Much of his philosophy was considered a threat to the establishment and society because it challenged conventional thought and order. He was also censured due to his confusing writing style and for the lack of rigour in his recording of history. Some commentators argued that Foucault could have addressed the more conventional modes of surveillance, rather than those used in a historical context. There are many aspects of his thoughts and ideas that are directly linked with education and the way in which we think about education. These aspects include the formation of policy, the questioning of what is considered good practice, his student-centred approach to teaching, and the use of his ideas as practical and theoretical instruments for educational research. Although not all of these aspects have direct application to practice, they are all important because they enable practitioners to think critically about education.

GLOSSARY OF TERMS

Discipline   Discipline is very much aligned with Foucault's idea of power/knowledge. There are three components of discipline set out in *Discipline and Punish: The Birth of the Prison* (1979): 'docile bodies', the 'means of corrective training' (this component is divided up into 'hierarchical observation', 'normalising judgement' and 'the examination') and 'panopticism'. Foucault stressed that within these three components discipline is not only imposed from those in power, but it is also enacted by people themselves as part of them flourishing both socially and economically.

Discourse   Foucault argues that meanings are generated in the association between power and knowledge, and this is entrenched in various social and political establishments. These meanings are transmitted through what he termed 'discourses'. These discourses are securely associated with the use of power. The discourses differ in the style of language used by distinct establishments and professions which are associated with their individual values and principles. These particular discourses tend to exclude those who are not part of the profession from taking part in communication; as such, the profession has power over those who are excluded. This is also the case in education where the discourse includes a particular style of language such as criteria, standards, assessment, curriculum and qualifications (Oliver, 2010).

Docile bodies   The notion of docile bodies, Foucault argued, was so that discipline could be enforced by producing people who could be controlled. It is the power that governs the individual so that they do what is desired and in the manner and time restraints that is desired by those in power. This is reflected in the organisation of school processes and the order of the school day with timetables and the imposition of differentiated subjects taught separately from each other. Docile bodies do not just refer to students, but also perhaps to a slightly lesser extent to teachers who are compelled to follow the needs of a timed and structured curriculum.

The examination   The examination is a culmination of hierarchical observation and the forming of judgements regarding what is normal and what is not. The examination has two functions: it observes and scrutinises, and then exposes individuals to assessment and grading. The result of the examination is to give individuals a distinct identity and status in relation to their graded examination score. The examination allows individuals to be shaped in a number of ways so that society has knowledge about them. A consequence of this is that it can generate groups of similar and dominant groups, who would be more inclined to participate in self-monitoring (Scott, 2008).

Hierarchical observation   Observation, Foucault thought, was the perfect way to instil discipline because through such surveillance by supervisors it was possible to watch everything continuously. Within this notion everyone is held responsible to the higher authority. As such, the efficiency of the supervision becomes assured for the reason that it is not feasible for individuals to know when they were being observed, so they act as if they were being observed at all times. This mode of observation is very apparent in school layouts with an abundance of windows, open spaces and now CCTV cameras. Pupils are not quite sure whether they are being watched, so they behave as if they are rather than suffer the consequence of punishment.

Normalising judgement   Normalising judgement is used to justify modes of oppression. For example, individuals can be categorised regarding the deviation from the recognised standards of behaviour. Those who deviate from the set standards are then subjected to different forms of discipline in the form of punishments and even exclusion. Normalisation is very much a part of Foucault's idea of discourse through labelling an individual's behaviour as 'normal' or 'disruptive'. In doing so, the individual begins to examine their own behaviour and then participates in the process of normalisation by recognising what is acceptable or not acceptable behaviour.

Panopticon   The prison structure of the 'panopticon', designed by Jeremy Bentham, is a central tower where prison officials can continuously observe the inmates in their cells. The prisoners, however, are not sure whether they are being observed or not. As a result, the 'control' is 'internalised by the prisoners themselves and the prisoner then becomes a thing of observable information. The function of the panopticon is 'to induce in the inmate a state of conscious and permanent visibility that assures the automatic functioning of power' (Foucault, 1979: 201).

Poststructuralism   Although Foucault would not have identified himself as such, many considered that much of his philosophy stemmed from poststructuralism. It is a somewhat complex term that was initiated by the scepticism of European scholars, including Foucault, who questioned and vigorously challenged conventional and time-honoured ways of thinking which emanated from the Age of Enlightenment. Poststructuralists' ways of thinking embraced a broad range of topics, such as justice, politics and equality. The poststructuralist standpoint is crucial in grasping Foucault's concept of power/knowledge.

Power/knowledge   Foucault's concept of power/knowledge contests that the established notion of knowledge is formidable because it makes people the subject of the different types of knowledge. Power, Foucault thought, could only be wielded on people who desired to be in the position of being powerless, although he also considered that the use of power was not always damaging. Power can be unwanted; it can also be a beneficial phenomenon.

Surveillance   Surveillance was an important notion for Foucault. In short, surveillance included the ways in which the means of correct training could be enforced; there were three methods that could be employed to ensure that people were controlled and then obliged to do as was required by those in power. These methods were hierarchical observation, normalising judgement and the examination; a brief outline of these three components can be found in this glossary. Surveillance is also central to Foucault's notion of the panopticon.

FURTHER READING

Deleuze, G. (1999) *Foucault*. London: The Athlone Press.
Written by a contemporary philosopher, this is an insightful analysis of Foucault's major ideas such as knowledge, power and subjectivity.

Gutting, G. (2005) *Foucault: A Very Short Introduction*. Oxford: Oxford University Press.
A brief illustrated introduction to Foucault which is biographical and clarifies his key themes and the development of his philosophy.

Mills, S. (2003) *Michel Foucault*. Abingdon: Routledge.
An introductory text which not only explores Foucault's main ideas, but offers some practical guidance for application in practice.

Rainbow, P. (ed.) (1984) *The Foucault Reader: An Introduction to Foucault's Thoughts*. London: Penguin.
This book is an authoritative review of Foucault's works, with many extracts from his writings and material from the interviews he gave.

REFERENCES

Allan, J. (2013a) 'Foucault and his acolytes: Discourse, power and ethics'. In: Murphy, M. (ed.) *Social Theory and Education Research*. London: Routledge.

Allan, K. (2013b) *Contemporary Social and Sociological Theory* (3rd edn). London: SAGE.

Ball, S. (ed.) (2010) *Foucault and Education: Disciplines and Knowledge*. London: Routledge.

Ball, S. (2013) *Foucault, Power, and Education*. London: Routledge.

Barry, P. (2002) *Beginning Theory: An Introduction to Literary and Cultural Theory* (2nd edn). Manchester: Manchester University Press.

Bartlett, S., Burton, D. and Peim, N. (2001) *Introduction to Education Studies*. London: Paul Chapman.

Bell, L. and Stevenson, H. (2006) *Education Policy: Process, Themes and Impact*. London: Routledge.

Chitty, C. (2014) *Education Policy in Britain* (3rd edn). Basingstoke: Palgrave Macmillan.

Cole, M. (2008) *Marxism and Educational Theory: Origins and Issues*. London: Routledge.

Danaher, G., Schirato, T. and Webb, J. (2000) *Understanding Foucault*. London: SAGE.

Denscombe, M. (2007) *The Good Research Guide* (3rd edn). Maidenhead: Open University Press.

Fejes, A. (2013) 'Foucault, confession and reflective practices'. In: Murphy, M. (ed.) *Social Theory and Education Research*. London: Routledge.

Fisher, R., Fulford, A., McNichols, B. and Thompson, R. (2010) 'The curriculum in the lifelong learning sector'. In: Avis, J., Fisher, R. and Thompson, R. (eds) *Teaching in Lifelong Learning: A Guide to Theory and Practice*. Maidenhead: Open University Press.

Foucault, M. (1961) *Madness and Civilization: A History of Insanity*. London: Routledge.

Foucault, M. (1963) *The Birth of the Clinic: An Archaeology of Medical Perception*. London: Routledge.

Foucault, M. (1966) *The Order of Things*. London: Routledge.

Foucault, M. (1969) *The Archaeology of Knowledge*. London: Routledge.

Foucault, M. (1976) *The History of Sexuality: The Will to Knowledge*, Vol. 1. London: Penguin.

Foucault, M. (1979) *Discipline and Punish: The Birth of the Prison*. London: Penguin.

Foucault, M. (1984a) *The History of Sexuality: The Use of Pleasure*, Vol. 2. London: Penguin.

Foucault, M. (1984b) *The History of Sexuality: The Care of the Self*, Vol. 3. London: Penguin.

Foucault, M. (2006) 'The means of correct training'. In: Lauder, H., Brown, P., Dillabough, J.-A. and Halsey, A. (eds) *Education, Globalisation and Social Change*. Oxford: Oxford University Press.

Hope, A. (2013) 'Foucault, panopticism and school surveillance research'. In: Murphy, M. (ed.) *Social Theory and Education Research*. London: Routledge.

Kumar, K. (1997) 'The post-modern condition'. In: Halsey, A., Lauder, H., Brown, P. and Stuart Wells, A. (eds) *Education: Culture, Economy, Society*. Oxford: Oxford University Press.

MacBlain, S. (2014) *How Children Learn*. London: SAGE.

MacLure, M. (2003) *Discourse in Education and Social Research*. Buckingham: Open University Press.

McNay, L. (1994) *Foucault: A Critical Introduction*. Cambridge: Polity Press.

Moore, A. (2000) *Teaching and Learning: Pedagogy, Curriculum and Culture*. London: RoutledgeFalmer.

Moore, A. (2004) *The Good Teacher: Dominant Discourses in Teaching and Teacher Education*. London: Routledge.

Murphy, M. (ed.) (2013) *Social Theory and Education Research*. London: Routledge.

Oksala, J. (2007) *How to Read Foucault*. London: Granta.

Oliver, P. (2010) *Foucault – the Key Ideas*. London: Hodder Education.

Peters, M. (2001) 'Michel Foucault, 1926–84'. In: Palmer, J. (ed.) *Fifty Modern Thinkers on Education: From Piaget to the Present*. London: Routledge.

Peters, M. and Besley, T. (2012) 'Education and postmodernism'. In: Arthur, J. and Peterson, A. (eds) *The Routledge Companion to Education*. London: Routledge.

Punch, K. (2009) *Introduction to Research Methods in Education*. London: SAGE.

Rawlings, V. (2019) '"It's not bullying", "It's just a joke": Teacher and student discursive manoeuvres around gendered violence'. *British Educational Research Journal*, 45(4): 698–716.

Schwan, A. and Shapiro, S. (2011) *How to Read Foucault's Discipline and Punish*. London: Pluto Press.

Scott, D. (2008) *Critical Essays on Major Curriculum Theorists*. Abingdon: Routledge.

Silverman, D. (2006) *Interpreting Qualitative Data* (3rd edn). London: SAGE.

Thomas, G. (2007) *Education and Theory: Strangers in Paradigms*. Maidenhead: Open University Press.

Weiner, G., Arnot, M. and David, M. (1997) 'Is the future female? Female success, male disadvantage, and changing gender patterns in education'. In: Halsey, A., Lauder, H., Brown, P. and Stuart Wells, A. (eds) *Education: Culture, Economy, Society*. Oxford: Oxford University Press.

Whitty, G. (1985) *Sociology and School Knowledge: Curriculum Theory, Research and Politics*. London: Methuen.

9
LORIS MALAGUZZI

THE REGGIO EMILIA EXPERIENCE

LEARNING OUTCOMES

After reading this chapter, you should be able to:

- understand the life and work of Loris Malaguzzi;
- recognise the relationship between Malaguzzi and the Reggio Emilia experience;
- understand the philosophy behind the Reggio Emelia experience;
- recognise the influence of constructivist theorists on Malaguzzi's philosophy;
- consider how the Reggio Emilia principles can be applied to practice.

KEY WORDS

Asili nido; atelier; Atelierista; documentation; The Hundred Languages of Children; municipality; provocations; *progettazione; scuola dell'infanzia.*

INTRODUCTION

Loris Malaguzzi can be credited with founding the educational philosophy that under-pins a network of municipal pre-schools and infant toddler centres in the Northern Italian town of Reggio Emilia. Malaguzzi trained as a teacher and commenced his career as a primary school teacher in 1946. However, his life course was set to change in the aftermath of the Second World War when he became aware of a group of peas-ant women who were building their own pre-school from the rubble of war. Deciding to see this for himself, Malaguzzi cycled to the village of Villa Cella and met the women, who, on realising he was a teacher, implored him to 'look after their children' (Featherstone, 2016; Jarvis et al., 2017). Thus, Malaguzzi's lifetime commitment to the **municipality** of Reggio Emilia was born.

Influenced by his own experiences during the war, especially the impact of fascism, Malaguzzi set out a vision of a schooling system that was free from the control of the Catholic Church, and which sought to promote the rights of the child. Building on the aspirations of the women of Villa Cella and with the support of the community, Malaguzzi sought to recognise the child's rights to be a protagonist and looked for ways to sustain the child's spontaneous creativity at the highest level (Rinaldi, 2006). Furthermore, the system of education which Malaguzzi developed promoted an environment that served the needs of children, the community and teachers equally.

What resulted from Malaguzzi's early philosophy, inspired by the women of Villa Cella, was a municipal education system, which has become world-renowned for its high-quality education system, providing a child-centred, community-oriented educa-tional experience for children under six years of age (Lazzari, 2012). Building on his initial promise to the women of Villa Cella that he would do his best to look after their children, Malaguzzi dedicated his life to the community of Reggio Emilia, and remained working alongside them, until control was transferred to the municipality in the early 1960s.

Even once the schools had come under the control of the municipality, Malaguzzi continued to play an active role in their development, being appointed the Consultant to the first municipal schools, ***scuolla del' infanzia***, for children aged three to six in 1963 and later becoming Director for the City Schools, overseeing their expansion and including provision for children under three in the ***asili nido*** (Moss, 2016). Despite formally retiring in 1984, Malaguzzi continued to be active in the field of early education, editing a national magazine for early years educators, *Bambini*, and becoming President of the Gruppo Nazionale Nidi which supported debate on issues for services for children under three years of age (Moss, 2016). In addition, he contin-ued to promote the Reggio experience by inviting visitors to view for themselves the unique system of education and by reaching out to the wider community by way of the travelling exhibition, **The Hundred Languages of Children**, which showcased the most significant project work from the municipal schools.

Malaguzzi died in 1994 and at the time of his death he was working on the creation of Reggio Children, which was another project designed to promote the Reggio Emilia approach around the world. As we will see in the following sections, while Malaguzzi was adamant that he did not wish for the Reggio experience to be replicated in its entirety, he hoped that through sharing his own vision it would empower others to develop their own vision for a better early childhood experience for all.

LORIS MALAGUZZI, THE PERSON

Loris Malaguzzi was born in 1920 in the province of Emilia Romagna, in the small town and commune of Correggio, near Reggio Emilia. Moving to the city of Reggio Emilia with his family in 1923, Malaguzzi remained there for much of his working life, with only brief periods away to study and when he was drafted by the Republic of Salo to work in a barracks in Bologna (Cagliari et al., 2016). Malaguzzi was a family man; he married Nilde Bonacini in 1944 and they had one son, Antonio, who was born in 1946. However, since he was an intensely private person, little more is known about Malaguzzi's personal life.

Malaguzzi's working life was dedicated to a career in education. Initially, he trained to be a primary school teacher, enrolling in a teacher training institution in 1939, a decision with which he credits his father, observing 'that I should take the path of teaching and becoming a primary school maestro [teacher] was written in my father's mind' (Cagliari et al., 2016: 19). Once qualified as a teacher, Malaguzzi taught in primary and secondary schools in Reggiolo, Sologno, Reggio Emilia and Guastello, beginning a course in pedagogy at the University of Urbino in 1940. Following the war, he studied psychology at the National Centre for Research in Rome, before returning to Reggio Emilia to work in a centre for children experiencing learning difficulties at school.

Despite knowing little of his personal life, it is well documented that Malaguzzi was heavily impacted by the fascist regime that had governed Italy in the period up to and during the Second World War (Brunson Day, 2001; Smidt, 2013; Jarvis et al., 2017). According to Brunson Day (2001), Malaguzzi stated that 'fascism had gobbled up my youth'. Furthermore, in a 1993 interview with Lella Gandini (2006), Malaguzzi observes:

> War in its tragic absurdity might have been the kind of experience that pushes a person toward the job of educating as a way to start anew and live and work for the future. This desire strikes a person, as the war finally ends and the symbols of life reappear with a violence equal to that of the time of destruction. (cited in Parker-Rees and Willan, 2006: 312)

This would then provide some insight into the factors that influenced Malaguzzi's philosophy as an educationalist, since his experience of war and fascism profoundly affected his thinking, his questions and his answers (Smidt, 2013). It is necessary, therefore, to set this in the context of the political situation in Reggio Emilia during the period in which Malaguzzi was working as a young teacher.

Reggio Emilia is set in the agricultural and industrial region of Emilia Romagna, an area that was identified as being in Italy's red belt during the war period. So called because the majority of people in the region joined the socialist and communist parties during the Second World War, the ideals of the people of Reggio Emilia were in direct opposition to the ruling fascist party of the time. While the area suffered great loss and hardship during the war, which touched and coloured the lives of its occupants, the inhabitants of Reggio Emilia still played a key part in the resistance movement during the war.

Post-war, the citizens of Reggio Emilia received the gold medal for military valour, Italy's highest honour (Hall et al., 2015), and moving on from the war strong support was given to socialist principles, including egalitarianism and the building of a solid community. Most significant in the post-war development of the region was the women of the community who set themselves the task of rebuilding the war-torn region, starting with provision of education for the very young. Thus, in June 1945 female members of the Union of Italian Women (UDI) requested funds from the public towards the establishment of nursery schools (Hall et al., 2015). Furthermore, in the village of Villa Cella, the women of the community raised an additional 800,000 lira from the sale of salvaged war materials, including an abandoned German tank, bricks, horses and trucks, money which they put towards building their own school.

It is significant that it was the women of the community who were driving the initiative, since women in Italy had lacked any power up to this point, having only received the right to vote in 1945. However, playing a significant role in the resistance movement during the war had empowered them to take action and this began with a desire to 'overcome the ideological divisions that had lasted for two decades' (Reggio Children, 2002: 6, cited in Hall et al., 2015) and to build a better future for the children who they saw as 'inhabitants of the new world that was rapidly being built' (2002: 6, cited in Hall et al., 2015).

Malaguzzi became aware of the actions of the women of Villa Cella and decided to see for himself if it were true. He stated: 'No-one in the city believed it. I went there by bicycle. Simply everything was true and the women were already there cleaning bricks collected from the ruins' (cited in Cagliari et al., 2016: 24).

He recalls that the women showed him around the area and told him their story, and as soon as they found out that he was a teacher, asked for his help. 'If that's true come here and teach with us' (Cagliari et al., 2016: 24).

The school, which was built by the community of Villa Cella, took eight months to complete and was officially opened by the mayor under the name 'The April 25th School' in honour of liberation day. The building of the school was a community effort and remained so in its organisation and management, being self-managed and dedicated to the children, in direct contrast to the Church-influenced ideals and philosophies of the time. Malaguzzi recalls that it was 'an exciting anomaly, an invention I liked immensely and from which many facts of my life would follow' (Cagliari et al., 2016: 24). The April 25th School was to spearhead a number of further schools built on the same principle of being entirely community financed and community run.

The following section will explore further the unique attributes of these early settings and their subsequent legacy. However, what is important in the context of this section is the impact that his experience in Villa Cella had on Malaguzzi and his future work. Malaguzzi observes that he made a pact of solidarity with the community of Villa Cello and six other schools run by women and the people's movement, a pact never to desert them (Cagliariet al., 2016). He subsequently built on a commitment to make a difference to the lives of these people, abandoning his career in teaching, in favour of work in municipal children's services, including the development of a centre for children with psychological problems and being appointed as Consultant to Reggio Emilia's first municipal schools, ***scuola dell' infanzia***, for children aged three to six years, and then Director of the city schools, which included the addition of schools for children under three years (Moss, 2016). It was in these roles that he was able to further influence policy, particularly as the municipality also took over control of the original *scuola dell' infanzia* at this time.

Malaguzzi was instrumental in raising awareness of the educational needs of children under six years of age and, along with a network of fellow educationalists, created a new secular public education, free from the control of the Church. His 'hands-on approach' meant that he became an educational expert and planner in the *scuola dell' infanzia* and played a key role when these early schools moved from local to municipal control. Despite his formal retirement in 1984, Malaguzzi continued to play an active role in the city schools (Moss, 2016). In addition, he edited *Bambini*, a national magazine for early years educators, and was president of the Gruppo Nazionale Nidi (National Nido Group) which focused on issues for children under three years of age. Malaguzzi also continued to promote the Reggio Emilia experience through the travelling exhibition, The Hundred Languages of Children, and through hosting overseas visitors to the municipal schools of Reggio Emilia.

Loris Malaguzzi worked tirelessly to create a system of education that was both democratic and radical, building on the collective responsibility of a community in which reciprocity and trust were implicit. In passing responsibility on to the municipality, Malaguzzi was instrumental in ensuring that the original ideologies were not lost, thereby creating a legacy of a world-renowned nursery education system. To date, there are more than eighty education centres for children from zero to six in the local territory of Reggio Emilia (Reggio Children, n.d.), and these centres are renowned in the field of early education. The philosophy behind Reggio Emilia and the influence of Malaguzzi in this will be discussed in the next section.

THE REGGIO EMILIA EXPERIENCE

In order to understand the impact of the Reggio Emilia philosophy, it is necessary to situate this in the political and educational climate of the time, since, as observed by Hall et al., 'if any system of education can be said to have grown out of the political landscape of a country it is Reggio Emilia' (2015: 8). As noted in the previous section, in the period prior to and during the Second World War, Italy had come under the control of the fascist dictator, Benito Mussolini, whose ideology was abhorred by the people of Reggio Emilia who sympathised with a socialist/communist ideology.

Under the fascist regime, the Church retained its control over the education system. Declaring Catholicism the official state religion of Italy, education policies were designed to ensure that Catholic principles were adhered to, with boys and girls taking on the traditional roles of boys being educated to become soldiers and girls to raise soldiers. The education system was expected to promote all aspects of fascism. Furthermore, Mussolini promoted a system of early years education inspired by the work of the Agassi sisters, whose ideas on early years education very much centred around how children used their natural abilities in environments closely resembling their home. Smidt (2015) questions how far these ideas on education had anything to do with learning. Nevertheless, impressed by their views Mussolini established the state-run ONMI services (National Organisation for Mothers and Infants) which supported the care and provision for children in large and poor families. Alongside this, he introduced the Gentile Reforms to the education system, declaring that education for children under the age of six was not a requirement, reinforcing a view that pre-school education was neither necessary nor important.

According to Hall et al. (2015), following the demise of fascism, Italy was a country that was left divided by its political history, with vast sections of the country alienated as a result of strong socialist/communist sentiments, a sentiment that was particularly felt by the citizens of Reggio Emilia. Thus, in creating a system of early education, a significant driver for the women responsible for building the school at Villa Cella was the need to rectify past injustices and create a better future for their children. This then became the founding principles of the Reggio Emilia experience.

While Jarvis et al. (2017) argue that a key driver for the setting up of pre-schools was a prudent one, with the women of Reggio Emilia being in desperate need of employment following the economic crisis triggered by the war, there was also a strong sense among the women that the education system they desired for their children was one that was very different from the traditional education they had received under the direction of the Catholic Church. This education instilled obedience and respect for authority, qualities that were further reinforced under the strict fascist regime. Thus, when setting out their vision for the school, the women were insistent that the education experience that was delivered should be one that would allow children to become non-conformist, critical young thinkers who were self-aware and intolerant of inequality and justice (Wortham, cited in Jarvis et al., 2017).

When asked by the women of Villa Cella to 'help to look after our children' since they were 'just as intelligent as the rich people's children' (Achtner, 1994, cited in Jarvis et al., 2017: 156), Malaguzzi made a commitment to learn as he was teaching the children. Acknowledging that he had little experience of working with such young children, Malaguzzi observed that this would be a reciprocal situation in which rather than being in charge of the children, they would learn as he worked alongside them (Smidt, 2013). Respecting the wishes of the women of Villa Cella to change history and create an education system that was truly child-led, Malaguzzi recognised the importance of involving parents and the community in providing a high-quality, liberating education system. He built on the commitment he made by continuing to learn on the hoof and engaging as widely as possible with the whole community by travelling around, promoting his aims and goals, and winning the trust of the communities he visited.

What emerged under the direction of Malaguzzi, but with the support of the communities and families, was an education system that was built around Malaguzzi's image of the child. As we will see later in the chapter, Malaguzzi was heavily influenced by constructivist theorists such as Dewey, Piaget and Vygotsky, and this led him to view the child as one who was rich in potential and a co-constructor of their world. He believed the child to be strong and powerful, and capable of developing their own theories of the world and how it worked. Staying faithful to his notion that the adult was a co-creator, rather than director, of knowledge, he believed that children should be allowed to explore ideas with adults and other children. His education philosophy was one that recognised the child as being a self-confident explorer and investigator with a strong sense of curiosity, being free of spirit to venture beyond what was known (Jarvis et al., 2017).

Malaguzzi is renowned for his ideology of the 'hundred languages of the child' which underpinned their learning and provided a vehicle by which to express themselves. Malaguzzi's hundred languages included talking, painting, writing, role-play, photography, sculpture and fabric work, to name but a few. Malaguzzi was keen to ensure that children were able to access these languages to express themselves and communicate their thoughts and feelings. To facilitate this, the environment is constructed as a third teacher, with a focus on the use of light, floor to ceiling windows, pale walls so children's artwork can be viewed uninhibited, and the use of mirrors to catch light and reflect the child's own self-image back to them. Furthermore, Reggio Emilia pre-schools are traditionally built around an *atelier*, managed by an ***Atelierista*** who is responsible for facilitating opportunities for children to communicate through their hundred languages. Since the 1980s, the hundred languages have been used as a basis for Malaguzzi's travelling exhibition, which he referred to as 'an exhibition of the possible' (Vecchi, 2010: 27 cited in Cagliari et al., 2016: 276). The exhibition provided Malaguzzi with the opportunity to share with a much wider audience the principles and philosophy of the Reggio experience.

The environment was one of three teachers identified by Malaguzzi, with parents being viewed as the first teacher, later joined by other adults, and the child as the second teacher (Featherstone, 2016). Malaguzzi stayed true to the original intention for the school as a community setting, and since the inception parents have been welcomed into the Reggio Emilia school as a partner in their children's learning. Furthermore, teachers believe firmly in the rights of parents, ensuring they are well informed and productive members of the school team. In acknowledgment of the growing number of working parents, exchanges with parents take place at the end of sessions where discussions can precede without pressure while children are resting. An important element of the Reggio Emilia philosophy is the detailed **documentation** prepared by teachers which forms the basis of many of these discussions. In this way, parents are truly involved in their child's learning journey.

What began as an ideal, first muted by a group of women wanting to make a difference to their children, grew into something extraordinary, which must be attributed to the unique vision and commitment of Malaguzzi. Thus, the original six pre-schools, run entirely by parents working alongside Malaguzzi, very quickly grew and emerged as a democratic and radical world-renowned education system. It is the strength of the vision and ideology underpinning the Reggio Emilia school system that ensured that even when the schools eventually came under the responsibility of the municipality in the 1950s, they remained as secular schools, free from Church control, and retained their unique approach to learning. However, as we will see in the following sections, the Reggio Emilia experience is not designed to be replicated in other settings, and Malaguzzi himself was hesitant in publishing a theory of any kind, since he believed that pedagogy should be fluid, open to change and informed by practice (Jarvis et al., 2017). Thus, in translating the philosophy to practice, Moss (2016) observes that the philosophy is not to be exported or copied, rather the alternatives presented should be used as a means by which to change and develop practice which is responsive to the uniqueness of each individual setting.

LINKS WITH OTHER THEORISTS

Dodd-Nufrio (2011) observes that comparisons between Montessori and Reggio Emilia settings are inevitable given their shared cultural contexts, and, according to Smidt (2013), as a young teacher Malaguzzi had followed what she was saying and doing. Certainly, elements of the Montessori approach are reflected in Malaguzzi's philosophy, specifically the child-centred approach to learning and the role of the adult as facilitator or director, rather than in the traditional role of the teacher. However, a more direct influence on Malaguzzi came from those theorists in the constructivist tradition, including Dewey, Piaget and Vygotsky.

Dewey specifically related his work to classroom practice and his principles can be seen influencing the Reggio Emilia school's value and practice. Dewey saw the child as oppressed, lacking a voice and subject to the control of the adults around them, and built a philosophy around the individual child. Dewey believed that schools should enable children to actively participate in their own learning with the help and guidance of teachers, and through learning to work co-operatively would change society accordingly (Smidt, 2013). As we have discussed in earlier sections, Dewey's ideas resonated with Malaguzzi who wanted children to have a voice when faced with the oppression he himself had experienced.

As a young teacher, Malaguzzi was heavily influenced by the work of Jean Piaget and, according to Rinaldi, was grateful for the guidance which Piaget's work offered him (Smidt, 2013). However, as he began to develop his own philosophy, Malaguzzi began to question the lack of historical, cultural and social emphasis in Piaget's work, and while he agreed with Piaget's view of the child as an active explorer, he became more heavily influenced by the work of Vygotsky and Bruner who both saw learning proceeding in a social context, in which language was essential to learning. Vygotsky believed that children work within a zone of proximal development and can achieve at a higher level when supported by a more knowledgeable other. Similarly, Bruner theorised that early learning could be extended through a more expert other scaffolding and supporting learning. This is seen throughout Reggio Emilia schools, in which interaction between adults and children is actively encouraged and facilitated throughout the learning environment. Furthermore, as will be seen in the next section, the ethos behind the Reggio Emilia environment is one that actively promotes learning in a social context.

Malaguzzi's emphasis on the interactions between parents and teachers in the Reggio School has parallels with Bronfenbrenner's work. Bronfenbrenner saw the environment in which the child lived as key to their learning experience, and he observed that the people within the environment were of particular influence on the developing child. Bronfenbrenner saw the environment as multi-layered, with the two layers closest to the child, the microsystem and the mesosystem, comprising the home and school. Thus, according to Bronfenbrenner, positive interactions between the adults in these layers was key to promoting a good learning experience for the developing child. As we have seen in the previous section, relationships between adults and children, and between children themselves, underpin the Reggio Emilia philosophy. Furthermore, as we will see in the later section, the design of the Reggio School is built around a central piazza, which Malaguzzi intended as a reflection of the city square which was traditionally seen as a meeting place in Italian culture, thereby reinforcing the community ethos of the school.

CRITIQUING THE THEORY

Jarvis et al. (2017) argue that the principles behind Malaguzzi's philosophy are out of keeping with the target-driven and outcomes-focused nature of the current early year's curriculum. Despite the fact that the Early Years Foundation Stage (EYFS) (2017) curriculum promotes a child-centred approach, it could be argued that tensions exist when teachers are under pressure to meet certain requirements set by a rigid and structured curriculum and increasingly demanding early learning goals; this makes it increasingly challenging to promote the child-led, project-driven curriculum underpinning the Reggio Emilia experience. Writing as an early year's educator who has adopted the Reggio approach, Priscilla Patti observes that 'from a teacher's perspective there is certainly a loss of control with the unknown' (2017: n.p.). Soler and Miller reinforce this view, arguing that 'in the absence of a written curriculum there is a lack of accountability to the wider society' (2003: 65).

Papathoedorou (2006) observes that the Reggio Emilia experience is underpinned by a pedagogy that values the everyday experiences of children, teachers, parents and the community. However, this is set in a context in which shared experience is common, whereas in the diversity of our own society it could be argued that this might highlight disadvantages for some children, particularly if their experiences could be construed as inferior to their more advantaged peers. This would certainly require a sensitive approach from those facilitating the experience. Furthermore, the Reggio Emilia system is built around community involvement, in which parents play a more active role in the education system, supporting the children's projects and being an active presence in the life of the school. Even once parents have returned to work, they continue to maintain this role. Despite the importance placed in the EYFS on the involvement of parents, it is questionable how far they would be able to, or want, to take on the level of commitment observed in the Reggio Emilia community.

It is difficult to critique a system which is so inherently linked to the environment in which it was created, and perhaps any criticisms here come not from what Malaguzzi created, since this was fitting to the time and circumstances of the period. Furthermore, the fact that it has endured for so long would suggest that it is fitting for the Reggio Emilia community. Any challenges that might exist outside of Reggio Emilia must surely emerge where practitioners try to replicate it in its entirety, since Malaguzzi was keen that the philosophy should only ever act as a stimulus to encourage others to develop a philosophy in keeping with their own individual circumstances. The Reggio Emilia experience is most certainly not a 'one-size-fits-all' approach.

APPLYING THE REGGIO EMILIA PRINCIPLES IN THE CLASSROOM

As noted earlier in the chapter, the Reggio Emilia approach was never intended to be replicated, and, as observed by Featherstone (2016), a key principle of Reggio School is that the unique method they developed could not be exported. 'Like a plant it can only flourish in the right soil' (Featherstone, 2016: 193). However, through opening settings to visitors and in touring The Hundred Languages of Children exhibition, it could be argued that Malaguzzi was keen to promote the ideology of the Reggio Emilia experience with the intention of empowering practitioners to 'take the essence of Reggio and build their own version' (Featherstone, 2016: 193).

This section will then commence with an account of the traditional approach to the Reggio Emilia experience and then consider how policy-makers might translate this practice into policy.

Central to practice in the Reggio Emilia setting is the image of the child, which Malaguzzi insisted was 'not only a necessary act of clarity and correctness, it is the necessary premise for any pedagogical theory, and any pedagogical project' (Cagliari et al., 2016: 374). Furthermore, Malaguzzi's image of the child was one of a rich child, stating that 'all children whatever their culture, whatever their lives are rich, better equipped, more talented, stronger and more intelligent than we can suppose' (Calgiari et al., 2016: 397). For Malaguzzi, the richness came from the hundred languages that children used to express themselves, and the principle of the Reggio experience was built around providing children with opportunities to express themselves in as many ways as possible, and in ways that suited them best.

The Reggio classroom provides, then, a nurturing experience for the child, with the teacher playing a central role. Here, Malaguzzi calls for an image of the rich teacher, since rich children 'request rich intelligence in others, rich curiosity in others, a very high and advanced capacity for fantasy, imagination, learning and culture in others (Calgiari et al., 2016: 397). The teacher must, however, view their own role as a partner and co-constructor of knowledge, learning with, rather than directing the children, through discovery and exploration. A key part of the teacher's role is documentation which teachers use as a means by which to reflect on the children's experience. Teachers look and listen to what is going on around them and use this to develop their knowledge of the child or groups of children. Any records made are shared with the children themselves, and parents and colleagues, showing the children that their work is valued and evidencing to parents how children have been engaged in individual or group projects. Documentation forms the professional discussions amongst teachers and supports them in their planning. Documentation is made visible and is usually seen lining the walls, providing a timeline of projects undertaken, and providing an insight into the depth and variety of the children's learning experiences (Jarvis et al., 2017).

Through the process of documentation, teachers are able to elicit children's thoughts, interests and ideas, and in doing so provide an environment which supports the interests of the child. Jarvis et al. (2017) observes that this allows teachers to create **provocations**, which are starting points directly driven by the children's interests. Provocations allow children to work in groups on extended exploration and problem solving (Hall et al., 2015) and generally lead to extended projects or topics, which involve extended studies on life, environment, science or culture. A project might last for a week or a whole term, and it is not unusual for children to drop a project for a period before returning to it at a later date. As explained by Rinaldi (2006), the flexibility and fluidity of the Reggio teaching and learning process is key to preventing it from becoming formulaic and inflexible, and while the original project may change direction, it continues to be documented and flexibly planned (Jarvis et al., 2017).

Teachers in the Reggio Emilia setting do not follow a structured curriculum and, according to Forman and Fyfe, 'the curriculum is not child-centred or teacher-directed. The curriculum is child-originated and teacher-framed' (2011: 240). Malaguzzi believed that a planned curriculum would push schools towards teaching without learning (Smidt, 2013) and instead substituted the term 'curriculum' for **progettazione** which described how staff, children, parents and the community come together to discuss how a project might evolve. Central to the process was the *Atelierista*, and while each classroom has two qualified teachers, the *Atelierista* has an entirely different background, having attended an Academy or Institute of Art (Hall et al., 2015). The role that the *Atelierista* fulfils is one of art director, selecting materials and ensuring that the environment is rich and inviting, and open to questioning for the children. According to Smidt (2013), the role of the *Atelierista* is complex and important, requiring them to be a researcher into both children's and adult's ways of knowing, and should bring a different perspective to the learning experience (Hall et al., 2015). Alongside the specific role of the *Atelierista*, Malaguzzi also insisted that all Reggio Emilia schools should have an *atelier*, or art studio, which is where the *Atelierista* works with groups of children on a variety of projects. These might include art, music, drawing and play; the *atelier* is resourced in such a way that children are not inhibited in their learning. Smidt observes that the *atelier* also serves the function of a laboratory, 'promoting enquiry, investigation and expression and encouraging the use of spoken and other languages' (2013: 101).

While the *atelier* is a fundamental part of the Reggio Emilia experience, this is, however, just one aspect of the unique learning environment that the settings provide. This includes a piazza, replicating the function and spirit of the town square, acting as a meeting place for people to exchange ideas and be sociable, and provides a public space celebrating what the children have been doing. The piazza will frequently contain large mirrors, performance areas and dressing-up capsules, encouraging children of all ages to come together and share the space. The Reggio Emilia setting also contains an open patio, or room without a ceiling, designed to illustrate the connection between indoor and outdoor spaces (Smidt, 2013). Classrooms come immediately off the central piazza, giving all children freedom of access to the patio area. The classrooms themselves mirror the piazza experience, providing flexible spaces for children to demonstrate their creativity, alongside especially created quiet spaces for those children who wish to sit and contemplate. Finally, functional areas such as kitchens, dining rooms and bathrooms continue to play their part in the learning process. Children are encouraged to go into the kitchens and interact with the staff, and dining areas are designed to be sociable areas building on the value of social interactions.

It can be seen, then, that the Reggio experience is indeed unique and largely built on the vision of one man, who believed that children should not be shaped by experience, but shape it themselves (Smidt, 2013). Nevertheless, while it would be extremely challenging and indeed ill advised to replicate the experience in its entirety, there are certainly elements of it that can be seen reflected in current Early Years policy and practice today. Furthermore, as discussed by Jarvis et al. (2017), many countries have attempted to replicate aspects of Malaguzzi's vision with varying degrees of success, with Reggio Emilia centres being set up successfully in Scotland, Sweden and the United States of America. Furthermore, Learning and Teaching Scotland adopted the Reggio framework when revising their early years framework in 2006.

On a more conservative scale, elements of Malaguzzi's ideology can be seen reflected in the revised Early Years Foundation Stage framework (2017), particularly in respect of the four guiding principles that shape practice in the early years, which state:

- every child is a unique child, who is constantly learning and can be resilient, capable, confident and self-assured;
- children learn to be strong and independent through positive relationships;
- children learn and develop well in enabling environments, in which their experiences respond to their individual needs and there is a strong partnership between practitioners and parents and/or carers;
- children develop and learn in different ways and at different rates. (DfE, 2017: 6)

The emphasis on the unique child echoes Malaguzzi's view of the child as being rich in potential, while the notion of building positive relationships reflects Malaguzzi's idea that children should explore ideas and collaborate with other children and adults (Jarvis, 2017). It should not be overlooked either that a focus on enabling environments and the partnership between practitioners and carers is in harmony with Malaguzzi's view of the environment as a third teacher.

While policy and practice gives some indication of how the Reggio Emilia experience might influence practice, there is also evidence in everyday practice that schools themselves have adopted elements of practice in their day-to-day running – for example, the EYFS requires that ongoing assessment is a fundamental part of the learning and development process (DfE, 2017). Moreover, evidence gathered should be used to ascertain each individual's 'level of achievement, interests and learning styles, and then to shape learning experiences for each child based on those observations' (DfE, 2017: 13). Furthermore, it is expected that learning experiences are also influenced by the information provided by parents and carers, with the expectation of the sharing of information between home and school. In much the same way that Reggio Emilia practitioners use documentation to share these observations, schools in England have adopted a variety of online approaches to this sharing of information – for example, through software programs such as 'tapestry' which provides an online journal for parents and practitioners to record the everyday experiences of children.

While Jarvis et al. (2017) argue that the target-driven and outcome-driven curriculum is not in alignment with Malaguzzi's vision, they do suggest that aspects can still be adapted even within these constraints. This includes building our own conception of the child, showing a willingness to share and collaborate with children, other professionals and parents, and taking a more creative look at the environment. They also suggest that a more lateral interpretation of the statutory frameworks might well present a more individual and inclusive view of the child (Jarvis, 2017).

REFLECTIVE TASK

Which aspect(s) of the Reggio Emilia experience do you think are most easily transferable to the Early Years Foundation Stage?

What changes could you make to your own practice to fit with the Reggio Emilia philosophy?

SUMMARY

In describing the working life of Loris Malaguzzi, Moss (2016) presents a picture that is both complex and multifaceted, observing that alongside his role as educator, he was also an administrator, pedagogical researcher and director, student and campaigner. However, ironically Moss (2016) goes on to observe that one role he did not fit comfortably in was that of leader, since throughout his life Malaguzzi sought to empower individuals to be in control of their own destiny. A fundamental aspect of the Reggio Emilia school was the distinct lack of a hierarchy, with each individual in the school encouraged to participate in their own way, through the sharing of knowledge and ongoing dialogue.

While it should not be forgotten that the impetus behind the Reggio Emilia experience came from the women who wanted a better life for their children, it could be argued that this would not have been realised without Malaguzzi's drive and vision to create a school system that was truly centred on the needs of the child and the communities in which they lived. Inspired by the work of constructivist theorists such as Vygotsky and Piaget, and influenced by Dewey's philosophy that learning is an active process rather than the traditional transmission of pre-packed knowledge common in schools of the time, Malaguzzi sought to find a means by which children could be supported in directing their own learning. This he achieved through creating a learning environment that facilitated active learning and redefining the role of the adult as that of the first teacher, who was responsible for enabling the child's learning.

Although Malaguzzi actively promoted the Reggio philosophy through inviting practitioners to view the schools for themselves, and through touring The Hundred Languages of Children exhibition, a key principle of the Reggio schools is that their unique methods could not be exported (Featherstone, 2016). Nevertheless, what has been encouraged is that practitioners are empowered to develop their own philosophies, taking aspects of the Reggio experience and translating it to their own settings. Thus, aspects of the Reggio Emilia experience can be seen mirrored in early years policy and practice across the world today.

GLOSSARY OF TERMS

Asili nido   The name given to the infant-toddler centres or nurseries, designed for children from three months to three years of age.

Atelier   A defining feature of the Reggio Emilia preschool setting, the *atelier* combines studio, workshop and laboratory, and provides a well-equipped area in which children can work on a range of projects.

Atelierista   The *Atelierista* is a qualified art teacher who works with the children in the *atelier*. Roughly translated as studio teacher, the *Atelierista* complements the work of teachers by guiding the children towards using their multiplicity of expressive languages.

Documentation   The record-keeping processes undertaken by teachers in the Reggio Emilia settings. Existing at two levels, one for adults and one for children, this detailed documentation provides a visual record of a child's progress and identifies opportunities for future development and projects.

Municipality   The name given to a city, town or village that has a shared territory and is managed by one local government.

The Hundred Languages of Children   How Malaguzzi defined the ways in which children express themselves. These were symbolic languages including art, dance, drama, puppetry and sculpture, and were open to the endless potential of students. Malaguzzi sought to find ways of facilitating these languages since he expressed that inhibiting them potentially silenced the children.

Provocation   An object that promotes or expands thought, ideas, discussions, questions and creativity in the Reggio Emilia preschool. They should provide an open invitation for a child to explore and express themselves. Provocations come in many forms, but ideally would be something simple and open-ended allowing for creative thought.

Progettazione   The name given to the more responsive, open-ended and culturally based education system used in Reggio Emilia settings, replacing the more traditional curriculum or *progammazione*.

Scuola dell' infanzia   The name given to the centre or nursery for children from three years of age up to the compulsory school age of six years.

FURTHER READING

Abbott, L. and Nutbrown, C. (eds) (2010) *Experiencing Reggio Emilia: Implications for Pre-school Provision*. Maidenhead: Open University Press.
Reflections from early years educators following a visit to the region. A range of key issues are discussed including the culture of early years, working with parents and play and learning. Viewed from the perspective of Reggio Emilia, it encourages thinking for practitioners and policy-makers.

Edwards, G., Gandini, L. and Forman, G. (eds) (2011) *The Hundred Languages of Children*. Norwood, NJ: Ablex Publishing.
An insight into the Reggio Emilia philosophy through the lens of The Hundred Languages of Children. The text includes contributions from key figures including Loris Malaguzzi, Carlina Rinaldi, Howard Gardner and Gunilla Dahlberg.

Kinney, L. and Wharton, P. (2008) *An Encounter with Reggio Emilia: Children's Early Learning Made Visible*. London: Routledge.
Charts the documentary approach that was implemented by Stirling Council in Scotland. It provides an account of why practitioners should use documentation and discusses how this can be implemented in early years settings.

Thornton, L. and Brunton, P. (2014) *Bringing the Reggio Emilia Approach to Your Early Years Setting*. London: Routledge.
Draws connections between the Reggio Emilia approach and the EYFS, offering practical suggestions as to how the approach can be applied to educational settings today.

REFERENCES

Achtner, W. (1994) *Obituary Loris Malaguzzi*. Available online at: www.independent.co.uk/news/people/obituary-loris-malaguzzi-1367204.html
Brunson Day, C. (2001) 'Loris Malaguzzi founder: The Reggio Emilia approach believing in the power of the child'. *Early Childhood Today*, 15 (8): 46.
Cagliari, P., Castagnetti. M., Giudici, C., Rinaldi, C., Vecchi, V. and Moss, P. (eds) (2016) *Loris Malaguzzi and the Schools of Reggio Emilia: A Selection of his Writings and Speeches, 1945–1993*. London: Routledge.
Department for Education (DfE) (2017) *Statutory Framework for The Early Years Foundation Stage: Setting the Standards for Learning, Development and Care for Children from Birth to Five Years*. London: Crown copyright.
Dodd-Nufria, A.T. (2011) 'Reggio Emilia, Maria Montessori, and John Dewey: Dispelling teachers' misconceptions and understanding theoretical foundations'. *Early Childhood Education*, 39: 235–7.
Featherstone, S. (2016) *An Anthology of Educational Thinkers: Putting Theory into Practice in the Early Years*. London: Bloomsbury.
Forman, G. and Fyfe, B. (2011) 'Negotiated learning through design, documentation and discourse'. In: Edwards, G., Gandini. L. and Forman, G. (eds) *The Hundred Languages of Children*. Norwood, NJ: Ablex Publishing.

Hall, K., Horgan, M., Ridgway, A., Murphy, R., Cunneen, M. and Cunnigham, D. (2015) *Loris Malaguzzi and the Reggio Emilia Experience*. London: Bloomsbury.

Jarvis, P., Swiniarski, L. and Holland, W. (2017) *Early Years Pioneers in Context*. London: Routledge.

Lazzari, A. (2012) 'The public good: Historical and political roots of municipal preschools in Emilia Romagna'. *European Journal of Education*, 47 (4): 556–68.

Moss, P. (2016) 'Loris Malaguzzi and the schools of Reggio Emilia: Provocation and hope for a renewed public education'. *Improving Schools*, 19 (2): 167–76.

Pappatheodorou, T. (2006) *Seeing the Wider Picture: Reflections on the Reggio Emilia Approach*. Available online at: www.researchgate.net/publication/237739730_Seeing_the_Wider_Picture_Reflections_on_the_Reggio_Emilia_Approach

Parker-Rees, R. and Willan, J. (eds) (2006) *Early Years Education: Major Themes in Education: Histories and Traditions*, Vol. 1. London: Routledge.

Patti, P. (2017) *Benefits and Challenges of a Reggio Emilia Education*. Available online at: www.rootsandwingsfc.com/blog/benefitschallengesreggio

Reggio Children (n.d.) Available online at: www.reggiochildren.it/?lang=en

Rinaldi, C. (2006) *In Dialogue with Reggio Emilia: Listening, Researching and Learning*. London: Routledge.

Smidt, S. (2013) *Introducing Malaguzzi*. London: Routledge.

Soler, J. and Miller, L. (2003) 'The struggle for early childhood curricula: A comparison of the English Foundation Stage Curriculum, Te Whāriki and Reggio Emilia'. *International Journal of Early Years Education*, 11 (1): 57–68.

10

NEL NODDINGS

CARING IN EDUCATION

LEARNING OUTCOMES

Having read this chapter, you should be able to:

- understand the work of Nel Noddings;
- distinguish between natural and ethical caring;
- recognise the difference between cared-for and carer, caring-for and caring-about;
- understand how ethics of caring can be applied to education;
- critique Noddings's theory of ethical caring.

KEY WORDS

Ethics of care; caring; cared-for; moral education; engrossment; motivational displacement; natural caring; modelling; dialogue; confirmation; practice.

INTRODUCTION

Nel Noddings is a well-known philosopher of education and feminist ethics who currently holds the role of Lee L. Jacks Professor of Education, Emerita, at Stanford University. She is perhaps best known for her work around the ethics of **caring**, which she has applied to education, seeking a means by which to apply the **ethics of care** to schooling. In so doing, Noddings has demonstrated how caring in education can be seen as an educational goal, particularly for those wishing to apply a more ethical and moral foundation to their teaching.

Despite her early training as a mathematics teacher, Noddings's doctoral studies saw her exploring philosophy and the study of ethics, and her early work centred on moral action and the basis for this. Noddings sought to reconceptualise evil from the perspective of women and began to consider how 'natural caring' – that is, the care of the mother for a child – could be seen as a moral attitude. In this respect, Noddings began to see how 'care' was transferable as individuals attempted to replicate their own memories of caring. From this, Noddings developed the concept of ethical caring, this being the moral obligation to care and something that is developed from the early experiences of natural caring. Noddings (1984) suggests that the human condition is one that wants to be seen as moral, and, in this respect, individuals will want to be seen as caring in order to remain in a caring relationship.

Noddings asserts that the home is the primary educator and, as such, recommends that 'schools should as far as possible, use the sorts of methods found in the best homes to educate' (2002: 289). Noddings also advises that schools should include education for home life as part of their curriculum, believing this to be important in the development of a good **moral education**.

Noddings has sought to transform education through her caring philosophy and suggests that education should be more personalised. She argues that the current curriculum fails to take account of the individual needs and talents of pupils and relies too heavily on standardised tests and attainment. In addition, Noddings proposes that more should be done to improve relations between students and teachers, suggesting that teachers who truly care are more interested in the individual needs of their students, rather than those whose caring only extends to coercing students into achieving at subjects they have little interest in.

Noddings draws from her own personal experiences in developing her philosophies. She has sought to develop student–teacher relationships because she recalls her own positive relationships with teachers when growing up (Flinders, 2001), and in reflecting on the importance of home she must surely draw from her first-hand experience of being married for over forty years (her husband died of cancer in 2012) and raising ten children.

NEL NODDINGS, THE PERSON

Nel Noddings has a long and illustrious career in the fields of education and philosophy, and it was her own positive experiences of being taught that motivated her to seek both a career in education, and also to focus on the place of care in education. Flinders (2001) observes that schooling played a central role in Noddings's life, most specifically her first-hand experience of caring teachers, which later led to an interest in the relationship between students and their teachers.

Noddings's career in education has spanned the full range of educational settings, from elementary through to secondary and post-secondary education. Noddings gained her bachelor's degree in mathematics and physical science from Montclair State College, New Jersey, followed by a master's degree in mathematics from Rutgers University in New Jersey (Smith, 2016). She taught in both elementary and high school following this, as well as working as an administrator in New Jersey public schools. Noddings's first job as a mathematics teacher reflected her early positive experiences of education since she chose subjects taught by the teachers she most admired. Flinders (2001) notes that it was only afterwards that she turned her attention to the subject matter itself.

While Noddings maintained an interest in mathematics through undertaking research into mathematics education, she became increasingly interested in educational theory and philosophy, gaining a doctorate in educational philosophy from Stanford University in 1975. After being awarded her PhD, Noddings served on the faculties of both Pennsylvania State University and the University of Chicago. At the University of Chicago, she directed the Universities Laboratory School, a role that Flinders (2001) suggests must have held particular appeal given the school's past associations with John Dewey, who has heavily influenced Noddings throughout her academic career.

In 1977, Noddings took a position in the education faculty at Stanford University where Flinders (2001) observes she served in all ranks, 'including as director of Stanford's teacher education program and as acting Dean' (2001: 210). In 1992, Noddings was appointed as an endowed chair and was named the Lee L. Jacks Professor of Child Education. Following her retirement from Stanford, she taught at Teachers College, Columbia, until 2000.

Despite officially retiring from Stanford in 1998, Noddings continued to hold a number of high-profile positions, including the A. Lindsay O'Connor Professorship of American Institutions at Colgate University and the Libra Professorship at the University of South Maine (Smith, 2016). At the time of writing, she is the Lee L. Jacks Professor of Education, Emerita, at Stanford University, and also holds the John W. Porter Chair in Urban Education at Eastern Michigan University. In addition, she is President of the Philosophy of Education Society and President of the John Dewey Society (Coleman et al., 2011).

While Noddings's early research was in the field of mathematics, a field in which she continues to make contributions, she became increasingly focused on philosophy and the study of ethics. In her first book, *Caring: A Feminine Approach to Ethics and Moral Education* (1984), Noddings raises the question: 'What is the basis for moral action?' This is a theme that has been consistent throughout her subsequent works, including thirteen published books and over 200 articles.

It was through her academic work that Noddings established herself as a leading feminist scholar, since she drew on a range of feminist theories to support analyses made. Her position as a feminist was further reinforced in her second book, *Women and Evil* (1989), which saw her drawing on the experiences of women in establishing the 'need for a morality that will help individuals understand and control their own tendencies towards evil' (Flinders, 2001: 212). Noddings suggests that courage is required as a defence against this evil, and believes it is through a caring approach that such courage is nurtured.

While it is without question that Noddings's work has made a 'significant contribution to ethics, phenomenology and feminist scholarship' (Flinders, 2001: 212), it should also be noted that her work has impacted on educational practice, an area that will be focused on in this chapter. Flinders (2001) suggests that this aspect of her work should be seen as transformational since she sought to transform the structures of teaching and schooling in order to encourage more caring relations and the growth of individuals. Noddings outlined her beliefs in her 1992 book *The Challenge to Care in Schools*, in which she critiqued liberal education in schools, the traditions of which she saw as being the best education for students (Flinders, 2001).

Noddings has, then, made some remarkable contributions to the fields of education and philosophy, and has received a number of accolades as testament to the contributions made. However, Noddings herself reflects on only three categories of things that matter to her: domestic life, learning and writing, and living life as a moral quest (O'Toole, 1998). In respect of her domestic life, O'Toole reports that she describes herself as 'incurably domestic' – she was married to the same man for forty-eight years and raised ten children. Noddings admits to liking 'order in the kitchen, a fresh tablecloth, flowers on the table and food for waiting guests', something she recognises may well be out of keeping with her feminist principles (O'Toole, 1998). However, despite her love for her family, she also acknowledges her love of learning and writing through the need to seek solitude in her study on a daily basis.

THE THEORY

Nel Noddings is perhaps best known for her writing on the ethics of care, setting out her philosophy in the aforementioned book *Caring* (1984), in which she identified the idea of care as a feminine ethic, applying it to the practice of moral education (Fieser and Dowden, n.d.). In defining caring, Smith (2016) suggests that, as a concept, it is not easy to establish, but from Noddings's point of view, the principle behind it is to consider the actual experience of caring from the perspective of those engaged in caring encounters. Noddings suggests that while engaging in such encounters, individuals discover that they are receptive and attentive in a special way (Noddings, 2002). For Noddings, care is basic in human life – that all people wanted to be cared for (2002: 11). Drawing largely from a feminist perspective, she suggests that caring relationships are fundamental to human existence and consciousness (Fieser and Dowden, n.d.).

Within a caring relationship Noddings identifies two discrete parties – the '**cared-for**' and the 'one-caring-for'. Noddings theorised that both parties are obliged to care reciprocally, meeting the other morally, but not in the same manner. Noddings's notion of caring was very much established on the basis of individuals being guided by an ethic of care – that is, 'natural caring' in which individuals have a natural propensity to care, such as the care a mother gives to a child (Flinders, 2001). Noddings sees this as something that is inbuilt, suggesting that 'natural caring, thus is a moral attitude – a longing for goodness that arises out of the experience or memory of being cared for' (1984: 220). Individuals who remember being cared for in the past will be able to model that caring as they latterly become the one-caring-for.

Noddings talks of the caring encounter in respect of the individual's response to it and suggests that caring is an act of **engrossment** (Fieser and Dowden, n.d.). For a successful caring encounter, the one doing the caring must receive the cared-for on their own terms and should resist the temptation to project the self on to the cared-for – that is, they should be open to what the cared-for is saying, which Noddings refers to as *receptive attention*. The encounter should be without judgement – that is, it should not be measured against some pre-established ideal (Noddings, 2005), and the motives to care should be inherently selfless – that is, the act is performed solely for the benefit of the cared-for, and the one doing the caring should expect nothing in return other than the acknowledgement that an act of caring has occurred. The carer should respond to the cared-for in ways that are helpful with the 'carer's motive energy flowing towards the cared-for' (Smith, 2016: 6), also known as **motivational displacement**. Noddings (2005) does acknowledge that in the case of motivational displacement the carer may not always approve of the wants of the cared-for and may ultimately lead the cared-for to a better set of values, but she emphasises the importance of taking account of the feelings and values evident at the time and responding as positively as possible.

In this respect, then, it would appear that the cared-for is benefiting the most from the caring encounter; however, Noddings also observes that there should be some connection between both parties with some degree of reciprocity. Both parties should gain from the encounter, but in different ways – for example, in a successful encounter the cared-for recognises the caring and will respond in some detectable manner such as an infant smiling and wriggling in response to a mother caregiving (Noddings, 2005: 2). The mother gains her satisfaction from the response of her child.

Noddings identifies three elements to the caring encounter:

1. A cares for B, that is A's consciousness is characterised by attention and motivational displacement, and
2. A performs some act in accordance with (1), and
3. B recognises that A cares for B.

(2002: 19)

Noddings views a caring person as one who is able to regularly establish caring relationships, maintained over a period of time when appropriate.

In addition to identifying the cared-for and the one-caring-for, Noddings also distinguishes between caring-for and caring-about, and locates this as a form of moral obligation. In the case of the cared-for, Noddings refers to first-hand, face-to-face encounters where one person cares directly for another (Smith, 2016). However, consideration must also be given to the caring-about, which Fieser and Dowden (n.d.) define as the nurturing of caring ideas or intentions. When caring-about something, this tends to be in more general terms and is of less personal concern. So, for example, we might care about poverty in a poorer country, and as a result carry out some charitable works to show we care. In her earlier writings Noddings proposed that caring-about involves a certain benign neglect, suggesting that

> One is attentive just so far. One assents with just so much enthusiasm. One acknowledges. One affirms. One contributes five dollars and goes onto other things. (1984: 112)

Noddings believed that caring needed to be reciprocal and in the case of caring-about, the more remote the object of care, then the less likely reciprocity was to occur, so the scope of caring was diminished. Noddings expressed that it was impossible to care for everyone, and while we might care for objects in our immediate environment, which might respond to but not reciprocate the care, this was less likely to occur where objects were so remote that care was unlikely to be completed.

Noddings's views on caring-about proved controversial (Fieser and Dowden, n.d.) and she later revised them, arguing that caring-about did, in fact, deserve more attention, and suggested that caring should encompass learning what it means to be cared-for, then learning to care for and finally learning to care about others (Noddings, 2002). Noddings began to view caring-about as being an important stage for inspiring local and global justice, although she maintained the view that it was impossible to care for all, especially for more distant others (Fieser and Dowden, n.d.).

↻ LINKS WITH OTHER THEORISTS

When considering Noddings's views on developing a curriculum that takes account of the individual needs of all pupils, parallels can be drawn with the work of John

Dewey, who himself favoured a curriculum tailored in such a way. Similarly, both Dewey and Noddings argue that the curriculum should not reflect social or occupational needs (Flinders, 2001) and Noddings has openly supported Dewey's argument that no subject is inherently more intellectual than another (Noddings, 2008). Dewey, too, talked of education as a vehicle for preparing students for 'public life' and firmly believed that a college degree should not be the means by which one earned respect (Dewey, 1927). Noddings's ideas reflect this notion, as she suggests that adolescents should be educated for life in a democratic society, regardless of their eventual occupation, stating 'not everyone needs to go to college, but everyone needs and deserves a genuine education' (2008: 37).

In respect of the relationship between pupils and teachers, Noddings argues that a relationship of care and trust should be developed, reflecting on research that indicates that challenges exist for developing relationships that would properly be labeled caring (Noddings, 2005). Noddings recommends that topics of mutual interest should be developed, with more attention being paid to the student's own interests. In this way, Noddings suggests that the teacher becomes engrossed in the needs of the cared-for (student) and the projects of the cared-for become their key priority. According to Vryza (n.d.), the relationship promoted by putting the needs of the student first is reflective of the work of Paulo Freire who sought to encourage a relationship of joy and happiness in the student–teacher relationship. Freire stated that 'democratic educators can only see the acts of teaching, of learning, of studying as serious, demanding tasks that not only generate satisfaction but are pleasurable in and of themselves' (1998: 90), and criticised an authoritarian teacher who failed to generate joy and happiness in the classroom.

Noddings has also criticised an education system that relies heavily on standardised testing as a means of measuring pupils' progress, and suggests that the pressures of standardised testing should be reduced so that teachers and pupils might spend more time exploring areas of mutual interest (Noddings, 2005). Furthermore, Noddings argues that pupils are being forced to take courses that are considered necessary to enter college education, rather than courses in which they have a genuine interest. She goes on to suggest that teachers are compromising the delivery of these courses in order to protect pupils from failure (Noddings, 2008). This is reminiscent of the work of John Holt, who argued that the testing regime in American schools was inhibiting pupils' learning and suggested that the fear of failure prevented pupils from accessing the form of learning that best met their individual needs. Holt believed that the school system was responsible for turning children away from learning, and this is echoed by Noddings who observes that 'youngsters who fail repeatedly in their school years are likely to reject opportunities for further learning' (2008: 37).

Noddings's work on care and moral education has clear links with the work of humanist theorists such as Carl Rogers, Abraham Maslow and Urie Bronfenbrenner. Like Rogers, she expounded the idea of the development of the 'true self', and claimed that '[selves] ... are under continual construction through encounters of all kinds, the effects these encounters produce and reflective evaluation of these efforts' (Bergman,

2004: 153). This would reflect Rogers's theory of self-actualisation, in which individuals strive towards the 'ideal self' in order to reach fulfilment. Like Rogers, Noddings firmly believes in the role of those closest to the child in supporting them through their journey to the ideal, or true, self.

Noddings sees the foundations of care theory as very much situated in the home and firmly believes that children should 'live in a home that has at least adequate material resources and attentive love' (2002: 289). This reflects the work of Urie Bronfenbrenner who, in his ecological systems theory, placed the influence of the home and family firmly at the centre of his model. Noddings believes that caring is learned and observes that the memory of being cared for is strong, and most often learned as a result of being cared for. She quotes Bronfenbrenner, saying, 'if we are lucky someone will have been "crazy about that kid"' (1984: 61; 2002: 25).

CRITIQUING THE THEORY

Noddings wrote from a largely feminist perspective and has been subject to some criticism from other feminist writers. When discussing 'natural caring', Noddings uses the maternal experience as a means of defining this as a concept. Noddings uses the physical and emotional experiences of women carrying and bringing a child into the world to explain the different roles of men and women in caring, and while she acknowledges that men can care, she suggests that this is a different kind of caring. This could be considered a somewhat controversial view at a time when the family unit is less traditional than it once was. Keller (1995) suggests that Noddings's work is reinforcing gender stereotypes of the woman as the homemaker, which goes against feminist principles. In addition, there is some conflict between women taking the role of carer and their own moral development since, as Carol Gilligan (1977) observes, a woman who sacrifices her needs for the needs of others would be at 'level two' of her own moral development model for women. Therefore, according to Gilligan, this woman would not yet be fully morally developed.

The notion of total engrossment, as outlined by Noddings, which sees the carer as supporting those cared-for without question or prejudice, has also been criticised. Davion (1993) warns that total engrossment in another individual can be dangerous and might see the carer compromising their own morals as they support the cared-for. This is particularly concerning if the moral path chosen is one that is lacking in good moral standing. Furthermore, Davion (1993) also cautions against a one-sided caring relationship in which caring is not reciprocated. She suggests that this reflects an unhealthy relationship in which the carer is sacrificing their own development of self.

From an educational perspective, Noddings considered that teachers and students should form a trusting and caring relationship, offering a pedagogic vision of authentic caring. Noddings saw this as teachers embracing students as individuals in a nurturing and caring manner. In opposition to this is aesthetic caring, in which teachers are only interested in caring from the perspective of how well students do in tests and assessments. While it would be difficult to argue against seeing students as individuals and planning their education accordingly, it must also be questioned how realistic this is in a society that is so driven by results and achievements. Noddings makes the assumption that teachers who are striving for the best for their students reflected through test results show caring at a largely superficial level. However, it could be argued that these teachers care enough to want their students to be the best they can, and sometimes 'tough love' is necessary to accomplish this.

NODDINGS AND CARING IN AN EDUCATIONAL CONTEXT

Noddings's early work on caring and evil saw her making 'significant contributions to ethics, phenomenology and feminist scholarship' (Flinders, 2001: 212); however, Flinders (2001) also observes that equally important was her application of philosophy to inform educational practice. Noddings saw how her work on caring and relations might encourage the growth of individuals, and she thus set out to transform school structures and curricula in a manner that might promote caring and moral education.

In her book *The Challenge to Care in Schools* (1992), Noddings criticised a curriculum that failed to acknowledge the individual interests and talents of its students, focusing instead on mathematics, science, languages, and so on (Flinders, 2001), and suggested that by delivering the same curriculum for everyone, teachers would be forced into coercion, which ultimately could undermine the positive relationships required for learning and growth. It is perhaps through her own experience as a mother of ten children that Noddings began to ask how parents would like to see a diverse group of children educated, and called for an education that is organised around the individual needs of its pupils.

Noddings believes that fundamental to providing a curriculum that serves the needs of individuals, a caring relationship needs to be forged between teachers and pupils. Noddings sees the challenge in this relationship as defining exactly what is meant by 'a caring teacher' and suggests that for some teachers, 'caring' in the virtues sense of the word might well be achieved. However, this does not assume a relation of care and trust, which, for Noddings, would be the ideal. Noddings states:

> But even for the majority [of teachers] who do 'care' in the virtues sense – that is they profess to care and work hard at their teaching – there are many who do not adopt the relational sense of caring. They 'care' in the sense that they conscientiously pursue certain goals for their students, and they often work hard at coercing students to achieve these goals. (2005: 1)

Noddings asserts that in order for an effective relationship to be forged, pupils need to know that they are cared for and suggests that the pupils themselves are able to distinguish between the teachers that care and those who care for them. Noddings observes that pupils might respect those teachers who care, but maintains that work is undertaken due to a sense of duty rather than through any love of learning. Noddings continues to look to the organisation of the school in seeking reasons for this apparent lack of care, suggesting that 'sometimes the conditions of schooling are so bad that teachers who want to care and students who want to be cared for cannot form the kind of relations we would properly label caring' (Noddings, 2005: 2). In this respect, Noddings suggests that more needs to be done to provide the right conditions for a caring relationship to form – for example, through smaller classes, so that more time can be spent on positive interaction, with less standardised testing allowing for the exploration of topics of mutual interest and the development of a curriculum which builds on pupils' interests. Noddings recognises the challenge of this task and acknowledges the importance of the need for time and encouragement in order for this to be achieved.

Noddings argues that education is key to the cultivation of caring in society, which she suggests provides a strong foundation for moral development. Noddings believes that moral education should play an important part in the curriculum and should be visible through purpose, policy and method, with a view to producing moral people. For Noddings, moral education should 'develop attitudes and skills required to sustain caring relations and the desire to do so' (1992: 21). Noddings recommends that moral education should be promoted through the application of four key components: **modelling**, **dialogue**, **practice** and **confirmation**.

MODELLING

For Noddings, care is not something that can be learned from a book, nor can students be told to care, instead 'we have to show in our behaviour what it means to care' (Noddings, 2012: 237). Noddings also advocates that the care shown must be sincere, so that it is not just shown for the purpose of modelling but is a by-product of genuine care. Teachers who model good caring support a student's moral development since they demonstrate what moral responsibility looks like. Noddings (2010) draws from the work of Slote when considering how modelling supports a child's moral education, and observes that children will seek moral role models, either fictitious or real, and this can be both conscious or unconscious. She goes on to observe that for the child with secure relationships, the caring adult can have a powerful effect. However, those with uncaring parents or teachers will often unconsciously internalise the uncaring ways of a poor role model, which may impact on behaviours at a later date.

DIALOGUE

It is not enough to show caring. Noddings advises that students should be engaged in dialogue about the care they are receiving. She suggests that dialogue is inherent to caring, but acknowledges that care can manifest itself in different ways so, in order to understand it, students may need help with the interpretation of care. It should also be noted that dialogue can also support the carer in reflecting on the care they give, and in this respect dialogue can open up a two-way discussion, which Noddings believes is important in raising ethical questions; she sees it as a stimulus to reflection and a powerful tool for promoting the building of students' ethical ideals (Noddings, 2012). Morally speaking, dialogue might be used as a means by which to support empathy in children. Noddings argues that by asking children the right questions, dialogue can open up discussions that serve to emphasise the feelings of others, while simultaneously reflecting on the impact of one's own behaviour. Noddings cites Stueber who suggests that the dialogue invites both empathic accuracy (an accurate assessment of what the other is feeling) and sympathetic response (Stueber, 2006, cited in Noddings 2010: 146).

PRACTICE

Where the teacher models and engages in dialogue about care, the role of the student is to practise caring for themselves, and for Noddings this should be through engagement in caring apprenticeships and subsequent reflections on this. Initially, Noddings advises that this may come through working with school custodians or as classroom aides to younger children, and suggests that good parents and teachers will provide caring opportunities for children to practise their skills in their immediate environment. Furthermore, good role models will watch to see if interactions meet the criteria for appropriate caring, and while Noddings does not advocate that such behaviours should be rewarded, she does argue that they should be acknowledged. Noddings also recommends that caring should be extended to the wider community through some form of community service, such as in nursing homes or animal shelters. Noddings states that 'children need to participate in caring with adult models who show them how to care, talk with them about the difficulties and rewards of such work, and demonstrate in their own work that caring is important' (2012: 239).

CONFIRMATION

Noddings observes that 'when we confirm someone, we identify a better self and encourage its development' (2012: 239). However, she is quick to point out that the aspiration is not a single ideal for all, but rather high expectations for all (Noddings, 2012). Through confirmation, Noddings suggests that the aim should be to 'recognise something admirable, or at least acceptable, struggling to emerge in each person we encounter' (2012: 239). Additionally, confirmation requires trust and continuity, with each seeing the goal to be achieved as worthy and credible. Interestingly, while Noddings advises that confirmation should not be given where ways are judged to be wrong, she does advocate recognising why an inappropriate behaviour might be exhibited – for example, recognising that a child might have cheated in an examination in order to get good results to please a parent. In this scenario, Noddings advocates engaging in dialogue, with a view to pointing the young person towards a better self. Noddings states that there is no recipe for confirmation and that 'The moral educator must know the child well enough to be able to pick out the best possible motive consonant with reality' (Noddings, 2010: 148).

While Noddings aspires for education to be seen as central to the development of a caring society, a tension does exist since, as Smith (2016) observes, the school system in capitalist societies is organised around a need to equip youngsters for business and the economy, and while some attention is paid to personal and social life, this is not sufficient to meet the demands of Noddings's vision of a system that promotes care theory. For Noddings, policy-makers should look to the home as a child's primary educator as a means of developing a model for a caring system, suggesting that 'schools should, as far as possible, use the sorts of methods found in best homes to educate' (Noddings, 2002: 289). Alongside this, Noddings advocates that children should 'live in a home that has at least adequate material resources and attentive love; and second, that schools should include education for home life in their curriculum' (2002: 289).

In considering education, Noddings (2006) also recommends that schools should create an environment that promotes critical thinking, suggesting that the incorporation of critical thinking skills and critical lessons will assist students in their daily lives. Noddings sees critical lessons as those that allow free discussion on topics viewed as controversial, such as Adam and Eve, and the invasion of Iraq, to give but two diverse examples, topics that Noddings believes have been avoided in schools. By allowing free debate on such issues Noddings suggests that students are being prepared for many aspects of adulthood that would not necessarily be learned through the more traditional curriculum subjects.

Noddings has therefore promoted an educational philosophy in which care is embedded, but also one that places less emphasis on the knowledge and skills required of the capitalist society and more on the personal growth of the individual. She argues against a system that focuses on the specification of what must be learned and on testing (Noddings, 2005) and advocates a system whereby teachers, working from the care perspective, focus on the individual needs of their students. She acknowledges the role of the family in the child's education and suggests that where secure relationships are formed between parents and teachers, and teachers and students, then there will be fewer calls for accountability. Finally, Noddings urges schools to tackle controversial issues through open debate and free speaking, giving students the confidence to voice their opinions in a safe and supportive environment.

REFLECTIVE TASK

Noddings believes that 'Classrooms should be places in which students can legitimately act on a rich variety of purposes, in which wonder and curiosity are alive, in which students and teachers live together and grow' (Noddings, 1992: 12).

Thinking back to your own experience of schools, do you recall experiencing this? How might you ensure that this is something you aspire to as a classroom practitioner?

SUMMARY

Nel Noddings is the author of thirteen books and over 200 articles, and despite retiring from Stanford in 1998, she has remained a prolific writer in the fields of philosophy and education, receiving a number of accolades that pay testament to the contributions she has made to both fields.

Noddings began her career as a teacher in both elementary and secondary school, and drew on her own positive experiences of school to help her develop a teaching philosophy. This was then followed by a doctorate in educational philosophy, which set the foundation for her subsequent work that saw her establish herself as a feminist writer. Noddings began to consider the question of moral education and how the ethics of caring could be used to help develop a moral attitude. Noddings saw how natural caring could be used to set the foundation for ethical caring, and set about applying her vision to school systems with the aim of encouraging a more personalised curriculum and improving relations between students and teachers.

Noddings has not been without her critics. Ironically, this has frequently come from feminist writers, the perspective from which her early work was written. Noddings has been accused of perpetuating the gender stereotype of caring as being a predominantly feminine role. It could also be considered that Noddings's ethic of caring encourages unequal relationships, in which the cared-for becomes dependent upon the carer, and the carer sacrifices their own true self in favour of carrying out the role of carer.

Nevertheless, as Smith writes, Noddings 'has made a significant contribution to deepening our understanding of what education entails' (2016: 17). She has brought to the fore the importance of caring, especially in respect of its place as a moral attitude, and has encouraged a more caring attitude between students and teachers. Noddings emphasises the importance of caring, and shows how by learning to care, we can not only care for others, but also care about others, which, in essence, provides the basis for a caring society, in which both the carer and cared-for receive mutual gratification.

GLOSSARY OF TERMS

Cared-for   Cared-for refers to the individual in receipt of a caring encounter. Noddings argues that the caring is completed in the other once the cared-for recognises and responds to the one doing the caring.

Caring   For Noddings, caring should be fundamental to ethical decision making and she argues that care is basic to human life since everyone wants to be cared-for. Furthermore, Noddings identifies a difference between responses from those doing the caring and those being cared-for, with those doing the caring being required to understand the needs of the one being cared-for, while the cared-for must in some way respond to the caring. For this to be effective, caring must be a reciprocal process.

Confirmation   Noddings defines confirmation as an act of affirming and encouraging the best in others. In order to do this, it is important that the carer does not set up an ideal for the other to live up to, but seeks to find something admirable or acceptable about each individual whom they encounter.

Dialogue   For Noddings, dialogue is necessary in a caring encounter, but she suggests that it should be open-ended with neither the carer nor the caregiver knowing what the outcome will be. Through dialogue, Noddings suggests that it is possible to search for understanding, empathy and appreciation, allowing individuals to talk about their actions, thus making connections and maintaining caring relationships.

Engrossment   Engrossment is the act of thinking about someone in order to gain a greater understanding of them. This is an essential component in caring, since it requires the carer to develop an understanding of a person's personal or physical situation in order that the caring encounter can be tailored specifically to the needs of the individual.

Ethics of care   Ethics of care is one of a number of ethical theories developed from a predominantly feminist perspective and builds from the premise that moral action is centred on interpersonal relationships and care. For Noddings, ethics are motivated by a sense of duty which she classifies into two distinctive caring types: 'natural caring' and 'ethical caring'. For Noddings, an ethics of caring is a virtue inherent in women.

Modelling   One of the four key components when using care in education, modelling refers to the way in which educators show what it means to care through their own behaviour and actions.

Moral education   Moral education is concerned with virtues such as honesty, responsibility and respect, with an overall aim of instilling such virtues into young people in order to help them to live good lives and become productive and contributing members of their community. For Noddings, care in education would assume caring teachers whose modelling of care contributes to the moral development of their students.

Motivational displacement Experienced by the carer, motivational displacement refers to the feelings experienced when a caring encounter is met positively. Noddings suggests that during an encounter motive, energy flows towards the needs and the wants of the cared-for, and while the carer may not always sympathise with the wants of others, they are able to respond as positively as their values and capacities will allow.

Natural caring Natural caring is a form of caring that does not require an ethical effort to motivate it. Noddings suggests that natural caring results from memories of being cared-for and is thus a moral attitude.

Practice According to Noddings, one of four components of ethics of care in education, practice is the practical application of allowing students to demonstrate care for themselves. Noddings argues that in order to encourage people to approach a moral life in which they are prepared to care for others, opportunities, through practice, need to be provided for them to do so.

FURTHER READING

Charney, R.S. and Noddings, N. (2015) *Teaching Children to Care: Classroom Management for Ethical and Academic Growth K-8*. Turner Falls, OK: Center for Responsive Schools.
A practical guide for teachers in adopting a classroom management style that encourages cooperation and the building of positive relationships.

Lake, R. (2012) *Dear Nel: Opening the Circles of Care (Letters to Nel Noddings)*. New York: Teachers College Press.
A series of open letters providing a moving tribute to Noddings.

Noddings, N. (2003) *Happiness and Education*. New York: Cambridge University Press.
A debate as to whether happiness and education can co-exist through a critique of the American education system, and a view of how the curriculum might look if happiness was included as part of it.

REFERENCES

Bergman, R. (2004) 'Caring for the ethical ideal: Nel Noddings on moral education'. *Journal of Moral Education*, 33 (2): 149–62.
Coleman, K., Depp, L. and O'Rourke, K. (2011) *The Educational Theory of Nel Noddings*. Available online at: www.newfoundations.com/GALLERY/Noddings.html
Davion, V. (1993) 'Autonomy, integrity, and care'. *Social Theory and Practice*, 19: 161–82.
Dewey, J. (1927) *The Public and Its Problems*. New York: Henry Holt.
Fieser, J. and Dowden, B. (eds) (n.d.) 'Care ethics'. *Internet Encyclopedia of Philosophy*. Available online at: www.iep.utm.edu/care-eth/#SH1b
Flinders, D.J. (2001) 'Nel Noddings, 1929–'. In: Palmer, J. (ed.) *Fifty Modern Thinkers on Education: From Piaget to the Present*. London: Routledge.

Freire, P. (1998) *Pedagogy of the Heart*. New York: Continuum.

Gilligan, C. (1977) 'In a different voice: Women's conceptions of self and morality'. *Harvard Educational Review*, 47: 481–517.

Keller, J. (1995) 'Autonomy, relationality, and feminist ethics'. *Hypatia*, 12: 128–33.

Noddings, N. (1984) *Caring: A Feminine Approach to Ethics and Moral Education*. Berkeley, CA: University of California Press.

Noddings, N. (1989) *Women and Evil*. Berkeley, CA: University of California Press.

Noddings, N. (1992) *The Challenge to Care in Schools*. New York: Teachers College Press.

Noddings, N. (2002) *Starting at Home: Caring and Social Policy*. Berkeley, CA: University of California Press.

Noddings, N. (2005) 'Caring in education'. *The Encyclopaedia of Informal Education*. Available online at: http://infed.org/mobi/caring-in-education

Noddings, N. (2006) *Critical Lessons: What Our Schools Should Teach*. New York: Cambridge University Press.

Noddings, N. (2008) 'Schooling for democracy'. *Phi Delta Kappan*, 90 (1): 34–7. Available online at: www.pdkmembers.org/members_online/publications/Archive/pdf/k0809nod.pdf

Noddings, N. (2010) 'Moral education and caring'. *Theory and Research in Education*, 8 (2): 145–1.

Noddings, N. (2012) *Philosophy of Education*. Boulder, CA: Westview Press.

O'Toole, K. (1998) *What Matters to Nel Noddings and Why*. Available online at: http://news.stanford.edu/news/1998/february4/noddings.html

Smith, M. (2016) 'Nel Noddings: The Ethics of Care and Education'. *The Encyclopaedia of Informal Education*. Available online at: http://infed.org/mobi/nel-noddings-the-ethics-of-care-and-education

Vryza, E. (n.d.) *Nel Nodding's and Paulo Freire's Pedagogies of the Heart for Social Justice*. Available online at: https://www.academia.edu/769213/Nel_Noddings_and_Paulo_Freires_Pedagogies_of_the_Heart_for_Social_Justice

11
LAWRENCE STENHOUSE

LINKING THE CURRICULUM WITH THEORY, RESEARCH AND PRACTICE

LEARNING OUTCOMES

After reading this chapter, you should be able to:

- appreciate Stenhouse's background and contribution to education;
- understand and identify his ideas regarding curriculum development and the teacher as a researcher;
- recognise the links between his work and other educational thinkers;
- critically evaluate Stenhouse's notions on curriculum development, classroom research and teacher professionalism;
- recognise how his ideas could be applied in practice.

KEY WORDS

Humanities Curriculum Project; Centre for Applied Research in Education; process curriculum model; objectives curriculum model; action research; restricted and extended teacher professionalism.

INTRODUCTION

Even though Lawrence Stenhouse died prematurely in 1982 while still working as an academic, he bequeaths a wealth of profound educational ideas. He was arguably the most prominent person in the field of curriculum development in the two decades leading up to his death. His work is exemplified by the thought that teaching should be informed by evidence-based classroom research; he also upheld the notion of teacher professionalism (Rudduck and Hopkins, 1985). His overriding contribution to educational thinking and practice was to emphasise the significance of artistry and self-improvement in teaching:

> More than any other contemporary educational theorist, Stenhouse grasped the peda-gogical significance of viewing education as a form of *praxis* rather than a technological process. He understood that good teaching was an art rather than the mastery of tech-niques. (Elliott, 2007: 19)

It was during his leadership of the controversial **Humanities Curriculum Project** (1967–72) that he was able to reinforce his interests in curriculum development and advance his ideas on the teacher as a researcher. Indeed, Stenhouse was probably 'the first person to argue that teachers, by dint of the fact that they were teachers, were also researchers' (Campbell et al., 2004: 9). In his plea for teachers to take a research perspective, he meant they should adopt 'a disposition to examine one's own practice critically and systematically' (Stenhouse, 1975: 156).

The Humanities Curriculum Project (HCP) was funded by the UK Schools Council and the Nuffield Foundation and was set up principally for pupils in secondary educa-tion to help them consider and make their own judgements regarding the contentious issues of the day such as race and international conflicts. It was controversial mainly because the project rejected the use of pre-set learning objectives and encouraged teachers to become impartial during classroom discussions (Rowntree, 1981). At the heart of the project was Stenhouse's quest to discover 'the relationship between knowledge, authority and emancipation' (Rudduck, 1995: 6). As the project was com-ing to a close, Stenhouse and a number of his fellow academics set up the **Centre for Applied Research in Education** (CARE) at the University of East Anglia. CARE evolved into a world-renowned centre of teacher research and curriculum design thinking (Rudduck, 1995).

Stenhouse's ideas were innovative and revolutionary; they focused on developing curricula that stressed the right of pupils to access knowledge, the use of classroom research to enable teachers to make judgements and the significance of collaboration in learning (Rudduck, 1995). He argued the case that teachers should be at the core of curriculum development. However, for them to be effective and to improve their practice, teachers needed to be reflective and communicate their experiences with others. He contested the notion of the **objectives curriculum model**, which he felt took knowledge to be preordained and also dampened student enquiry, the teacher being the expert and the student a passive partner in the learning. Stenhouse championed the **process curriculum model** in which there were no set objectives and that allowed pupils to make their own meaning of the world through questioning and discussion with the teacher. This process model advanced learning as research, which in turn becomes the foundation for teaching – therefore, research and teaching become implicitly linked (Stenhouse, 1975; Burton and Bartlett, 2005). For Stenhouse, the curriculum is not really about knowledge which is 'to be transmitted, but about how that knowledge is handled – or even how it is transcended – by teachers to enable understanding by their charges' (Thomas, 2013: 95). Whitty argues that Stenhouse's work on curriculum development may well attract those who have come to gradually challenge the traditional standard in curriculum studies. In particular, it could attract 'those who see their own work in education as contributing to a quest for greater democracy and social justice in society' (Whitty, 1985: 57). Stenhouse's ideas on curriculum development and design, his views on teacher research, and his enthusiastic support for teacher improvement and professionalism are all valid even in today's competitive and assessment-dominated educational environment. These ideas, as well as the censures they have attracted, the links with other educational thinkers and suggestions on how his thoughts could be applied in practice will be covered later in this chapter.

STENHOUSE, THE PERSON

Although born in Scotland in 1926, Lawrence Stenhouse's secondary education took place at Manchester Grammar School. He returned to Scotland to study for his first degree at St Andrew's University and then on to Glasgow University for his MEd, which he completed in 1956. By this time he had begun to develop an idea that he wished to explore – the issue of student emancipation. It was Stenhouse's own secondary education that helped to develop his ideas and he was very aware of how some of his own teachers had enabled him to realise his own potential. However, when he began his teaching career, he soon came to grasp the fact that schools were inhibited by conventional ideas about access to knowledge. Unlike his own, perhaps advantaged, experience of secondary school, the pupils he taught were not so fortunate in having such an enlightened school environment.

Following his foray into teaching, Stenhouse took up a staff tutorship in psychology and secondary education at the Institute of Education of the University of Durham, which was resolute in its purpose of developing teaching practice in schools (Stenhouse, 1983). Stenhouse's next move was a return to Scotland as a principal lecturer in education at Jordanhill College. In 1966 while at Jordanhill, he visited the United States for a conference where he met Joslyn Owen from the new Schools Council for Curriculum and Examination, who suggested that he should apply for the leadership of the HCP. Stenhouse, as we have seen, became the leader of the HCP until its demise; he then set up and led CARE at the University of East Anglia (Rudduck, 1995).

During his time at the HCP and CARE, Stenhouse drew together a number of like-minded progressive educational thinkers on curriculum development and research, such as Jean Rudduck, David Hopkins and John Elliott. Stenhouse himself went on to write a number of texts that gathered international acclaim. These included *Culture and Education* (1971a) and in 1975 his seminal text *An Introduction to Curriculum Research and Development*, a book heralded by Kelly as 'the definitive statement of the notion of curriculum as process' (2004: 224). Then, just before his untimely death, he collated his major writings in *Authority, Education and Emancipation*, which was published in 1983. Up until his death, Stenhouse continued with his research interests on the curriculum. He also advanced a further body of knowledge on the relationship between theory and practice to demonstrate how practitioner research can help teachers to develop their understanding and practice in classrooms (Rudduck, 1995).

THE IDEAS OF LAWRENCE STENHOUSE

Any attempt at chronologically outlining Stenhouse's ideas would be meaningless because his ideas, by their very nature, complement each other. With this in mind, this section will only offer a rudimentary structure, which in turn will hopefully illustrate the synergy between his thoughts and concepts. Therefore, we will explore Stenhouse's work with the HCP and CARE in a little more detail, examine his ideas regarding curriculum design and development, and consider his views on practitioner research and how this is linked with teacher professionalism.

Perhaps the pinnacle of innovative thinking about curriculum development and the championing of teacher research was during the 1970s; at the heart of this pioneering movement was the Schools Council, which part-funded the HCP. The HCP worked very closely with schools and teachers to improve the manner in which contentious topics were taught. We have already discovered that the HCP shunned the use of prescribed learning objectives. As it was trying to empower secondary age pupils to engage in discussion about controversial matters and to arrive at their own conclusions, the HCP team argued that using set objectives at the start would 'pre-empt the very questions they wanted to raise' (Kelly, 2004: 151). The project tried to create an environment where pupils felt comfortable in evolving a culture of their own during their group discussions; in doing so, they would be more adept at making sense of other cultures and the more formal language styles they encountered (Stenhouse, 1975). In short, the aim of the HCP was to develop resources for pupils 'of average and below average ability, with the emphasis on enquiry and interdisciplinary work. The role of the teacher is radically transformed from information-transmitter to debate-leader' (Stenhouse, 1971b: 336).

The HCP and Stenhouse were also at the centre of the advancement of **action research**. His work with the HCP and in promoting action research greatly contributed to developing classroom practice and 'to the thinking about the role of research in engaging with everyday processes' (Schostak and Schostak, 2008: 134). Stenhouse argued that meaningful development of the curriculum could only come from teachers themselves as they were at the core of classroom practice:

> [For Stenhouse] it was essential that teachers reflected upon practice, shared experiences and evaluated their work if the education of pupils was to improve. For Stenhouse, each classroom could be seen as a laboratory and each teacher a member of a research community ... Stenhouse believed in the professional desire of teachers to improve education for their pupils and so benefit society ... In this way a social democratic ideology ran through the work of the Schools Council. Curriculum reform was visualised as happening at the grass-roots level and involving all those with a stake in education. (Bartlett and Burton, 2016: 59)

It is interesting to note that aversion to the ideas of teachers being active and innovative in curriculum development, and the notion of teachers as influential authorities in education, eventually convinced Margaret Thatcher's Conservative government to close the Schools Council (Burton and Bartlett, 2005). However, much of the work of the HCP moved on to CARE with Stenhouse as its leader. The importance of CARE was indicative of the growth of applied research and action research at the time (Goodson, 2005). CARE at the University of East Anglia was, until its closure in 2015, at the forefront of taking research outside universities and the promotion of democratic evaluation, action research, case study and ethnography. The CARE team worked not only with schools but with other public bodies (CARE, 2015). Because of the work of Stenhouse and the work of CARE, it is argued that practitioner research is now supported by departments of education at numerous universities.

At the beginning of his book *An Introduction to Curriculum Research and Development*, Stenhouse makes an exploratory attempt at defining 'curriculum' as:

> an attempt to communicate the essential principles and features of an educational proposal in such a form that it is open to critical scrutiny and capable of effective translation into practice. (1975: 4)

In other words, for Stenhouse, the curriculum is a way of offering an idea for a learning experience which is open to criticism and ongoing evaluation – a process curriculum model. This notion was at odds with the widespread objectives model used in specific subject curricula, which focused on prescribed lists of learning outcomes that students have to passively achieve. This objectives model focuses on the training of skills and changing behaviours, as well as on the testing of students' attainment; it is also more concerned with stipulated instructional methods rather than allowing the teachers the liberty to think for themselves. As Kelly points out, the objectives model 'substitutes teacher accountability for teacher responsibility ...

it gives teachers responsibility without freedom' (Kelly, 2004: 151), the process model, on the other hand, is a process where the teacher invites active student enquiry rather than students submissively accepting given knowledge. It is related to the distinctiveness of the individual classroom and school; it allows students and teachers to work in harmony and gives the students opportunities – all of which Stenhouse argues will enable 'the attention [to shift] … from teaching to learning' (Stenhouse, 1975: 13).

The process model concentrates on the learning experience, which focuses on the roles and activities of the teacher and the learner, as well as the learning environment. In focusing on these factors rather than prescribed learning objectives, the 'process model appears to emphasise means rather than ends' (Neary, 2002: 62). Stenhouse makes the point that the process model is far more challenging in practice, as it 'rests with teacher judgement rather than teacher direction … but it offers a higher degree of personal and professional development' (1975: 96–7). Unlike the objectives model, the process model also has the advantage of presenting a theoretical basis which more truthfully mirrors what actually is involved in classroom practice. In contrast to the mainly subject-specific objectives model, it is more to do with the making of numerous decisions and the 'complex process of dynamic interaction between the teacher and taught' (Kelly, 2004: 96). Some of the benefits of the process model include the weight given to dynamic positions of both teachers and learners, and the stress given to learning skills that can be transferable to other subjects and for life in general (Neary, 2002). For Stenhouse, the process model fostered learner empowerment and emancipation, and gave teachers the freedom to improve their professional practice through research and evaluation.

Stenhouse advocated a closer link between research and teaching practice, and called for this to be encouraged from an early stage in teachers' careers:

> Students in training often notice a gap between the educationalist and the school not unlike that between Haig's headquarters and the mud of Flanders. So many seem elated by the discussion of educational ideas: so few are encouraged by close critical scrutiny of their own classrooms. The gap between aspiration and practice is a real and frustrating one. The gap can be closed only by adopting a research and development approach to one's own teaching, whether alone or in a group of co-operating teachers. (1975: 3)

He argued that more experienced teachers should also be supported in engaging with a research community through in-service education and links with university education departments. Teachers, he thought, would be ideal researchers as they were always trying to improve their practice by knowingly, through reflection, recognising features of their teaching which they needed to develop. Stenhouse considered that this notion of the teacher researcher could be further advanced by teachers engaging more closely with the research community so they could access and link with other research, and hence aim to build upon education theory from a practical viewpoint. The type of research he was promoting to achieve this aim was one 'which disciplines curiosity and calls certainty into question' (Rudduck and Hopkins, 1985: 112). Action research was what Stenhouse believed could be employed by teachers in their class-rooms to develop their professional practice and further augment educational theory. This augmentation of theory, from the perspective of Thomas, though, was a personal sort of theory that stemmed from the analysis of practice 'from reflective practitioners employing and developing their own "tacit theories" "personal theories" or "theories-in-use"' (Thomas, 2007: 5). According to Punch and Oancea (2014: 375), action research employs 'empirical procedures, in iterative cycles of action and research, to solve practical problems'. Action research presented teachers with the opportunity to participate in aspects of their own professional practice which they considered to be either issues to address, or aspects in which they were particularly interested, to ulti-mately improve the quality of the learning experience (Markless, 2003).

Stenhouse argued that curriculum development and the role of the teacher as a researcher should be the foundation for teacher professionalism. He was critical of the perceived demise of teacher professionalism, especially in the form of the 'teacher proof curriculum package' presented in the form of the objectives model (Rudduck, 1995: 4). Stenhouse alluded to the idea of a teacher being either a **restricted professional** or an **extended professional**. The restricted professional was competent, adept at working with children, engaged in short training courses and even evaluated their own classroom performance. The extended professional has all these attributes, as well as skills and values that involve engagement with curriculum development and research. The extended professional considers the broader issues of school and community, participates in a wide range of professional activities, seeks synergy between theory and practice, and is aligned with the critical evaluation of classroom teaching (Stenhouse, 1975). What was paramount for Stenhouse's principle for teacher professionalism was that 'Professionalism is based upon understanding as a framework for action and knowledge is always provisional' (1983: 192).

To sum up this section, it is probably fitting to consider what Kelly considered 'The end of the "Golden Age"' of curriculum development by Stenhouse and his fellow researchers, and indeed the passing of Stenhouse in 1982. In his text *The Curriculum: Theory and Practice* (2004), Kelly reflects on the progress that had been made in cur-riculum development which was leading to much more advanced methods of curriculum planning. Reflecting on the demise of that Golden Age, he states:

> We were beginning to understand more clearly what it means to claim that education entails more than the mere acquisition of knowledge; we were questioning the sanctity of traditional divisions of this knowledge into subjects; we were becoming aware of the inadequacies of curriculum planning based on achievement of simple behavioural objec-tives; we were learning more about the problems of educational equality, or rather educational inequality; and in particular we were coming to appreciate how far such inequality is a function not so much of society or even of the education system as of the curriculum itself. (Kelly, 2004: 169)

⟳ LINKS WITH OTHER THEORISTS

Stenhouse was particularly inspired by the sociologist Richard Peters's views on the process curriculum and the role of the teacher, but prior to the influence from Peters on the curriculum, Stenhouse was also aware of the similarity between Bruner's 'Man: A Course of Study' and his own HCP, both of which were devised without the use of behavioural objectives. Bruner's study was similar to the HCP in that it focused on areas of the social sciences and the experiences of differing cultures. There are also parallels with Dewey, particularly with regard to the importance of reflective practice and democracy for teaching practice. Furthermore, like Stenhouse, Dewey believed that classrooms should be like laboratories where teachers tested out their ideas to improve their professional practice. Dewey even set up a laboratory school in Chicago as early as 1894 when he was Professor of Pedagogy (Pring, 2004). Both Dewey and Stenhouse viewed the school as a community of pupils and teachers, where teaching was grounded in classroom research and such research was not only recognised but encouraged (Pring, 2004). Furthermore, Pring states that Stenhouse would have gained Dewey's approval of the HCP because the humanities were seen as an important concern for young people, and Stenhouse provided a supportive environment where controversial issues of 'public knowledge and experience' in a culture which students inhabit could be discussed openly (Pring, 2007: 105).

Stenhouse's concepts of restricted and extended teacher professionalism, albeit with some specific criticism about child-centredness and autonomy, emerged from the work of Eric Hoyle, who tried to capture the impact of teachers who were actively involved in curriculum development (Stenhouse, 1975). The origins of action research are located in the 1940s in the work of Kurt Lewin, who undertook a range of social experiments with a view to improving the opportunities of underprivileged groups in society. Stenhouse drew upon Lewin's ideas and adapted them for improving teaching and learning (Punch and Oancea, 2014). Furthermore, Stenhouse's notion of the teacher as researcher endeavouring to continually improve professional practice aligns closely with Schön's concept of the reflective practitioner, which suggests that action research is valuable in the construction of professional knowledge and practice (Wilson, 2013).

Stenhouse was the trailblazer for educational research in the UK and in many other countries and, as we have discovered, the centres for action research were the HCP and CARE, where he worked closely with schools and teachers to encourage and foster the notion of the teacher as researcher and curriculum developer. Stenhouse's criticism of the narrowness of the product curriculum model was also shared by the American progressive and critical educator Michael Apple, who argued that the curriculum was driven and controlled by society's dominant culture and class structure. Another critical American educator, Henry Giroux, had similar ideas to Stenhouse, particularly with regard to how students can become integral parts of the education process by facilitating them to critically question society. He also worked very closely with colleagues, who, in turn, carried forward and further developed Stenhouse's ideas with zeal and success. For example, Rudduck, Elliott and Hopkins have advanced classroom research and practice, 'while Carr and Kemiss continue to promote emancipatory notions of action research, and Whitehead and McNiff publish living theories' (Wilson, 2013: 235). Furthermore, his ideas regarding the curriculum, pedagogy and professional development are also shared with Ivor Goodson, an associate from the HCP and CARE projects. So the spirit of Stenhouse's ideas on curricula, research and teacher professionalism lives on. However, some of his work has attracted a degree of disapproval.

CRITIQUING THE THEORY

It is perhaps not surprising in view of Stenhouse's idea of professional critical scrutiny that many of the most pertinent censures came from himself. He has been criticised for his sexist language in his writings, and in the introduction of his 1983 book *Authority, Education and Emancipation*, he offered an apology 'to all readers who for "he" must read "she", and my regrets to readers of whichever sex'. He was also very aware of the difficulties that were inherent in his process curriculum, particularly when it came to assessing student achievement. Even though he argued that assessment and examination were not altogether impossible accomplishments with the process curriculum model, he did concede that it was a difficult undertaking for teachers and students alike. He particularly acknowledged that the process curriculum could not be used to help low-ability students to pass examinations, as he argued the process model was a 'critical model, not a marking model' (Stenhouse, 1975: 95). Furthermore, he recognised the importance of examinations in modern society and admitted that most teachers would shape their teaching towards giving their students a greater opportunity for success in their examinations (Stenhouse, 1975). Another problem with the process curriculum model is that it relies heavily on the teachers. If they do not have the flexible skills needed for classroom discussion and the student-centred approach called for, they will not have the back-up of the direction and accompanying resources available with the prescribed objectives curriculum model (Smith, 2000).

Stenhouse additionally accepted that the notion of the teacher as researcher is not a realistic option for most teachers given the increasing demands on their time in schools. Practitioner research takes time and a great deal of effort to develop good quality research methodology skills, as well as some awkward critical professional scrutiny and reflection. It was for this reason that he urged education departments at universities to support teachers in schools and to play a part in teacher professional development. There is further criticism of the use of Stenhouse's idea of teacher research. Kemmis suggests that the purpose of Stenhouse's notion of teacher research is somewhat vague:

It was not clear, for instance, whether teachers were to contribute to public knowledge by writing about their work or whether it was enough that they deepen their own understanding and enhance their own practice. Nor was it clear whether the role of the practitioner in relation to theory-building was merely to test in the laboratory of the classroom, the ideas of professional researchers. (1995: 4)

It is suggested that these limitations of time and the possible vagueness of the purpose of practitioner research are genuine factors in hampering the notion of teachers becoming extended professionals. Stenhouse granted that for this notion to become a reality for the majority of teachers, 'the teacher's professional self-image and conditions of work will have to change' (1975: 142). Despite these criticisms, there are many facets of Stenhouse's work that can be adopted in schools to advance his ideas of curriculum development, research and professionalism.

APPLYING STENHOUSE'S IDEAS IN PRACTICE

Stenhouse did not see the role of teachers as being the experts who deliver knowledge to students, but as people who are adept at teaching because of their education and teacher training. He saw the role of teachers as providing access to a world of knowledge and skills to students. Indeed, he argued that teachers should see themselves as learners alongside their students rather than experts; this mode he contested fosters mutual learning through 'teaching by discovery or inquiry methods rather than by instruction' (Stenhouse, 1975: 91). He further suggested that if there were a generally accepted professional notion that teachers are also learners, there would be less of a threatening element in colleagues observing each other in classrooms (Stenhouse, 1975). The importance of peer observation, reflection and peer discussion following observation is central to Stenhouse's concept of 'systematic self-critical enquiry' to enhance not only the teacher and observer's skills as researchers, but also to appraise and evaluate their teaching (Scott and Morrison, 2007).

These ideas of teachers as learners and the quest for self-critical enquiry are evident in Stenhouse's three aspects of what a curriculum should offer:

A. In planning:

1. Principles for the selection of content – what is to be learned and taught.
2. Principles for the development of a teaching strategy – how it is to be learned and taught.
3. Principles for the making of decisions about sequence.
4. Principles on which to diagnose the strengths and weaknesses of individual students and differentiate the general principles 1, 2 and 3 above, to meet individual cases.

B. In empirical study:

    1. Principles on which to study and evaluate the progress of students.
    2. Principles on which to study and evaluate the progress of teachers.
    3. Guidance as to the feasibility of implementing the curriculum in varying school contexts, pupil contexts, environments and peer-group situations.
    4. Information about the variability of effects in differing contexts and on different pupils and an understanding of the causes of the variation.

C. In relation to justification:

A formation of the intention or aim of the curriculum which is accessible to critical scrutiny.

(Stenhouse, 1975: 5)

It is this idea of what a curriculum should offer which, Stenhouse felt, should be adopted when discussing controversial issues with adolescent students. Controversial issues are by their nature divisive, in that society as a whole will have differing opinions, and this will include teachers, students and their parents. Therefore, it is paramount that teachers should not use their own standing to promote their viewpoint in an attempt to influence the students' thinking (Scott, 2008), but rather the teacher should facilitate a discussion between the students in which the divergence of views is defended without trying to gain a compromise, with the teacher acting as a chairperson to ensure that learning is taking place (Stenhouse, 1975). The discussions around the controversial topics is evidenced through such mediums as science, the arts, poetry, history literature, and theology (Pring, 2004). The teacher's role also includes creating an environment that stimulates communication between all group members and promotes a spirit of cooperation. These points were the outcomes from Stenhouse's observations of discussion-based teaching while at the HCP. First, these observations also revealed that group dynamics were enhanced by placing the chairs in such a way that encouraged discussion across the group – a slow-paced discussion usually widens the participation. Second, understanding of a controversial issue is gained by sensitive listening to opinions and then employing questioning for elaboration 'rather than arguing against opponents and attempting to resolve divergence' (Stenhouse, 1975: 94).

Stenhouse stressed the significance of active learning as opposed to the passive learning evident in instruction. According to Harkin et al. (2001) active learning involved the three elements of creating, solving and 'hands-on' experience. Learners create meaning for themselves and are encouraged to interpret information in novel ways. Teachers should also give students the opportunity to use their experiences to solve problems, which not only helps with developing the decision-making process, but also empowers and emancipates student learning. Hands-on experiences help students to be proficient and assured when using new tools and processes. It is certainly the case that the process curriculum model is appropriate for the student-centred approach to teaching, which promotes active enquiry. To facilitate this active learning, Neary (2002) suggests that the teacher must be someone who is willing to change and develop, and be open to the unpredictability of the classroom. Furthermore, they should have 'empathy – the ability to see someone else's problem through one's own eyes and to communicate that understanding' (Neary, 2002: 63). Active learning for Neary (2002: 63) requires the characteristics of a 'facilitator' rather than those she considered inherent in a traditional 'teacher'; below, she highlights the contrasting characteristics of these two notions:

Teacher	Facilitator
Focuses on teaching	Focuses on learning
Teacher centred	Student centred
Control	Sharing
Superior–subordinate relationships	Partnership
Director	Participant
Knowledge given	Knowledge available
Treats all the same	Perceives individual learning needs
Focuses on groups	Focuses on individuals
Closed learning environment	Open learning
Controls parameters of learning	Lets learners set parameters
Narrow horizon	Wider horizon

With a call for teachers to be facilitators, it is interesting to note that Stenhouse favoured a formal approach between student and teacher, not a formality that was impersonal, but a relationship that was fundamentally 'contractual' in its nature. This contract was a two-way process that required teachers to extend ways of thinking, and chances to discuss alternative ways of learning and the making of judgements in the classroom. The contract entailed students being responsible for their learning, and that instead of acting up when being taught by a teacher who is easily unsettled by unacceptable behaviour, they should make the most of what that teacher has to impart – 'otherwise they are wasting their time and the teacher's, and disadvantaging themselves in terms of their right to learn' (Rudduck, 1995: 9). Such a contract would, Stenhouse believed, negate any personal partiality felt between the teacher and the student. Learning contracts also have a part to play in the somewhat problematic area of assessment in the process curriculum model. Within the process model, assessment, instead of coming at the end of the learning, occurs in every aspect of the process.

The outcomes of this ongoing assessment are used to give feedback to students on their progress as a diagnostic or formative tool. As Neary (2002: 64) explains, the teacher takes a position of a 'critical appraiser of the learners' work with the emphasis on developing self-appraisal and self-assessment in the learners'. Stenhouse emphasises this point:

> The process model implies that in assessment or appraisal the teacher ought to be a critic, not a marker ... improving students' capacity to work to such criteria by critical reaction to work done. In this sense assessment is about the teaching of self-assessment. (1975: 94–5)

One final feature of Stenhouse's ideas which is offered for consideration for application in practice revolves around the links he made between the extended professional and the teacher as a researcher. As we have seen, central to his notion of the extended professional was that teachers should demonstrate a willingness and readiness to allow fellow teachers to observe them in the classroom, and then talk about the observation in an open and frank manner. It is argued that this was the basis of his notion of a teacher as a researcher, where teachers work systematically and honestly with others by analysing ideas identified through classroom research techniques in order to develop their professional practice (Stenhouse, 1975). He highlighted a number of critical traits that characterise extended professionalism:

> The commitment to systematic questioning of one's own teaching as a basis for development;
>
> The commitment and skills to study one's own teaching;
>
> The concern to question and to test theory in practice by the use of those skills.
>
> In short, the outstanding characteristics of the extended professional is a capacity for autonomous professional self-development through systematic self-study, through the study of the work of other teachers and through the testing of ideas by classroom research procedures. (Stenhouse, 1975: 144)

Atkins and Wallace (2012: 249–50) summarise Stenhouse's idea of a research-based model from an extended professional perspective as involving 'concerns around linking theory and practice; in other words, undertaking research and contributing to making those links'. To further develop the role of teacher as researcher, Stenhouse argued that student teachers should be introduced to the role of researcher with the help of experienced teachers in their initial teacher education process (Stenhouse, 1975).

While this critical enquiry into teachers' own practice can produce a new body of knowledge and indeed inform and develop practice, Stenhouse argues that this could be further enhanced by teachers engaging with the wider research community. Perhaps by collaborating with university education departments, similar to the work of CARE, teachers have the opportunity not only to develop themselves as researchers in their own classrooms, but to be involved in larger collaborative projects. As Davies summarises, teachers can then enter

A research culture, located within the university–school partnership and supported by seminars, conferences, web-based dialogue and publication, [which] can involve students, staff and schools researching together. (2013: 218)

It is acknowledged that applying some of Stenhouse's ideas in practice could be somewhat difficult with the constraints of the national curriculum and the time available. However, it is argued that many of his ideas are worth pursuing in the quest for a student-centred approach to learning as well as development of teacher professionalism through self-evaluation and research.

REFLECTIVE TASK

Consider the two aspects of a teacher as a facilitator and a teacher as a learner. What opportunities are there currently available for you to pursue these two aspects within the confines of the learning processes in your setting or placement? Try to think of ways in which you could develop these opportunities in the future.

SUMMARY

Even though Stenhouse died possibly at the peak of his academic career, he is recognised as having had a significant impact on education both in the UK and globally. His influence as an advocate for curriculum research and development and the promotion of teacher professionalism has been an inspiration for embryonic classroom researchers. The focal point of his work was the HCP and then CARE, where, with like-minded colleagues, he championed the process curriculum as opposed to the prescribed 'teacher-proof' objectives curriculum model. It was also at the HCP and particularly CARE that he encouraged teachers to collaborate with practitioner research activities. For Stenhouse, the process curriculum model was a way of providing a learning experience that involved honest criticism and ongoing reflection and evaluation, which in turn resulted in student empowerment and emancipation.

Stenhouse's ideas had similarities with those of a number of educational thinkers, specifically Dewey's thoughts on the importance of reflection and of schools being democratic communities where teachers developed their practice through research. Links are also evident between Bruner and Stenhouse regarding the rejection of the behaviourist objectives curriculum model. Stenhouse drew upon Lewin's action research approach and adapted this for developing and improving classroom practice. There are also close links with the American progressive and critical educators, Michael Apple and Henry Giroux. Furthermore, there are associations with his contemporaries and colleagues at HCP and CARE, such as Rudduck, Elliot, Hopkins, Goodson, Carr, Kemis, Whitehead and McNiff. Interestingly, Stenhouse himself was the originator of a number of criticisms of his own work. He acknowledged the difficulties encountered, especially in the demands and expectations for high examination results, in assessment using the process curriculum model. There is also a high dependency on the teacher's skills for the process curriculum model to succeed, as it relies on active learning and the non-controlling teacher role. Finally, many consider that the restrictions of time for an increasingly overburdened workforce hamper the efforts of teachers to become extended professionals and researchers in their own right.

Notwithstanding these criticisms, there are many possibilities for using active approaches to learning that involve students, and encourage them to air their beliefs and values without unnecessary judgement, through the process of discussion. There are also opportunities for teachers to research their own practice and to be self-critical by being open to peer observation. This could then lead to involvement in wider research projects through collaboration with teachers from other schools and departments of education in universities. As a closing statement, Stenhouse argues the case for, and the reason behind, practitioner research: 'A research tradition which is accessible to teachers and which feeds teaching must be created if education is to be significantly improved' (1975: 165).

GLOSSARY OF TERMS

Action research   For Stenhouse, action research was a practical approach for teachers to employ in their classroom not only to improve student learning and their own professional development, but also to add to educational theory. Action research offers teachers the prospect of engaging in facets of their own professional practice which they felt were either matters for development or features in which they were specifically interested, eventually to advance the value of the learning experience (Markless, 2003). The process of action research involves a series of repeated cycles of research and reflection to unravel everyday teaching and learning problems (Punch and Oancea, 2014).

Centre for Applied Research in Education   When the HCP closed, Stenhouse and much of the team moved to set up CARE where their innovative work continued. The significance of CARE was that the work advanced the growth of practitioner research and action research. The team at CARE took their work outside the university and into schools and public organisations to promote the use of democratic evaluation, action research, case study and ethnography (CARE, 2015). The work carried out by Stenhouse and his team at CARE has led to many other education departments at universities being engaged in supporting practitioner research. CARE remained very active at the University of East Anglia until its closure in 2015.

Humanities Curriculum Project   Stenhouse led the HCP for five years until its closure in 1972. The HCP was a pioneering project that focused on the way that curriculum development was thought about; it also championed teacher research. It was also a contentious project that worked very closely with secondary schools and teachers to advance the way in which controversial topics in society were covered and discussed in schools. The idea of the project was that teachers facilitated students in helping them to explore and reach their own enlightened conclusions, the teacher acting as a non-judgemental chairperson. The project was distinctive in that it shunned the use of set learning outcomes. The discussions were held in an environment where students felt comfortable in developing a culture of their own; in this way, they would be more skilled in understanding the cultures and formal language they encountered.

Objectives curriculum model   Contrary to the process curriculum model, the objectives curriculum model is generally more prescribed in its formation and content. Its use is widespread in education and relates mainly to subject-specific curricula. It is also centred on the prescribed lists of learning outcomes, which students have to achieve submissively. This model concentrates mainly on the training of skills and in modifying behaviours; it also focuses on assessment and the testing of learners' achievement. This model is mainly involved with specific and set instructional methods instead of giving teachers the freedom to reflect and make up their own decisions about learning and teaching approaches.

Process curriculum model   Stenhouse argued that the process curriculum model nurtured student empowerment and emancipation; it also gave teachers the freedom to develop their professional practice by way of research and evaluation. The process model focuses on the learning experience, and the roles and activities of both the student and the teacher, as well as the classroom environment. The teacher welcomes active student enquiry rather than students pacifically accepting given knowledge. It sanctions teachers and learners to work in accord and to allow students to access further opportunities. However, Stenhouse emphasises that the process model is more challenging (than the product curriculum model) in practice, as it 'rests with teacher judgement rather than teacher direction ... but offers a higher degree of personal and professional development' (1975: 96–7).

Restricted and extended teacher professionalism   Stenhouse was disapproving of the steady demise of teacher professionalism, which he thought was mainly brought about by the increased use of the objectives curriculum model. He offered two modes of teacher professionalism: restricted and extended. Restricted professionals were capable teachers, skilled at working with young people, self-evaluated their own classroom practice and attended staff development programmes. Extended professionals possessed all these attributes, but they also had the skills and values that enabled them to engage with research and curriculum development activities. Extended professionals also reflected upon the wider issues of the school and the community, the links between theory and practice, and actively participated in the critical evaluation of their teaching. Furthermore, extended professionals were open and agreeable to others observing their teaching and then discussing the observation honestly (Stenhouse, 1975).

FURTHER READING

Carr, D. (2000) *Professionalism and Ethics in Teaching*. London: Routledge.
A thoughtful analysis of ethical and professional issues in relation to education theory and the role of the teacher.

Elliott, J. and Norris, N. (eds) (2012) *Curriculum, Pedagogy and Educational Research: The Work of Lawrence Stenhouse*. London: Routledge.
An informative and detailed text about Stenhouse's work, as well as a contemporary insight into the meaning and application of his ideas.

Rudduck, J. and McIntyre, D. (2007) *Improving Learning through Consulting Pupils*. Abingdon: Routledge.
A research-based text that explores the realities of using pupils' voices in classrooms and aligned to Stenhouse's notions of the roles of teachers and students.

Stenhouse, L. (ed.) (1967) *Discipline in Schools: A Symposium*. Oxford: Pergamon Press.
A dated, yet useful guide to classroom management for student or newly qualified teachers.

REFERENCES

Atkins, L. and Wallace, S. (2012) *Qualitative Research in Education*. London: SAGE.

Bartlett, S. and Burton, D. (2016) *Introduction to Education Studies* (4th edn). London: SAGE.

Burton, D. and Bartlett, S. (2005) *Practitioner Research for Teachers*. London: Paul Chapman Publishing.

Campbell, A., McNamara, O. and Gilroy, P. (2004) *Practitioner Research and Professional Development in Education*. London: Paul Chapman Publishing.

CARE (2015) *Centre for Applied Research in Education – University of East Anglia (CARE)*. Available online at: www.uea.ac.uk/education/research/care

Davies, D. (2013) 'Education research: So what?' In: Ward, S. (ed.) *A Student's Guide to Education Studies* (3rd edn). London: Routledge.

Elliott, J. (2007) *Reflecting Where the Action Is: The Selected Works of John Elliott*. London: Routledge.

Goodson, I. (2005) *Learning, Curriculum and Life Politics: The Selected Works of Ivor F. Goodson*. Abingdon: Routledge.

Harkin, J., Turner, G. and Dawn, T. (2001) *Teaching Young Adults: A Handbook for Teachers in Post-compulsory Education*. London: RoutledgeFalmer.

Kelly, A.V. (2004) *The Curriculum: Theory and Practice* (5th edn). London: SAGE.

Kemmis, S. (1995) 'Some ambiguities in Stenhouse's notion of "the teacher as researcher"'. In: Rudduck, J. (ed.) *An Education that Empowers: A Collection of Lectures in Memory of Lawrence Stenhouse*. Clevedon: Multilingual Matters/BERA.

Markless, S. (2003) 'The case for action research'. In: Lea, J., Hayes, D., Armitage, A., Lomas, L. and Markless, S. (eds) *Working in Post-compulsory Education*. Maidenhead: Open University Press.

Neary, M. (2002) *Curriculum Studies in Post-compulsory and Adult Education*. Cheltenham: Nelson Thornes.

Pring, R. (2004) *Philosophy of Educational Research* (2nd edn). London: Continuum.

Pring, R. (2007) *John Dewey*. London: Bloomsbury.

Punch, K. and Oancea, A. (2014) *Introduction to Research Methods in Education* (2nd edn). London: SAGE.

Rowntree, R. (1981) *A Dictionary of Education*. London: Harper & Row.

Rudduck, J. (ed.) (1995) *An Education that Empowers: A Collection of Lectures in Memory of Lawrence Stenhouse*. Clevedon: Multilingual Matters/BERA.

Rudduck, J. and Hopkins, D. (1985) *Research as a Basis for Teaching: Readings from the Work of Lawrence Stenhouse*. London: Heinemann.

Schostak, J. and Schostak, J. (2008) *Radical Research: Designing, Developing and Writing Research to Make a Difference*. London: Routledge.

Scott, D. (2008) *Critical Essays on Major Curriculum Theorists*. London: Routledge.

Scott, D. and Morrison, M. (2007) *Key Ideas in Educational Research*. London: Continuum.

Smith, M. (2000) 'Curriculum theory and practice'. *The Encyclopaedia of Informal Education*. Available online at: www.infed.org/biblio/b-curric.htm

Stenhouse, L. (1971a) *Culture and Education*. London: Nelson.

Stenhouse, L. (1971b) 'The Humanities Curriculum Project'. In: Hooper, R. (ed.) *The Curriculum: Context, Design and Development*. Edinburgh: Oliver & Boyd.

Stenhouse, L. (1975) *An Introduction to Curriculum Research and Development*. London: Heinemann.

Stenhouse, L. (1983) *Authority, Education and Emancipation: A Collection of Papers*. London: Heinemann.

Thomas, G. (2007) *Education and Theory: Strangers in Paradigms*. Maidenhead: Oxford University Press.

Thomas, G. (2013) *Education: A Very Short History*. Oxford: Oxford University Press.

Whitty, G. (1985) *Sociology and School Knowledge: Curriculum Theory, Research and Politics*. London: Methuen.

Wilson, E. (2013) 'What is educational action research?' In: Wilson, E. (ed.) *School-based Research: A Guide for Education Students*. London: SAGE.

12

MICHAEL APPLE

IDEOLOGY, KNOWLEDGE, POWER AND THE CURRICULUM

LEARNING OUTCOMES

After reading this chapter, you should be able to:

*   appreciate Michael Apple's background and his role as a critical educational thinker;
*   understand his concepts which challenge the conventional ideas of education;
*   recognise the associations between his ideas and those of other educational thinkers;
*   critically evaluate Apple's work;
*   appraise his thinking from a practical educational perspective.

KEY WORDS

Ideology; official knowledge; reproduction; democracy; marketisation; critical pedagogy.

INTRODUCTION

Michael Apple is considered one of the foremost international progressive educational thinkers and a renowned advocate for critical education. Together with the likes of Henry Giroux and Paulo Freire, he has championed the cause of critical education to counter the increasingly predominant influence of conservative **ideology** and market forces evident in education. His interests and his writings have included a wide range of educational themes such as the curriculum, standardised testing, policy, finance and governance (Torre, 2001). Apple is an intellectual and social activist who has dedicated his career to promoting education as the conduit that can empower and transform people. His forte is scrutinising the associations between education and the concept of power. Throughout his career, he has maintained strong links with 'educators, unions, dissident and disadvantaged groups throughout the world on democratising educational policy and practice' (Peters, 2015: 1). The scrutiny that Apple employs analyses educational structures in the United States and other countries, particularly other capitalist nations; the results of his analysis are both thought-provoking and troubling. A key factor throughout Apple's works is that of **democracy**; he advocates that the democratic ideals which should be inherent in schooling should also be mirrored in society as a whole. His notion of democracy, he argues, is at odds with the growing emphasis on business and **marketisation** which is driving the curriculum in the majority of schools (Torre, 2001).

Although it is convenient to place Apple under the loose umbrella of being a critical educational thinker, which he most certainly is, it is quite tricky to locate his ideas into a particular pigeon-hole. Nevertheless, he does align with other critical and progressive educational thinkers who debate the effect of the forms of **reproduction**. Torre indicates that social reproduction is evident in schools as they 'tend to reproduce the *status quo* instead of fostering upward mobility' (Torre, 2001: 265). However, there is also common ground between Apple and other progressive/critical educators in that they all endeavour to expose the realities and inequities that are concealed within educational structures. Much of this common ground is underpinned by elements of neo-Marxism, principally regarding the insights of power relationships in schools (Howlett, 2013). Neo-Marxist ideas were introduced in the 1970s and 1980s into education discourse. It gave thinkers like Apple 'a vocabulary to talk about the social context of education, and the social struggles in and surrounding it' (Anyon, 2011: 1). To give greater context of what follows, it is fitting at this early stage, particularly when trying to locate Apple's place as a critical educator, to define the term 'ideology', which he frequently uses in his writing. According to Apple, ideology is 'a form of false consciousness which distorts one's picture of social reality and serves the interests of the dominant classes in society' (Apple, 1979: 20).

Michael Apple's radical ideas have sparked educational debate in the United States where the curriculum, along with other matters of class, gender, race and the economy, are major points for national discussion. His writings have advocated that educators have a role to play in resisting government and business influences on the structures evident in schools, structures which he feels relate to the economy rather than the individual aspirations of learners. These structures for Apple are organised curricula, set standards of achievement, and national assessments and evaluations (Scott, 2008). He has written extensively regarding these structures, as well as the social and cultural disparities evident in education. Apple's most renowned earlier books are *Ideology and the Curriculum* (1979) and *Education and Power* (1982) in which he explored the links between the curriculum, teaching and assessment and the forms of inequality in society. These texts also considered the associations relating to schooling, political and cultural power, and the state. *Teachers and Texts: A Political Economy of Class and Gender Relations in Education* (1988) considered positive ways in which teachers could take more control of the curriculum, including an analysis of class, gender and pedagogy. Later writings of note include *Official Knowledge: Democratic Education in a Conservative Age* (2000); *The State and the Politics of Knowledge* (2003); *Can Education Change Society?* (2013) and *The Struggle for Democracy in Education: Lessons from Social Realities* (2018). To fully comprehend how Apple's ideas and his role as a social activist developed, we need to explore the influence of his family and social background, and his career as a teacher and academic.

MICHAEL APPLE, THE PERSON 🔍

Michael Apple was born in 1942 in Paterson, New Jersey, to working-class parents who were active trade unionists and heavily involved in left-wing politics. In an interview with Michael Peters, Apple explains the significance of his family and local community:

> In order to understand some of the reasons I look at the world in particular ways, it is important to understand that I am what has been called a 'red diaper baby'. I come from a deeply committed leftist family, one that lived in a poor neighbourhood of one of the most political cities in the United States ... My grandfather was a Russian immigrant who as a young man in the late nineteenth century ... left Russia for economic reasons. As a communist, he was always in danger ... Like other immigrant working class folks in inner city Paterson, New Jersey – the home of some of the most important struggles in the history of the US – life wasn't life without being consumed by politics. (Peters, 2015: 2–3)

Apple's mother was a communist and anti-racist activist; his father was a printer who came from a socialist family. His mother was a founding member of the Paterson branch of the Congress of Racial Equality (CORE); Apple himself became the publicity director of CORE at the age of fifteen. Both parents were profoundly secular in their thinking and held a deep mistrust of right-wing religious groups. Michael Apple attended night school at two small state teacher training colleges and worked as a printer during the day (Torre, 2001; Peters, 2015). This experience in the printing workshop enabled him to value and respect the skills of his fellow workers; he also developed a lifelong affection for the printed word (Peters, 2015). Apple recalled that his parents were very pleased that he decided to become a teacher. For them, being a teacher was a commendable vocation and a tribute to the family: 'teaching was about critical literacy, about giving people power to understand the world and – maybe – change it' (Peters, 2015: 4).

However, before he could fulfil his ambition of becoming a teacher, he was drafted into the army where he spent his time as an instructor, an experience that helped confirm his aspirations of a teaching career. Due to a teacher shortage in Paterson's public schools, Apple was appointed as a substitute teacher even though he did not yet have a degree. His involvement with CORE and his work with African-American and Hispanic groups led him to be allocated to schools within these communities (Peters, 2015). During his time as a teacher, he absorbed himself in teacher politics and eventually became president of a teachers' union. He gained a BA degree in Education from Glassboro State College, New Jersey, while teaching in Paterson's public schools. He then gained an MA in Curriculum and Philosophy in 1967, and an EdD in Curriculum and Teaching in 1970 from Columbia University, New York. For the duration of Apple's postgraduate studies at Columbia University, the USA experienced protests from the civil rights and Vietnam anti-war movements; these protests were accompanied by radical literature and dissident debate. Following his doctorate, he was accepted for an academic post at the University of Wisconsin at Madison. When he was being interviewed for this post, army tanks were sent into the campus to quell hostile and persistent student anti-war protests and the building filled with tear gas. As a result of this experience, 'In Apple's own words, he knew when he was being interviewed that this was the place he wanted to be' (Torre, 2001: 264). His association with the University of Wisconsin, Madison, has lasted throughout his career, becoming the John Bascom Professor of Curriculum and Instruction and Educational Policy Studies at the university (Torre, 2001).

Apple's main teaching areas are around curriculum theory and the sociology of the curriculum. He travels widely and has held visiting professorships in Australia, New Zealand, Brazil, Norway and Mexico. Apart from finding time to write and research, he also participates in local, national and international politics (Torre, 2001). Apple has received many awards and honours during his career, including honorary doctorates from McGill University, Canada; University of Rosario, Argentina; and the Institute of Education, London, where he is World Scholar (much of Apple's research and writings feature education in the United Kingdom). He is also the recipient of the Medal for Distinguished Academic Achievement from the University of California (Peters, 2015). Despite these distinguished awards and honours, Michael Apple retains a grounded approach to his work in seeking a more democratic approach to schooling.

APPLE AND HIS IDEAS ON EDUCATION

The major aspects of Apple's thinking centre around his vision of social justice and democracy, including class, race and gender equality. As these aspects are all inter-related, the structure of this section will reflect this. Moreover, this section will explore his notion of reproduction; the curriculum; **official knowledge** and textbooks; marketisation and **critical pedagogy**. Before this, though, it is appropriate to consider some of the broader issues of his ideology, starting with the foundations from which his thinking emerged. It is contended that critical educators such as Apple can be identified as being progressive because their thinking advocates a political viewpoint in forming their philosophy, which locates its doctrine in the social analytical writings of the Frankfurt School of thought which arose in the period between the two world wars. The school's subversive and anti-establishment tenor was resurrected with enthusiasm by critical educators throughout the social activism of the 1960s and 1970s. Essentially, they were disapproving of the growth of what they saw as a consumer culture that was being fuelled by the different forms of mass media which, they thought, was a form of ideological brainwashing (Howlett, 2013). The Frankfurt School constructed their philosophy and methods on the writings of Marx and Freud. The school proffered articulate and dismissive evaluations of capitalism and capitalist societies with specific emphasis on 'the concepts of "false realities" generated by all-pervading forms of media which acted as an updated version of Marx's "opium of the masses"' (Howlett, 2013: 249).

The concept of neoliberalism attracts considerable condemnation from Apple because he perceived neoliberalism as a political principle that reinforces the Western world view – it involves the conviction that human character is innately competitive (Hicks, 2013). As such, competition between individuals, institutions and different countries will result in widespread advantages and therefore governments should not hinder this free-market approach. Apple claims that this view also shapes the manner in which education is seen, planned and structured (Hicks, 2013). Apple argued that there was a distinct difference between democratic and neoliberal notions of schooling. The democratic notion focuses on improving people's entitlements regarding the practices and policies of schooling, with the aim of involving politics to refresh democratic practice by creating methods of encouraging public discourse and arbitration. This is founded on the concept of democracy being an educative practice in itself. Conversely, the neoliberal notion of schooling places the emphasis on privatisation and marketisation by seeking not only to restrain politics, but also to reduce all political discourse to economics (Apple, 1997). It is interesting, but unsurprising, that Apple's ideas relating to neoliberalism are often linked to education in the United Kingdom since he has collaborated in a number of research projects in the UK. Apple (2006) suggests that he finds similarities between the neoliberalism approach to education and the rise of conservatism in both the US and the UK.

Another key and fundamental aspect of Apple's ideology is that of economic, social and cultural reproduction, which are particularly significant for their interrelationship with his views on the curriculum (Apple, 1997). Apple argues, following the writings of Bourdieu, that school has been used as an instrument for the reproduction of control and power by the dominant classes. For Apple, power and culture are not separate entities, but rather characteristics interlinked with the economic relations of institutions within society. Apple (1997) considers that schools are guided by the dominant structures employed by other institutions, such as business and industry, which are fundamentally unequal in the manner in which power and resources are apportioned. Schools, then, strengthen and reproduce these inequalities 'through their curricular, pedagogical, and evaluative activities in day-to-day life in classrooms, schools play a significant role in preserving if not generating ... inequalities' (Apple, 1979: 64). By doing so, schools turn the dominant culture into cultural capital or a commodity; as such, it acts as a safeguard in ensuring the preservation of the status quo (Apple, 1979; Hall et al., 2010). This process is also boosted by more affluent parents who have access to a greater range of material resources, which in turn frequently results in the 'successful conversions of economic and social capital into cultural capital. And this is exactly what is happening in England' (Apple, 2006: 473–4).

Apple (1979) argues that the school curriculum is not neutral, but is culturally biased in its subjective selection of the knowledge and skills that are included. This cultural bias in the curriculum is not only concealed, but it operates by presenting a 'false picture of "able" (often middle-class) and "less able" (typically working-class) students, which itself can be used as a justification for unequal distribution of jobs and pay' (Moore, 2000: 92). Apple cautions that the dominant discourse around the curriculum and the language used in its formation has become increasingly 'the language of production, rationalisation and standardisation. The language of democracy, participation, and equality is being muted' (Apple, 1988: 27). He is also wary of the escalating influence of the 'authoritarian populist' religious conservatives who have endeavoured to change the content and form of the curriculum in the United States to mirror their own narrow religious viewpoints (Peters, 2015: 9). These influences on the curriculum are all part of what Apple termed the 'conservative restoration' which happened in the 1980s and 1990s. Then there was concentrated lobbying by the main companies to boost the flagging economic competitiveness of United States businesses, particularly in the light of the less expensive and technically superior goods coming into the country from South East Asia. Business groups cited the failure of the education system as a reason for the decline in their economic fortunes. Business leaders in the United States contested that the South East Asia workforce had a better technical education, which enabled their businesses to compete in the global marketplace, resulting in an increasingly neoliberal curriculum in form and content (Anyon, 2011).

The curriculum according to Apple (1979) is not impartial in its content or form, which is especially the case regarding matters such as race, class and power. The selection of what is included and what is not, as we have seen, comes from the dominant culture. Citing the British Marxist academic Raymond Williams, Apple states that the process for selecting what is included in the curriculum is the '*selective tradition*: that which, within the terms of an effective dominant culture, is always passed off as, "the tradition," *the* significant past' (Apple, 1979: 6). For Apple, it is the selectivity of what is to be included, and excluded, from the present and the past which is significant and often results in the curriculum being:

> vacuous, ahistorical, one-sided, and ideologically laden ... There are few serious attempts at dealing with conflict (class conflict, scientific conflict, or other). Instead, one 'inquires' into a consensus ideology that bears little resemblance to the complex nexus and contradictions surrounding the control and organisation of social life (Apple, 1979: 7).

As such:

> the knowledge, and ways of seeing the world of dominant white (male) elites in US society are validated by being included in the school curriculum, and students study the lives of presidents and generals, but not of the working class, blacks, or women. (Anyon, 2011: 34)

The outcome of this is that knowledge that does not fit into the dominant discourse is rejected from the curriculum. What remains is what Apple terms 'official knowledge'. The consequence of this is the emphasis on 'the performance of "competence" and the positioning of education as a service to business becomes orthodoxies of policy' (Fisher et al., 2010: 110).

Apple's notion of official knowledge is a demonstration of how the dominant ideology underpins the reproduction of inequities in society. At the same time, official knowledge disguises its own function in the 'processes of social reproduction by masquerading as neutral and universal' (Gewirtz and Cribb, 2009: 114). Official knowledge is evident throughout the conservative discourse on education, which is mainly apparent in textbooks where students gain much of their knowledge. Textbooks are far from being the neutral resources they may appear to be. The deliberations that go into selecting textbooks for any given curriculum involve a combination of powerful drivers including those not only from schools, but also from governments. In their book *The Politics of the Textbook* (1991), Apple and Christian-Smith posit that textbooks can be seen as methods of moral regulation by powerful factions to create and enhance political and cultural consensus. Textbooks are conceived and written by individuals with their own concerns and interests; they are also printed and circulated within the economic and political limitations of the dominant culture and market forces. Apple and Christian-Smith (1991) blame difficult economic times and the insecurity regarding authority for the conservative attacks on schooling:

> "Authoritarian populism" is in the air, and a New Right has been more than a little successful in bringing its own power to bear on the goals, content, and process of schooling ... The ideology that stands behind this is often very complex. It combines a

commitment to both the 'traditional family' and clear gender roles with the commitment to 'traditional values' and literal religiosity. Often packed into this is also a defence of capitalist economies, patriotism, the "Western tradition", anti-communism, and a deep mistrust of the "welfare state". (Apple and Christian-Smith, 1991: 2–3)

For Apple, then, official knowledge in the curriculum and textbooks is shaped in order to enhance state economic growth or else to meet the neoconservative traditional programme (Scott, 2008).

A major facet of Apple's thinking and criticism centres on the emergent rise of a powerful alliance of capitalist intellectuals who are dedicated in using neoliberal marketisation to resolve the perceived problems in education. This alliance is uncompromising in its goal to ensure that systems of measurement, accountability, competition and management used in business are established and strengthened in education. They cited progressivism in schooling as the ruin of their romanticised and traditional view of education. Apple emphasised that the alliances' goal could not be achieved 'without setting the market loose on schools so as to ensure that only "good" ones survive' (Apple, 2006: 470). Within marketisation, then, educational values are frequently compromised, and commercial matters such as resource distribution and curriculum design take priority. The rise in the drive by governments for increasing standards and performance is exemplified by the publication of examination league tables, which have cultivated an environment of competition between schools (Apple, 2006). In Britain, the 1993 Education Act extended the principle of marketisation by allowing greater choice and giving schools more autonomy in their day-to-day management. This allowed schools, to some extent, to function as private-sector organisations, which in turn led 'families to treat educational decisions in a similar way to other decisions about private consumption' (Whitty, 1998). Another outcome of marketisation is the rising marketness of teachers' work, which involves extracting the maximum value from their work and time (Robertson, 2000). The relationship between teachers and the state has changed in this rise of marketisation. This has come about because of a shift to a small but potent state which is guided by the requirements of the market, and as such seems to have resulted in a decline of teachers' professional status and power (Apple, 2006).

By urging educators to confront the curricula and educational structures that validate and reproduce dominant authority, Apple was a catalyst for the development of critical pedagogy among US neo-Marxist educators. Over a period of twenty years, this faction of educators developed a comprehensive theoretical body 'of knowledge concerning critical teaching for student empowerment' (Anyon, 2011: 35). Henry Giroux, one of the key proponents of critical pedagogy, felt that there was a need to challenge the school culture in the US, which functioned for the benefit of the privileged students to the detriment of the hopes of the less represented members of society. Giroux (2003) argued that schools needed to foster environments where students could be actively critical and mature into vigorous democratic participants in society as a whole. Apple explains:

> Critical educators emphasise the importance of not predetermining the learning act through the rigid predetermination of the curriculum and instructional techniques. The teacher is viewed as assuming a central role in guiding and facilitating the learning process in dialogue with students in response to the emerging situation at hand. (Carlson and Apple, 1989: 24)

This radical approach to critical classroom teaching was condemned by conservative education policy-makers who endeavoured to 'teacher-proof' the curriculum during the 1970s and 1980s (Carlson and Apple, 1998). Within the notion of critical pedagogy, Apple was suspicious of the instrumentalist use of technology in classrooms. His main cause for concern was the manner in which new technologies were being promoted for use in classrooms. There was, he thought, an overemphasis on 'how to' use technology rather than the 'why'; therefore, it was a form of thinking that was more technical rather than of substance, and excluded political and cultural considerations. Apple also questioned some of the future outcomes of the unrestricted use of technology. These included the effect on teaching and the curriculum, and the effect of an increasing focus on computer expertise in relation to opportunities for social interactions, particularly for the more disadvantaged learners (Apple, 1988).

Michael Apple's ideology and notions of reproduction, democracy and critical pedagogy are in tune with other like-minded progressive educators.

LINKS WITH OTHER THEORISTS

We have already revealed how Apple was inspired by the Frankfurt School of thought (particularly Marxism), and this influence is deeply evident throughout his work and life. In an interview with Peters (2015), Apple stressed the importance of the work of Habermas and Gramsci in relation to his thinking and personal belief on the importance of social change and how thinking is a human activity that cannot be disassociated from human culture. This is personified in what Gramsci termed 'an "organic intellectual" this would seem to be demonstrated in the way your personal and family background influenced your outlook and life-long commitments' (Peters, 2015: 10–11). The progressive and critical works of Paulo Freire, Ivan Illich, Peter McLaren and Henry Giroux are also synonymous with Apple. Principally, these associations are that all have argued for the inter-linked connection between schools and politics, especially in the United States and other neoliberal free market nations. Despite Freire's work being positioned mainly in South America, his visions of education being located within the social, cultural and political domains resonates firmly with Apple's thinking (Schugurensky, 2014). Freire's seminal work *Pedagogy of the Oppressed* (first published in 1970, revised in 1996) emphasised that learning to read and write enabled students to appreciate the role of language in the production of culture, as well as using the power of language and reason to liberate (Carlson and Apple, 1998). Similar to Apple, Giroux, one of the founders of the concept of critical pedagogy, also considered that politics and the understanding of the social structure of knowledge were key to learners seeking actions to advance social justice and eradicate inequalities of power (Aubrey and Riley, 2019).

Apple introduced a number of American educational scholars to the works of contemporary European thinkers, including Pierre Bourdieu and Basil Bernstein, who had been evaluating dominant cultures and the influence they had on society. Apple explained Bourdieu's notion of cultural capital as how 'language patterns, ways of knowing, and specific bodies of knowledge of dominant groups are what the US educational system validates as legitimate and therefore correct' (Anyon, 2011: 33). Bernstein's work encompassed three interrelated themes, all of which mirror the work of Apple: 'language codes and social class; classification, framing and the construction of the curriculum; and the construction of knowledge systems and pedagogies' (Aubrey and Riley, 2017: 73). Bernstein also gave great emphasis to the provision of a democratic education, and he set out three democratic rights for students: enhancement, inclusion and participation (Bernstein, 2000). Lawrence Stenhouse, the British curriculum scholar, thought, similarly to Apple, that the curriculum was excessively guided by the dominant class and culture of society (Stenhouse, 1975). Other US educational thinkers associated with Apple's thoughts are John Goodlad and his search for an ethical, moral and democratic schooling system, and his interest in the notion of power and the curriculum. Linda Darling-Hammond, an educational reformer who advocated a more equitable schooling system, as well as promotion of teacher professionalism, also has meaningful connections with Apple. Last but certainly not least to be associated with Michael Apple is the founder of the concept of democratic education – John Dewey, who also advanced the idea that schools should be democratic environments that prepared students to become active participants in society. It is clear that Apple has been influenced by, and linked with, a number of progressive and critical scholars, which could be the reason for much of the criticism his ideas attracted.

⊛ CRITIQUING THE THEORY

Apple's language can at times make him sound like a conspiracy theorist, which is especially the case when he writes about the ideologies involved in his thinking. He uses such terms as 'The Right, neoliberals, neo-conservatives, neo-Gramscians to show that conservative thinking is underpinned to protect the "merit-based" class hierarchy in the United States' (Torre, 2001: 269). However, it is contested that the overuse of such terms almost reduces the importance of his arguments by being too ideologically focused. This also renders his writing rather repetitive at times. Similarly, his language can occasionally be somewhat emotive, although, on the other hand, it is also a reflection of his undoubtable commitment to social justice. For example, Apple himself expresses his wrath and the justification of such anger when writing about the impact that conservative policies have had on the poor and disfranchised pupils, 'if we cannot allow ourselves to be angry about the lives of our children, what can we be angry about?' (Apple, 1997: 598).

Apple is clear in his emphasis of the importance of creating radical and utopian principles in finding answers to the problems in conservative educational structures (Apple, 2006). Then again, Apple rarely proposes any clear practical solutions for remedying the problems he raises (Torre, 2001). This is possibly because he is out of touch with the current realities of what teachers face in classrooms. Scott (2008) offers an illustration of this by exploring Apple's principal notion that teachers should embrace a reflexive position in their practice. Scott highlights two key problems with this notion. The first is regarding the manner in which knowledge is created by individual students who are learning in actual classrooms; their everyday worries may originate not only outside schools, but also outside the locations where official knowledge is being generated. The second problem develops from the first in that disenfranchised and oppressed students, for the most part, are inclined to act in a manner in which liberal scholars such as Apple would possibly object to. Consequently, by taking away structural inequities and reforming curriculum and teaching methods so that students who have previously been deprived of expressing their opinion are given their opportunity to do so may result in disorder, requiring an autocratic rather than a democratic resolution (Scott, 2008).

There does appear to be a lack of unity among the radical educational scholars in pressing ahead with transforming their commendable ideas of social justice into practice. An example is the difference of opinion between Apple and Bernstein in what to include within their ideas for a democratic set of social and cultural arrangements. For Bernstein, the key aspect of his idea was social class; however, Apple stressed 'the importance of taking gender and race relations as seriously as those of class if we were to act in more progressive ways' (Apple, 1988: 183). Apple confessed also that there was some confusion on what was meant by the term 'critical pedagogy'. He thought it was a term that had 'become something of a "sliding signifier" – a slogan that is employed to mean multiple things' (Carlson and Apple, 1998: 25). Possibly it is the fault of these radical scholars in not being united in their ideas that they were unable to take their ideas forward in more practical ways and supported by policy. Apple recognised, though, that internationally the conservative restoration was very powerful and was now used to running schools; therefore, perhaps the fault lies with 'the inability of the left to mobilise itself in defence of equity and social justice' (Scott, 2008: 71). Although these criticisms may appear to negate putting his ideas into practice within the constraints evident in the national curriculum and the increasing use of standardised assessment, his idea of striving to enhance social justice is a vital aspect of a practitioner's role.

⚙ APPLE'S THOUGHTS IN RELATION TO EDUCATION PRACTICE

Before we explore some thoughts about the possibility of applying Apple's ideas in practice, and some of the constraints involved, it is worth reminding ourselves of the radical impact that his concepts have made in progressive educational thinking. His *Ideology and the Curriculum* (1979) was one of a few texts that shifted the thinking about children's learning. Up until the late 1970s, the main notions of how children learn were the concern of psychological thinkers – for example, Piaget and his staged cognitive development. Research into child learning was 'positivistic and orientated toward control, as in the Skinner stimulus and response paradigm ... Most education conversations centred on technocratic, mechanistic, and behavioural aims' (Anyon, 2011: 1–2). However, Apple and his fellow progressive educators adopted a different stance that focused on educational issues in a wider context (Apple, 1988), a position that governments could implement, given the resolve, to ensure that we develop democratic citizens for the future. It is understandable to assume that it is somewhat difficult for practitioners to take an active stance to confront the imposed anti-democratic structures that Apple perceives are in place in schools. Yet Apple argues that schools, like other institutions, were formed because of conflict and are fragmented by conflict. As such, he suggests that practitioners, where necessary, 'will mediate, transform, and attempt to generally set limits on what is being imposed from the outside' (Apple, 1988: 26). This section offers some considerations for what *could* be done as part of national policy reforms, and what *can* be done by practitioners in classrooms to create a more progressive and democratic environment in schools.

Kelly laments what he sees in the increasing influence of the New Right in the curriculum; he argues that this ideology does not reflect the essential principles and morals of democracy.

> Democracy is not about privilege nor even solely about freedom; it is also about equality. And equality in education cannot be achieved unless we provide an appropriate curriculum, planned and implemented in such a way as to combat privilege, along with the freedom of licence, and promote equity for all, regardless of social or ethnic origin. (Kelly, 2004: 215–16)

For Kelly (2004), this ideology, which is evident in the national curriculum, has resulted in the reduction of the core moral ideals of democracy which young people require to be active and critical participants in society. Hatcher also states that a curriculum can be constructed which is comprehensible to all students and which enables working-class students to understand and participate in the world. This, he suggests, can be achieved by:

> Bringing the experiences and concerns of the child and young person into the curriculum and reconstructing the curriculum on the basis which combines high intellectual quality with the perspectives of the socially deprived and oppressed rather than those of the

privileged and powerful ... This provides the basis both for high academic achievement within the system and wider goals of education for emancipation. (Hatcher, 2006: 221)

This notion of emancipation is central to Apple's progressive notion of critical pedagogic practice which strives to reveal the realities of inequality within the educational structures (Howlett, 2013). Critical practice requires practitioners to continually examine the values, form and content of their teaching to see whether there is any bias. It also attempts to connect with the student's knowledge and voice in a collaborative manner by investigating what is fair and what is unfair (Hall et al., 2010).

Moore (2000) queries the feasibility of practitioners applying Apple's progressive ideas in their classrooms because of the power of the educational institution and structures, as well as the effectiveness of teachers in making any meaningful changes to society. Yet, it is argued that practitioners can adopt progressive ideas in their classrooms with the aim of creating democratic learning environments despite the imposed constraints – for example, the interpretation of official knowledge, particularly in the form of the text and the curriculum. Apple and Christian-Smith (1991) argue that the meanings and politics of texts can be multiple and conflicting; as such, we should be willing to interpret our own meaning of texts. They go on to argue that teachers can, and do, mediate and transform text when teaching. Students too 'bring their own classed, raced, gendered, and sexual biographies with them as well. They, too, selectively accept, interpret, and reject what counts as legitimate knowledge' (Apple and Christian-Smith, 1991: 14). They go on to suggest that there are three ways in which people can respond to texts: dominated, negotiated and oppositional. In the dominated reading, the reader accepts the meaning; in the negotiated response the reader accepts, with reservations, the interpretation of the text; in the oppositional response the reader discards 'these dominant tendencies and interpretations ... [and] takes on the position of the oppressed' (Apple and Christian-Smith, 1991: 14).

Although the ideological and structural contexts that are evident in education can make it difficult for teachers to actively participate in political and collaborative social events, they have incredible capacity to continue to strive to preserve their dignity and unity in labour (Robertson, 2000). However, Apple (1988) argues that for this capacity to flourish, it is important that progressive academics should have rigorous and continuous links with teachers and their classroom practice. These links should also involve students, parents, feminist groups, different races and unions (Apple, 1988). Working closely with practitioners, Apple thought, was essential in gaining a feeling of what is actually happening in classrooms and schools; he encouraged progressive educational scholars to listen and learn from teachers about their experiences. By doing this, he believed that it would help both practitioners and academics in asking critical questions about the nature of teaching and the relationship between teachers and the wider ideological, political and economic undercurrents. This connection between progressive scholars and teachers added to the struggle and opposition against the dominant ideology, even if it did not result in overt action; 'sometimes, just thinking seriously can be a form of resistance itself' (Apple, 1988: 182).

Apple (1988) notes that the main positive force that leads to greater democratisation in schools is what he saw as the increasing number of practitioners who are willing to actively participate and collaborate to enhance social justice. He thought that this growing willingness to be actively engaged would 'foster the growth of new social movements and coalitions that will bring pressure on the school for greater equality' (1988: 196). This idea of forming alliances between those parties who are worried by the inequalities evident in schooling has been mirrored by Frank Coffield and Bill Williamson's 2012 book *From Exam Factories to Communities of Discovery: The Democratic Route*, which has partly been influenced by Apple's work. It advocates the forming of a broad set of alliances that include the world of work, local communities and other interested parties. It also calls for alliances with and between school management and practitioners 'which pull together changes instigated from the top with those demanded from the bottom' (Coffield and Williamson, 2011: 71). Their aim is to create 'communities of discovery, educators and learners become experimenters, researchers, thinkers, pragmatists and joint developers of a new curriculum' (2011: 71). Working in these communities of discovery enables them to become influential democratic professionals, exclusively for the benefit of others (2011). For these alliances to work, Apple (2006) argues that they must be active in facing up to the dominant ideology regarding schooling, as well as thinking tactically in countering the threat to a progressive and democratic education.

Educators have the independence and interdependence when working in alliances to make changes through progressive and critical practice. They have, regardless of systematic constraints, the ability to highlight specific facets of the curriculum which correspond to their values and social context (Avis and Orr, 2010). It is contested that education is firmly rooted in the social world; Apple seeks 'to place educational issues back in their social context, to situate what is happening to teachers, textbooks, curriculum, and technology in the larger social movements of which they are a part' (1988: 177).

REFLECTIVE TASK

Apple argues that educators should resist the increasing power of the dominant culture on education in general, but in particular the use of official knowledge, the standardised curriculum, the return to traditional teaching methods, and the growing associations between education and marketisation. It is understandably tricky for some educators to overtly and actively resist, but Apple makes a profound and intriguing statement in *Teachers and Texts: A Political Economy of*

Class and Gender Relations in Education (1988: 182): 'sometimes, just thinking seriously can be a form of resistance itself'.

Consider and reflect on your 'thinking seriously' about injustices that could hamper a democratic education, either from your own experiences as a student or from what you have witnessed in your practice. List your thoughts on resistance. How, if at all, could these thoughts be transformed into practical actions?

SUMMARY

Michael Apple is a key progressive educator and social activist of international prominence. Along with other like-minded educators, Apple has campaigned against the increasing power of the conservative and neoliberal ideology, and the accompanying market forces that affect schooling. He has advanced his idea that education should be transformational, emancipatory and empowering. His distinctive forte is in analysing educational structures in his native United States and in other capitalist countries, in particular regarding the curriculum with matters such as class, gender, race and the economy. The main aspect underpinning his work is democracy, which he feels is being eroded with the growing involvement of business and free markets in education. Apple cites his family as the reason for his left-wing lens on life and society. The major elements of his thinking relate to the concepts of reproduction, the curriculum, official knowledge and textbooks, marketisation and critical pedagogy. Apple considered that economic, social and cultural reproduction were linked to the neoliberal influence on schooling, especially in relation to the form and content of the curriculum. He thought that the curriculum was not a neutral phenomenon, but was biased in favour of the dominant middle-classes to the detriment of the issues of gender, race and the working-classes. The curriculum, he argued, was bolstered by what he termed official knowledge – knowledge included in textbooks created, approved and marketed by the dominant right-wing ideology. What was important, Apple contended, was that to counter this ideology educators needed to foster an environment that encouraged students to be critical in their analysis of the curriculum and sceptical of official knowledge.

Apple was influenced by the Frankfurt School philosophy. The school was active between the two world wars, during which time their thinking was shaped by the thoughts of Marx and Freud. It was a school of thought that was subversive and anti-establishment; their ideas were enthusiastically revived by critical educators during the 1960s and 1970s. Apple emphasised the significance that Habermas and Gramsci had on his thinking, which stressed that human activity cannot be separated from human culture and transformation in education. Apple's views on critical and progressive education can also be aligned with Freire, Ivan Illich, Peter McLaren and Giroux with their notion of linking politics with education. There are close associations also with Pierre Bourdieu and Basil Bernstein with their notion of social and cultural capital, and the significance they placed on language acquisition being associated with social class. Lawrence Stenhouse's argument that the curriculum should be free from the influence of the dominant culture and class of society also resonates with Apple's work. There are also similarities with fellow American Linda Darling-Hammond who advocated a more equitable form of education and the need for greater teacher professionalism. Apple's ideas also have strong links with John Dewey's notion of democratic education. Some of the criticisms he attracts centre on his writing. The language he uses is somewhat conspiratorial and emotive in nature. His ideas were deemed too radical and he seldom offered practical resolutions to the issues he presented. His ideas are quite problematic to put into practice for educators working within set curricula and standardised assessment. Nevertheless, his struggle for democracy in education merits practical consideration where possible.

GLOSSARY OF TERMS

Critical pedagogy   For Apple and other like-minded critical educational scholars, students should be encouraged to understand the origin and social composition of the knowledge they encounter. He feels that this can be achieved by helping students to expose the inequalities that are present but obscured in the curriculum and in other educational structures. The aim is to empower students by providing a democratic classroom environment that promotes social justice through active critical discourse.

Democracy   Apple's notion of democracy was similar to that of Dewey's in that democracy in education led to, and was synonymous with, democracy in society, where students became actively critical and questioning participants. Apple specifically considers that democracy encompasses aspects of social justice, and includes class, race and gender equality.

Ideology   As a broad definition, ideology is a classification of beliefs which is shaped by social, cultural, economic and political viewpoints. The ideology that Apple contested was that espoused by the conservatives and neoliberals who were influential in shaping education policy. He argues that it is an ideology that is deceptive in misrepresenting what really happens in society for the benefit of the dominant classes (Apple, 1979).

Marketisation   Marketisation is a neoliberal notion that education is a commodity. This involves allowing schools greater autonomy by offering a wider choice to parents and students. Neoliberal policy-makers felt this would lead to greater competition and as such would not only improve the quality of education available, but would create better economic outcomes. It embraces the structures of measurement, accountability, competition and management used in business.

Official knowledge   Official knowledge is constructed by those responsible to create education policy that seeks to replicate the status quo and inequalities in society to the detriment of those people who are not of the dominant culture and social class. It is endorsed and legitimised in the school curriculum and in school textbooks. Official knowledge stresses the requirement of competence, and as such places education as a prerequisite of the industry and business sectors.

Reproduction   A process closely linked with Apple's notion of official knowledge, whereby society continues to replicate itself. Reproduction can be represented as being economic, social or cultural, or a combination of all three. In education, it is perceived as a means of supplying passive employees for the economic needs of the state.

FURTHER READING

Apple, M. (2006) *Educating the Right Way: Markets, Standards, God, and Inequality* (2nd edn). Abingdon: Routledge.
An examination of how the right-wing conservative restoration has been increasingly involved in determining education policy in the United States, and internationally.

Apple, M. (2013) *Knowledge, Power, and Education: The Selected Works of Michael W. Apple* (World Library of Educationalists). Abingdon: Routledge.
An overview of Apple's writing spanning some thirty years, including excerpts from books, articles and papers. The book explores the development of his thinking and offers ideas of what can still be done in the field of progressive/critical education.

Apple, M. (ed.) (2017) *Cultural and Economic Reproduction in Education: Essays on Class, Ideology and the State.* Abingdon: Routledge.
This book is a wide-ranging review from a number of critical educators regarding the role of schooling and the effects of reproduction. This is a revised version that was first published in 1982.

Apple, M., Ball, S. and Gandin, L.-A. (eds) (2010) *The Routledge International Handbook for the Sociology of Education.* Abingdon: Routledge.
A comprehensive range of issues within thirty-seven chapters from leading progressive educational scholars. The topics covered include theoretical aspects, issues for practice, and forms of disparities and struggles.

REFERENCES

Anyon, J. (2011) *Marx and Education*. Abingdon: Routledge.
Apple, M. (1979) *Ideology and Curriculum*. Boston, MA: Routledge & Kegan Paul.
Apple, M. (1982) *Education and Power*. New York: Routledge.
Apple, M. (1988) *Teachers and Texts: A Political Economy of Class and Gender Relations in Education*. New York: Routledge.

Apple, M. (1997) 'What postmodernists forget: Cultural capital and official knowledge'. In: Halsey, A., Lauder, H., Brown, P. and Stuart Wells, A. (eds) *Education: Culture, Economy, Society*. Oxford: Oxford University Press.

Apple, M. (2000) *Official Knowledge: Democratic Education in a Conservative Age* (2nd edn). New York: Routledge.

Apple, M. (2003) *The State and the Politics of Knowledge*. New York: Routledge.

Apple, M. (2006) 'Producing inequalities: Neo-liberalism, neo-conservatism, and the politics of educational reform'. In: Lauder, H., Brown, P., Dillabough, J.-A. and Halsey, A. *Education, Globalization and Social Change*. Oxford: Oxford University Press.

Apple, M. (2013) *Can Education Change Society?* New York: Routledge.

Apple, M. (2018) *The Struggle for Democracy in Education: Lessons from Social Realities*. New York: Routledge.

Apple, M. and Christian-Smith, L. (eds) (1991) *The Politics of the Textbook*. New York: Routledge.

Aubrey, K. and Riley, A. (2017) *Understanding and Using Challenging Educational Theories*. London: Sage.

Aubrey, K. and Riley, A. (2019) *Understanding and Using Educational Theories* (2nd edn). London: Sage.

Avis, J. and Orr, K. (2010) 'Theory and practice' In: Avis, J., Fisher, R. and Thompson, R. *Teaching in Lifelong Learning: A Guide to Theory and Practice*. Maidenhead: Oxford University Press.

Bernstein, B. (2000) *Pedagogy, Symbolic Control and Identity: Theory, Research, Critique* (revised edn). Lanham, MD: Rowman & Littlefield.

Carlson, D. and Apple, M. (eds) (1998) *Power, Knowledge and Pedagogy: The Meaning of Democratic Education in Unsettling Times*. Oxford: Westview Press.

Coffield, S. and Williamson, B. (2012) *From Exam Factories to Communities of Discovery: The Democratic Route*. London: Institute of Education, University of London.

Fisher, R., Fulford, A., McNicholas, B. and Thompson, R. (2010) 'The curriculum in the lifelong learning sector'. In: Avis, J., Fisher, R. and Thompson, R. (eds) *Teaching in Lifelong Learning: A Guide to Theory and Practice*. Maidenhead: Oxford University Press.

Freire, P. (1970 [1996]) *Pedagogy of the Oppressed*. London: Penguin.

Gewirtz, S. and Cribb, A. (2009) *Understanding Education: A Sociological Perspective*. Cambridge: Polity Press.

Giroux, H. (2003) 'Critical theory and educational practice'. In: Darder, A., Baltodano, M. and Torres, R. (eds) *The Critical Pedagogy Reader*. New York: Continuum.

Hall, K., Horan, M., Ridgway, R., Murphy, M. and Cunningham, D. (2010) *Loris Malaguzzi and the Reggio Emilia Experience*. London: Bloomsbury.

Hatcher, R. (2006) 'Social class and schooling: Differentiation or democracy?' In: Cole, M. (ed.) *Education, Equality and Human Rights: Issues of Gender, 'Race', Sexuality, Disability and Social Class* (2nd edn). Abingdon: Routledge.

Hicks, D. (2013) 'Education for sustainability'. In: Ward, S. (ed.) *A Student's Guide to Education Studies* (3rd edn). London: Routledge.

Howlett, J. (2013) *Progressive Education: A Critical Introduction*. London: Bloomsbury.

Kelly, A. (2004) *The Curriculum: Theory and Practice* (5th edn). London: SAGE.

Moore, A. (2000) *Teaching and Learning: Pedagogy, Curriculum and Culture*. London: RoutledgeFalmer.

Peters, M. (2015) 'Interview with Michael Apple: The biography of a public intellectual'. *Open Review of Educational Research*, 2 (1): 105–17.

Robertson, S. (2000) *A Class Act: Changing Teachers' Work, the State, and Globalisation*. London: Falmer Press.

Schugurensky, D. (2014) *Paulo Freire*. London: Bloomsbury.

Scott, D. (2008) *Critical Essays on Major Curriculum Theorists*. London: Routledge.

Stenhouse, L. (1975) *An Introduction to Curriculum Research and Development*. Oxford: Heinemann Educational.

Torre, C. A. (2001) 'Michael W. Apple, 1942– '. In: Palmer, J. (ed.) *Fifty Modern Thinkers on Education: From Piaget to the Present*. Abingdon: Routledge.

Whitty, G. (1998) 'Citizens or consumers? Continuity and change in contemporary education policy'. In: Carlson, D. and Apple, M. (eds) *Power, Knowledge and Pedagogy: The Meaning of Democratic Education in Unsettling Times*. Oxford: Westview Press.

13
HENRY GIROUX

CRITICAL PEDAGOGY

LEARNING OUTCOMES

After reading this chapter, you should be able to:

- appreciate Giroux's background and his impact on education;
- understand his theoretical perspectives, in particular critical pedagogy;
- recognise the links between Giroux's ideas and those of other key educational thinkers;
- critically appraise his works;
- identify which aspects of Giroux's theories could be applied in practice.

KEY WORDS

Critical pedagogy; border pedagogy; radical education; corporate public pedagogy; postmodernism and feminism; transformative intellectuals; hidden curriculum; praxis curriculum model.

INTRODUCTION

Henry Giroux can be considered one of the most notable present-day thinkers and writers on education, but in particular on **critical pedagogy**, the role of schools and universities, the effects of neoliberalism and the plight of young people. He argues that the neoliberal economy has been a major driving force in the neglect and oppression of the younger generation. His central themes call for an emphasis on an education that embraces the community, and focuses on democracy, fairness and social justice. For these themes to be realised, he contends that teachers and others concerned with education should be politically active. It is only through democratic processes and the advance of a critical and progressive pedagogy that neoliberalism and what Giroux considers a society riven by class structures can be challenged. His writing is optimistic and promotes the idea of teachers developing the notions of human empowerment and participatory democracy, regardless of their specific subject field (Nicholls, 2010).

Giroux has striven to extend our understanding of the nexus between schools and politics. In doing so, he has defied the conventional positions of teachers and students within the schools and universities where they encounter each other. At the heart of Giroux's teaching and writing is a moral responsibility towards encouraging all those involved in education to engage in democratic practices and shared governance. These practices, he argues, cannot be handed down from previous generations; they need to be continuously discovered and rediscovered. It was with these underpinning thoughts that Giroux became a prominent and vocal advocate of the critical pedagogy group of thinkers, which was a fusion of the progressive educational ideas initiated by the Brazilian philosopher Paulo Freire. Freire's actions led him to evaluate the roles of teachers and students in view of an oppressive political environment and then plan for new and revolutionary curricula (Giroux et al., 1988). It was Freire who emphasised the notion of criticality and its relationship with Giroux's idea of **radical education** and pedagogy for both student and teacher:

> The more we live critically (this is what I would call a radical pedagogy in Giroux's sense), the more we internalise a radical and critical practice of education and the more we discover the impossibility of separating teaching and learning. The very practice of teaching involves learning on the part of those we are teaching, as well as learning, or relearning, on the part of those who teach. (1985: 177)

For Giroux, schools ought to be centres of cultural creativity and transformation but not reproduction. They should be the focus for critical and participatory democracy which welcomes diversity and a range of different cultural and social alliances. In this idea of democracy, schools accept and greet such diversity instead of 'serving the agenda of the elite, powerful minority or ideology' (Morrison, 2001: 280). Although his views developed and changed over the years, Giroux's radical stance, together with his visions of humanitarianism and social justice, are evident throughout his writing: 'Education is not only about issues of work and economics, but also about questions of justice, social freedom, and the capacity for democratic agency, action, and change as well as the related issues of power, exclusion, and citizenship' (2011: 121).

In the Preface of Giroux's *Ideology, Culture and the Process of Schooling* (1981), Aronowitz emphasises how Giroux's work is an enduring 'exploration of how education may contribute to the emancipation of human beings' (Aronowitz, 1981: 3). Such longevity continues in Giroux's writing some thirty-five years later. Giroux's thoughts, as well as the criticisms he encountered, together with the connections he has with other educational thinkers, and some ways in which his thoughts could be applied in practice, will be covered in this chapter.

GIROUX, THE PERSON

Henry Giroux was born into a working-class family in 1943, in Providence, Rhode Island. He entered academia almost by default, gaining a basketball scholarship which enabled him eventually to enrol in a teacher training college. He enjoyed the collective shared aims of student life and he became acutely aware of the unjust aspects of racism, sexism and class division (Nicholls, 2010). With the United States' involvement in the Vietnam War he also developed a strong sense of social justice, and the more he read about social theory the more he became attracted to teaching: 'Not only did I see [teaching] as a way to make an impact but I saw teaching as a wonderfully noble profession' (Giroux, 1992: 14). Giroux went on to complete a master's degree in history, after which he was employed as a high school social science teacher as well as being deeply involved as a community activist. He worked with the black community in Baltimore, which, at that time, was a highly segregated city. In the schools where he taught, he was recognised for his radical approaches to the curriculum (Nicholls, 2010).

In 1977, Giroux received his doctorate from Carnegie Mellon University; his thesis was written on curriculum theory, sociology and the sociology of education. He then relocated to Boston University where he taught from 1977 to 1983. It is interesting to note that while at Boston University, Giroux originally had his academic contract rejected because senior university staff were at odds with the radical views in his two early books: *Ideology, Culture and the Process of Schooling* (1981) and *Theory and Resistance in Education: A Pedagogy for the Opposition* (1983) (Nicholls, 2010). His next post was as Professor of Education and Renowned Scholar in Residence at Miami University, Ohio, from 1983 to 1992. Then, from 1992, he became Waterbury Chair Professor of Secondary Education at Penn State University. Later he assumed the role of the Global Television Network Chair in English and Cultural Studies at McMaster University, Canada (Morrison, 2001).

Giroux is often regarded as a leading light for the concept of critical pedagogy. He has a gift of making even the most complicated concept clear and comprehensible.

Furthermore, he writes with a conviction that has emanated from his past experience as a teacher. He has written numerous articles and books, mostly within the field of education, but lately his writing has also encompassed issues of culture (Howlett, 2013). His ideas in relation to his advancement of critical pedagogy are best discovered in his seminal work *Border Crossings: Cultural Workers and the Politics of Education* (1992) where he lists nine characteristics required for critical pedagogy (Scott, 2008). However, it is likely that Giroux himself would assert that critical pedagogy has evolved from an amalgamation of previous notions about social thought and radical education movements that have endeavoured to connect teaching and schools 'to democratic principles of society and to transformative social action in the interests of oppressed communities' (Darder et al., 2003: 3). The next section will explore the theoretical aspects of Giroux's work.

THE BACKGROUND AND THEORY OF CRITICAL PEDAGOGY

Giroux is best known for his ideas on critical pedagogy. However, to fully appreciate the context it is appropriate to explore the notion of radical education and how politics, culture, **postmodernism and feminism** underpin his philosophy. This section will then consider Giroux's notion of critical pedagogy, before reflecting on his thoughts on **border pedagogy**, the curriculum and teacher professionalism.

Radical educators such as Giroux examined and interrogated the very foundations of teaching. As a group, they contested the conventional sociopolitical and philosophical justifications for learning and teaching. The aim of the radical educator is to give power to the student by transforming the association between learners and teachers, with the long-term goal of achieving social reformation and equality (Preece and Griffin, 2006). However, to achieve this goal, radical educators contend that the education systems themselves also need to be transformed:

> Educational systems and the people within them need to problematise what seems normal. Within that the notion of how knowledge is perceived at all needs to be re-examined.
> (Preece and Griffin, 2006: 68)

For Giroux, radical education is not a stand-alone concept that relates to a specific subject or speciality, nor does it describe a form of knowledge. He argues that radical education has three features: 'it is interdisciplinary ... it questions the fundamental categories of all disciplines, and it has a public mission of making society more democratic' (Giroux, 1992: 10).

Giroux was incensed by the increasing use of neoliberal and corporate strategies, which he saw as encroaching on education in the United States, contradicting his notion of education being an active agent for social justice. Giroux saw such neoliberalism as serving the needs of private advantage where economic advancement becomes more important than matters of social democracy. Neoliberalism came at the expense of the marginalised in society and caused the stripping down of the welfare state. Giroux termed this '**corporate public pedagogy**', the purpose of which was to serve the individual in a competitive environment where material gain was to the fore. In the culture of corporate public pedagogy, matters of social injustice such as gender, race and social class issues are all undervalued and normalised for the sake of economic gain. Giroux described this as 'an all-encompassing cultural horizon for producing market identities, values and practices' (2011: 134).

Giroux would also argue that the idea of corporate public pedagogy would not take into account the rapidly changing and diverse multicultural society. Giroux felt that school culture served the needs of the privileged learners of the governing and middle classes at the expense of the aspirations of the disadvantaged, diverse and often neglected sections of society. Radical educators contested that the United States, by way of its discriminatory policies, funding and legal powers, 'shaped school practice in the interest of capitalist rationality' (Giroux, 1985: xv). What was needed was a culture that promoted an environment where learners could be critically active and develop into democratically spirited members of society (Giroux, 2003).

Both postmodernism and feminism underpin Giroux's notion of critical pedagogy. Like other similar postmodernist thinkers, his stance opposes the established ways of understanding and the formation of knowledge (Bartlett et al., 2001). For Giroux, education is far too complex and ever-changing, and he is sceptical of the conventional importance placed upon histories, society and knowledge itself. The postmodernist ideas which are the basis for critical pedagogy value the notion that there are no right or wrong answers to problems. Indeed, 'there are *many* sides to a problem, and often these sides are linked to certain class, race and gender interests' (McLaren, 2003: 71). Postmodernists take into account the differences and complexities of educational settings and cultures with a view to empowering learners to prevail against social limitations. Szkudlarek contests that education is not 'collective nor individual; it is a postmodern subject within which social, cultural, and political processes create a sphere of conflict and negotiation' (1993: 111). This view of postmodernism aligns itself with feminism; both emphasise that people's social and cultural circumstances affect their lives (Ormston et al., 2014). Giroux has argued for the feminist cause – a cause which called for women to have an equal say in pedagogical practice and in the formation of the curriculum, as well as advancing feminist educational theoretical standpoints (Preece and Griffin, 2006).

The purpose of critical pedagogy, for Giroux, is to reveal the disparities that are often concealed in different educational establishments. This is achieved first by emancipating students in the classrooms (Howlett, 2013). To achieve student emancipation as part of the critical pedagogy process, teachers should endeavour to

> Take young people beyond the world they are familiar with and [make] clear how classroom knowledge, values, desires, and social relations are always implicated in power ... critical pedagogy becomes a project that stresses the need for teachers and students to actively transform knowledge rather than simply consume it. (Giroux, 2011: 6–7)

As such, the student becomes an integral element of the education process and in doing so strives to critically question society and its problems to look for fundamentally different solutions; thus, the role of critical pedagogy 'is to transform teachers, schools, and ultimately society' (Sadovnik et al., 2013: 196). According to Morrison (2001), a number of principles are required for Giroux's notion of critical pedagogy:

- Attention needs to be paid to pedagogy as much as to traditional scholarship, (re)constructing schools as democratic public spheres.
- Ethics are of central concern in critical pedagogy, questioning educative practices that perpetuate inequality, exploitation and human suffering.
- The political implications of celebration of difference in democratic societies must be addressed.
- A language that embraces several versions of solidarity and politics needs to be developed.
- There is no single script or grand narrative, but rather, several scripts, several curricula, several versions of education which need to be critically interrogated, just as there are several versions and areas of exploitation and oppression in society which mediate each other.
- Cultural representations in curricula have to be regarded as discourses of power and asymmetrical relations of power.
- The curriculum is a 'cultural script' whose messages should be susceptible to critique.
- The politics of voice require an affirmation of diversity and of the rights of oppressed groups for recognition in education.

(Morrison, 2001: 282)

Giroux amplified his notion of critical pedagogy to challenge current boundaries of knowledge, which he termed 'border pedagogy'. A key facet of border pedagogy is the acceptance of the connections between knowledge and power, and how in practice this is used to bolster certain forms of authority (Giroux, 1992). He felt that for equality to be truly achieved in society, the function of power should be unmasked and refigured (Morrison, 2001). For Giroux, border pedagogy, as a process, was meant to cultivate a 'democratic public philosophy that respects the notion of difference as part of a common struggle to extend the quality of public life' (Giroux, 1992: 28). For this to happen, he argued that students and teachers alike should examine and confront conventional boundaries (or borders) 'of power ... decision-making, cultural and social representation in the curricula' (Morrison, 2001: 283). Border pedagogy, then, is an opportunity for educators and students to destroy the boundaries that exist in education that fortify authority. He contended that learners ought to 'engage knowledge as border-crossers, as people moving in and out of borders constructed around coordinates of difference and power' (Giroux, 1992: 29).

These aspects of power and difference are very noticeable in Giroux's thoughts on the curriculum. He describes what he called the '**hidden curriculum**' as the way in which authority tacitly embeds sets of values and beliefs by way of ordered and structural school procedures and routines. The hidden curriculum is an intervention to promote 'social control, one that functions to provide differential forms of schooling for different classes of children' (Giroux, 1983: 47). He also contested that the hidden curriculum was not just about social control, but it was additionally 'the ground on which ideological and political struggles were fought and hence a potential for change' (Whitty, 1985: 47). Further to this, Giroux extended Stenhouse's model of the process curriculum (Stenhouse, 1975). He, like other critical pedagogy theorists, advanced the **praxis curriculum model**, which had at its core the idea of social transformation and the nexus between theory and practice. The praxis model perceives knowledge as provisional and accessible to criticism; it confronts traditional notions of knowledge, and the opinion of authority and coercion. The praxis model is valuable because it has explicit application to students' everyday lives (Curtis and Pettigrew, 2010). The intention of the praxis model is to nurture 'critical consciousness: The cultivation of informed action as a foundation for hope in the future' (Curtis and Pettigrew, 2010: 38).

As a final point in this section, and very much in line with critical and border pedagogy, Giroux took an interest in teacher professionalism and in particular how this was shaped at an early stage during initial teacher education. He criticised teacher education programmes, which he thought reinforced traditional practice with its rules and ways of thinking about measures of achievement, the transmission of knowledge and teacher competence. Furthermore, he thought that teacher education programmes in the United States focused on the dominant languages of competencies and standards (Moore, 2004). These practices were, he considered, left unchallenged, which in turn resulted in a move away from the perception of a teacher as a professional to that of a teacher as a technician (Giroux, 1981). Teachers, he contested, were not educated or encouraged to apply the different cultural and personal aspirations of students in their teaching practice: 'The result is a form of pedagogical violence that prevents teachers establishing conditions which allow students to speak with an authentic voice' (Giroux, 1981: 155).

Such restricted and didactic methods he thought were opposite to the democratic, experimental and emancipatory approaches to teaching espoused by Dewey. The connections with Dewey, and other progressive and radical educators, are outlined in the next section.

LINKS WITH OTHER THEORISTS

There is a clear-cut affiliation with John Dewey's desire to create a democratic form of education, which also encourages citizenship (Aronowitz, 1981). Giroux considered that critical pedagogy with its contention of critical reflection, thoughtful reasoning and the fostering of community spirit is 'central to the cultivation of what John Dewey once called "democracy as a way of life"' (Giroux, 2011: 8). Giroux's notion of democracy is directly related to Dewey's ideas and his conviction in the positive power of education as a force for social justice; like Dewey, Giroux also criticised the traditional didactic methods of teaching and learning (Howlett, 2013).

There are also strong links between the Brazilian philosopher Paulo Freire and Giroux. Both considered that their work had a much wider application than in schools. They both sought to emancipate students and their communities, and in doing so they believed that organised oppression would be abolished (Morrison, 2001). Freire facilitated learners to create an awareness of freedom, to identify and understand oppressive leanings and language, 'and learn to read the word and the world as part of a broader struggle for justice and democracy' (Giroux, 2011: 152). For Freire, then, critical pedagogy was not just a matter of students learning specific skills in literacy; it was also an approach to learning about literacy as a way of actively engaging in the world. It was more than learning facts; rather, it was a way of questioning and confronting conventions and beliefs, and engaging in critical discussions with the past to look forward to a future that would not just be a replication of the present (Giroux, 2011). Freire was a leading light for Giroux and other radical educators. It is suggested that from Freire, Giroux was inspired to reconfigure 'some of the implicit utopianism of the romantic tradition through the addition of a healthy dose of urban and inter-cultural pedagogical experience' (Irwin, 2012: 5). Other critical and progressive educators who have associations with Giroux are Peter McLaren, Ivan Illich and Michael Apple. In particular, Apple developed Giroux's notion of the teacher as a 'transformative intellectual, siding with the oppressed and committed to the advancement of progressive projects through the educative process' (Carlson and Apple, 1998: 26).

There are also some similarities and differences between the work of Giroux and Pierre Bourdieu. According to Giroux, schools are places of cultural and social reproduction that exemplify what Bourdieu terms 'cultural capital' (Aronowitz, 1981). Bourdieu argued that it is through cultural capital that the middle classes can retain their place in the 'process of social reproduction while making this inequality legitimate ... to keep social order and perpetuate the existing inequalities' (Bartlett et al., 2001: 9). Although the similarities between the two regarding inequalities of social reproduction are acknowledged, Giroux differed in that he considered any analysis of social reproduction should also take into consideration matters of race and gender as well as social class (Gewirtz and Cribb, 2009).

Giroux thought that schools that take students from subgroups of class and race are typified by over-restrictive systems and regulations, which in turn results in a passive and powerless student body for the marginalised. Basil Bernstein argued that such a regulation-dominated oppressive school environment is detrimental to the learning and social relations of students; Bernstein termed this a visible pedagogy. This type of teaching is an anathema to the critical and border pedagogy espoused by Giroux. Like

Giroux, Bernstein felt that such a controlling and hierarchical teacher–student relationship was unjust, and that it favoured the students who were from the dominant race and class of the school. These students were able to 'operate within a classroom experience where flexible and interpersonal relations (soft socialisation), replace overt rule conformity' (Giroux, 1981: 75). Stenhouse and Giroux had similar ideas regarding the way in which students can become important parts of the education process by teachers facilitating them to critically question society. Furthermore, it is suggested that Stenhouse's process curriculum model was a prototype for Giroux's notion of the praxis curriculum model.

CRITIQUING THE THEORY

Giroux's radical ideas have been criticised as being over-optimistic and unachievable in today's schools. The main criticisms are concerned with the impracticality of his ideas as well as their overtly political nature. Morrison questions whether Giroux's writings have any explicit effect on teaching practice, or whether his work is too idealistic and does nothing more than 'put fire into one's belly' (Morrison, 2001: 284). Furthermore, the central theme to critical pedagogy is that teachers encourage their students to question education practices. Gore, a teacher educator, found when she tried to do this with her students, it resulted in some unpredicted and not so positive outcomes. A number of her students felt they could not tolerate working in such restrictive working environments and never started their teaching careers; some of those who did take up teaching did so for a short time before changing careers. Others who persevered with a critical and questioning approach to practice were sometimes shunned by their colleagues and jeopardised their salary as a result of doing so; some others just accepted the status quo (Gore, 2003: 339).

There are also concerns with the term 'critical pedagogy'. Carlson and Apple argue that

> It has often become something of a 'sliding signifier' – a slogan that is employed to mean multiple things, some of which unfortunately have either lost their critical edge or are simply restatements in a new and more difficult language of things that radical educators have been doing for years. (1998: 25–6)

Other criticisms of Giroux's idea of critical pedagogy include that it has not been accepted or endorsed by any Western government as a structure for learning and teaching; neither did Giroux clarify how critical pedagogy could be of benefit to students in gaining transferable skills to enhance employability (Howlett, 2013). Moreover, an overtly politicised form of education, particularly one that is led by teachers themselves, in school systems that are increasingly being compelled to focus on results and standards, is a very contentious proposition (Howlett, 2013). Similar criticism is also levelled at Giroux's praxis curriculum model, which Curtis and

Pettigrew suggest 'risks representing to learners a partial and overtly critical standpoint on the world' (2010: 380).

Much of Giroux's work criticises the traditional role of schools as being authoritative and retaining power over students. This, however, disregards the student-centred innovations that are evident in practice in schools; despite the highly regulated curriculum in an ever-increasingly managerial profession, teachers do strive for a democratic model of professionalism that values matters of reflection, collegiality and collaboration between students and teachers and other stakeholders (Sachs, 2003). Such collaboration is explained by hooks as 'mapping-out terrains of commonality, connection, and shared concern with teaching practices' (1994: 130).

⚙ APPLYING GIROUX'S IDEAS IN PRACTICE

Even though Giroux's thinking has undoubtedly given progressive teachers food for thought to apply in their classrooms, Preece and Griffin contend that his ideas 'present ideological, rather than practitioner perspectives on pedagogy' (2006: 60). Most of Giroux's suggestions for practical applications for his ideas are found in *On Critical Pedagogy* (2011); however, he does question just how much teachers can influence the curriculum and the decisions made in classrooms in schools today (Giroux, 2011). Yet he maintains that teachers should cultivate a critical pedagogy that connects classroom practice with society as a whole: teachers need to become '**transformative intellectuals**' (Morrison, 2001). Transformative intellectuals make learning and teaching political acts by fostering students' own life experiences and their consciousness about subjects of contention, hence enabling students themselves to become critics; in doing so the aim is

> to expose oppression, inequality and the constrictions of social identities within asymmetrical relations of power of different groups in society, with a view to transforming students' ways of looking at their lives, life situations and life chances, so that they experience empowerment and emancipation as members of diverse cultures and communities. They develop their 'voice' within participatory democracies. (Morrison, 2001: 282–3)

Being a transformational intellectual requires unconventional and progressive methods of teaching, which need to be complemented by a form of student–teacher relationship that involves discussion, negotiation, questioning and communication; it also needs self-reflection to be embedded into teachers' practice (Giroux, 2011). Such self-reflection needs to be augmented by research and action so that they can, with other teachers, help influence aspects of school experiences in the name of social justice (Goodson, 2005). In doing so, teachers begin to create their own classroom theories and reform their practices, which will hopefully go beyond the confines of the classroom with the promise of transforming society as a whole. Giroux thought that teachers could achieve this in their practice by actively questioning traditionally held beliefs about teaching methods, forms of knowledge and assessment techniques. By taking such a critical standpoint, together with a self-reflective and enquiry-based approach, 'teachers can help to raise the political consciousness of themselves, their fellow teachers, and their students' (Giroux, 2011: 42).

What is of importance is the understanding and recognition of the different issues in education and in their everyday lives that students experience. The use of these different experiences in teaching gives a meaningful basis of learning and underlines notions of principles, power and politics – all of which Giroux suggests are essential for students and teachers to develop their communication and collaboration (Giroux, 2011). Furthermore, encouraging students to question and argue from the basis of their own experiences within a democratically enriched classroom helps develop a sense of resistance to oppression; it also enhances their progress in thinking critically about the broader issues of inequality and injustice in the world. Giroux argued that students resist the dominant cultural systems more than we would expect; such resistance is not only confined to anti-authoritarian behaviour, but also through membership of subcultures that challenge the controlling culture (Giroux, 1983; Anyon, 2011). The student voice could be used within school councils to fulfil their democratic rights, along with teachers, parents and school administrators (Apple, 2013). Even though Giroux argues that traditional authority in classroom relations needs to change to allow a greater contribution for students to air their voice and resistance, he was also clear that certain pedagogy practices are expected for schools to function:

> These are: a respect for the views of others; the possibility of communicating; an orderly exchange of views; an acceptance that one may be wrong; and the need to be tolerant of other people's viewpoints. (Scott, 2008: 108)

Giroux laments the lack of self-reflection, critical thinking and imagination evident in public schools in the United States: schooling has become a 'dead zone' where teaching to assessment and seeking ways to exclude badly performing students have become priorities (Giroux, 2011: 153). To counter such passivity, where students because of their race or class are both voiceless and powerless, Giroux offers a practical example, which is very much associated with Freirean pedagogy:

> Students could be asked to write short papers that speculate on the meaning and the power of literacy and why it was so central to the civil rights movement. These may be read by the entire class with each student elaborating on his or her position and offering commentary as a way of entering into a critical discussion of the history of racial exclusion, reflecting on how its ideologies and formations still haunt American society in spite of the triumphal dawn of an allegedly post-racial Obama era. (Giroux, 2011: 155)

This teaching method is aligned to the seminar approach favoured by Giroux because it encourages student engagement with discussion. Giroux, although he prescribes the issues and topics for discussion, wishes to let students have the opportunity to take a position they believe in from their experience and their personal history, and then to defend that position. Although it does not matter what position is taken, the student should appreciate the effect that position has on others. In doing this, Giroux is politicising his teaching and the subject being discussed. Students are then agents in their learning and as such become 'self-conscious about the social relationships that undergird the learning process' (Giroux, 1992: 16). What is central to Giroux in the use of discussions and seminars is the significance of the student voice in the stories of their experiences which help them to justify their point of view. Giroux felt that these stories opened up even larger issues of education philosophy – for example, using the actual voices of young black people to 'talk about the hidden curriculum of racism, about what black kids have to give up to become academically successful' (Giroux, 1992: 16). Giroux would argue that all students have experiences and that these are influenced, for better or worse, by their personal feelings, religious beliefs, languages, culture and family ties (1992).

Once students feel comfortable in discussing their own histories and experiences in matters of social justice, they should be encouraged to put these into practice in the classroom so they actually act as if they are living and learning in a democracy. Striving for social justice and democracy in the world is an ongoing struggle, which Peterson (2003) suggests could begin in the classroom by emphasising that many marginalised people have gained from such struggles, and students should decide whether or not to be involved in the struggles. Like Giroux, Peterson argues that the specific subject content areas are not so important, as they can be intertwined around themes of democracy and social justice. Current national and international social issues can be raised with recourse to curricula resources and texts that empower students (Peterson, 2003). This form of teaching, as we have seen, should be a form of critical enquiry and 'of building a social imagination that works within a language of hope' (McLaren, 2003: 92). It is this shared understanding of language that students can use not only as a debating tool with other students in classrooms, but also as a means of helping teachers and students to construct the foundations for democracy and justice in society as a whole (McLaren, 2003).

From a teacher's own developmental point of view within critical pedagogy, they also need to listen critically to the voice of their students during seminar discussions. This critical listening is of importance because it allows the teacher to adopt a more self-reflective understanding of the boundaries of their bias regarding their own political standpoint, and personal and pedagogical values. In doing so, teachers, while perhaps not agreeing with the views listened to, respect and acknowledge the student's history and experience. This critical listening enables teachers to become self-critical and reflective of their own experiences and stories, and reinforces the notion of teachers as intellectuals. This in turn keeps the discussions and seminars unfettered and subject to continuing criticality (Giroux, 1992).

It is recognised that it is somewhat troublesome to put into practice some of Giroux's ideas of critical pedagogy, particularly because of their ideological nature and the restrictions of a national curriculum. Nevertheless, his views on student voice and his altogether inclusive approach to teaching and learning are all embedded in the continuing struggles for social justice. Just having an awareness of the inequalities of oppression will help us develop our classroom practice and seek to address these issues. Finally, there are some areas, such as the celebration of student difference and the use of seminars and discussions, and self-reflection, which are indeed of a practical nature.

REFLECTIVE TASK

One of the principles of Giroux's notion of critical pedagogy is to encourage the student voice in education to confirm and celebrate diversity, and the rights of marginalised groups.

What procedures are there in your setting that enable the voice of difference to be heard?

What other processes could be put in place to develop this voice even further?

SUMMARY

Henry Giroux is arguably one of the most influential progressive and radical thinkers and writers on education today. He has railed against the effects that neoliberal ideology has had on public education, which he argues has had negative connotations for many young people, particularly those from oppressed groups by virtue of their race, culture, class or gender. He has been relentless in trying to demonstrate the need for a link between politics and schools, where schools and those who work and study in them take a moral responsibility to engage in democratic practices through his notion of critical pedagogy. For Giroux, education is more than just economic gain; it should be about issues of social justice, democracy, and being an agent for change and fairness for all. His ideas of critical pedagogy and border pedagogy are, to some extent, ideological stances, but they also have very profound practical implications and applications for progressive teachers with the emphasis on self-reflection and self-criticism, the use of enquiry, and the striving for democratic teacher–student relationships.

Giroux is one of a number of radical educators who took a revolutionary approach to teaching and learning which questioned traditional thoughts on education starting with John Dewey. He can also readily be associated with the anti-oppression position taken by Paulo Freire, and, to a certain degree, with Pierre Bourdieu and Basil Bernstein who stressed the relevance of culture and social reproduction on the education aspirations and achievements of students. There are further similarities with other progressive thinkers such as Michael Apple, Ivan Illich, Peter McLaren and the curriculum theorist Lawrence Stenhouse. A number of criticisms are levelled at his ideas, particularly the meaning and practicality of his critical pedagogy. Many of his ideas, however, are worthwhile for practice, such as his inclusive approach to learning and teaching, the notion of teachers as transformative intellectuals and the promotion of the student voice. Giroux's writings are filled with hope and visions of social justice, even within increasingly restrictive and market-driven educational systems. Finally, perhaps a fitting overview of the value of Giroux's work should come from Morrison:

> His work holds out hope for a better life for us all. His work is profoundly humanitarian; that is unsettling as it is optimistic. Education needs its visionaries. (Morrison, 2001: 284)

GLOSSARY OF TERMS

Border pedagogy   Giroux expanded the idea of critical pedagogy to contest the boundaries of knowledge, which he termed 'border pedagogy'. The main aspect of border pedagogy is the recognition of the relationship between knowledge and power, and how this is employed to strengthen particular forms of authority. He argued that for equality to be genuinely reached in society, power should be exposed and refigured (Morrison, 2011). Border pedagogy therefore offers students and teachers the prospect to demolish the boundaries that occur in education that reinforce authority.

Critical pedagogy   For Giroux, the aim of critical pedagogy is to uncover the inequalities that are frequently hidden in schools and other learning establishments; the idea is to emancipate the students in the classroom. This is achieved through a process that 'stresses the need for teachers and students to actively transform knowledge rather than simply consume it' (Giroux, 2011: 7). In doing so, the student becomes an integral part of the education process by endeavouring to critically challenge society and its problems (Sadovnik et al., 2013).

Hidden curriculum   Giroux argues that the hidden curriculum is a way in which authority implicitly embeds sets of values and beliefs by way of ordered and structural school procedures and routines. The hidden curriculum is an imposition to advance 'social control, one that functions to provide differential forms of schooling for different classes of children' (Giroux, 1983: 47).

Corporate public pedagogy   Giroux thought that neoliberalism functioned as a tool for private advantage where economic gain becomes more important than the advancement of social democracy. He argued that education in the USA was being increasingly driven by neoliberal and corporate strategies, which conflicted with his idea of education being a dynamic instrument for social justice. Neoliberalisim disadvantaged the maginalised of society and was the demise of many of the functions of the welfare state. Giroux named this 'corporate public pedagogy', a form of pedagogy that served the individual in an economic competitive environment. Within the culture of corporate public pedagogy, issues of social injustices, social class and race are all devalued for the sake of financial advantage.

Postmodernism and feminism   Both postmodernism and feminism are the foundations of Giroux's notion of critical pedagogy. Postmodern thinkers such as Giroux challenge the conventional ways of understanding the formation of knowledge (Bartlett et al., 2001). Giroux thought that education was far too complex and fluid, and he was distrustful of the established importance given to histories, society and knowledge itself. Postmodernist ideas are fundamental to critical pedagogy, as they value the concept that there are no right or wrong answers to problems.

Feminism is very much associated with postmodernism as both stress that people's social and cultural situations affect their lives (Ormston et al., 2014).

Praxis curriculum model   The praxis curriculum model is an extension of Lawrence Stenhouse's model of the process curriculum (Stenhouse, 1975). Giroux, like other critical pedagogy thinkers, advanced the praxis curriculum model, which has at its core the idea of social transformation and the link between practice and theory. It recognises knowledge as provisional and accessible to criticism, and challenges traditional notions about knowledge, as well as the view of authority and oppression.

Radical education   Radical education examines and scrutinises the foundations of teaching; it also contests the conventional socio-political and philosophical foundations that underpin learning and teaching. The aim of radical education and radical educators is to empower learners by transforming the relationship between students and teachers with the eventual goal of achieving social reformation and equality (Preece and Griffin, 2006).

Transformative intellectuals   Transformative intellectuals are teachers who make learning and teaching political acts by nurturing learners' personal life experiences as well as their consciousness about topics of contention; this in turn empowers learners to become critics. 'They develop their "voice" within participatory democracies' (Morrison, 2001: 283). Transformative intellectuals require alternative and progressive teaching methods that are complemented by the form of teacher–student relationship that includes discussion, negotiation, questioning and communication; self-reflection also needs to be grounded in teachers' practice (Giroux, 2011).

FURTHER READING

Giroux, H. (1988) *Teachers as Intellectuals: Towards a Critical Pedagogy of Learning?* South Hadley, MA: Bergen & Garvey.
Giroux explores the matters of transformation and empowerment, and the relationships between schools and society at large.

Giroux, H. (1997) 'Crossing the boundaries of education discourse: Modernism, postmodernism and feminism'. In: Halsey, A., Lauder, H., Brown, P. and Wells, A. (eds) *Education: Culture, Economy and Society*. Oxford: Oxford University Press.
An analysis of how modernism, postmodernism and feminism shape radical education.

Giroux, H. (2000) *Breaking in to the Movies: Film and the Culture of Politics*. New York: Routledge.
This book uncovers the role of films as powerful teaching methods when exploring issues of society and culture.

Giroux. H. (2009) *Youth in a Suspect Society: Democracy or Disposability?* New York: Palgrave-Macmillan.
Giroux reveals how public policy has forsaken the aspirations of young people.

McLaren, P. (2006) *Life in Schools: An Introduction to Critical Pedagogy in the Foundations of Education*. Boston, MA: Pearson.
An example of how teachers can practically apply critical pedagogy into their classrooms through the formation of communities of practice.

REFERENCES

Anyon, J. (2011) *Marx and Education*. London: Routledge.
Apple, M. (2013) *Can Education Change Society?* London: Routledge.
Aronowitz, S. (1981) 'Preface'. In: Giroux, H. (ed.) *Ideology, Culture and the Process of Schooling*. London: Falmer Press.
Bartlett, S., Burton, D. and Peim, N. (2001) *Introduction to Education Studies*. London: Paul Chapman.
Carlson, D. and Apple, M. (eds) (1998) *Power/Knowledge/Pedagogy: The Meaning of Democratic Education in Unsettling Times*. Oxford: Westview Press.
Curtis, W. and Pettigrew, A. (2010) *Education Studies Reflective Reader*. Exeter: Learning Matters.
Darder, A., Baltodano, M. and Torres, R. (eds) (2003) *The Critical Pedagogy Reader*. London: RoutledgeFalmer.
Freire, P. (1985) *The Politics of Education: Culture, Power and Liberation*. London: Bergin & Garvey.
Gewirtz, S. and Cribb, A. (2009) *Understanding Education: A Sociological Perspective*. Cambridge: Polity Press.
Giroux, H. (1981) *Ideology, Culture and the Process of Schooling*. London: Falmer Press.
Giroux, H. (1983) *Theory and Resistance in Education: A Pedagogy for the Opposition*. London: Heinemann Educational.

Giroux, H. (1985) 'Introduction'. In: Freire, P. (ed.) *The Politics of Education: Culture, Power and Liberation*. Westport, CT: Bergin & Garvey.

Giroux, H. (1992) *Border Crossings: Cultural Workers and the Politics of Education*. New York: Routledge.

Giroux, H. (2003) 'Critical theory and educational practice'. In: Darder, A., Baltodano, M. and Torres, R. (eds) *The Critical Pedagogy Reader*. London: RoutledgeFalmer.

Giroux, H. (2011) *On Critical Pedagogy*. New York: Continuum.

Giroux, H., Shumway, D., Smith, P. and Sosnoski, T. (1988) 'The need for cultural studies'. In: Giroux, H. (ed.) *Teachers as Intellectuals: Towards a Critical Pedagogy of Learning?* South Hadley, MA: Bergen & Garvey.

Goodson, I. (2005) *Learning, Curriculum and Life Politics: The Selected Works of Ivor F. Goodson*. London: Routledge.

Gore, J. (2003) 'What we can do for you! What can "we" do for "you"? Struggling over empowerment in critical and feminist pedagogy'. In: Darder, A., Baltodano, M. and Torres, R. (eds) *The Critical Pedagogy Reader*. London: RoutledgeFalmer.

hooks, b. (1994) *Teaching to Transgress: Education as the Practice of Freedom*. London: Routledge.

Howlett, J. (2013) *Progressive Education: A Critical Introduction*. London: Bloomsbury.

Irwin, J. (2012) *Paulo Freire's Philosophy of Education*. London: Continuum.

McLaren, P. (2003) 'Critical pedagogy: A look at the major concepts'. In: Darder, A., Baltodano, M. and Torres, R. (eds) *The Critical Pedagogy Reader*. London: RoutledgeFalmer.

Moore, A. (2004) *The Good Teacher: Dominant Discourses in Teaching and Teacher Education*. London: Routledge.

Morrison, K. (2001) 'Henry Giroux, 1943–'. In: Palmer, J. (ed.) *Fifty Modern Thinkers on Education: From Piaget to the Present*. Abingdon: Routledge.

Nicholls, D. (2010) 'Henry Giroux: Neoliberalism's nemesis'. *The Encyclopaedia of Informal Education*. Available online at: http://infed.org/mobi/henry-a-giroux

Ormston, R., Spencer, L., Barnard, M. and Snape, D. (2014) 'The foundations of qualitative research'. In: Richie, J., Lewis, J., McNaughton Nicholls, C. and Ormston, R. (eds) *Qualitative Research Practice* (2nd edn). London: SAGE.

Peterson, R. (2003) 'Teaching how to read the world and change it: Critical pedagogy in the intermediate grades'. In: Darder, A., Baltodano, M. and Torres, R. (eds) *The Critical Pedagogy Reader*. London: RoutledgeFalmer.

Preece, J. and Griffin, C. (2006) 'Radical and feminist pedagogies'. In: Jarvis, P. (ed.) *The Theory and Practice of Teaching* (2nd edn). London: Routledge.

Sachs, J. (2003) *The Activist Teaching Profession*. Buckingham: Open University Press.

Sadovnik, A., Cookson, P. and Semel, S. (eds) (2013) *Exploring Education* (4th edn). London: Routledge.

Scott, D. (2008) *Critical Essays on Major Curriculum Theorists*. London: Routledge.

Stenhouse, L. (1975) *An Introduction to Curriculum Research and Development*. Oxford: Heinemann.

Szkudlarek, T. (1993) *The Problem of Freedom in Postmodern Education*. West Westport, CT: Bergin and Garvey.

Whitty, G. (1985) *Sociology and School Knowledge: Curriculum Theory, Research and Politics*. London: Methuen.

14

HOWARD GARDNER

MULTIPLE INTELLIGENCES AND EDUCATION

LEARNING OUTCOMES

After reading this chapter, you should be able to:

- understand the life and works of Howard Gardner;
- critically appraise the theory of multiple intelligences;
- compare and contrast the work of Gardner with other contemporary theorists;
- recognise how Gardner's work can be applied to the classroom.

KEY WORDS

Multiple intelligences: linguistic, logical–mathematical, musical, bodily-kinaesthetic, spatial, interpersonal, intrapersonal, naturalistic; Project Zero.

INTRODUCTION

Howard Gardner currently holds the position of John H. and Elisabeth A. Hobbs Professor of Cognition and Education at the Harvard Graduate School of Education. He has had an academic career spanning five decades, the majority of which have been spent at Harvard University. Gardner has published over thirty books and several hundred articles, and is perhaps most well known for his theory on **multiple intelligences**.

Gardner showed a passion for learning from the early days of his schooling, and, despite attending a mainstream preparatory school, he managed to secure a place at Harvard with the original intention of studying law or medicine. However, after meeting a number of influential people at Harvard, and with the support of some high-profile mentors, including Jerome Bruner and Erik Erikson, Gardner changed his focus of study to that of developmental psychology and later cognitive development. Gardner was heavily influenced by some of the key thinkers in the field of neurobiology, the most significant of whom was renowned neurologist Norman Geschwind, who encouraged Gardner to work with brain-damaged patients in a local hospital (Winner, 2012). It was through this work that Gardner became interested in brain pathology, which he used when formulating his theory on multiple intelligence (MI) and identifying the characteristics of the initial seven intelligences.

While Gardner is most well known for his MI theory, he was also a founding member of **Project Zero** at Harvard University, and remains active in the project to this day. Originally led by Geschwind, Project Zero looks at the higher cognitive processes of individuals, with a specific focus on creativity and the arts (Winner, 2012). Project Zero has since resulted in further areas of focus for Gardner and his colleagues, including linking to the development of a personalised curriculum in respect of his work on MIs. Project Zero also led to Gardner's involvement in the Good Project, 'a group of initiatives that investigate work, collaboration, citizenship, digital life, and more' (Howard Gardner, online biography: https://howardgardner.com/biography); he has also sought to gain a greater understanding of good work among young people.

It would be fair to say that Howard Gardner has ensured currency in his work, with current foci on digital media and an examination of current college provision from a national and international perspective. Winner (2012) describes Gardner as an accomplished grant-getter who has been responsible for bringing significant funds into Harvard University. Gardner sees himself as an independent scholar and public intellectual. He describes himself as a happy workaholic, who enjoys spending his free time with his close-knit family (Winner, 2012).

⌕ HOWARD GARDNER, THE PERSON

Howard Gardner was born in 1943 in Scranton, a mid-sized former coal-mining city, in north-east Pennsylvania (Winner, 2012). Gardner's parents, Ralph and Hilde Gardner, arrived in America as Jewish immigrants on 9 November 1938, the day of the infamous 'Kristallnacht' (Night of Broken Glass) in Nazi Germany. Gardner comments that his parents had a traumatic history, having been forced out of Germany and the business they ran there by the Nazis (Amrein-Beardsley, 2013). Gardner explains that, prior to their arrival in America, his mother and his brother Eric were held hostage in Germany for three years while his father tried to find someone who would sign an affidavit so they could leave for the United States. The family arrived in America with very few material possessions, in stark contrast to their life in Germany, where they had lived reasonably comfortably. Gardner observes that his mother had never cooked a meal or made a bed before coming to America as this had always been done by the people who worked for the family (Amrein-Beardsley, 2013). Tragedy hit Gardner's family just prior to his birth when his brother Eric was killed in a sleighing accident. Nevertheless, Gardner recalls having a fairly uneventful upbringing, asserting that he was largely unaware of the trauma experienced by his family prior to his birth, stating that 'my parents did not talk about the Holocaust. They did not talk about my brother. In fact, I only discovered that he had died by finding some old clippings' (Gardner, in Amrein-Beardsley, 2013).

Although his parents did not talk directly with Gardner about those events prior to his birth, he does suggest that they indirectly impacted on his upbringing (Amrein-Beardsley, 2013); dangerous pastimes were understandably discouraged and his parents were keen for him to get a good education, encouraging creative and intellectual pursuits. Gardner was, in fact, an excellent student, both academically and musically, being a gifted pianist. While his parents were keen for him to attend the renowned Phillips Academy in Andover, Massachusetts, Gardner refused and instead attended the nearby preparatory school in Kingston, Pennsylvania, where he proved himself to be a conscientious student, embracing opportunities and gaining the support and interest of his teachers.

Gardner was the first of his extended family to attend university, commencing study at Harvard in 1966, where he claims his education began in earnest (Winner, 2012). It was during his time at Harvard that he began to develop a love of learning, which ultimately led to him pursuing an academic career. Gardner states: '[on entering college] I immediately liked studying. I liked taking courses. I probably audited more courses than anybody in the history of Harvard – dozens and dozens of courses' (Amrein-Beardsley, 2013).

During his early days at Harvard, Gardner was able to work with a number of eminent people, including David Reisman and Jerome Bruner, with whom he worked on the 'Man: A Course of Study' (MACOS) programme, a social studies curriculum programme. As an undergraduate, he also worked with renowned psychoanalyst Erik Erikson (Winner, 2012), after which he spent a postgraduate year as a Harvard Fellow at the London School of Economics, reading philosophy and sociology. Of his time in London, Gardner states: 'I have to admit that I was rarely seen there [London School of Economics]. But I loved going to theatre and plays.

I actually wrote a novel – it was terrible – concerts, and so on' (Amrein-Beardsley, 2013). However, he also explains that his time in London led to some reflection on the work of cognitive psychologists Piaget and Bruner. Gardner began to question the scientific focus that Piaget had emphasised in his theory of cognitive development, and began to examine how those who had an interest in the arts looked at works, acknowledging that they too had a mind, and a way in which to view the world. This ultimately led to Gardner's early work on style perception in the visual arts and latterly to his involvement in Project Zero.

Following his year at the London School of Economics, Gardner decided to continue graduate studies in developmental psychology at Harvard, where he had the opportunity to work with psycholinguist Roger Brown and epistemologist Nelson Goodman. Following the completion of his doctorate, Gardner worked with Norman Geschwind, a renowned and brilliant neurologist (Winner, 2012). Gardner was inspired by Geschwind to research into neuropsychology and combined this with his interest in the arts, studying the 'breakdown of artistic and other high-level skills under various forms of brain pathology' (Winner, 2012: 2). His interest in the higher cognitive processes and the arts also resulted in the aforementioned Project Zero undertaken at Harvard University, which also inspired his work on MIs, for which he is probably most well known, and which will be explored in more detail in this chapter.

Gardner has spent his entire academic career associated with Harvard University. As a doctoral student, he held a tutoring position there and, following his doctorate, he held a teaching positon at Clark University for a short period, while maintaining his contact with Harvard through Project Zero. Gardner recalls that despite teaching some well-received courses at Harvard, he failed to get a tenure there. As a result, he was forced to live off grants, including a MacArthur Fellowship in 1981 that supported him for five years (Amrein-Beardsley, 2013), which was later followed by a fellowship from the John S. Guggenheim Memorial Foundation in 2000.

Gardner has had a phenomenally successful career as an academic and has received honorary degrees from twenty-nine colleges and universities across the world. He was also selected by *Foreign Policy* and *Prospect* magazines as one of the hundred most influential public intellectuals in the world in 2005 and 2008. In addition to holding the position of John H. and Elisabeth A. Hobbs Professor of Cognition and Education at the Harvard Graduate School of Education, he is also an adjunct professor of psychology at Harvard University.

THE THEORY OF MULTIPLE INTELLIGENCES

Gardner first began to develop his MI theory in the late 1970s and early 1980s (Davis et al., n.d.). In this theory, Gardner challenges some of the early perceptions of intelligence which assume that it is a singular, inherited entity, measurable by a single IQ test. Instead, Gardner proposed that humans have several, or multiple, intelligences, which the individual is able to draw upon 'individually and corporately, to create products and solve problems that are relevant to the societies in which they live' (Gardner, 1983, 1993a, 1999a, 2006). He also observed that the only intelligences really valued and tested in schools related to **linguistic** and **logical–mathematical intelligence**, suggesting that this language–logic combination was seen as 'academic' or 'scholarly intelligence' (Davis et al., n.d.).

For Gardner, there was much more to intelligence than those factors that were associated with more scholarly endeavours, and he postulated that there were, in fact, 'a multitude of intelligences, quite independent of each other; that each intelligence has its own strengths and constraints' (Gardner, 1993a: xxiii). Gardner set out his first full-length statement on the theory of MI in the text *Frames of Mind* (1983, 1993a), where he drew on his interest in the work of cognitive psychologists, and more recent developments in neurobiology. He suggested that the brain had certain areas that roughly corresponded to specific forms of cognition, and which also proved 'hospitable to the notion of different forms of information processing' (Gardner 1993a: 59). In this respect, the way that an individual processed information was unique to them and their brain structure, and hence each individual would form knowledge in different ways. Ironically, Gardner also goes on to say that there will never be a 'single irrefutable and universally accepted list of human intelligences' (Gardner, 1993a: 60), suggesting that this could only really be achieved through the application of one level of analysis.

Nevertheless, in the early model of Gardner's MI theory, he formulated a provisional list of seven intelligences, which were a combination of the typical intelligences most valued in schools: intelligences more commonly associated with the arts; and intelligences that relate to the personal attributes of an individual. Gardner suggested that each form of intelligence could be subdivided and that the list could be rearranged (Gardner, 1993b). He also recognised that each individual had their own intelligence profile, which might be subject to change as the individual grew and developed, and in respect of the influence of environmental factors.

GARDNER'S MULTIPLE INTELLIGENCES

We will now examine the intelligences that Gardner identified, commencing with the initial seven intelligences proposed by Gardner in his early work. This will then be followed by an examination of the two intelligences that Gardner added at a later date.

LINGUISTIC INTELLIGENCE

Linguistic intelligence relates to the knowing that comes through the various forms of language transmission: spoken language, reading and writing. Gardner saw the gift of language as being universal and consistent across all cultures. He suggested that even in deaf populations, where manual sign languages may not be taught, children will devise their own forms of communication (Gardner, 1993b). Those with a mastery of language will understand the meaning and order of words – spoken and written – and will have an understanding of the sociocultural nuances of language, such as word play, idioms and humour in language. An individual showing linguistic intelligence is likely to have highly developed skills in reading, writing and speaking, and will have 'the capacity to use language to accomplish certain goals' (Gardner, 1999b: 41). Gardner (1999b) suggested that people likely to be high in linguistic intelligence would include lawyers, speakers, writers and poets.

LOGICAL–MATHEMATICAL INTELLIGENCE

As the name suggests, **logical–mathematical intelligence** relates to people who use numbers, mathematics and logic to make sense of the world. A person with a logical–mathematical intelligence 'is able to analyse problems logically, carry out mathematical operations and investigate issues scientifically' (Gardner, 1999b: 42). A person inclined towards logical–mathematical intelligence is likely to be able to think conceptually and abstractly, and can often see patterns and relationships that others may not. For Gardner, the process for solving problems is rapid and often involves coping with many variables and creating multiple hypotheses (Gardner, 1999b).

Gardner identified that it was both linguistic and logical–mathematical intelligences that formed the basis for the traditional IQ test, and as such both types of intelligence had been heavily investigated by traditional psychologists. He also suggests that an individual blessed with both of these intelligences is at a significant advantage when it comes to traditional tests and examinations, since these invariably are the areas most commonly tested. Gardner also postulates that since most psychologists and academics exhibit a combination of linguistic and logical intelligence, it is inevitable that these faculties dominate tests of intelligence (Gardner, 1999b).

For Gardner, it was important, then, to acknowledge that for some people intelligence may not fall into these traditionally tested areas of intelligence, hence the following three intelligences had much more in common with the arts, an area that we have already seen was of particular interest to Gardner.

MUSICAL INTELLIGENCE

Gardner defined **musical intelligence** as 'entail[ing] skill in the performance, composition and appreciation of musical patterns' (Gardner, 1999b: 42). Knowledge is formulated through sounds and vibration, and captures sound, tones, beats and vibrational patterns; those high in musical intelligence are likely to be very sensitive to sounds around them in the environment. Gardner (1999b) saw a direct parallel between musical intelligence and linguistic intelligence, and indeed a person high in musical intelligence is likely to be particularly sensitive to voice tone and intonation, and likely to be skilled in mimicking speech patterns and accents. Gardner (1999b) questioned, then, why one should be called an intelligence (linguistic) and the other a talent (musical), when the two are so very similar.

BODILY–KINAESTHETIC INTELLIGENCE

Gardner linked **bodily–kinaesthetic intelligence** to both the control of one's bodily motions and the capacity to handle objects skilfully (Gardner, 1993b). Therefore, he identified individuals such as dancers and swimmers alongside artisans, ball players and instrumentalists as being high in bodily–kinaesthetic intelligence (Gardner, 1993b). For Gardner, bodily–kinaesthetic related to the capacity to use the body or parts of the body to solve problems or fashion products (Gardner, 1999b). People with this intelligence have a great sense of body awareness and can often communicate well through body language and physical expression.

SPATIAL INTELLIGENCE

Like logical–mathematical intelligence, **spatial intelligence** relates to people who are able to see things through shapes, images, patterns, designs and textures. Patterns can be seen and manipulated in wide open spaces, but also in confined areas, so those with spatial intelligence might include navigators and pilots, but equally sculptors, surgeons and architects.

In the final two intelligences, Gardner focused his attention on personal intelligences.

INTERPERSONAL INTELLIGENCE

Gardner saw **interpersonal intelligence** as being 'a person's capacity to understand the intentions, motivations and desires of other people' (Gardner, 1999b: 43). A person strong in this intelligence works effectively with others as part of a team, having well-developed social skills to work person-to-person. Those most requiring good interpersonal intelligence unsurprisingly include salespeople, teachers, politicians and religious leaders.

INTRAPERSONAL INTELLIGENCE

In this final intelligence, Gardner looked at the capacity for a person to understand themselves, 'to have an effective working model of oneself – including one's own desires, fears and capacities – and to use such information effectively in regulating one's own life' (Gardner, 1999b: 43). In **intrapersonal intelligence**, a person shows skills in self-reflection and is able to recognise emotions, values and beliefs as they apply to their self; they tend to be internally motivated and highly intuitive. People high in intrapersonal intelligence might include writers, poets and philosophers.

While Gardner initially identified seven intelligences, he continued to research intelligences throughout his academic career, and in the mid-1990s identified an eighth intelligence, **naturalistic intelligence**, which, for him, met the criteria for identification as an intelligence (Davis et al., n.d.). As the name suggests, someone high in naturalistic intelligence is able to develop knowledge through their encounters with the natural world, having a propensity towards plants, animals and environmental factors. Gardner has since alluded to a ninth intelligence, existential intelligence, which, as a preliminary definition, he offers as 'Individuals who exhibit the proclivity to pose and ponder questions about life, death, and ultimate realities' (cited in Sortino, 2020: 24), suggesting that this might apply to someone who is concerned about the fundamental questions about existence or who questions the intricacies of existence (Afamasaga, 2009). However, as observed by Afamasaga (2009), Gardner has avoided committing to this intelligence, with Wilson (2020) suggesting that 'since Gardner's work is situated in neurological evidence it may well be risky to definitively pinpoint the exact biological seat of spiritual wonder or cosmic awareness' (para. 3).

As we will see in the following section, Gardner was influenced by many key thinkers in the field of psychology; however, his work also met with criticism from his contemporaries. It is testament to Gardner that he was able to respond to these critics in developing and adapting his theories in response to these observations.

⟳ LINKS WITH OTHER THEORISTS

As we have seen, Gardner worked with a number of eminent psychologists and neurobiologists, and his critique of the work of cognitive psychologists Piaget and Bruner was influential in the formation of his MI theory. Gardner observes that Bruner 'was part of a generation of intellectual giants who roamed across the disciplinary terrain. Bruner and his colleagues gave us a language to see how we make sense of the world' (2016a: para. 2). Gardner goes on to state that 'he [Jerome Bruner] is the most important thinker and writer about education in our time, equal in importance to John Dewey in an earlier epoch' (2016b: 25). Gardner cites Jerome Bruner as being highly influential. Following a period of working with Bruner on the development of a curriculum in social studies, Gardner became interested in cognitive and developmental psychology. This is particularly noteworthy since, prior to this, Gardner was set to study clinical psychology; thus, it could be argued that this marked a turning point in his life, setting him on the course to the academic career for which he is renowned.

Gardner was also influenced by Jean Piaget, stating that 'Intellectually ... Piaget was probably the single biggest influence in my life' (2013: 12). However, despite the assertion that he was heavily influenced by Piaget, he also suggests that 'the bulk of my scholarly career has been a critique of the principal claims that Piaget put forth' (Gardner, 2008). It may well be that his work with neuropsychologist Norman Geschwind contributed to his questioning Piaget's work, since this resulted in Gardner working with brain-damaged patients, which raised questions regarding Piaget's views on intelligence. Where Piaget saw intelligence as 'a single general capacity that developed pretty much in the same way across individuals' (Gardner, 2008), Gardner came to believe that 'humans possess a number of relatively independent intelligences and these can function and interact in idiosyncratic ways' (Gardner, 2008).

Gardner was mentored by both Erik Erikson and David Reisman while at Harvard and he acknowledges their influence in setting him on the course to study how humans think. Gardner refers to Erikson as 'intellectually charismatic' and recalls him as being 'the most arresting figure on campus' (2013: para. 13). Like Gardner, Erikson had taken an unconventional route into psychology, being first a painter and then a primary school teacher. Gardner suggests that this interdisciplinary route led to a richness of seeing problems through the lens of different disciplines. Reisman, too, had taken an unconventional route to his chosen discipline of sociology from a distinguished law career. Gardner has continued to draw from both Reisman's sociological perspective and Erikison's psychological perspective in more recent work on digital technology, co-authoring the text *The App Generation* with media scholar Katie Davis, which argues that the digital generation is 'app-directed', suggesting that this encourages superficial relationships and stifles creativity. Gardner credits his old mentors with this work, observing that 'my intellectual lineage endures today ... I'm still using their ideas for what I do' (2013: para. 18)

While Gardner was influenced by a number of eminent thinkers in the field of psychology and neurobiology, he has continued to work with more contemporary psychologists. As his field of study has widened, so too has the range of people Gardner has worked with, each project seemingly presenting the opportunity to work with an increasingly diverse range of people. Winner (2012) outlines some of his more recent projects and accomplishments, including working with Dennie Wolf on tracing the development of young children in using symbols and working with his then wife, Judy Gardner, demonstrating the imitative capacities in early infancy.

It has also been noted that Gardner has continued his association with Project Zero, which was first developed at Harvard University in the late 1960s. Alongside founding member and project leader Nelson Goodman, work focused on artistic knowledge and practice, with a view to examining how artistic skills and understanding can be enhanced through school- and museum-run projects. Gardner names Goodman as a further influence on him, suggesting that he encouraged scepticism in Gardner, leading him to search for evidence through asking questions, which is reflected throughout Gardner's work.

In a long and illustrious career, Gardner has always sought to work with, and learn from, a wide range of people on a number of different projects. It is no surprise, then, that with such a wide range of influences and foci, Gardner's work has at times met with some criticism, which we shall look at in the next section.

CRITIQUING THE THEORY

Despite a successful academic career spanning five decades, and with over thirty books and hundreds of articles to his name, Gardner's work has been met with some criticism over the years. However, far from being troubled by this criticism, he appears to have relished the opportunity to respond to his critics, reflected, for example, in the text *Howard Gardner Under Fire* (Schaler, 2006), an edited volume to which he has contributed a 'reply to my critics' for every chapter and through the article 'Reflections on multiple intelligences: Myths and messages' (1995). Gardner has also shown a willingness to amend and develop his theories in response to criticism or observations made.

White questions just how far Gardner's work on intelligence is either unique or new, suggesting that for centuries philosophers and psychologists have acknowledged the existence of intelligence, and furthermore have recognised it as something 'flexible in pursuit of one's goals' (2005: 2). White goes on to suggest that Gardner's identification of seven (later eight) intelligences is understating the range of intelligence, and that 'there are as many types of human intelligence as there are types of human goal. Gardner has corralled this huge variety into a small number of categories' (2005: 2). Perhaps, then, Gardner has oversimplified the true nature of intelligence.

A further criticism of Gardner's work is the lack of empirical evidence available to support his claims, with the suggestion that Gardner's work is founded on his own intuition and reasoning rather than any research evidence. Gardner (1995) himself disputes this criticism, however, stating that in the book *Frames of Mind*, hundreds of empirical studies have been reviewed, and the seven intelligences were identified and delineated through a review of this evidence.

The question of measuring the seven intelligences is also an area of interest when applying MI theory. In the same way that traditional intelligence is measurable through the conventional IQ test, some of Gardner's critics suggest that the seven intelligences identified by Gardner should also be measurable. Again, Gardner defends this by observing that 'a battery of MI tests is inconsistent with the major tenets of the theory' (1995: 202). The principle of MI theory is in direct contrast to the measuring of intelligence through linguistic and numerical means, so for Gardner to attempt to measure intelligence in this way is in discord with the theory. Additionally, Gardner raises concerns regarding labelling and stigmatisation, which inevitably come with testing.

Despite the criticisms levelled at Gardner's work, as we will see in the next section, his work can be applied in educational settings, and while initially application was most commonly seen in the field of gifted education and among isolated schools in the United States (Armstrong, 2000), it has since gathered global recognition. As observed by Armstrong (2000), 'educators have applied multiple intelligences concepts to a wide range of settings' (2000: vii).

APPLYING GARDNER IN THE CLASSROOM

Gardner suggests that due to his criticism of the views on intelligence within the field of psychology, his MI theory was not well received by fellow psychologists; however, he also admits to being unprepared for the impact that his work had in the field of education (Gardner, 1995). In fact, MI theory potentially lends itself well to the classroom and might offer educationalists a means by which to approach teaching and learning, offering an alternative to the traditional mode of learning through predominantly academic subjects.

Gardner (1995) observes that he saw numerous approaches to the application of MI theory in the classroom, and, given that he admits 'to having presented an "ensemble of ideas" (or "memes") to the outer world', he states that he was 'inclined to let those "memes" fend for themselves' (Gardner, 1995: 200). Gardner does, however, question the purpose to which schools used ideas about the mind, suggesting that

> MI ideas and practices cannot be an end in themselves; they cannot serve as a goal for a school or an educational system. Rather, every educational institution must reflect on its goals, mission, and purposes continuously, and, at least at times, explicitly. Only after such reflections can MI ideas be usefully implemented. (1999a: 143)

Gardner was keen, then, that MI theory should not be seen as a quick fix to teaching, something he saw frequently in American schools in which new practices were embraced for a short period until the next trend was adopted. For Gardner, MI theory saw a change in the way that intelligences were viewed and, as such, in order for MI theory to work at an educational level, it is necessary for education systems to be responsive. If MI theory were to be adopted in schools, then the ways in which children are tested and assessed must also change to reflect this.

We can see, then, that there is no fixed approach to the application of MI theory, and it was never Gardner's intention when he first introduced MI theory that it should be an educational approach. By its very nature, the application of MI theory should be responsive to the needs of the learners for whom it is being applied. Nevertheless, White (2005) proposes that in British schools MI theory was adopted as a basis for a more flexible approach to teaching and learning, a response to the recognition that children have different preferred learning styles. As Gardner himself identified, not all children have a propensity to learn through the more traditional literate and numerate means; as such, MI theory allows opportunities for children to bring to their learning other means – for example, through music or movement, areas in which they may show greater intelligence.

When applying MI to the classroom, it is necessary for the practitioner to plan work which is outside the traditional modes of learning – for example, when writing about a historical event, it may be the case that for those children who show high musical intelligence, the event could be written as a rap or performed as a song as an alternative to the more traditional essay. In this way, learning is presented in a way that is more accessible to the child and is then more likely to be retained. White (2005) suggests that a further advantage of applying MI theory is that it raises a child's self-esteem, and a child who might have previously considered themselves not as clever as their peers can be allowed to shine through, for example, their musical or bodily–kinaesthetic endeavours.

However, for MI theory to be fully capitalised on, there is a need for a curriculum that embraces this mode of learning, since as long as knowledge is tested in the manner of the more traditional examination, those children lacking in linguistic and logical–mathematical intelligence will still find themselves at a disadvantage compared with their more academic peers. White suggests that ideas linked to MI theory may well have been inadvertently responsible for educational policies and practices that led to 'selection, specialisation, individualisation of learning, and assessment' (2005: 16). Certainly, the 1999 DfEE report *All Our Futures* called for a creative curriculum that 'develops young people's capacities for original ideas and action' (DfEE, 1999: 2). This was followed by further reports (Alexander, 2008; Williams, 2008; Rose, 2009), all of which called for a curriculum that placed less emphasis on the academic subjects and instead allowed children to realise their creative potential.

Such measures would certainly have lent themselves well to MI theory, allowing teachers to teach in a way that actively promoted those subjects not deemed to be as academic as others, and therefore allowing those children with intelligences outside of linguistic and logical–mathematical to shine. Indeed, this would reflect Gardner's own liberal approach to education in which he suggests that

> Education in our time should provide the basis for enhanced understanding of our several worlds – the physical world, the biological world, the world of human beings, the world of human artifacts, and the world of the self. (1999b: 158)

He also advocates a curriculum that favours 'the pursuit of knowledge for its own sake over the obeisance to utility' (1999b: 39).

Unfortunately, a change in the UK government in 2010 meant that the creative curriculum was never fully realised. Instead, government policy saw a return to a more formal curriculum, in which subjects were to be taught as disciplines in their own right, and in which there was a heavy emphasis on the core subjects of English, mathematics and science. Additionally, a heavy emphasis on the assessment of these core subjects saw a return to a more formal style of teaching, since a less traditional mode of learning could be seen as a risky business. This trend towards a more formal, subject-based curriculum was cemented with the publication of the National Curriculum in England documentation (DfE, 2014), in which programmes of study were set out on the basis of key stages and individual subject content. The document firmly emphasised that twelve subjects should be taught to pupils of compulsory age, including three core subjects of English, mathematics and science. Highlighting these subjects as core subjects would reflect Gardner's observation of a curriculum built around literacy and numeracy, while marginalising those subjects deemed less academic. This is further emphasised by an assessment programme that focuses solely on English and mathematics at Primary level, and in which a requirement to pass GCSE English and mathematics was made compulsory up until the age of 18 following the raising of the educational participation age in 2014.

In many ways, this reflects the fear that Gardner had that MI theory could be seen as a passing fad, a trend that lasts for only as long as government policy dictates. Certainly, while educational attainment is still tested by traditional means, some students will remain at a disadvantage. However, it could be argued that Gardner's MI theory did open the doors to a new way of thinking about how children learn. Gardner has always maintained that MI theory was never intended as an 'educational prescription' (1995: 206), but suggests instead that it should be down to educators to decide how MI theory should be applied in their settings, if at all. This reflects previous observations that MI theory should always be about a best fit, and Gardner cautions against trying to force such a fit, arguing that some topics lend themselves well to MI theory and others not so well, in which case a common-sense approach should be applied. However, what Gardner does advocate, where MI theory is concerned, is that educators consider an alternative approach to education, approaching topics from a number of perspectives in the hope that more children will be reached.

REFLECTIVE TASK

Take a topic traditionally taught in schools, such as the Victorians, forces and energy, or the water cycle:

How would you apply each of Gardner's intelligences to delivering this topic?

What do you see as the advantages of this method of delivery?

What are the challenges?

SUMMARY

Howard Gardner has had a long and illustrious academic career; from his own early experiences with education he showed a propensity for learning which he has capitalised on throughout his life. With the advantage of supportive and encouraging parents, and then later through working alongside a number of high-profile mentors,

Gardner has made significant contributions to the fields of both psychology and education. Gardner is best known for his theory on multiple intelligences, which emerged from the two main themes of his work: looking at how the mind develops, particularly when developing abilities in the arts; and, as a result of his work with patients with brain trauma, looking at how the mind processes break down under special conditions.

Gardner challenged some of the traditional theories of cognitive development and also some of the thinking on intelligence. He suggested that measurement of intelligence through the traditional IQ test did not fully reflect the extent of intelligences available to the individual and proposed that there were seven key intelligences that should be taken account of when looking at learning. It was his MI theory that propelled him to the forefront of education, with educationalists adopting his theory to find an alternative means of content delivery.

Gardner's work has not been without its critics; however, it is testament to his conviction and tenacity that he has faced his critics head-on, showing a willingness to adapt his theories, but also defending his work publicly.

In conclusion, it should be noted that while MI theory is the best-known area of Gardner's work, this is only part of an academic career that spans five decades. Gardner has been involved in numerous recent projects and has been responsible for significant funding at Harvard University through research grants. He has worked, and continues to work, with a range of academics in the field, showing a diversity of ideas in a variety of projects.

GLOSSARY OF TERMS

Bodily–kinaesthetic intelligence According to Gardner's theory of multiple intelligences, those with bodily–kinaesthetic intelligence have the ability to process information physically, through hand and body movement. People with this intelligence will have good hand–eye coordination and dexterity, and tend to excel at sport and dance or creative activities. In learning, they favour hands-on activities rather than dissemination through hearing or seeing.

Interpersonal intelligence Interpersonal intelligence relates to those individuals whose strengths lie in their interactions with others. People who are strong in interpersonal intelligence tend to be skilled at recognising emotions, motivations and desires in others and are able to see situations from different perspectives. Communication skills are good, which means that those with interpersonal intelligence are able to form and maintain secure relationships.

Intrapersonal intelligence Intrapersonal intelligence relates to how well a person understands themselves. These people are self-aware and introspective, qualities which they are able to apply to solving personal problems. Gardner defines intrapersonal intelligence as being sensitive to one's own feelings, wants and fears, with an awareness of one's own strengths and weaknesses.

Linguistic intelligence   Linguistic intelligence refers to a sensitivity to language, including the meaning and order of words, and the different functions and usage of words. Those with linguistic intelligence have the ability to understand the nuances of spoken and written language, as well as being proficient in their own use of language.

Logical–mathematical intelligence   Those with logical–mathematical intelligence are proficient in solving problems logically. They have the ability to analyse situations and apply deductive reasoning to aid them in solving logical–mathematical problems. They will process information through logic and reasoning, preferring to apply a scientific method.

Multiple intelligences   A theory proposed by Gardner in 1983 in response to his observation that psychometric intelligence testing was too limited. Gardner initially identified eight distinct intelligences, later adding a ninth, suggesting that individuals were not just limited to intellectual intelligence, but could have intelligences or talents in many different areas.

Musical intelligence   An individual with musical intelligence is able to think in pattern, rhythm and sound. They are able to recognise pitch, timbre and tone, and show a deep appreciation for musical compositions.

Naturalistic intelligence   Naturalistic intelligence was the eighth intelligence, added later by Gardner in his text *Intelligence Reframed* (1999b). A person with naturalistic intelligence has a strong affinity with the natural world and is highly sensitive to the patterns and changes in their immediate environment.

Project Zero   A research centre founded by Nelson Goodman in 1967, starting with a focus in research into learning through the arts. The centre now focuses on preparing learners for work in the worlds in which they live, work and develop. Gardner was one of the founding research assistants for Project Zero and later became director for the project, which provided him with a platform to develop his research into human cognition.

Spatial intelligence   Spatial intelligence refers to the way in which information is processed through visual representation. A person with strong spatial intelligence is able to visualise objects in one or more dimensions, and can rotate, manipulate and transform them. Engineeers, scientists and architects tend to excel in spatial intelligence.

FURTHER READING

Baum, S., Viens, J., Slatin, B. and Gardner, H. (2005) *Multiple Intelligences in the Elementary Classroom: A Teacher's Toolkit*. New York: Teachers College Press.
A practical guide to supporting teachers in meeting the needs of a diverse group of learners in the classroom through the application of pathways related to MI theory.

Craft, A., Gardner, H. and Claxton, G. (eds) (2008) *Creativity, Wisdom and Trusteeship: Exploring the Role of Education*. Thousand Oaks, CA: Corwin.
An examination of creativity and wisdom, and how they relate to classroom practice. Contributions are made by scholars and educators in the fields of cognitive psychology and the neurosciences.

Gardner, H. (2006) *Five Minds for the Future*. Boston, MA: Harvard Business School Publishing.
Some of Gardner's more recent work which looks at the 'five minds' that Gardner believes individuals will need to face a fast-paced future.

Komhaber, M., Fierros, E. and Veenema, S. (2003) *Multiple Intelligences: Best Ideas from Research and Practice*. Cambridge: Pearson.
Using original research from Project Zero, this book shows how MI theory can be applied in schools and classrooms.

Schaler, J.A. (ed.) (2006) *Howard Gardner under Fire: The Rebel Psychologist Faces His Critics*. Chicago, IL: Carus Publishing Company.
In this text, Gardner has the opportunity to respond to some of the fiercest critics of various aspects of his work.

REFERENCES

Afamasaga, B.A. (2009). *Understanding your DNA and Mind*. New York: iUniverse.
Alexander, R. (2008 [2010]) *Children, Their World, Their Education* (The Cambridge Primary Review). London: Routledge.
Amrein-Beardsley, A. (2013) *Inside the Academy*. Video interviews with Dr Howard Gardner, 16 March. Available online at: http://insidetheacademy.asu.edu/howard-gardner
Armstrong, T. (2000). *Multiple Intelligences in the Classroom* (2nd edn). Alexandria: ACSD.
Davis, K., Christodoulou, J., Seider, S. and Gardner, H. (n.d.) *The Theory of Multiple Intelligences*. Available online at: www.pz.harvard.edu/sites/default/files/Theory%20of%20MI.pdf
Department for Education (DfE) (2014) *National Curriculum in England: Framework for Key Stages 1 and 4*. London: Crown copyright.
Department for Employment and Education (DfEE) (1999) *All Our Futures*. London: Crown copyright.
Gardner, H. (1983) *Frames of Mind: The Theory of Multiple Intelligences*. New York: Basic Books.
Gardner, H. (1993a) *Frames of Mind: The Theory of Multiple Intelligences* (10th anniversary edn). New York: Basic Books.
Gardner, H. (1993b) *Multiple Intelligences: The Theory in Practice*. New York: Basic Books.
Gardner, H. (1995) 'Reflections on multiple intelligences: Myths and messages'. *Phi Delta Kappan*, 77: 200–9.
Gardner, H. (1999a) *The Disciplined Mind: What All Students Should Understand*. New York: Simon & Schuster.
Gardner, H. (1999b) *Intelligence Reframed*. New York: Basic Books.
Gardner, H. (2006) *Multiple Intelligences: New Horizons*. New York: Basic Books.
Gardner, H. (2008) *Wrestling with Jean Piaget, My Paragon*. Available online at: www.edge.org/q2008/q08_1.html#gardner

Gardner, H. (2013) 'Howard Gardner: "A blessing of influences."' *The Harvard Gazette*. Available online at: https://news.harvard.edu/gazette/story/2013/10/the-mentors-of-howard-gardner/

Gardner, H. (2016a) *Remembering Jerome Bruner*. Available online at: https://howardgardner.com/2016/06/13/remembering-jerome-bruner/

Gardner, H. (2016b) 'Remembering Jerome Bruner'. In: *Innovations in Early Education: The International Reggio Emilia Exchange* (quarterly periodical of the North America Reggio Emilia exchange). Available online at: https://inservice.ascd.org/remembering-jerome-bruner/

Gardner, H. and Davis, K. (2013) *The APP Generation: How Today's Youth Navigate Identity, Intimacy and Imagination in a Digital World*. London: Yale University Press.

Rose, J. (2009) *Independent Review of the Primary Curriculum*. London: DfE.

Schaler, J.A. (ed.) (2006) *Howard Gardner under Fire: The Rebel Psychologist Faces His Critics*. Chicago, IL: Carus Publishing Company.

Sortino, D.P. (2020) *Brain Changers: Major Advances in Children's Learning and Intelligence*. London: Rowman & Littlefield.

White, J. (2005) *Howard Gardner: The Myth of Multiple Intelligences*. Available online at: http://eprints.ioe.ac.uk/1263/1/WhiteJ2005HowardGardner1.pdf

Williams, P. (2008) *Independent Review of Mathematics Teaching in Early Years Settings and Primary Schools*. London: DCSFT.

Wilson, L.O. (2020) *The Second Principle: The Ninth Intelligence – Existential or Cosmic Smarts*. Available online at: https://thesecondprinciple.com/optimal-learning/ninth-intelligence-existential-cosmic-smarts-2/

Winner, E. (2012) *The History of Howard Gardner*. Available online at: https://howardgardner01.files.wordpress.com/2012/06/ellenwinnerbio.pdf

15

JOHN HOLT

UNSCHOOLING OR HOME-SCHOOLING

LEARNING OUTCOMES

After reading this chapter, you should be able to:

- show an appreciation for the philosophy of John Holt;
- recognise Holt's notion of unschooling;
- critically evaluate Holt's work;
- reflect on your own views of the schooling system.

KEY WORDS

Growing Without Schooling; home-schooling; learning exchanges; unschooling; free schools.

INTRODUCTION

John Holt was a key figure in American education during the 1960s and 1970s who was perhaps best known for his work with the **home-schooling** movement in America. Holt coined the phrase '**unschooling**' to explain a system of home-schooling which did not rely on traditional teaching methods or a set curriculum, and which allowed children to learn at their own pace in a way that best responded to their individual needs.

Holt's work with the home-schooling movement arose from his discontent with the American school system, which he believed to be flawed, and his frustration with policy-makers who seemed reluctant to change it. Holt appeared well placed to make these observations in his capacity as a classroom teacher, and, despite having no formal teaching qualifications, he spent fourteen years teaching grade school in America. During his time as a teacher, Holt observed that his colleagues failed to make the best use of the pedagogical techniques available to them, and as a result bright and competent children were becoming 'self-centred, self-protective students who aimed above all else to avoid trouble, embarrassment, punishment, disapproval or loss of status' (Lant, 1976–7: 329). Holt carried out a number of observations on his own classroom practice and that of his co-teacher Bill Hunt, and used these observations and his commentary on them in his seminal texts *How Children Fail* (1964; revised 1982) and *How Children Learn* (1967; revised 1983). It was these texts that launched Holt's career as an education lecturer and consultant, and he was praised for his work, which seemed to show what really happened in schools.

Despite his contention that compulsory schooling was destroying children's natural curiosity (Gaither, 2015), Holt's work was well received by his contemporaries and his books sold well (Lant, 1976–7). Released at a time when social reform was being welcomed, Holt continued to offer suggestions as to how classroom practices and school systems might be reformed to better meet the needs of their pupils through a further series of books. However, as Holt's ideas became increasingly radical, he soon met with resistance from teachers and policy-makers, leading him to conclude that it was a waste of time trying to reform schools (Farenga, n.d.).

In turning his attention away from the school system and the classroom, Holt became increasingly interested in the rights of the child and their position in society. In his books *Freedom and Beyond* (1972) and *Escape from Childhood* (1974) Holt challenged the notion of childhood and suggested that society was responsible for suppressing a child's rights until they reached the age of eighteen. At this time he also began to support those parents who were looking to extricate their children from compulsory education. He became an advocate for these parents, offering practical support through the bi-monthly newsletter ***Growing Without Schooling***, first published in 1977.

Holt's untimely death from cancer at the age of sixty-two meant that he did not see the legacy of an ever-growing home-schooling movement in America; however, his name remains synonymous with both home-schooling and unschooling, and the periodical *Growing Without Schooling*, which he founded, continues to be published today.

JOHN HOLT, THE PERSON

John Holt was born in New York in 1923 to parents Henry and Elizabeth Holt. He had a privileged upbringing and attended one of the more prestigious private schools in New England (Farenga, n.d.). He later went on to graduate from Yale University with a degree in industrial administration, although Farenga suggests that he was later somewhat scathing about this qualification, often adding 'whatever that means' after it. Indeed, as Holt's philosophies developed, he became increasingly reticent in talking about his academic accomplishments, and, despite having an excellent academic record, he believed his experiences of formal education to be mostly worthless. Holt is often quoted as saying:

> I have come to believe that a person's schooling is as much a part of his private business as his politics or religion, and that no one should be required to answer questions about it. May I say instead that most of what I know I did not learn in school, and indeed was not even taught. (cited by Farenga, n.d.)

On graduating from Yale, Holt served in the Navy as a lieutenant aboard the submarine *USS Barbero* (Lant, 1976–7), an experience which he later reflected on as being hugely significant in terms of the learning he gained from it. Holt expressed the notion that while no one was talking or thinking about learning, the demanding work that was jointly accomplished, alongside the experience and skills gained, were far more powerful than any formal learning experience previously undertaken (Lant, 1976–7). Holt's three-year stint in the Navy also led him to reflect on war in the nuclear age, which he considered to be 'suicidal for mankind' (Farenga, n.d.); as a result, on leaving the Navy he began to work for the World Federalist Movement, a group intent on bringing peace to the planet through the organisation of a one-world government.

Holt's work with the World Federalist Movement led him to the role of lay missionary, which saw him spending six years travelling the world promoting 'a visionary postwar program of international unity' (Lant, 1976–7: 328). Unfortunately, after six years Holt became disillusioned with the ineffective work of the movement and as a result he left the organisation.

It is the period following this that saw Holt direct his attention to the education system, encouraged by his sister, who suggested that he visit the newly opened Colorado Rocky Mountain School. Holt was so impressed by what he saw that he began teaching there. It is perhaps fortuitous that this school was unconventional (being co-educational and maintained by faculty and students) since without a formal teaching qualification Holt was restricted in where he was allowed to teach. Holt related how he was unable to seek work in public schools without such qualifications and was unable to gain the required degree having limited time or financial resources to do so.

Nevertheless, Holt spent four years at the Colorado Rocky Mountain School before moving to Boston 'to experience city life again' (Farenga, n.d.). Here he found work teaching fifth grade in a private school in Cambridge, Massachusetts, and it was during this time that he met 'his intellectual comrade and collaborator Bill Hunt' (Gaither, 2015). While working in this school, Hunt and Holt began to observe one another's classes, making notes of their observations and engaging in discussion around their shared interest in children's learning. Through their observations, both Hunt and Holt began to reflect on their own teaching, particularly around seeking a means by which children could become better learners. They began to question what it was they wanted the children to achieve and how this could best be accomplished (Farenga, n.d.).

It was the notes from his observations with Bill Hunt that provided Holt with the material for his first two texts and, after eleven years of teaching and observing, Holt published his first book, *How Children Fail* (1964, revised 1982), swiftly followed by his second, *How Children Learn* (1967, revised 1983). In these texts, Holt is critical of an educational system that fails to make the best use of the pedagogical techniques available and suggests that children's fear of the education system stifles their creativity and ability to learn effectively. Holt and Hunt had both begun to make changes to their own classroom practice in the light of their observations, and attempted to encourage other faculty members to do the same.

Despite believing the school to be supportive of his 'new ideas and new thinking about education' (Lant, 1976–7: 329), Holt soon found that this was his undoing, since 'many of his fellow teachers were not happy about what the upstart Holt was doing' (Lant, 1976–7: 329), and in addition his application of classroom strategies which saw him downplaying grades, cutting back on tests and decreasing classroom stress and competition (Lant, 1976–7) ultimately led to him being fired; as Holt observed, 'I only found out later that they were interested in old "new ideas" not new "new ideas"' (Lant, 1976–7: 329).

Holt continued to attempt to pursue a career in teaching following his firing from Cambridge; however, his increasingly radical ideas led to him being fired from several more positions. Nevertheless, despite being unpopular with his colleagues and superiors, Holt was rapidly becoming a mainstream figure in American education in the mid-1960s, and, alongside his other commitments, he frequently contributed to magazines such as *Life, the Saturday Evening Post* and *Redbook* (Gaither, 2015).

Holt left teaching in 1968 and became a lecturer at Harvard Graduate School of Education and the University of California, Berkeley. His experience as an academic spurred him on to write *The Underachieving School* (1969 [2005]), which saw him turn his attention away from his earlier classroom case studies to the school system itself. This book reflected Holt's increasing frustration at what he perceived to be a flawed system which appeared to show no signs of changing. He concluded that the school system was both self-serving and demeaning to its pupils (Farenga, n.d.).

Throughout the 1970s, Holt's ideas became increasingly radical, particularly after he became interested in the work of social critic Ivan Illich, with whom he worked for two weeks in Cuarnavaca, Mexico, in 1969 (Meighan, 2007). Illich's work resonated with Holt since he, too, believed that 'the concept of mass education was inherently self-defeating' (Gaither, 2015). Illich believed that schools were a disastrous idea in poor countries, locking them into poverty, dependency and helplessness. He latterly turned his attention to the effect of the school system in richer countries, a discussion to which Holt contributed. Following the time spent with Illich, Holt went on to publish further texts which showed his increasing frustration at the reluctance of policy-makers to change the education system, including *Freedom and Beyond* in 1972 and *Escape from Childhood* in 1974.

The more radical his ideas became, the more marginalised Holt found himself, which resulted in him turning his attention to the American home-schooling movement; Holt's final work was very much centred on this. Despairing of the American education system, Holt theorised that children would be better educated from home, proposing his ideas in *Instead of Education: Ways to Help People Do Things Better* (1976) and *Teach your Own* (1981); latterly, Holt published his ideas through the fortnightly newsletter *Growing Without Schooling*. Thus, Holt spent his final years offering advice and guidance to parents who chose to eduate their child from home and working towards securing a legal framework for home-schooling in America. Holt's untimely death from cancer in 1985 meant that this work was largely unfinished; however, the home-schooling movement is Holt's enduring legacy, remaining, as it does, an important part of the American education system today.

THE EDUCATION SYSTEM ACCORDING TO HOLT

As we have seen, Holt's work was based predominantly on his own first-hand experiences and observations of classroom practice and school systems, and, along with his colleague and friend Bill Hunt, he set out to address some of the perceived flaws identified through these observations. As such, what was developed from this work could be considered more of a philosophy than a theory, since Holt wanted teachers themselves to mirror the work that he and Bill Hunt were doing by reflecting on their own classroom practices and challenging the systems that he believed were harming children's learning.

Lant (1976–7) suggests that it may well have been the lack of formal training as an educator that led Holt to view classroom practices in such a disparaging way, since he was entering the classroom without the insight of one who had been formally trained in the art of teaching. For the trained teacher, there was already an awareness of the constraints that a curriculum and school system could place on the educator. However, for Holt, who was entering the system oblivious to such restrictions, there was a sudden realisation of 'the disjunction between what the school said it was doing and what was in fact going on in the classroom' (Lant, 1976–7: 328).

Through his observations, Holt identified that the pedagogical techniques and methodological approaches applied in the classroom were actually resulting in potentially bright and competent children becoming increasingly self-centred and self-protective. He believed that the fear of failure inherent in the education system was leading children to avoid situations that might lead to 'trouble, embarrassment, punishment, disapproval or loss of status' (Lant, 1976–7: 329). In short, children were constrained in their educational endeavours, preferring to play safe to protect themselves.

Holt was frustrated by what he observed in classrooms since he recognised that children were indeed by their very nature curious and showed a natural desire to learn. He observed that 'babies are not blobs but true scientists' (Holt, 1982: xxv) and as such he believed that schools should be places where children should be allowed and encouraged to explore and make sense of the world around them, in the ways that most interested them (Holt, 1982). Holt recognised that human beings are learning animals who don't need to be shown how to learn; however, he also believed that what killed the process was people interfering with or trying to regulate or control it (Bumgarner, 1980).

Holt believed that the most powerful learning happened before the child entered the school system, and ideally learning in the classroom should be a natural progression from the learning already experienced. However, while he observed that children had a style of learning unique to their individual characteristics, he also believed that the educator trains them out of this natural desire to learn. In the Preface to his book *How Children Learn*, Holt states:

> we like to say that we send children to school to teach them to think. What we do, all too often, is to teach them to think badly, to give up a natural and powerful way of thinking in favour of a method that does not work well for them and that we rarely use ourselves. (1983: xi)

Holt believed that children developed their own coping mechanisms to deal with the challenges of the school system, often becoming distracted from the learning experience by trying to second-guess what the teacher wanted from them. While he acknowledged that a few children did learn in school, for the majority he suggested that they used their minds not to learn, but to get out of the things teachers were trying to make them do to make them learn (Holt, 1983).

However, despite Holt's somewhat disparaging assessment of the education system, in his early observations he maintained that the school system could indeed be changed for the better. In both books *How Children Fail* (1964) and *How Children Learn* (1967), he used his own reflections on the observations he made to demonstrate what could be learned from the situation described, and also how classroom practice could be changed to better meet the needs of the pupils. His vision was that school should become the place where all children could grow, not just in size and knowledge, but in 'curiosity, courage, confidence, independence, resourcefulness, resilience, patience, competence and understanding' (Holt, 1983: viii). He believed that this could best be achieved by developing a better understanding of 'the ways, conditions and spirit in which children do their best learning' (Holt, 1983: viii); schools should then become places where children could improve their own style of thinking and learning.

As we have noted, it was during the 1970s that Holt's vision of the school system became increasingly radical, and the more opposition he met, the more frustrated he became by the lack of desire for schools to change. In the opening chapter of his book *Instead of Education* (1976), Holt's disillusionment is expressed as follows:

> Do not waste your time trying to reform these schools. They cannot be reformed. It may be possible for a few of you, in a few places, to make a place called school which will be a humane and useful doing (as distinct from educating) place for the young. If so, by all means do it. In most places, not even this will be possible. (1976: 8)

Holt turned his attention away from reforming the school system, which he now believed to be 'among the most authoritarian and destructive of all the inventions of man' (Farenga, n.d.), and instead looked to working around it. He explored the notion of **free schools** and **learning exchanges** which offered free courses to all-comers, run by volunteers from the community utlising local community resources. Furthermore, as his interest in the home-schooling movement grew, Holt began to offer practical support to parents who themselves sought to remove their children from the school system. While parents had been schooling their children from home for some time, Holt recognised that he could use his own experience to offer advice and guidance, from which a network of like-minded people was formed.

In order to offer support to these parents, Holt began to publish the bi-monthly newsletter *Growing Without Schooling*, in which he offered practical support to parents who preferred to educate their children from home. However, Holt's vision of home-schooling very much reflected his early ideas of how children should be educated, through taking their own interests and needs into account. So, rather than simply replicate the school curriculum in the home environment, Holt advocated what he called *unschooling*, in that the learning experience developed should be directed solely by the child. For Holt, unschooling is the natural way to learn, and while it is conceivable that curriculum materials and traditional teaching materials could be used, this would be decided by the child and parent. Holt expressed that it was unnatural for learners to learn things in a particular way as decided by policy-makers, and postulated that learners would learn what they need to learn when it made sense to them. In this way, they are learning what others learn, but not necessarily in the same order. According to Holt and Farenga, 'it isn't unusual to find unschoolers who are barely eight-years-old studying astronomy or who are ten-years-old and just learning to read' (2003: 239).

Although in his later years Holt reverted back to the term 'home-schooling', finding that the term 'unschooling' led people to assume that it meant being uneducated, Holt's name remains synonymous with unschooling, and his work is still closely tied to the home-schooling movement in the United States. Regardless of the term used, Holt sought to support parents who wanted to present children with a more natural way to learn, in which the quest for knowledge seen in the preschool years could be continued, and in which learning was no longer impeded by a fear of failure, and natural curiosity was not quashed because something wasn't on the curriculum.

⟳ LINKS WITH OTHER THEORISTS

Holt's work was celebrated throughout the 1960s and 1970s, a period that saw an abundance of new ideas about education emerging (Farenga, 1999). Holt himself was heavily influenced by the work of philosopher and social critic Ivan Illich, who himself believed that 'the concept of mass education was inherently self-defeating' (Gaither, 2015). In his book *Deschooling Society* Illich wrote:

> universal education through schooling is not feasible. It would be no more feasible if it were attempted by means of alternative institutions built on the style of present schools. (1970: 2)

Illich then goes on to discuss the negative impact of the school system on the child, particularly with regard to the relationship between teacher and student, which he believed impacted on the child's individual freedom. Illich argued that the function of education in society should be to provide information to the individual when and how they wanted it. He believed that individuals should have access to information and should have a means by which to share their knowledge through distinct channels or learning exchanges. This was echoed in Holt's later work as he, too, sought to turn schools into resource centres and teachers into guides in his own vision to reform the education sector (Farenga, n.d.). Holt's vision of unschooling was undoubtedly influenced by Illich's *Deschooling Society* (1970), which encouraged people to become less dependent on institutions and therefore 'deschool' themselves.

Similarities with the work of A.S. Neill can also be seen in Holt's vision for education. Holt and Neill first met in 1965 (Allen, 1981) and Holt supported Neill's belief that children could be trusted to learn about the world without interference from adults (Allen, 1981). Both men shared a vision for an education system that sought an alternative to the more traditional school and encouraged pupils to take responsibility for their own learning. The difference between the two was that Neill was able to realise his dream of a more progressive school system, being the founder of the renowned Summerhill School, whose principles lay in the ideal that children learn best when free from coercion (see Chapter 3). Holt visited the Summerhill School shortly before Neill's death in 1973.

Meighan (2007) observes that Holt was inspired by the work of Paulo Freire when justifying his observations that the schooling system did little to improve conditions for the very poor in society. Holt cites the work of Freire and his colleagues in which the inhabitants of some of the poorest villages in north-eastern Brazil were encouraged to discuss their lives, interests, needs and concerns. While reticent in the first instance, Freire noted that the more they talked, the more they gained the courage to share their thoughts, from which common words and themes emerged. Freire would write these words down and this became the starting point for evening classes in functional literacy. From these observations, Holt suggested that learning to read could proceed without the need for formal schooling. He went on to develop the volunteer reading guide scheme in which guides would wear identifying clothing such as an armband or hat, which would indicate that they were available for support. Any interested party could then approach the guide and ask for help with understanding a word or assistance with spelling (Meighan, 2007).

CRITIQUING THE THEORY

Despite being a mainstream figure in American education during the 1960s (Gaither, 2015), Holt's increasingly radical ideas about the American education system saw him rapidly falling out of favour with policy-makers. It could be argued that the more extreme his ideas became, the less credible he became, which is unfortunate given that his aspiration was always that the education system should be responsive to the individual needs of the child.

Holt's philosophy was a result of his observations and discussions with his colleague Bill Hunt; however, as Lant observes, these observations resulted in a series of 'explosive descriptive data about schools' (1976–7: 330), from which Holt himself was unable to draw any significant conclusions. It must also be considered that Holt's early observations were small in scale, being restricted to his own and Hunt's practice, which would call into question any generalisations formed. Alongside this, Holt's lack of formal qualifications meant that he was restricted to teaching in private schools, which would also have a significant impact on the data he was collecting, since we must question how far what he was observing in the private school sector was reflective of the education system as a whole. Parents opting for a private school education for their children would surely have been expecting a formal education, resulting in the best academic performance, which would be underpinned by examinations and test results.

It must be questioned how realistic Holt's unschooling philosophy was, since leaving a child's education to chance must surely be a risky business. Holt believed that allowing a child to follow their own interests would ultimately lead to the child learning what needed to be learned, albeit not always in the order that a formal curriculum might dictate. However, without testing this philosophy on a wider scale, it cannot be assumed that all children would be motivated to learn in this way, and it would surely not be ethical to risk a child's education based on this premise. Similarly, Holt spoke out about the use of testing and assessments in school. However, he himself acknowledged that this is a culture so heavily ingrained in schools that while pupils themselves complain and rebel against testing, they also defend the system asking, 'if we're not tested and graded how can we tell whether we're learning anything, whether we're doing well or poorly?' (Holt, 1969 [2005]: 40).

In conclusion, when considering Holt's work, we must question how far his observations were simply based on his own preconceived ideas about the shortcomings of the education system. It could be argued that Holt had become so disillusioned by the system that he failed to see the positives in his observations, and perhaps what he assumed about children's feelings towards their education was not in reality an accurate assumption.

⚙ APPLYING HOLT IN AND OUT OF THE CLASSROOM

Although Holt was unsuccessful in persuading his contemporaries to adopt his ideas in their classrooms, it could be argued that the ideas he was proposing can now be seen reflected in many of the curriculum developments in the UK, and to some extent in the changes to the English school system, which now encourages the development of free schools and academies.

Holt was a keen advocate for learning which began with the child, using their own interests as a starting point. He recounts an example of a fifth grader with a deep interest in snakes, and while snakes were not part of the curriculum, Holt suggested that 'any time he spent learning about snakes was better spent than in ways I could think to spend it' (1982: 292). Holt goes on to say that in the process of learning about snakes, the child is learning about many other things which he would not otherwise be learning (1982). He sums this up by suggesting that 'It is not the subject matter that makes some learning more valuable than others, but the spirit in which the work is done' (1982: 293).

Evidence of such personalised learning in the UK was observed for a brief period in the early 2000s, in which the Department for Education and Skills (DfES) (2004) proposed that education should be tailored to meet the needs of each individual, and should be responsive to their interests and aptitude, thus allowing every young person to fulfil their potential. In a speech at the North of England conference, David Miliband defined this as

> High expectations of every child, given practical form by high quality teaching based on a sound knowledge and understanding of each child's needs. It is not individualised learning where pupils sit alone. Nor is it pupils left to their own devices – which too often reinforces low aspirations. It means shaping teaching around the way different youngsters learn; it means taking the care to nurture the unique talents of every pupil. (2004: 3)

While this is an ethos that would reflect Holt's ideals on developing a curriculum around the individual needs of the child, since it promoted an ideal that accepted and assumed that each individual enters the education system with their own unique knowledge base and skills which should be used as a starting point for a personalised learning agenda (DfES, 2004), Meighan suggests that this agenda lacked real commitment to personalised learning. Meighan argues that the version of personalised learning promoted by the government was 'heavily teacher controlled and can be caricatured as "the teacher devises an individual learning program, which can look very much like that of everybody else, and the learner signs it"' (2007: 152).

Policies pertaining to personalised learning were not sustained and by 2016 documentation was withdrawn, although arguably the notion remains in the Early Years Foundation Stage in which the revised Statutory Framework for the Early Years Foundation Stage continues to promote a curriculum in which

> Practitioners must consider the individual needs, interests, and stages of development for experiences for each child in all of the areas of learning and development for each child in their care and must use this information to plan challenging and enjoyable activities. (DfE, 2017: 9)

One possible suggestion why the ethos of an individualised curriculum sustained in the Early Years Foundation and not in subsequent stages could well be that this is much easier to achieve in the formative stages, where there are far fewer pressures to meet standards and pass assessments. In this respect, a more formal curriculum might well be considered a requirement beyond the foundation stage to ensure that children meet the standards set out by government policy. This notion of meeting set standards, measured through formal examinations and tests, was a further area of contention for Holt, who suggested that 'the test-examination-marks business is a gigantic racket' (1982: 232). Holt believed that the sole purpose of assessments was to be a joint pretence to show that 'students know everything they are supposed to know; when in fact they only know a small part of it' (1982: 232). He suggested that the very fact that tests are announced to the students in advance is to ensure that students prepare themselves in the best way possible, in order that the best results might be achieved.

Similar views were suggested by Black and Wiliam in 2001 with the publication of *Inside the Black Box* in which they proposed that rather than assessing children summatively at the end of a module or scheme of work, assessment should take more of a formative form. Through the formative assessment model, teachers would carry out ongoing assessments of the learning process, allowing them to address any issues as they arise, rather than at the end when it is often too late to do anything about it. This way, teachers could adapt their teaching to meet the needs of each individual child. Black and Wiliam's work was reflective of Holt's in that they were more interested in the process than the product – understanding how an answer had been reached rather than the answer itself. For Holt, his interest was in how the mind worked, something he suggested was almost impossible to measure (Holt, 1969 [2005]).

Black and Wiliam's work had a significant impact on assessment in schools through the assessment for learning strategy, introduced in England by the Department for

Children, Schools and Families in 2008. Here, the then Minister of State for Schools and Learners, Jim Knight, set out his aims to personalise learning and teaching through embedding assessment for learning in all classrooms. Building on the work of Black and Wiliam, the assessment reform group, responsible for the implementation of the strategy, highlighted the importance of assessment in the classroom, which placed less emphasis on the more traditional formal assessments used in schools. Instead, they presented a vision that saw assessment as an ongoing system of continuous monitoring, central to classroom practice and designed to inform planning and teaching methods. More importantly, it saw pupils at the heart of the process, involved in the assessment of their own work and that of their peers, a notion that Holt himself certainly embraced, suggesting that 'all serious practice can be seen as a way in which the learner tests his own skill and knowledge' (1969 [2005]: 37). While a change in government in 2010 saw a return to a more traditional style of assessment in schools, it could be argued that the assessment for learning strategy has left a legacy in schools that sees teachers continuing to use ongoing formative assessment to help inform and personalise the learning experience for children, which Holt would surely have approved of.

By the late 1970s, Holt had turned his attention away from classroom practice and instead began to focus on the school system as a whole. In his book *Instead of Education* (1976) he provided examples and methods for running free schools and learning exchanges as an alternative to compulsory schooling. Although not as radical as Holt's ideas, free schools came to the fore in British politics following the election of the coalition government in 2010. In their academies and free school's policy document, the government set out their aim to reform the school system to prevent standards in England from falling behind those of other countries (DfE, 2010). Through the models of both academies and free schools, more control was given to the setting to decide on their own curriculum, decide their own term dates and school times, and control staffing and budgets in the best interests of the stakeholders. Of course, we cannot overlook the impetus for this policy change, since for the coalition government this was about raising standards, a concept that would have held no appeal for Holt unless it was in the best interests of the child. However, arguably the sense of control, if in the right hands, could well reflect Holt's ideal of an education system tailor-made for its intended audience.

It would be an oversight not to consider the home-school movement when evaluating the impact of Holt's work on practice, since in abandoning all attempts to change the education system, it is in the American home-school movement that Holt has perhaps had the most significant and lasting impact. Holt was keen, however, when encouraging parents to take their children out of compulsory schooling that they did not simply replicate the school system in their homes. Holt urged the parents of home-schoolers to make the most of their natural environment in the learning process, taking education into the environment and creating a secure foundation for lifelong learning. Holt suggests:

Experience being the greatest of all teachers, homeschoolers can make their children part of their everyday adult lives. By being accepted into the continuum of their parents' lives, a child learns by doing, by seeing other people work and do things and wanting to do them themselves. (cited in Farenga, n.d.)

To this end, Holt believed that the home-schooler should be allowed autonomy over their own learning, learning what they wanted when they wanted without the pressure of a set curriculum that showed no respect for a child's individual needs. This may well be seen reflected in the most recent government guidelines, which state that home-schooling is a right for all parents and children, and there is no legal obligation to follow the national curriculum in England (Gov.uk, 2015). However, we must question the reality of this notion set against a society that relies so heavily on the standards set by formal examinations.

REFLECTIVE TASK

What is most important and valuable about the home as a base for children's growth into the world is not that it is a better school than the schools but that it isn't a school at all. It is not an artificial place, set up to make 'learning' happen and in which nothing except 'learning' ever happens. (Holt and Farenga, 2003: 279)

Holt believed that children should be educated at home, following their own needs and interests. In this way he believed they would learn what they needed to learn when they needed to learn it.

How practical do you think this is in today's society? Make a list of advantages and disadvantages of this approach to schooling.

SUMMARY

It is testament to Holt's tenacity that, despite being met with resistance from both policy-makers and colleagues, he never gave up on his desire to promote a more positive learning experience for children. His attempts to reform education saw him turn his attention away from classroom practice into policy and school reform, and latterly to the rights of the child and home-schooling.

Aside from his influence on the home-schooling movement in America, Holt is probably best known for his two seminal texts, *How Children Fail* and *How Children Learn*, in which he presents a somewhat disparaging view of the American education system. However, despite his initial contention that 'school is a place where children learn to be stupid' (Holt, 1964, cited in Lant, 1976–7), Holt continued to offer practical suggestions to help parents and teachers improve matters for children, before eventually concluding that schools simply did not want to change.

Despite setting out to be neither an educationalist nor a writer, Holt made a significant impact in both fields at the height of his success in the 1960s and 1970s. His books sold well, and there continues to be a market for those seeking an alternative to traditional schooling even today. It is unfortunate that his ideals became too radical, even during the heady times of social reform.

GLOSSARY OF TERMS

Free schools   Schools that are set up by local community groups and are free from local authority control, allowing greater independent control of operating procedures.

Growing Without Schooling   The home-schooling newsletter that was founded by Holt in 1977. The newsletter focused predominantly on unschooling and deschooling, and was a reflection of Holt's antipathy towards the education system and what he construed to be an unwillingness from educators to elicit change.

Home-schooling   Home-schooling in the traditional sense refers to educating the child in the home environment, whether full or part-time. Parents who wish to home-school their child have a legal obligation to inform the local education authority, and while there is no requirement to follow a set curriculum, parents must evidence that their children are receiving a suitable education from home.

Learning exchanges   A community-operated project in which those with skills offer guidance and instruction to those who wish to develop skills. Holt promoted the use of community resources as a means by which to access such tutelage and recommended that this should be self-managed and governed. Holt was also keen to point out that those with advanced qualifications should have no more merit than those with technical skills, emphasising the importance of the promotion of skills and knowledge to which others placed value.

Holt proposed a radical overhaul of the American education system in which he advised that extreme changes needed to be made to current practice requiring policy-makers to question the purpose of education. Holt's observation of the education system was one that engendered fear and compliance in children, and he sought to create a system that encouraged creativity and spontaneity. For this to be achieved, radical reform was required.

Unschooling   Holt coined the term 'unschooling' to distinguish it from the more traditional 'home-schooling'. Parents who choose to unschool their children are not required to follow a set curriculum, nor is education directed by an adult. In unschooling, children are encouraged to follow their own interests, with the onus on freedom to learn at their own pace. Choice and control are in the hands of the learner, with children choosing what to learn, when to learn and how to learn.

FURTHER READING

Gatto, J.T. (2002) *Dumbing Us Down: The Hidden Curriculum of Contemporary Schooling*. Gabriola Island: New Society Publishers.
An account of the impact of compulsory schooling on children in America.

Holt, J. and Scheffer, S. (1990) *A Life Worth Living: The Selected Letters of John Holt*. Athens, OH: Ohio State University Press.
A selection of letters written by John Holt providing an insight into some of his thoughts on educational reform, schooling and politics.

Miller, R.J. (2005) *Free Schools, Free People: Education and Democracy after the 1960s*. New York: State University of New York Press.
An account of the free school movement of the 1960s, charting the works of some of the key figures of the time, including John Holt and A.S. Neill.

REFERENCES

Allen, M. (1981) *The Education of John Holt*. Available online at: www.holtgws.com/educationofjh.html

Black, P. and Wiliam, D. (2001) *Inside the Black Box: Raising Standards through Classroom Assessment*. British Educational Research Association. Available online at: https://weaeducation.typepad.co.uk/files/blackbox-1.pdf

Bumgarner, M. (1980) *A Conversation with John Holt*. The Natural Child Project. Available online at: www.naturalchild.org/guest/marlene_bumgarner.html

Department for Education (DfE) (2010) 2010–2015 *Government Policy: Academies and Free Schools*. London: Crown copyright.

Department for Education (DfE) (2017) *Statutory Framework for the Early Years Foundation Stage*. London: Crown copyright.

Department for Education and Skills (DfES) (2004) *A National Conversation about Personalised Learning*. London: Crown copyright.

Farenga, P. (n.d.) *Homeschooling and John Holt's Vision*. Available online at: http://spinninglobe.net/spinninglobe_html/hs%26jholt.htm

Farenga. P. (1999) *John Holt and the Origins of Contemporary Homeschooling*. Available online at: http://mhla.org/information/resourcesarticles/holtorigins.htm

Gaither, M. (2015) 'John Holt'. *Encyclopaedia Britannica Online*. Available online at: www.britannica.com/biography/John-Holt

Gov.uk (2015) *Home Education*. Available online at: www.gov.uk/home-education

Holt, J. (1964) *How Children Fail*. London: Penguin Books.

Holt, J. (1967) *How Children Learn*. London: Penguin Books.

Holt, J. (1969 [2005]) *The Underachieving School*. Boulder, CO: Sentient Publications.

Holt, J. (1972) *Freedom and Beyond*. New York: E.P. Dutton.

Holt, J. (1974) *Escape from Childhood*. New York: Holt Associates.

Holt, J. (1976) *Instead of Education: Ways to Help People Do Things Better*. New York: E.P. Dutton.

Holt, J. (1981) *Teach Your Own: A Hopeful Path for Education*. New York: Delacorte.

Holt, J. (1982) *How Children Fail* (revised edn). London: Penguin Books.

Holt, J. (1983) *How Children Learn* (revised edn). London: Penguin Books.

Holt, J. and Farenga, P. (2003) *Teach Your Own: The John Holt Book of Homeschooling*. New York: Perseus Books Group.

Illich, I. (1970) *Deschooling Society*. London: Marion Boyars Publishers.

Lant, J.L. (1976–7) 'Considering John Holt'. *Educational Studies*, 7: 327–35.

Meighan, R. (2007) *John Holt*. London: Bloomsbury Academia.

Miliband, D. (2004) *Personalised Learning: Building a New Relationship with Schools*. North of England Education Conference, Belfast. London: Department for Education and Skills. Available online at: https://webarchive.nationalarchives.gov.uk/20130323075319/https:/www.education.gov.uk/publications/eOrderingDownload/DfES%200919%20200MIG186.pdf

16
BELL HOOKS

EDUCATION AS THE PRACTICE OF FREEDOM

LEARNING OUTCOMES

After reading this chapter, you should be able to:

- understand how hooks's upbringing influenced her teaching and writing;
- appreciate the impact of hooks's notion of education as the practice of freedom;
- identify and understand hooks's concern with issues of race, gender and class as they relate to education;
- apply the principles of engaged pedagogy to your practice;
- critically evaluate hooks's writing and her views on educational practice.

KEY WORDS

Engaged pedagogy; critical thinking; democratic education; spirituality; learning community; practical wisdom.

INTRODUCTION

bell hooks is an American scholar, author, feminist, progressive educator and social activist, born in 1952 in Hopkinsville, Kentucky, USA. Her actual name is Gloria Watkins; she adopted the pen name bell hooks, written in lower case, from her great-grandmother Bell Blair Hooks (Burke, 2004). Although she is probably more renowned for her writings on the black female in US culture, this chapter will mainly focus on her significant contributions to the practice of progressive and democratic higher education. These significant contributions to education have emerged and are embedded in her convictions of the inequality that is still evident where matters of race, gender and social class are concerned. From these convictions, hooks has campaigned for a powerful and active form of **engaged pedagogy** with which to defy how conventional education is practised, and has called for 'education as the practice of freedom' (hooks, 1994; Thomas, 1997) – a notion of education that is both influenced by, and closely related to, Freire's antipathy to a 'banking' system of education (Freire, 1970 [1996]).

The motivation for her writing on education came from her own experiences of how she was influenced by teachers from her time at school and as an undergraduate and postgraduate student at university. Her writing also stemmed from her positive, and not so positive, experiences as a teacher:

> Nurturing the self-development and self-actualization of students in the classroom I soon learned to love teaching. I loved the students. I loved the classroom. I also found it profoundly disturbing that many of the abuses of power that I had experienced during my education were still commonplace, and I wanted to write about it. (hooks, 2010: 3)

She was furthermore moved to write because of what she saw as a widespread lack of black women writers in present-day scholarly works that tackled the inequities of gender, race and class issues (hooks, 1994). A complementary comparison has been offered between hooks and Nina Simone, the musical phenomenon known as 'the High Priestess of the Civil Rights Movement ... [because she] brought a critical creative expression to her work that parallels some of the principles that are supported by hooks' (Tisdell and Tolliver, 2009: 96). Writing in 2010, hooks comments: 'although our nation has made significant strides in the area of civil rights, the United States remains a society where segregation is the norm'; this she feels was particularly the case in education and on university campuses (2010: 95).

hooks has written a trilogy of influential, and radical, educational books: *Teaching to Transgress: Education as the Practice of Freedom* (1994), *Teaching Community: A Pedagogy of Hope* (2003a) and *Teaching Critical Thinking: Practical Wisdom* (2010). All are written in the autobiographical memoire style of the storyteller, which uses a combination of reflection and narrative (Cole and Knowles, 2001). Each book is a collection of critical essays in which she shares some quite personal issues, particularly about her family; this style is not written to disturb, but rather to confront honestly those issues that normally go unspoken (Cheng, 1997; hooks, 2003a).

The first of the trilogy, *Teaching to Transgress* (1994), is a set of fourteen essays that endeavour to consider the associations between engaged pedagogy and matters of gender, race and class. In addition, it reflects on the influence that Freire's philosophy has had on hooks's writing. In this work she also urges teachers to move on from traditional practices to surmount the *ennui* of what is currently experienced in the classroom (Thomas, 1997). The second book of sixteen essays, *Teaching Community* (2003a), enabled hooks to build on the success of the first in that the broad and diverse essays were drawn from a wide section of society, not just those directly involved in teaching; as such, she was able to reach out and promote her ideas and the importance of a more progressive education to a wider community. In the final part of the trilogy, *Teaching Critical Thinking* (2010), hooks again covers a diverse range of issues, nevertheless with the same focus on gender, race and class. In this work, the thirty-two essays (or 'teachings' as she calls them) have arisen from conversations with teachers and students in a 'collected desire to understand how to make the classroom a place of fierce engagement and intense learning' (hooks, 2010: 5).

To gain a full insight into what shaped hooks's notions of education as the practice of freedom and engaged pedagogy, we need to consider the culture of her upbringing as a black female child in the 1950s and 1960s in the South of the United States, and to examine her experiences during her academic career in higher education.

BELL HOOKS, THE PERSON

hooks was brought up in a black working-class neighbourhood and her rise to become a distinguished scholar is a phenomenon. She appreciated the meaning of gender inequity as a young girl growing up in a patriarchal family where 'our daily life was full of patriarchal drama – the use of coercion, violent punishment, verbal harassment to maintain male domination' (hooks, 1994: 119). She, like her siblings, realised that her father's authority held more weight than her mother's. These early experiences, together with what she felt as a student regarding the effect of racism and sexism for black women, were explored in her first feminist book *Ain't I a Woman: Black Women and Feminism* (1982). Until the publication of this book, feminist writers found it difficult to include matters of diversity such as 'racial, cultural, or sexual, and tended to universalise the experience of white, middle-class, urban heterosexual women' (Barry, 2002: 140). These early experiences have shaped her current thinking, and today she is an anti-racist and committed feminist; however, the core theme of her work stresses that issues of 'gender, race and class distinctions are not viewed as being more than the other', but they are all interlocked (Burke, 2004: 2).

Because of the racial apartheid at the time, hooks's early education took place in segregated schools. It was in these black schools, with black teachers

where I experienced learning as a revolution ... black children who were deemed excep-
tional, gifted, were given special care. Teachers worked with us to ensure that we would
fulfil our intellectual destiny and by doing so uplift the race. My teachers were on a mission. (hooks, 1994: 2)

At this stage, school, for hooks, was a place of happiness and discovery, 'where I could
forget ... and, through ideas, reinvent myself' (1994: 3). Teachers knew their students'
family backgrounds and, as such, teaching was culturally meaningful. However, this
changed dramatically with racial integration in the 1960s, when the enthusiasm of her
teachers to strive to improve students' learning was gone. Now knowledge was concerned with gathering information and it had no links with black culture. Black
children were now 'bussed to white schools, we soon learned that obedience, and not
a zealous will to learn, was what was expected of us' (1994: 3). She is very critical about
her teachers when she attended her new white school, who she said considered
themselves racially superior and thought that black students were unable to learn.
Her comments about this period of her education are thought-provoking and quite
disturbing – for example, she states: 'Imagine what it is like to be taught by a teacher
who does not believe you are fully human' (2010: 2). These feelings about race domination stayed with her through her time at university both as an undergraduate and
postgraduate student. She was, in the main, not impressed by her lecturers, but 'learned
a lot about the kind of teacher I did not want to become' (1994: 5).

Despite her unhappiness as a university student within a dominant culture, hooks
progressed well in her academic studies. She was awarded a scholarship to study at
Stanford University where she gained a BA in 1973, then in 1976 she achieved an MA
from the University of Wisconsin before her PhD in 1983 at the University of Santa
Cruz (Burke, 2004). She went on to become a prolific writer of many books and journal articles on race, feminism, film and class, as well as education. She has taught for
many years in a variety of higher education institutions in the United States, becoming
Distinguished Professor of English at the City College of New York (Burke, 2004). In
2014, she founded the bell hooks Institute in Berea, Kentucky, which endeavours to
encourage the ending of domination and discrimination through **critical thinking**
and teaching (bell hooks Institute, 2015). She has remained active in the anti-hegemonic
movement challenging the dominant culture throughout her time as a student and
during her academic career. Apple (2013) argues that it is difficult to understand the
impact of dominance if one is not involved in such anti-hegemonic movements. Her
ideas on education and teaching were shaped by the anti-racist civil rights movement,
feminism and her wish to become an active cultural critic (hooks, 2010).

HOOKS AND HER NOTIONS OF LEARNING

Before exploring the specific notions held by hooks, such as engaged pedagogy,
critical thinking, learning communities and **practical wisdom**, it is appropriate at this

stage to consider her overall rationale for changes in teaching practice and her untiring quest for education as a practice of freedom. hooks feels that **democratic education** in the United States has been weakened because 'business and corporate capitalism encourage students to see education solely as a means to material success' (hooks, 2010: 16). This materialistic notion of education values the gathering of information, whereas the democratic model of education values the process of attaining knowledge and critical thinking. She laments that progressive university lecturers who strive for a democratic education are often ostracised or urged to leave academia. Yet she calls for lecturers to continue the struggle to create a democratic environment in their classrooms where learning and thinking critically are appreciated and esteemed, where student voice and dissent are not just allowed but also promoted (hooks, 2010). Such a democratic learning environment needs to be 'a place that is life-sustaining and mind-expanding, a place of liberating mutuality where teacher and student together work in partnership' (hooks, 2003a: xv).

Drawing upon events from her own education where teachers in her segregated schools acknowledged and valued individual students' experiences as part of the learning process, hooks explains how this was certainly not the case when she later attended desegregated schools where black children were 'regarded as objects and not subjects' (hooks, 1994: 37). For her, student experiences are explicitly linked with the politics of gender, race and issues of class. As such, teachers should not submissively consent to use pedagogies that mirror the prejudices of the dominant standpoint of education by the 'imperialist white-supremacist capitalist patriarchy' (hooks, 2003a: 166). Her aim of creating education as the practice of freedom is focused on hope for the future, a future away from segregation towards a radical vision which endeavours to salvage the full potential of anti-racist and democratic integration (hooks, 2003a). Central to this aim is her notion of engaged pedagogy (hooks, 1994).

Engaged pedagogy, hooks argues, should embrace and celebrate student experiences; it is a way of defining a process of interactive learning and teaching where everyone's existence and voice in the classroom is acknowledged (Collins et al., 2002). However, engaged pedagogy has a more all-inclusive advantage:

> When education is the practice of freedom, students are not the only ones asked to share, to confess. Engaged pedagogy does not seek simply to empower students. As any classroom that employs a holistic model of learning will also be a place where teachers grow, and are empowered by the process. (hooks, 1994: 21)

hooks concedes that engaged pedagogy is a demanding practice that involves both teachers and students taking risks, and stresses that 'teachers must be actively committed to a process of self-actualization that promotes their own well-being' in order to empower students (hooks, 1994: 15). For hooks, engaged pedagogy involves 'a flexible agenda, spontaneity, interaction and critical reflection' (Collins et al., 2002: 106).

Engaged pedagogy challenges the traditional and dominant way of thinking that all classrooms are the same, even when there are differences in students' gender, race and class. hooks argues that with engaged pedagogy the classroom is in a constant state of flux: 'It's dynamic. It's fluid. It's *always* changing' (hooks, 1994: 158). As such, engaged practice fosters discussion and interpersonal associations that enable critical reflection to flourish between students and teachers: 'it allows students to recognize their own and others' humanity and assists them in becoming critical citizens' (Carolissen et al., 2011: 158). Engaged pedagogy is a teaching approach that strives to re-establish students' motivation to think critically as part of the learning process. This, she argues, is not an easy process as the majority of students are more secure with passive learning (hooks, 2010).

For hooks, critical thinking is a process that insists on students and teachers openly and honestly participating together to deconstruct and delve below the surface in their search for knowledge, and together building what she terms 'learning communities' (hooks, 2010). She sees critical thinking as a perceptive way to uncover knowledge that can be shared and valued despite differences. According to hooks, what is crucial for successful critical thinking practice is not so much the analysis of the debate, but rather the capabilities of students to 'transcend race, class, and gender biases to transform their lives, moving beyond these into places of power and possibility' (Lim, 2011: 5). Key to the success of critical thinking is the building of trusting classroom relationships in a safe environment for students to openly discuss topics of contention and sensitivity. Engaged pedagogy that involves critical thinking enables students and teachers to face their feelings and rebuild their connections with others in secure and trusting learning communities (hooks, 2003a).

Building trusting learning communities involves finding out what similarities we have, as well as what divides us and creates differences. Many students, and teachers, avoid facing up to difference because they think this will lead to discord. However, hooks (2003a) argues that it is our refusal to encounter the existence of difference that creates continuing discord; instead, she suggests that we should connect with, and celebrate, our differences and confront any frictions as they are encountered. Therefore, she promotes the creation of learning communities that have 'unity within diversity' (hooks, 2003a: 109). She cites the dominator culture as blameworthy for students and teachers preferring uniformity over difference. In its place we should discover what aspects connect us and also rejoice in our differences. This in turn will bring individuals nearer to each other with a set of shared values to form meaningful learning communities, both inside classrooms and in the world (hooks, 2003a).

Her last book in the teaching trilogy (hooks, 2010) makes links with engaged pedagogy, critical thinking, learning communities and what she calls practical wisdom. This is the awareness of the interconnections between theory and knowledge and the fact that knowledge cannot be detached from experience. Engaged pedagogy and critical thinking encourage us to think for ourselves and to be self-critical, which are essential for practical wisdom. By being critical and reflective about our lives and the world we live in

> Practical wisdom shows us that all genuine learning requires of us a constant open approach, a willingness to engage invention and reinvention, so that we may discover those places of transparency where knowledge can empower ... learning to reflect, to broaden our vision so that we can see the whole picture. (hooks, 2010: 187)

The notion that knowledge is embedded in experience affects not only how we came about our knowledge, but also how we utilise it (hooks, 2010). Furthermore, practical wisdom helps us combine knowledge, theory and personal skills in a practical approach to learning (hooks, 2010).

The use of dialogue is central throughout all hooks's notions of learning. She particularly emphasises the significance of language and voice in education as a practice of freedom. In her own writing, she uses autobiographical narrative to uncover the realities of the marginalised, in so doing enlightening her readership about significant issues of social justice, and also 'how the personal is fundamentally political' (Carolissen et al., 2011: 158). It is the English language which she feels is used in a political context by the dominant culture and 'what the oppressors do with it, how they shape it to become a territory that limits and defines, how they make it a weapon that can shame, humiliate, colonize' (hooks, 1994: 168). She criticises the reality that, in teaching and in writing, and in academia as a whole, there has been scant endeavour to use black colloquial speech or anything that is not 'normal' English. Furthermore, she contests that those students who come from ethnically diverse or working-class backgrounds can be disadvantaged, as she explains: 'To insist on speaking in any manner that did not conform to privileged class ideas and mannerisms placed one always in the position of interloper' (hooks, 1994: 182).

Despite these possible disadvantages, hooks has always encouraged and enthused about the use of student voice as being a vital part of engaged pedagogy within trusting learning communities (hooks, 2003a).

Throughout her works, hooks stresses the significance of well-being for teachers and students, and interweaves notions of care, love, **spirituality** and imagination as underpinning such well-being and personal growth (Sewell, 2010). She likens teaching to a caring profession but considers that, like other caring professions in the United States, teaching is unappreciated. Moreover, she proposes that those teachers who care for their students in the wider sense are usually acting in conflict with their institutions because, she argues, these establishments are places where knowledge has been designed to bolster the dominant culture (hooks, 2003b). hooks's claim that teaching involves love goes against conventional wisdom, which states that teachers should remain emotionally detached from their students. For hooks, the idea of love in teaching ought to 'be a practice that validates the whole person and not only that which they can produce in a test' (Carolissen et al., 2011: 159). She argues that teachers should not be anxious that love will result in favouritism or rivalry, because love will act as a deterrent to domination: 'love will always challenge and change us' (hooks, 2010: 163). A lack of clarity about the notion of love

278 UNDERSTANDING AND USING CHALLENGING EDUCATIONAL THEORIES

is the core of any difficulty involved in the act of loving; love for hooks 'is a matter of will, action and choice. It is a matter of education' (Back, 2007: 82).

Central to her idea of care are the aspects of the human spirit such as kindness, tolerance and forgiveness. All of these aspects can create a classroom environment where learning becomes meaningful and worthwhile, and students develop a sense of self-determination and take responsibility for their growth as learners. By involving these aspects of the human spirit students have an insight into the emotional and caring features of their inner self, which helps to create spirituality in the classroom (hooks, 2010). She cautions that

> Schooling that does not honour the needs of the spirit simply intensifies the sense of being lost, of being unable to connect ... [and furthermore] it is the failure to achieve harmony of mind, body, and spirit that has furthered anti-intellectualism in our culture and made of our schools mere factories. (hooks, 2003a: 180–1).

For hooks, living in a community, love and spirituality are synonymous with each other, but these are impeded by a culture of domination:

> To be guided by love is to live in community with all life. However, a culture of domination, like ours, does not strive to teach us how to live in a community. As a consequence, learning to live in a community must be core practice for all of us who desire spirituality in education. (hooks, 2003a: 163)

Imagination, like spirituality, is not encouraged within the dominant culture of higher education establishments, which value information over the process of learning. Even though young children are encouraged to use their imagination, as they get older 'imagination is seen as dangerous, a force that could possibly impede knowledge acquisition' (hooks, 2010: 60). For the most part, university discourages imagination in favour of data and information-gathering. The dominant culture, hooks contends, is trying to quash imagination as a way of repression; arguing that, 'imagination is one of the most powerful modes of resistance that oppressed and exploited folks can and do use' (hooks, 2010: 61). These sentiments of resistance over oppression and the notion of democratic education are in common with other progressive educational thinkers and social activists.

LINKS WITH OTHER THEORISTS

Possibly the most influential thinker to promote democratic education was John Dewey in his 1916 seminal text *Democracy and Education: An Introduction to the Philosophy of Education*. Like Dewey, hooks advances the notion of a democratic education that embraces experiences from real life and the world at large. Also, for both of them, education is not limited to the formal curricula of schools and universities;

rather, learning takes place in the real world and is a continual process (hooks, 2003a). Her ideas are also very comparable to those of Dewey, who argued for a move away from the traditional passive notion of teaching to a more active, participatory practice that valued difference and the building of democratic learning communities (Dewey, 1938). hooks and Dewey advocated a progressive and democratic form of education in which experiences from different cultures were used to resolve problems through discussion and where students learned from each other (Dewey, 1938).

The thinker who has had the most influence upon hooks was Paulo Freire, the Brazilian educational philosopher. When she discovered Freire, hooks 'found a mentor and a guide, someone who understood that learning could be liberatory' and not a process of 'banking' information given (hooks, 1994: 6). Undoubtedly, Freire has had an overwhelming impact on hooks's practice and her writing, especially concerning language and consciousness (Burke, 2004). It was Freire's notions of freedom from oppression (Freire, 1970 [1996]) that inspired hooks to generate approaches to her teaching that were aligned to his idea of 'conscientisation' – a term she interpreted and associated with her notions of engaged pedagogy and critical thinking. She was thereafter convinced that it 'was crucial for me and every other student to be an active participant, not a passive consumer' (hooks, 1994: 14). Both also considered that education should be rooted in hope. Like Freire, hooks saw hope appear from 'places of struggle where I witness individuals positively transforming their lives and the world around them' (hooks, 2003a: xiv). Although hooks considered that Freire's philosophy was in many ways attuned with her own feminist thinking, she did censure his use of sexist language which was apparent in his earlier writing (Irwin, 2012).

There are many similarities between Henry Giroux and hooks in their standpoints on education and teaching practice. Giroux's critical pedagogy emphasises the need for teachers to reach out to all students by taking into consideration matters of gender, race and class (Giroux, 1992). Giroux also stresses the importance of situating students' experiences and cultural differences in the process of learning. He also highlights the significance of encouraging the student voice, otherwise students become passive recipients of the dominant and oppressive culture (hooks, 1994). Giroux, similar to hooks, also felt that feminist activists should not concentrate entirely on issues of gender differences, but should look at how they overlap with other sources of power, especially with respect to race and class (Giroux, 1992). Her ideas of empowerment, engagement and criticality are also similar to other progressive educators such as Ivan Illich, Michael Apple and Peter McLaren. hooks's view that traditional education and the curriculum were constructed and controlled by the dominant culture to maintain the status quo is very much aligned with Foucault's ideas outlined in *Discipline and Punish: The Birth of the Prison* (1979). This, hooks argues, thwarts opportunities for critical thinking and students soon learn 'via a model of discipline and punish that it is better to choose obedience over self-awareness and self-determination' (2010: 8). hooks's progressive ideas have influenced other educational thinkers, and her inclusive and caring approach to teaching have had a positive impact on engaged classroom practice.

⊛ CRITIQUING THE THEORY

hooks attracts censure because her work does not conform to the conventions of academic writing (Cheng, 1997). This is a matter that hooks herself acknowledges, and she regrets that students are discouraged from citing her work as their professors do not consider it of a scholarly quality. She puts this down to her standpoint on issues of gender:

> Any of us who create feminist theory and feminist writing in academic settings in which we are continually evaluated know that work deemed 'not scholarly' or 'not theoretical' can result in one not receiving deserved recognition and reward. (hooks, 1994: 72)

Non-compliance to the conventions of academic writing includes her not citing scholarly sources and a style of writing that, as we have seen, is very personal and confessional in its nature. Therefore, by using this personal style of writing there is a danger that she could be accused of exaggeration and giving an excessive degree of bias to her ideas. In doing so, she risks losing the regard from those in academia who would prefer a more reasoned and critically logical analytical approach (Cheng, 1997).

There are very real practical problems as well in the telling of stories and divulging personal experiences in the classroom, which hooks fully concedes. This can be seen by some students as an opportunity to try to divert the lesson away from the designated course reading and planned content, which can result in some students dominating while others are passive (hooks, 2010). She has also been criticised as a teacher, as well as during her time as a student, 'for having too much passion, for being too emotional' (hooks, 2003a: 127). She makes a strong case for promoting a notion of love between students and teachers as being a component of caring and open relationships, as long as that love is contained within the appropriate boundaries. However, there is a very real concern for some teachers who might feel overwhelmed at being too emotionally involved in students' problems (hooks, 2003a).

The practice of engaged pedagogy, ensuring that all students are participating, is very tiring. It is made worse by an ever-increasing number of students entering her classrooms. When this happens, engaged practice becomes impractical: 'overcrowded classes are like overcrowded buildings – the structure can collapse' (hooks, 1994: 160). There is also a risk with large groups of teacher over-exhaustion and consequently a return to the traditional didactic method of teaching (hooks, 1994). Moreover, there is a question over the validity of her emphasis on the use of an equity of dialogue between teacher and student. Berry argues that 'engaged pedagogy does not alleviate the historical power of the teacher/professor and thereby can limit the freedom of speech in the classroom' (Berry, 2010: 21).

A regular criticism of hooks's essays in all three teaching trilogy books is that they offer an abundance of passion and insight about gender and race issues, but little in the way of concrete advice for practical application (Thomas, 1997; Carolissen et al., 2011). Irrespective of these criticisms, hooks's work offers a range of inclusive and progressive ideas that can be adapted for practice to create participatory learning opportunities.

APPLYING HOOKS'S IDEAS IN PRACTICE

Although hooks may not propose a set of detailed guidelines for pedagogical practice, it is argued that her notions of engaged pedagogy, critical thinking and the use of student experience and voice presents practitioners with a plethora of ideas for class-room practice. These ideas emerge from her optimistic and passionate vision of the liberatory form of higher education teaching, which is highlighted in the concluding paragraph of the first book of her teaching trilogy:

> The academy is not paradise. But learning is a place where paradise can be created. The classroom with all its limitations, remains a location of possibility. In that field of possibility we have the opportunity to labor for freedom, to demand of ourselves and our comrades, an openness of mind and heart that allows us to face reality even if we collectively imagine ways to move beyond boundaries, to transgress. This is education as the practice of freedom. (hooks, 1994: 207)

She emphasises that the engaged pedagogy approach has also had benefits for her as a developing intellectual and teacher because at the core to this approach is critical thinking. To do this requires teachers to employ a range of learning and teaching strategies to promote an active **learning community**. However, she accepts that at times students become quite uncomfortable when teaching deviates from the passive 'banking' system (hooks, 1994).

To encourage and embrace the active learning which is embedded in the spirit of engaged pedagogy, teachers must act as performers, although not in the conventional meaning of the term. Such performances should endeavour to create flexibility and spontaneity to allow opportunities that empower all students. However, empowerment invites students to take risks – for example, taking part in confessional discussions that could possibly expose their vulnerability. According to hooks, teachers should not ask students to take risks that they are unwilling to take themselves; if they do, the teachers are 'exercising power in a manner that could be coercive' (hooks, 1994: 21). Therefore, it is this willingness on behalf of teachers to be at one with the students, to be open and share each other's vulnerability that is the essence of engaged pedagogy.

Engaged pedagogy, for the teacher, is the belief that the most valuable learning takes place when there is a shared and active rapport with the students. For this to happen, the teacher must determine what the students already know, as well as what it is they wish to learn. This in turn means that the teacher must delve deep to uncover the different levels of emotional awareness and consciousness that exist in the classroom. In practice, this takes a considerable amount of time and can be quite disconcerting for teachers who are anxious about ensuring that they cover the assigned material that is expected of them. However, hooks contends that we should take the time to get to know the students at the start of programmes of study by making time to let them introduce themselves and to share with the rest of the group where they have come from, and what their expectations and aspirations are. Making time to do this, she argues, creates a more favourable and positive learning environment – the start of an engaged and active learning community (hooks, 2010).

She offers some practical examples of how she ensures such engagement and sharing of experiences, so teachers can begin to understand who the students actually are and where they stand emotionally. To do this, she frequently asks students to write a brief paragraph (an activity in which she also takes part):

> We might all write a spontaneous paragraph beginning with a phrase like 'My most courageous moment happened when ...' or we might bring a small object to class and all write a short paragraph about its value and importance. Reading these short paragraphs aloud to each other, we have the opportunity to see and hear each unique voice ... Writing and reading paragraphs together acknowledges the power of each student's voice and creates the space for everyone to speak when they have meaningful comments to make. (hooks, 2010: 20)

Another strategy that she employs to build a learning community where every student voice is valued is to ask the students to keep journals, and she encourages them to write in them during her classes and then to read them to one another. This practice ensures that no student is passive and hidden within the classroom. This she maintains also encourages active listening and a recognition of each other's voice and viewpoints (hooks, 1994).

The use of voice, and in particular active listening, she stresses is a crucial component of engaged pedagogy and in the promotion of critical thinking. The use of voice, hooks argues, is more than about the telling of stories of experience; it is about developing a voice so that students can speak openly about other topics. hooks maintains that many students from working-class backgrounds believe that their lecturers think they have nothing of worth to say. The teaching strategy she offers to overcome this belief is to reduce the emphasis on her voice as a teacher and to encourage students to actively listen to each other. From her experience, she feels this happens quite rapidly when students share their experiences in union with the academic topic in question (hooks, 1994). She does accept, however, that although the use of encouraging student voice through conversation and discussion enhances the notion of a learning community, it can in practice lead to what could be conceived as quite disruptive and argumentative behaviour. For many students from a middle-class background, such behaviour is seen as aggressive. Nevertheless, she states that 'those of us from working-class backgrounds may feel that discussion is deeper and richer if it arouses intense responses' and, as such, teachers should continue to be open to such frank exchanges (hooks, 1994: 187).

A further consideration for practice is hooks's notion of the importance of the body in teaching and how the body is employed as a means of power in the classroom. She suggests that many teachers think it does not matter where they position themselves in the classroom. However, there are those teachers who, quite understandably, feel a loss of control if they move from behind the lectern or desk. Conversely, hooks feels more comfortable when she is among the students and being close to them. For her, accepting that both teachers and students are bodies is a crucial aspect of engaged pedagogy in her 'efforts to disrupt the notion of professor as [an] omnipotent, all-knowing mind' (hooks, 1994: 138). This idea of the teacher as the font of all knowledge who is always right, hooks argues, has no place in engaged pedagogy. She calls instead for an openness to recognise what teachers do not know and a 'radical commitment to openness which maintains the integrity of the critical thinking process and its central role in education' (hooks, 2010: 10). These are all linked to hooks's viewpoint on the importance of trust and love in the classroom.

One of the major facets of engaged pedagogy is the promotion of students' self-esteem; this for hooks is done by demonstrating appropriate approval and a recognition of students' capabilities. This she suggests is not achieved through lavish and uncritical praise. However, it does mean that teachers should provide feedback to students which recognises strengths, which in turn builds their confidence and leads to their self-esteem as learners. hooks's own practice encourages students to self-evaluate their progress so they are working for themselves rather than trying to satisfy the wishes of their teachers (2010). Students

> are empowered by working in a manner where they recognize their responsibility and accountability for the grade they receive. That empowerment reinforces healthy self-esteem. (hooks, 2010: 125)

This empowerment, then, not only raises the student's self-esteem, but promotes the concept of critical thinking. These ideas form a basis for the application of an active engaged pedagogy and what hooks calls 'education as the practice of freedom'.

REFLECTIVE TASK

hooks's notion of engaged pedagogy promotes the idea of encouraging the student voice and also the idea that all students should play an active part in the classroom. From your experiences as a student, answer the following two questions:

1. What are the barriers, both practical and philosophical, to achieving these aspects of engaged pedagogy?
2. If you had a free hand, and the opportunity to do so, how could these barriers be overcome in the future?

SUMMARY

bell hooks has had a profound impact as a social activist, feminist and scholar. Her work has also been of great significance for educators throughout the world. Her ideas of democratic education have been shaped by her beliefs, which are rooted in the inequalities she still sees in matters of gender, race and social class. These viewpoints have arisen from, and are deeply embedded in, her own experiences growing up as a black female in the South of the United States, as well as her experiences as a pupil first in a segregated school for black children and later as a black child in an integrated school. Her experiences as an undergraduate and postgraduate student affirmed what she saw as the oppressive and controlling nature of the dominant culture of the 'imperialist white-supremacist capitalist patriarchy' (hooks, 2003a: 166).

hooks is a prolific writer and wrote a trilogy of teaching books that offers a series of essays regarding education as a practice of freedom. These essays cover a range of topics that advocate a progressive and somewhat radical approach to teaching, especially in higher education. Her particular contributions to teaching are the notions of engaged pedagogy, critical thinking, creating learning communities and practical wisdom. Throughout all these ideas are the threads of active student learning through participation and the recognition of student voice and experience. Furthermore, she promotes aspects of love, spirituality and imagination, which are quite radical and innovative strategies in higher education teaching.

Her ideas of education have strong associations with John Dewey and democratic education that espouses the concepts of embracing the student experience, and encouraging active participatory learning. However, she was greatly influenced by Paulo Freire and his writing on overcoming oppression. She found Freire's works an inspiration that helped shape her ideas on engaged pedagogy and critical thinking, despite her criticism of his sexist language. Her views on teaching practice and issues of gender were very much in tune with Giroux's critical pedagogy, as well as the other progressive educators such as Illich, Apple and McLaren. She also shared with Foucault an aversion to the over-controlling and punitive systems in place in education to ensure the dominant culture maintains the status quo. The criticisms of hooks's work focus on the lack of scholarly application to her writing, her overly emotional approach to her pedagogical ideas and the risks involved in teachers being too close to their students. Furthermore, she receives criticism that her writings offer little practical guidance for classroom practice. This final point is contested. Although she does not set out a prescribed step-by-step guide for teachers, her emphasis on every student participating and the promotion of the student voice offer many inclusive and refreshing ideas for practice in university classrooms.

GLOSSARY OF TERMS

Critical thinking   This is the process whereby teachers and learners participate in an open and candid way to deconstruct and reach under the surface to seek knowledge, and in so doing build meaningful learning communities. hooks perceives critical thinking as a way to reveal knowledge that can be owned by all in spite of their differences. The key to critical thinking is the creation of trusting relationships in a secure environment for people to discuss ideas of opinion with understanding. The aim of critical thinking is that students go beyond matters of class, race and gender 'biases to transform their lives, moving beyond these into places of power and possibility' (Lim, 2011: 5).

Democratic education   The democratic model of education gives great importance to the actual process of gaining knowledge, as well as critical thinking. hooks urges educators to make every effort to create and provide a democratic environment where learning and critical thinking are valued and highly regarded, where student voice and dissent are not only allowed but also actively encouraged, and where students and teachers work equally together (hooks, 2010).

Engaged pedagogy   Engaged pedagogy supports and welcomes students' own experiences as a method of defining a process of interactive teaching and learning. It also celebrates and acknowledges everyone's contribution and voice in the classroom. It empowers learners and uses an all-inclusive mode of learning where both students and teachers develop and are enabled by the process. Engaged pedagogy is a demanding undertaking that involves teachers and students taking risks; it also includes being flexible, unplanned and dynamic, and using critical reflection. It challenges the dominant and conventional notion of classroom practice, and promotes interpersonal relationships that celebrate similarities and differences.

Learning community   The creation of learning communities involves finding out what we have in common and what creates differences between us. Many learners and teachers tend to stay clear of voicing differences because they think it will result in confrontation and dispute. hooks, however, argues that the rejection of facing up to differences just creates a continuance of discord; instead, she contests that we should welcome and celebrate differences and tackle any tensions as they are met. She advances the notion of building learning communities that have 'unity within diversity' (hooks, 2003a: 109).

Practical wisdom   Practical wisdom is the appreciation of the interconnections between theory and knowledge, and the point that knowledge cannot be separated from experience. Engaged pedagogy and critical thinking promotes us to be self-critical and to think for ourselves, which are central to practical wisdom. The idea that knowledge is rooted in experience influences not just how we came about knowledge, but also how we use such knowledge; practical wisdom enables us to align knowledge, theory and personal skills in a practical approach to learning (hooks, 2010).

Spirituality   hooks believed that by fostering students' human spirits, such as kindness, tolerance and forgiveness, they develop a sense of self-determination and accept accountability for their advancement as learners. By embracing these aspects of human spirit, learners have an awareness of the emotional and caring aspects of their inner self; this in turn creates spirituality in the classroom. Spirituality, living in a community and love are all synonymous with each other in developing worthwhile and meaningful learning. However, hooks warns that these are obstructed by a culture of domination (2003a).

FURTHER READING

Atkinson, E. (2006) 'Sexualities and resistance: Queer(y)ing identity and discourse in education'. In: Lauder, H., Brown, P., Dillabough, J.-A. and Halsey, A. (eds) *Education, Globalization and Social Change*. Oxford: Oxford University Press.
This chapter explores the notion of gender and sexuality as a process of resistance to the oppressive dominant culture in education.

hooks, b. (1996) *Reel to Real: Race, Sex and Class at the Movies*. London: Routledge.
A series of essays in which hooks considers the value of films in a pedagogical sense, and the ways in which watching films can teach the viewers about race, gender and class.

hooks, b. (2000a) *Where We Stand: Class Matters*. London: Routledge.
Using her experiences as a child and an adult, hooks presents a personal account of how the issues of class and race are interlocked; she also offers approaches to move these matters forward.

hooks, b. (2000b) *All About Love: New Visions*. New York: HarperCollins.
A candid and personal account of what hooks perceives of the danger of love, as well as the joys when we return to love.

Scapp, R. (2002) *Critical Perspectives on Education, Politics, and Culture*. London: Routledge. Written by a close friend and colleague of hooks, this work explores value-based teaching and learning in opposition to traditionalist models of education and includes an affirmation of the role of citizenship.

REFERENCES

Apple, M. (2013) *Can Education Change Society?* Abingdon: Routledge.

Back, L. (2007) *The Art of Listening*. London: Bloomsbury.

Barry, P. (2002) *Beginning Theory: An Introduction to Literary and Cultural Theory* (2nd edn). Manchester: Manchester University Press.

bell hooks Institute (2015) *About the bell hooks Institute*. Available online at: www.bellhooksinstitute.com

Berry, T. (2010) 'Engaged pedagogy and critical race feminism'. *Education Foundations*, Summer–Fall: 19–26.

Burke, B. (2004) 'bell hooks on education'. *The Encyclopaedia of Informal Education*. Available online at: www.infed.org/mobi/bell-hooks-on-education

Carolissen, R., Bozalek, V., Nicholls, L., Leibowitz. B., Rohleder, P. and Swartz, L. (2011) 'bell hooks and the enactment of emotion in teaching and learning across boundaries: A pedagogy of hope?' *South African Journal of Higher Education*, 25 (1): 157–67.

Cheng, C. (1997) 'A review essay on the books of bell hooks: Organizational diversity lessons from a thoughtful race and gender heretic'. *The Academy of Management Review*, 22 (2): 553–64.

Cole, S. and Knowles, J. (eds) (2001) *Lives in Context: The Art of Life History Research*. Lanham, MD: AltaMira Press.

Collins, J., Harkin, J. and Nind, M. (2002) *Manifesto for Learning*. London: Continuum.

Dewey, J. (1916) *Democracy and Education: An Introduction to the Philosophy of Education*. New York: The Macmillan Company.

Dewey, J. (1938) *Experience and Education*. New York: Kappa Delta Pi.

Foucault, M. (1979) *Discipline and Punish: The Birth of Prison*. London: Penguin.

Freire, P. (1970 [1996]) *Pedagogy of the Oppressed*. London: Penguin.

Giroux, H. (1992) *Border Crossings: Cultural Workers and the Politics of Education*. New York: Routledge.

hooks, b. (1982) *Ain't I a Woman: Black Women and Feminism*. London: Pluto Press.

hooks, b. (1994) *Teaching to Transgress: Education as the Practice of Freedom*. London: Routledge.

hooks, b. (2003a) *Teaching Community: A Pedagogy of Hope*. London: Routledge.

hooks, b. (2003b) 'Confronting class in the classroom'. In: Darder, A., Baltodano, M. and Torres, R. (eds) *The Critical Pedagogy Reader*. London: RoutledgeFalmer.

hooks, b. (2010) *Teaching Critical Thinking: Practical Wisdom*. London: Routledge.

Irwin, J. (2012) *Paulo Freire's Philosophy of Education*. London: Continuum.

Lim, L. (2011) 'Review: Teaching critical thinking: Practical wisdom'. *Education Review*, April: 1–7.

Sewell, A. (2010) 'Review: Teaching community: A pedagogy of hope'. *International Journal of Children's Spirituality*, 15 (2): 341–3.

Thomas, R. (1997) 'Review: Teaching to transgress: Education as the practice of freedom'. *Contemporary Education*, 68 (3): 204.

Tisdell, E. and Tolliver, D. (2009) 'Transformative approaches to culturally responsive teaching'. In: Mezirow, J., Taylor, E. and associates (eds) *Transformative Learning in Practice: Insights from Community, Workplace, and Higher Education*. San Francisco, CA: Jossey Bass.

17

JACK MEZIROW

TRANSFORMATIVE LEARNING

LEARNING OUTCOMES

After reading this chapter, you should be able to:

- appreciate Mezirow's background and his contribution to adult education;
- understand and identify his development of transformative learning and the implications for adult educators and their learners;
- appreciate the links between his work and other educational thinkers;
- critically appraise Mezirow's works;
- recognise how his work could be applied in practice.

KEY WORDS

Transformative learning; emancipatory education; reflection; critical reflection; critical self-reflection; meaning perspective; meaning schemes; instrumental learning; communicative learning; frames of reference; discourse.

INTRODUCTION

Jack Mezirow, who died in 2014 aged ninety-one, had a profound effect on the development of adult education theory. Before his notion of **transformative learning** was published, the main focus for adult education was ensuring that students mastered basic skills; the theoretical basis for adult learning centred on self-directed learning and the notion of andragogy (Brookfield, 2005). The theory of transformative learning acted as a catalyst which generated far-reaching changes and heated discussions in adult education, and also in other areas such as higher education, professional development, health and social activism (Columbia University, 2014). Mezirow's 1978 book *Education for Perspective Transformation: Women's Re-entry Programs in Community Colleges* set out his initial thoughts regarding transformative learning. This notion was originally prompted by the experiences of Edee, Mezirow's wife, when she went to college to study in middle age; it was also very much influenced by Habermas's earlier work on transformation. The research for Mezirow's transformative learning theory was based on a wide-ranging study in the United States of women returning to community colleges (Mezirow, 2006).

Transformative learning involves experience, **critical reflection** and personal change. The development of transformation starts with an experience, followed by critical reflection on that experience and then a **discourse** to allow for a change in the learner's actions (Hutchings, 2013). Mezirow noted that emotion and critical reflection on beliefs and attitudes are important features in an adult's transformative learning 'which involve changes in self-awareness and learner identity' (Carlile and Jordan, 2012: 101). The idea of transformative theory is that adults may be empowered to learn and that they can free themselves 'from unexamined ways of thinking that impede effective judgement and action' (Mezirow, 1998: 73). Furthermore, it foresaw a 'society composed of educated learners engaged in a continuing collaborative inquiry' (Mezirow, 1998: 73). Overall, for Mezirow transformative learning was a democratic process that used critical reflection and critical action to enable adults to change and develop as learners.

The basis of Mezirow's work in adult education is embedded in the efforts taken in the United States to encourage community cohesion by integrating people from differing ethnic and social backgrounds. Moreover, Mezirow came from the state of Minnesota which had been very strongly influenced by 'Scandinavian social-democratic and even socialist ideas [therefore] his concern with community development in a social perspective is quite natural' (Finger and Asun, 2001: 54). Even though his professional background was as an educationalist rather than a sociologist, Mezirow's work placed a significant degree of emphasis on social justice, and aligned adult learning with social development and progression (Finger and Asun, 2001).

Mezirow's notion of transformative learning is a contested concept that has drawn considerable criticism, some of which has come from fellow adult educators mainly because it is seen by a few as being 'complex and multi-faceted' (Kitchenham, 2008: 104).

Nevertheless, as a result of his work, a number of transformative learning groups were formed, which involved global conferences, numerous journal articles and books being published, and the concept of transformative learning was the main focus for many a doctoral thesis (Mezirow, 2006). Mezirow published many articles that developed and defended his theory of transformative learning. He also wrote a number of books that mapped and demonstrated the progression of his ideas. These included, with Darkenwald and Knox, *Last Gamble on Education: Dynamics of Adult Basic Education* (1975); with associates, *Fostering Critical Reflection in Adulthood* (1990); *Transformative Dimensions of Adult Education* (1991); with associates, *Learning as Transformation: Critical Perspectives on a Theory in Progress* (2000); and with Taylor and associates, *Transformative Learning in Practice: Insights from Community, Workplace, and Higher Education* (2009). To understand further the manner in which Mezirow's ideas emerged and how his theory developed, we now need to consider his background and his progress as an academic in the field of adult education.

MEZIROW, THE PERSON

'Jack' was born John D. Mezirow in 1923 in Fargo, North Dakota, USA. His career as an adult educator began in a teaching capacity working with communities, a role he never relinquished, even when he achieved a high degree of academic acclaim (Finger and Asun, 2001). Mezirow gained his first degree and then his master's degree in social sciences from the University of Minnesota. Next, after prompting from Malcolm Knowles, who was at the time the Director of the National Adult Education Association, Mezirow went on to study for his doctorate in adult education at the University of California at Los Angeles. Following graduation, he worked internationally in adult education and community development in Asia, Africa and South America. In this capacity, he worked for the following organisations: The United Nations Development Programme; the United Nations Educational, Social and Cultural Organisation (UNESCO); the United States Agency for International Development; the Asia Foundation; and World Education. He became an associate dean for a number of extension and human resource programmes at the University of California, before joining Teachers College, Columbia University, in 1968 as the Professor of Adult and Continuing Education (Mezirow and associates, 2000; Finger and Asun, 2001; Columbia University, 2014).

Mezirow's ideas on transformative learning grew from his wife's experience when she enrolled at Sarah Lawrence College in the early 1970s to complete her undergraduate degree. The experience, for both Jack and Edee, was truly 'transformative'. Moved by Edee's experiences, Mezirow set out on his seminal research work, which sought to uncover the factors that helped and hindered learning for women who were returning to study at community colleges in the United States. For most of the women returners to study, he found that they had gone through an individual transformation and had experienced a staged process of personal growth and change. This process included the questioning of taken-for-granted assumptions and an examination of the possibilities for new opportunities. This in turn led to the development of competence and self-assurance (Columbia University, 2014). These outcomes were the beginning of Adult Education Guided Intensive Study (AEGIS), a distinctive and innovative adult education doctoral programme established by Mezirow in 1982 at Teachers College, Columbia University. The idea of AEGIS has since been reproduced internationally (Columbia University, 2014).

At AEGIS, Mezirow endeavoured to promote the creation of a learning community that valued collaborative enquiry (Mezirow, 2006), and the learning and teaching methods Mezirow encouraged at AEGIS will be explored later in this chapter. To further this collaborative theme, AEGIS took in postgraduate students from a variety of disciplines and areas, which included private and government sector employees from adult education, school education, healthcare, social and community work, as well as religious organisations. In recruiting this variety, Mezirow was trying to get students together so that they could question their fundamental beliefs and develop an appreciation of the viewpoints and beliefs of others. Apart from the work with AEGIS, Mezirow continued to develop his notion of transformative learning, particularly with regard to other disciplines. In the later stages of his career, he became interested in the chemistry of the brain, and after retirement he kept in touch with academics worldwide who were interested in transformative learning (Columbia University, 2014). The meaning and development of his notion of transformative learning will be explored in the next section.

💡 MEZIROW AND HIS THEORY OF TRANSFORMATIVE LEARNING

This section will first define the key themes involved in Mezirow's ideas and then explore some of the significant aspects of his work, before considering the origins and influences of the theory of transformative learning. Core to Mezirow's notion of transformative learning was **emancipatory education** with its emphasis on 'effecting social change [to] modify oppressive practices, norms, institutions and socio-economic structures to allow everyone to participate more fully and freely' (Mezirow, 2006: 30). For Mezirow, emancipatory education required a combination of key themes. Before the main thrust of his ideas is discussed in more detail, it is useful to define these key themes, even though the terminology used may be unfamiliar at this early stage:

Meaning perspective: The structure of assumptions that constitutes a frame of reference for interpreting the meaning of an experience.

Reflection: Examination of the justification for one's beliefs, primarily to guide action and to reassess the efficacy of the strategies and procedures used in problem solving.

Critical reflection: Assessment of the validity of the presuppositions of one's meaning perceptions, and examination of their sources and consequences.

Critical self-reflection: Assessment of the way one has posed problems and one's own meaning perspectives.

Transformative learning: The process of learning through critical self-reflection, which results in the reformulation of a meaning perspective to allow a more inclusive, discriminatory and integrative understanding of one's experience. Learning includes acting on these insights.

Emancipatory education: An organized effort to precipitate or facilitate transformative learning in others.

(Mezirow and associates, 1990: xvi)

Mezirow's notion of transformative learning is centred upon adult learners' use of experience, critical reflection and discourse. Discourse here signifies a dialogue that engages with learners' evaluation of beliefs, emotions and values. This discourse concerns matters raised from a specific **frame of reference** (Mezirow, 2003). According to Mezirow:

> Frames of reference are the structures of culture and language through which we construe meaning by attributing coherence and significance to our experience. They selectively shape and delimit our perception, cognition and feelings by predisposing our intentions, beliefs, expectations and purposes. These preconceptions set our 'line of action'. Once set or programmed, we automatically move from one specific mental or behavioral activity to another, we have a strong tendency to reject ideas that fail to fit our preconceptions. (2009: 92)

For Mezirow, transformative learning begins with the manner in which problematic frames of reference are tackled – 'to make them more inclusive, discriminating, open, reflective and emotionally able to change' (Mezirow, 2009: 92). For Mezirow, 'a frame of reference involves both habit of mind and a point of view. Both suggest that, at its root, a frame of reference is a way of knowing' (Kegan, 2009: 44). Mezirow offered two frames of reference that could be considered in unlocking these problematic frames and beginning the process of transformative learning; these were **meaning schemes** and meaning perspective. The term 'meaning' here is significant to transformative learning, as it is a process of how learners understand, use and change their perceptions: 'transformative learning is an adult dimension of reason assessment involving the validation and reformation of meaning structures' (Mezirow, 2009: 93). Jarvis et al. posit that for Mezirow 'meaning is an interpretation of experience based upon our previous experiences, our meaning systems and the language we use' (2003: 39).

Mezirow differentiates between the two dimensions of meaning schemes and meaning perspectives. Meaning schemes are 'habitual expectations governing if–then, cause–effect' – for example, 'we expect food to satisfy hunger ... that the sun will rise in the east and set in the west – they are habitual, implicit *rules* for interpreting' (Mezirow and associates, 1990: 2). These meaning schemes efficiently shield the person from confronting 'existing assumptions and beliefs, acting as a mechanism through which new information, advice and experience are accommodated within an essentially unchanging philosophy' (Moore, 2004: 15). On the other hand, meaning perspectives are of a much higher order; they comprise theories, concepts, values, beliefs and evaluations. Meaning perspectives also concern the specific ways in which a learner interprets experience, which includes the phases of reflection before making value judgements. Mezirow cites the women's movement as an exemplar of meaning perspectives and transformative learning:

> Within a few years, hundreds of thousands of women whose personal identity, self-concept, and values had been derived principally from prescribed social norms and from acting out sex-stereotypical roles came to challenge these assumptions and to redefine their lives in their own terms. The women's movement provided a support climate for this kind of personal reappraisal by publicizing the constraints on personal development, autonomy, and self-determination imposed by such stereotypes and by providing support groups and role models. (Mezirow and associates, 1990: 3)

Both meaning perspectives and meaning schemes that are considered unviable can be transformed by reflection. Meaning perspectives that establish what, how and why we learn may be transformed through critical reflection – 'reflection on one's own premises can lead to transformative learning' (Mezirow and associates, 1990: 18). This reflection 'on one's own premises' involves the learners delving deeply into well-established beliefs and expectations that are both socially and culturally formed over the learner's lifetime. The resultant transformation could be radical in the way the learners regard themselves and the world in which they live; it could also enable them to have a deeper insight into their long-standing values and beliefs (Hutchings, 2013). This emphasis on profound change taking place in transformative learning is a constructivist process and an outcome of personal intellectual conflict (Dennick, 2008). The role of reflection is crucial, creating a transformation of perspective as it enables learners to critically appraise their learning, as well as being more creative, open and receptive to new knowledge and experiences (Mezirow, 1991; Kennett, 2010).

Transformative learning could happen suddenly, which is often associated with important life-changing crises, or it could occur in an accumulative manner, which is manifested by a series of understandings, which in turn produces different points of view. 'Most transformative learning takes place outside of awareness; intuition substitutes for critical reflection of assumptions' (Mezirow, 2009: 94). The role of the adult educator is to facilitate learners to bring awareness into the process. This in turn will enhance the learners' competence and encourage proactive involvement in the transformative learning process. Using the outcomes from his study regarding women returners to college education, Mezirow (2009) identified ten sequential phases of meaning and becoming which learners followed in their transformative learning journey. Apart from the first – 'a disorientating dilemma' – the other phases are quite self-explanatory. According to Taylor, a disorientating dilemma is 'some experience that problematizes current understandings and frames of reference' (Mezirow, Taylor and associates, 2009: 155). The phases are:

- a disorientating dilemma;
- self-examination with feelings of fear, anger, guilt or shame;
- a critical assessment of assumptions;
- recognition that one's discontent and the process of transformation is shared;
- exploration of options for new roles, relationships and action;
- planning a course of action;
- acquiring knowledge and skills for implementing one's plans;
- provisional trying of new roles;
- building competence and self-confidence in new roles and relationships;
- a reintegration into one's life on the basis of conditions dictated by one's new perspective.

(Mezirow, 2009: 94)

Mezirow reinforces the two central elements of transformative learning that are necessary during this phased process: 'First, critical reflection or critical self-reflection on assumptions ... second, participating fully and freely in dialectical discourse to validate a best reflective judgement' (2009: 94).

Much of Mezirow's work, particularly the overarching theory of transformative learning, originates from, and has been influenced by, the German sociologist and philosopher Jürgen Habermas. This is specifically the case with Habermas's ideas on the differences between instrumental and **communicative learning**. For Mezirow, **instrumental learning** concerns controlling and influencing the environment with the intention of enhancing performance and outcomes. In essence, instrumental learning is about appraising assertions of truth. It is about measuring 'changes resulting from our learning to solve problems in terms of productivity, performance, or behavior ... canonized by natural sciences, that we all use or misuse in learning how to *do* things' (Mezirow and associates, 1990: 8). Conversely, communicative learning is deemed of greater importance to adult learning as it is about '*understanding the meaning* of what others communicate concerning values, ideals, feelings, moral decisions and such concepts as freedom, justice, love, labor, autonomy, commitment, and democracy' (Mezirow and associates, 1990: 8). Central to both communicative learning and Mezirow's transformative learning is the concept of discourse. Mezirow gives two very fitting examples of the application of discourse and understanding involved in communicative learning:

This understanding involves being aware of the assumptions, intentions and qualifications of the person communicating. When a stranger strikes up a conversation on a bus, one needs to know whether he or she is simply passing the time, intends to proselytize, or is trying to pick you up. When a stranger recommends a new medicine or an investment, one needs to know whether he or she is qualified to make such recommendation or judgment. (2003: 58)

Transformative learning may happen in either instrumental or communicative learning; 'the former is about prescription whereas the latter is about "insight and attaining common ground through symbolic interaction" with other persons' (Jarvis et al., 2003: 40). Instrumental learning normally entails task-orientated activities, whereas in communicative learning it demands critical self-reflection (Mezirow, 2009).

Dirkx and Smith provide a thought-provoking evaluation of where the experience of transformation lies and what transformative learning means to them:

Ultimately whether a learning experience is transformative rests with the learner, not us as instructors or facilitators. Our work is to help learners make the deep connections with the subject matter that we know is possible. Where those connections lead is not under our control, and it may not be in the conscious control of the learner. There is a kind of mystery to the idea of transformative learning, a way of learning that is more an expression of the creative and artistic dimensions of our being rather than the rational, literal and scientific. Like the unfolding and metamorphosis of the caterpillar into a beautiful, majestic, and soaring butterfly, the process of transformative learning touches on and reminds us of the fundamental mystery that is being human. (2009: 65)

Mezirow's ideas regarding personal change, reflection and democracy in the learning process can be linked to other like-minded educational thinkers.

↻ LINKS WITH OTHER THEORISTS

Despite the gap of some eight hundred years, it is possible to trace Mezirow's notion of transformative learning to the renowned medieval philosopher Robert Grosseteste (Bishop of Lincoln) and his concept of illumination. Both these concepts involve profound aspects of learning. Although Mezirow does not include a theological dimension to his notion of transformative learning, it is interesting that both of their ideas place a high degree of significance on education being a life-changing experience. Furthermore, both thinkers also championed emancipation and that deep learning requires active participation. They were absorbed in a number of fields of learning, including the broader science subjects, as well as having a trust in social justice (Aubrey, 2019). The significant influence of Habermas's instrumental and communicative learning domains on Mezirow's theory of transformative learning has already been covered. At the heart of Mezirow's thinking was John Dewey's progressive and democratic notion of learning, which contested the traditional didactic methods of learning and teaching, and emphasised the primacy of the student in the education process (Columbia University, 2014). Mezirow was also guided by Thomas Kuhn, particularly by his seminal work *The Structure of Scientific Revolutions* (1962). In his work, Kuhn explored the paradigm shift that happens in the revolution of ideas to progress the understanding of science. As Mezirow explains, these paradigm shifts can also be associated with the way we interpret the meaning of experience:

> As we encounter new meaning perspectives that help us account for disturbing anomalies in the way we understand our reality, personal as well as scientific paradigm shifts can redirect the way we engage the world. (Mezirow and associates, 1990: 13)

These paradigm shifts of Kuhn's, which influenced Mezirow's thinking, were seen as progressive and transformative processes; old theories were considered dated and redundant, while new theories were being developed (Dennick, 2008).

Mezirow was also influenced by the radical educator Paulo Freire who was responsible for setting up emancipatory adult education programmes in Brazil as a prelude to a broader revolutionary mission with the aim of achieving social empowerment of the people (Mezirow and associates, 1990). Mezirow considered that the concept of 'conscientisation', which Freire introduced in his book *Pedagogy of the Oppressed* (1970 [1996]), was a significant factor in transformative learning. Conscientisation was the raising of people's consciousness with a view to being freed from the oppression of the established social order. Freire felt that this was only feasible through the process of critical reflection, dialogue and problem-posing learning (Freire, 1970 [1996]; Mezirow and associates, 1990). Although not considered such a revolutionary educator as Freire, Knowles's concept of andragogy – the teaching of adults using learner experience – has links with Mezirow's thinking. Knowles, like Freire and Mezirow, has altered the relationship between the adult student and the teacher, so that it becomes less about the delivering of information and more about creating a dialogical process (Preece and Griffin, 2006).

Core to Mezirow's transformative learning is the idea of personal change in individual students. This is comparable, and indeed evident, in Kolb's theory of experiential learning and constructivist theory. Mezirow, like Kolb, stresses the importance of critical reflection for the process of change. In Kolb's experiential learning cycle, learners are encouraged to reflect and, with the help of their teachers, transform their own points of view and create their own ideas (Mezirow and associates, 2000). Like Kolb, and Mezirow, Schön places great emphasis on the use of reflection as a social action. Additionally, Schön advocated the use of reflection on experience in understanding and solving problems. He used the terms 'reflection on action' and 'reflection in action'. Both of these are cyclical, ongoing processes where learners can discover their own theories and in so doing develop their personal transformative learning (Mezirow and associates, 1990). It is evident that Mezirow has been heavily influenced by other thinkers in his development of transformative learning theory, which could be the basis of some of the criticism that he encountered.

⊛ CRITIQUING THE THEORY

Some of the criticism that came Mezirow's way was from other adult educators who felt that he had abandoned his stance on social activism. This criticism centred on their perception of his notion of transformative learning which increasingly focused on the growth and development of the individual at the expense of the wider principles and effects involved in the social activism of adult education. Finger and Asun (2001) argue that Mezirow's ideas of transformation have not truly incorporated the notions of Freire and Habermas regarding social change. They state that, more accurately, Mezirow's transformative learning focuses on how the 'learners adapt to rather than criticise society' (Finger and Asun, 2001: 59). There was also some disquiet from community and other not-for-profit bodies that adult education was being taken over by corporate business organisations with a view to gaining an advantage over their competitors. Mezirow himself was associated with, and acted as a consultant for, corporations, and his ideas were taught at Harvard Business School (Columbia University, 2014).

There was also censure that the teaching and learning of transformative learning were not for everyone. There were certain challenges for both teachers and adult learners. These included aspects of ethics, confidentiality and conflicts between students (Cooper, n.d.). Undoubtedly, some adults find the notion of transformative learning stimulating and inspirational. Conversely, many adults strongly anticipate what they need, what they want and how that education should be taught (Cross, 1981). Furthermore, there is some anxiety about the elusive nature of the teaching in relation to transformative learning. Taylor offers a warning about the practice of transformative learning from a teacher's point of view:

> Much of it remains unknown and poorly understood. Like any other educational approach, it is rooted in ideals, and when the realities of practice are explored, it becomes difficult to get a handle on how it plays out in the classroom. It is laced with contradictions and oversights. (Taylor, 2009: 3)

Taylor also argues that using transformative learning involves 'personal risk, a genuine concern for the learners' betterment, and the ability to draw on a variety of methods and techniques' (2009: 14).

Finger and Asun contest that Mezirow's ideas are an amalgamation of differing notions and philosophies that require further development to validate the claims made (Finger and Asun, 2001). Mezirow was quite aware of the criticism. He wrote a number of articles, particularly in *Adult Education Quarterly*, accepting these criticisms and sometimes defending his ideas. However, there are some aspects of his theory which he acknowledged required further development. Jarvis et al. add to this criticism, arguing that his theory needs further extensive research, something that Mezirow attempts to provide by involving 'a number of writers whose work, they claim, falls within the ambit of transformative learning' (Jarvis et al., 2003: 40). Moreover, the language used in transformative learning can become so alluring that it starts to be employed for many principles, which in turn results in its meaning being so unrecognisable that its original meaning can be lost. 'It can take on quasi-religious qualities, in this case of dramatic "conversion". Transformation begins to refer to any kind of changes or process at all' (Kegan, 2009: 41). Possibly the main area for Mezirow that needed further work was the explanation and importance of the role played by emotions, intuition and imagination in the process of transformation. He confessed that this is a difficulty in his work because the process we use to interpret our own beliefs may encompass assumed values (Mezirow, 2009). Notwithstanding these criticisms, the process of transformative learning has profound implications for the practice of emancipatory adult learning.

APPLYING MEZIROW'S IDEAS IN PRACTICE

This section will first explore an overview of the practice of transformative learning before offering some specific examples for application. Although Mezirow was an adult educator and his major work of transformative learning was focused around the adult learning experience, there are, it is argued, many elements of his ideas that could be applied in universities, colleges and even schools. From a practical point of view, there are three forms of experience in the classroom that can end with transformative learning taking place: experience, critical reflection and discourse. They frequently follow on from each other; an intense emotional experience raises critical reflection and thoughts about parallel past experiences, which in turn is discussed with others who hold similar or different viewpoints, which can then lead to a transformation of perspectives (Learning Theories, 2017).

There is a generally acknowledged mode of adult education that entails the handing over of authority from the teacher to the learner. This in turn requires the adult educators to respect all adult students 'as self-directed learners, almost by the virtue of their adult status alone' (Kegan, 2009: 50). The idea that effective learning relies on effective teaching is an accepted concept, and educational thinkers such as Mezirow have 'argued that effective learning is self-actualising, self-directed, self-planned and transformative' (Griffin, 2006: 83). According to Moon, there are five progressive phases, with transformative learning being the most valuable; these five phases are:

- noticing;
- making sense;
- making meaning;
- working with meaning;
- transformative learning.

(1999 [2000]: 16)

Moon further explains that a learner at this transformative phase will be:

> Self-motivating and self-motivated, but may derive support from discussion and an environment in which their ideas can be tested by others ... In formal education terms, 'transformative learning' is a place of intellectual excitement and of deeply satisfying discourse that can occur in good-quality tutorial work. (1999 [2000]: 146)

Most teachers and students have experienced the moment in their learning when something has 'clicked'; this, it is suggested, is where learning shifts from being the accumulative to a transformative process. At this stage, the topic is being considered from a changed perspective. When something 'clicks', it does not mean that the student has a greater knowledge of the idea than his or her peers, 'but, rather, that he or she has put it together in new ways that transformed the idea' (Cross, 1981: 232).

Mezirow argues that the function of the adult educator is to nurture the manner of transformative learning, which enables students to make informed judgements and take valuable and applicable actions. A teacher's role is to assist students 'to think, judge, and learn – and to act – with greater insight not to prescribe what they think and learn' (Mezirow, 1998: 73). Moreover, for transformative learning to be successful, Mezirow advocated collaboration not only between students but, possibly more importantly, between students and teachers. Although in many instances at the start of the learning process the teacher will have more knowledge than the student, what the teacher needs to do is to

> Relearn what is known in the context of the learners' efforts to interpret these insights in terms of their own lives. This is what adults mean when they write of collaborative learning ... the educator actively seeks to know learners' expectations and aspirations to enable the educator to understand learners' levels of perception, their language, and the difficulties they may have understanding the academic language or the nature of the instruction. (Mezirow and associates, 1990: 368–9)

What is also required when nurturing collaboration in transformative learning is for the teacher to take into consideration what the student wishes to learn. This will then instigate a discourse, which in turn will lead to a critical exploration of the assumptions that underpin the value judgements of both student and teacher. Mezirow thought that for true transformative learning to occur there should be an unlocking of the traditional power relationships created between teachers and students. At the heart of adult education for Mezirow was the process of facilitating students in developing their awareness of their understandings and values, and to be 'more critically reflective on their assumptions and those of others, more fully and freely engaged in discourse' (Mezirow and associates, 2000: 31).

Mezirow borrowed from Habermas's ideal foundations for conditions for adult learning. These conditions also offer a medium for adult educators to provide a social commitment for students to participate freely and fully in discourse. Overall students, for their part, must take responsibility for their own learning and for establishing a congenial learning environment (Learning Theories, 2017). However, in particular, for these conditions to be met, students must:

- have accurate and complete information;
- be free from coercion, distorting self-deception or immobilizing anxiety; be open to alternate points of view – empathetic, caring about how others think and feel, withholding judgement;
- be able to understand, to weigh evidence and to assess arguments objectively;
- be able to become aware of the context of ideas and critically reflect on assumptions, including their own;
- have equal opportunity to participate in the various roles of discourse;
- have a test of validity until new perspective evidence or arguments are encountered and validated through discourse as yielding a better judgement.

(Mezirow, 2009: 92)

One of the attributes that Mezirow argues is crucial for students to acquire in the transformative learning process is the ability to 'imagine how things could be different' (Mezirow, 2009: 103).

Cooper (n.d.) outlines the characteristics and roles that teachers and students need to facilitate successful transformative learning as follows:

Teacher characteristics and roles which facilitate transformative learning

- Encourage students to reflect on and share their feelings and thoughts in class.
- Be holistically oriented, aware of body, mind, and spirit in the learning process.
- Become transcendent of his [or her] beliefs and accepting of others' beliefs.
- Cultivate awareness of alternate ways of learning.
- Establish an environment characterised by trust and care.
- Facilitate sensitive relationships among the participants.
- Demonstrate ability to serve as an experienced mentor reflecting on his [or her] own journey.
- Help students question reality in ways that promote shifts in their worldview.

Student characteristics and roles which facilitate transformative learning

- Students must be free to determine their own reality, as opposed to social realities defined by others or by cultural institutions.
- Students must be ready for and open to change.
- Those with a wider variety of life experiences, including prior stressful life events, are likely to experience more transformation.
- Cultivate the ability to transcend past contexts of learning and experience.
- Students must be willing and able to integrate critical reflection into their school work and personal life.

- Students must be able to access both rational and affective mental functioning.
- Have sufficient maturity to deal with paradigm shifts and material which differs from their current beliefs.

(Cooper, n.d.)

Mezirow explains how he facilitated transformative learning in his graduate AEGIS doctoral programme at Teachers College, where great significance was placed on the establishment of learning communities for collaborative enquiry (Mezirow, 2006). Students on the programme were required to take part in a number of transformative learning-related activities. For example, they were asked to write papers that posed arguments on both sides, describing each viewpoint as well as their own, and then to analyse their own beliefs. Topics offered on the programme included 'assumption analysis, involving comparative assessment of key turning points in the lives of the students' (Mezirow, 2006: 36). Art, literature and the work of adult educators such as Paulo Freire were used to inspire students to consider alternative methods of interpreting experiences. Methods such as critical incidents, life histories, media analysis, metaphor analysis, action learning sets and journal writing were all found helpful in developing critical self-reflection of assumptions and discourse (Mezirow, 2006). Lukinsky (1990: 233) offers a range of ideas, processes and methodologies for critical reflective journal writing 'to help us, as persons, learn to listen and, as educators, to help others to do so'.

The use of self-assessment in adult and higher education is very closely associated with the notion of transformative learning. Taylor argues that self-assessment encompasses much more than students being autonomous in their own marking and progression. The proficiencies that students develop when self-assessing include the use of deep questioning, and understanding and framing of the benchmarks for them to make judgements regarding their own learning. The use of self-assessment 'is likely to lead to habits of questioning criteria for performance and noticing the extent to which one's work meets these criteria' (Taylor, 2000: 177). Taylor suggests that students can use self-assessment to check progress, self-diagnose and self-remediate, consolidate learning, and gain self-knowledge and self-understanding (Taylor, 2000).

Finally, it is interesting to note that transformative learning in the form of collaborative enquiry can take place online, in the form of emails and blogs, as well as in classrooms. Dirkx and Smith found that online collaborative enquiry provided an environment that promoted deep levels of discourse and reflection from students whose previous experiences of group work were not always positive (Dirkx and Smith, 2009).

REFLECTIVE TASK

Reflecting on your own learning as an adult in relation to Mezirow's transformative learning theory:

1. Give examples of the aspects of the theory that you are comfortable with in your own learning and suggest ways that you could enhance these further.
2. Give examples of the aspects of the theory you are anxious about and suggest ways that you could overcome such anxieties.

SUMMARY

Jack Mezirow was an adult educator whose notion of transformative learning has not only added to the theory of adult education, but has also changed the way in which teachers perceive their practice. Transformative learning is now embedded in adult education, higher education, professional development, and health and social activism (Columbia University, 2014). Critical reflection, experience and discourse are all fundamental to successful transformative learning. The foundation for Mezirow's theory came from Habermas's previous work on transformation. Mezirow's research involved a wide-ranging study in the United States which explored the transformations evidenced by women who returned to community colleges. He worked as an adult educator and community developer in the United States and internationally. In 1982, he set up the renowned AEGIS adult education doctoral programme in Teachers College, Columbia University, where transformative learning was core to the learning and teaching process.

Apart from being influenced by Habermas's prior work on instrumental and communicative learning domains, Mezirow's notion of transformative learning was also shaped by Kuhn's idea of paradigm shifts. Dewey's concept of a democratic pedagogy was at the heart of Mezirow's work, as well as his drive for social activism. Like Knowles's idea of andragogy, Mezirow added to the growing repertoire of adult education theory. Mezirow was inspired by Freire's concept of conscientisation and the need for critical reflection, discourse and problem-posing learning. There are also close links, particularly related to the importance of social interaction, with Kolb's experiential learning theory and Schön's notions of reflection on action and reflection in action. Furthermore, in spite of the huge time difference, it is feasible to offer the suggestion that the deep changes in Mezirow's notion of transformative learning could be aligned with the medieval philosopher Robert Grosseteste's concept of illumination.

Mezirow's work has drawn considerable criticism, mainly from adult educators. He has been accused of abandoning his social activism principles, and some see his work on transformative learning as a blend of theories. There has also been censure about the lack of research underpinning some of his ideas on transformative learning, especially regarding the processes of emotion, intuition and imagination.

It is contested that transformative learning can be an emancipatory experience for many learners in adult education. However, transformative learning is not for everyone; it is a practice that requires experience from the teacher and a willingness from the learner to undergo personal change. Nevertheless, despite these criticisms, Mezirow's work still has the potential to make positive changes to the lives of adult learners.

GLOSSARY OF TERMS

Communicative learning   Unlike instrumental learning, communicative learning is considered of greater significance to adult learning because it is believed to be about '*understanding the meaning* of what others communicate concerning values, ideals, feelings, moral decisions and such concepts as freedom, justice, love, labor, autonomy, commitment, and democracy' (Mezirow and associates, 1990: 8). Communicative learning requires critical self-reflection. Communicative learning and transformative learning are closely linked with Mezirow's concept of discourse.

Critical reflection   Critical reflection is an appraisal of the validity of the *presuppositions* of a person's meaning perceptions, and the scrutiny of their foundations and consequences (Mezirow and associates, 1990). It helps learners to critically evaluate their learning and also to be more creative and receptive to new experience and knowledge (Mezirow, 1991).

Critical self-reflection   Critical self-reflection is an evaluation of the way a person has presented problems and their own meaning perspectives (Mezirow and associates, 1990).

Discourse   Discourse involves a dialogue that concerns adult learners' use of experience and critical reflection. This resulting dialogue draws together learners' appraisal of their beliefs, emotions and values. This discourse relates to issues raised from a particular frame of reference (Mezirow, 2003). It is used to change a person's actions. Discourse is closely aligned with the concepts of communicative learning and transformative learning.

Emancipatory education   Central to Mezirow's idea of transformative learning was his notion of emancipatory education and its stress on making social change, and to restrain oppressive educational practices, their 'norms, institutions and socio-economic structures to allow everyone to participate more fully and freely' (Mezirow, 2006: 30). The key themes of emancipatory education are meaning perspectives, reflection, critical reflection, critical self-reflection, transformative learning, which then results in emancipatory education (Mezirow and associates, 1990).

Frames of reference   'These are the structures of culture and language through which we construe meaning by attributing coherence and significance to our experience' (Mezirow, 2009: 92). Frames of reference form and define people's perceptions in how they act. When these preconceptions are conditioned, people habitually shift from one activity to the next. For Mezirow, a 'frame of reference involves both a habit of mind and a point of view. Both these suggest that, at its root, a frame of reference is a way of knowing' (Kegan, 2009: 44). Both meaning perspective and meaning schemes make up frames of reference, which in turn could be employed to unlock problematic frames and in doing so start the process of transformative learning by challenging preconceptions and assumptions through reflection.

Instrumental learning   Instrumental learning is about influencing and controlling the environment with the aim of improving results and performance. For Mezirow, it is about evaluating statements of truth. It involves assessing 'changes resulting from our learning to solve problems in terms of productivity, performance, or behaviour' (Mezirow and associates, 1990: 8). It usually entails task-orientated activities.

Meaning perspective   One of two frames of reference that could be used to begin the process of transformative learning: meaning schemes and meaning perspective. Meaning perspective includes the formation of assumptions that creates a frame of reference for making sense of an experience (Mezirow and associates, 1990). It is a process of how learners understand, use and change their perceptions. It also concerns the specific ways a learner interprets experience, which includes the phases of reflection before making value judgements. A meaning perspective is of a much higher order than meaning schemes as it comprises theories, concepts, values, beliefs and evaluations. It also concerns the specific ways a learner interprets experience, which includes the phases of reflection before making value judgements.

Meaning schemes (see also above, meaning perspective)   Meaning schemes are customary expectations gained from an accumulation of experiences that adults acquire over their lifetimes through associations, concepts, beliefs, values and feelings. These in turn result in a number of different meaning schemes for particular experiences. Collectively, meaning schemes can help in creating a meaning perspective a person has of the world (Learning Theories, 2017).

Reflection   Reflection is an evaluation of a person's beliefs and principles in order to guide any action, and to re-examine the value of the methods and processes used to solve problems (Mezirow and associates, 1990).

Transformative learning   Transformative learning includes the use of experience, critical reflection, discourse and personal change. Mezirow observed that emotion and critical reflection on beliefs and attitudes were significant characteristics of adult learning, and included changes in self-awareness and learner identity. Transformative learning is defined as 'the process of learning through critical self-reflection, which results in the reformation of a meaning perspective to allow a more inclusive, discriminatory and integrative understanding of a person's experience. Learning includes acting on these insights' (Mezirow and associates, 1990: xvi).

FURTHER READING

Habermas, J. (1975) *Legitimation Crisis.* Boston, MA: Beacon Press.
This is a review of what Habermas considers as two general forms of learning: non-reflexive and reflexive. It is a notion that Mezirow adopts throughout his theory of adult transformative learning.

Schön, D. (1983) *The Reflective Practitioner: How Professionals Think in Action.* New York: Basic Books.
This is a helpful book for teachers working with adults. It explains the value of the reflective process in enhancing students' and teachers' development in their professional lives.

Welton, M. (ed.) (1995) *In Defense of the Lifeworld: Critical Perspectives on Adult Learning.* Albany, NY: State University of New York Press.
A very informative text on the relationship and engagement of Mezirow with Habermas with regard to the distinction concerning technical, communicative and emancipatory knowledge.

REFERENCES

Aubrey, K. (2019) 'Robert Grosseteste and Illumination, and Jack Mezirow and Transformative Learning: An educational appraisal'. In: Cunningham, J. and Puttick, S. (eds) *Robert Grosseteste and Theories of Education: The Ordered Human.* London: Routledge.

Brookfield, S. (2005) *The Power of Critical Theory for Adult Learning and Teaching.* Maidenhead: Open University Press.

Carlile, O. and Jordan, A. (2012) 'Learning'. In: Arthur, J. and Peterson, A. (eds) *The Routledge Companion to Education.* London: Routledge.

Columbia University (2014) *In Memoriam: Jack Mezirow.* Available online at: www.tc.columbia. edu/news.htm?articleID=9698

Cooper, S. (n.d.) *Transformational Learning.* Available online at: www.lifecircles-inc.com/ Learningtheories/humanist/mezirow.html

Cross, K. (1981) *Adults as Learners: Increasing Participation and Facilitating Learning.* San Francisco, CA: Jossey Bass.

Dennick, R. (2008) 'Theories of learning: Constructive experience'. In: Matheson, D. (ed.) *An Introduction to the Study of Education* (3rd edn). London: Routledge.

Dirkx, J. and Smith, R. (2009) 'Facilitating transformative learning: Engaging emotions in an online context'. In: Mezirow, J., Taylor, E. and associates. *Transformative Learning in Practice: Insights from Community, Workplace, and Higher Education.* San Francisco, CA: Jossey Bass.

Finger, M. and Asun, J. (2001) *Adult Education at the Crossroads: Learning Our Way Out.* London: Zed Books.

Freire, P. (1970 [1996]) *Pedagogy of the Oppressed.* London: Penguin.

Griffin, C. (2006) 'Didacticism'. In: Jarvis, P. (ed.) *The Theory and Practice of Teaching* (2nd edn). London: Routledge.

Hutchings, M. (2013) 'Arriving in a new place: The ecology of learning'. In: Ward, S. (ed.) *A Student's Guide to Education Studies* (3rd edn). London: Routledge.

Jarvis, P., Holford, J. and Griffin, C. (2003) *The Theory and Practice of Learning* (2nd edn). London: Routledge.

Kegan, R. (2009) 'What "form" transforms? A constructive-developmental approach to transformative learning. In: Illeris, K. (ed.) *Contemporary Theories of Learning*. Abingdon: Routledge.

Kennett, K. (2010) 'Professionalism and reflective practice'. In: Wallace, S. (ed.) *The Lifelong Learning Sector Reflective Reader*. Exeter: Learning Matters.

Kitchenham, A. (2008) 'The evolution of John Mezirow's transformative learning theory'. *Journal of Transformative Education*, 6 (2): 104–23.

Kuhn, T. (1962) *The Structure of Scientific Revolutions*. Chicago, IL: Chicago University Press.

Learning Theories (2017) *Transformative Learning Theory*. Available online at: www.learning_theories/transformative_learning_theory.txt

Lukinsky, J. (1990) 'Reflective withdrawal through journal writing'. In: Mezirow, J. and associates. *Fostering Critical Reflection in Adulthood*. San Francisco, CA: Jossey Bass.

Mezirow, J. (1978) *Education for Perspective Transformation: Women's Re-entry Programs in Community Colleges*. New York: Teachers College, Columbia University.

Mezirow, J. (1991) *Transformative Dimensions of Adult Education*. San Francisco, CA: Jossey Bass.

Mezirow, J. (1998) 'Transformational learning and social action'. *Adult Education Quarterly*, 49 (1): 70–3.

Mezirow, J. (2003) 'Transformative learning as discourse'. *Journal of Transformative Education*, 1 (1): 58–63.

Mezirow, J. (2006) 'An overview of transformative learning'. In: Sutherland, P. and Crowther, J. (eds) *Lifelong Learning: Concepts and Contexts*. London: Routledge.

Mezirow, J. (2009) 'An overview on transformative learning'. In: Illeris, K. (ed.) *Contemporary Theories of Learning*. Abingdon: Routledge.

Mezirow, J. and associates (1990) *Fostering Critical Reflection in Adulthood*. San Francisco, CA: Jossey Bass.

Mezirow, J. and associates (2000) *Learning as Transformation: Critical Perspectives on a Theory in Progress*. San Francisco, CA: Jossey Bass.

Mezirow, J., Darkenwald, G. and Knox, A. (1975) *Last Gamble on Education: Dynamics of Adult Basic Education*. Ann Arbor, MI: University of Michigan, Adult Education Association of the USA.

Mezirow, J., Taylor, E. and associates (2009) *Transformative Learning in Practice: Insights from Community, Workplace, and Higher Education*. San Francisco, CA: Jossey Bass.

Moon, J. (1999 [2000]) *Reflection in Learning and Professional Development: Theory and Practice*. London: Kogan Page.

Moore, A. (2004) *The Good Teacher: Dominant Discourses in Teaching and Teacher Education*. London: Routledge.

Preece, J. and Griffin, C. (2006) 'Radical and feminist pedagogies'. In: Jarvis, P. (ed.) *The Theory and Practice of Teaching* (2nd edn). London: Routledge.

Taylor, E. (2009) 'Fostering transformative learning'. In: Mezirow, J., Taylor, E. and associates. *Transformative Learning in Practice: Insights from Community, Workplace, and Higher Education*. San Francisco, CA: Jossey Bass.

Taylor, K. (2000) 'Teaching with developmental intention'. In: Mezirow, J. and associates. *Learning as Transformation: Critical Perspectives on a Theory in Progress*. San Francisco, CA: Jossey Bass.

18
LINDA DARLING-HAMMOND

EQUITY IN EDUCATION: POLICY, TEACHERS AND TEACHING

LEARNING OUTCOMES

After reading this chapter, you should be able to:

- be aware of Darling-Hammond's background and her contribution to education;
- understand and identify her ideas regarding educational policy for equitable education, teaching and teacher development;
- appreciate the links between her work and other educationalists;
- critically appraise some of Darling-Hammond's notions;
- recognise how her ideas could be applied in schools and classrooms.

KEY WORDS

Teacher preparation and teacher education; teacher professionalism; performance assessment; collaboration; Professional Development Schools.

INTRODUCTION

Linda Darling-Hammond, the renowned American educator, is one of the most influential, respected and active leaders calling for an equitable education system for all learners, which includes reforms of schools and **teacher education**. Although her work is internationally known, and she uses extensive data from other developed countries' educational systems, her main aim is to strive to inform and create inclusive educational policies in the United States. Her talents embrace the ability to relate her scholarship to school reform by way of her writing, and her determined efforts to facilitate policies that support successful learning for students regardless of their background. Darling-Hammond has provided educators and policy-makers with the leadership and insight needed for schools to be seen as democratic communities, resulting in a 'more just and equitable society' (Lieberman, 2001: 289).

One of the most significant policy documents she was involved in was as the Director of the National Commission on Teaching and America's Future, which maintained the need to generate educational policies that would reinforce innovative pedagogies and professional practices. The Commission (NCTAF) report was published in 1996 and her own book, *The Right to Learn: A Blueprint for Creating Schools That Work*, which related to her work on the Commission, was published in 2001. Both the report and Darling-Hammond's companion book were very well received by educators. The report offered the country a proposal for rethinking the manner in which teachers and school leaders were recruited, prepared, supported and inducted. Educators throughout the United States were enthused by its brief but forthright recommendations:

- get serious about standards, for both students and teachers;
- reinvent **teacher preparation** and professional development;
- fix teacher recruitment and put qualified teachers in every classroom;
- encourage and reward teacher knowledge and skill;
- create schools that are organized for student and teacher success.

(Lieberman, 2001: 288)

Her book *The Right to Learn: A Blueprint for Creating Schools That Work* (2001a) augmented the findings of the report in that it explored the research practice involved in the production of the Commission report, the possible policies to be implemented and the rationale behind creating a more democratic system of schools. The outcomes of the report still remain the basis for her ideas for educational reform.

Darling-Hammond has fought to foster the notion of **teacher professionalism**. She has spurned the use of older mechanistic, tick-box methods in teacher assessment and evaluation for a more rigorous and professional set of teaching standards. Darling-Hammond has worked closely with many schools and school authorities in the United

States in her research into educational policy. Disturbed by the poor state of many urban public schools, she was inspired to become an activist in enhancing teacher professionalism and championing the cause of students from disadvantaged backgrounds. As a new teacher, she acknowledged that she was inadequately equipped for teaching. Furthermore, she considered that the 'factory model' schools she taught in had an unequal allocation of resources and funding, and the paucity of assistance for teachers' development was discouraging (Amrein-Beardsley, 2011).

Overall, Darling-Hammond's interests and work have focused on education policy, teaching and assessment, and teacher professionalism and education. She has forged an extraordinary career path that encompasses two apparently opposing standpoints – that of social activist/researcher and policy-maker (Lieberman, 2001). To appreciate how she reconciled and managed to blend these two seemingly conflicting positions, we need to have an understanding of her upbringing, and her progress in academia and her role in educational policy.

DARLING-HAMMOND, THE PERSON

Linda Darling-Hammond was born in Cleveland, Ohio, in 1951. She came from a working-class family and when she was a young child the family moved home several times so that the children could attend what the parents thought were better schools. During the 1950s and 1960s, schools in Cleveland were supported to offer students greater choice, and problem-solving activities and project work were encouraged at the expense of rote learning. The curriculum movement of the 1960s appealed to teachers to consider realistic methods of teaching that offered learners the opportunity to experience authentic experiences, such as being an engineer, geographer or scientist. Darling-Hammond was an excellent student who benefited from a progressive educational system and the interaction of considerate and skilful teachers. She was the first woman in her family to go to college; she was also one of the first women to attend Yale University. Although she attributed her own experience of public education as the inspiration to become a teacher, it was during her time at Yale that she noticed the very dissimilar schooling experiences of her fellow students, many of whom had had a private education (Lieberman, 2001; Amrein-Beardsley, 2011).

Furthermore, while she was at university, the United States was embroiled in the Vietnam War and protest rallies were staged on many university campuses; it was also a time of an increasingly active civil rights movement. University, then, for Darling-Hammond was a potent experience of protest and fostered a growing awareness of the inequities in social justice. She knew from her own education that life prospects could be determined by having entry into a quality educational experience; the matter of universal access to quality education was to be at the heart of her future work. Despite the distractions of protests during her undergraduate years, she was a hard-working student who graduated from Yale in 1973 with distinction. Following this, she trained as a public school teacher and became a student teacher in a large urban school in Camden, New Jersey, an experience that further strengthened her conviction of the inequities of the public school system. She achieved her doctorate in urban education from Temple University in 1978 (Lieberman, 2001; Banks, 2010).

Apart from leading the NCTAF, Darling-Hammond has been involved in numerous research and policy-making organisations such as The American Educational Research Association, the National Board for Professional Teaching Standards and the National Academy of Education. She has also been a member of the White House Advisory Panel's Resource Group for the National Education Goals and the Foundation for the Advancement of Teaching (Darling-Hammond, 2010). She was also the leader of President Obama's education policy transition team. She was seen by some as a probable choice for the Secretary of Education position in President Obama's new government. However, this idea was of concern to many politicians who were in favour of corporate-type educational reforms. They thought Darling-Hammond was a champion of teacher professionalism, a close ally of the teacher unions, a supporter of teacher tenure and a critic of the fast-track teacher education programme Teach for America (Sadovnik et al., 2013). She has written extensively, including both journal articles and books. Apart from *The Right to Learn: A Blueprint for Creating Schools That Work* in 2001, some of her other major works include *Authentic Assessment and School Development*, with Ancess, in 1994; *Powerful Teacher Education: Lessons from Exemplary Programs* (2006); *Preparing Teachers for a Changing World: What Teachers Should Learn and Be Able to Do*, with Bransford, in 2005; and in 2010, *The Flat World and Education: How America's Commitment to Equity Will Determine Our Future*. All of these works and others set out her ideas.

DARLING-HAMMOND AND HER IDEAS OF AN EQUITABLE EDUCATIONAL SYSTEM, TEACHERS AND TEACHING

Darling-Hammond's ideas evolve from her drive for an education system that has social justice at its core. Although the themes of her work are very much interrelated in seeking an equitable education for all, this section will first briefly explore the challenges faced by the public education system in the United States; then broadly consider the aspects of educational policy related to and championed by her; examine her thoughts on teacher professionalism and teacher education; and finally, appraise her notions of student-centred teaching and assessment.

There is an overriding view that the corporate model of schooling in the United States affects most aspects of education: teaching practice, curriculum content and many features of education reform and subsequent policies. Those who promote such corporate school models also advocate privatisation and the deregulation of schools; they 'imagine public schools as private businesses, districts [education authorities] as markets, students as consumers, and knowledge as a product' (Saltman, 2012: 674).

Darling-Hammond paints a gloomy picture of the state secondary schools in urban areas:

> Schools are huge warehouses, with three thousand or more students. They are focused substantially on the control of behaviour rather than the development of community. With a locker as their only stable point of contact, a schedule that cycles them through a series of seven to ten overloaded teachers ... Most students are likely to experience such high schools, heavily stratified within and substantially dehumanised throughout, as non-caring or even adversarial environments. (1997: 333)

This perception of education which associates schools with markets she terms the 'factory conception of the school' (Darling-Hammond, 2010: 62). This resonates with Coffield and Williamson's concept of the market turning UK schools, colleges and universities into skills factories; instead, they offer an alternative which, like Darling-Hammond, calls for **collaboration** and cooperation, which they refer to as 'communities of discovery'. Communities of discovery means that students and teachers work collectively and democratically to enhance their creativity (Coffield and Williamson, 2012).

Unlike many other developed countries, the United States does not have nationalised healthcare or housing support systems. In other developed countries, children are, for the most part, well supported by society as a whole; should it be needed, assistance is provided by the government for meals, healthcare and housing. This social support is not so evident in the United States and, as a result, much of the funding which is allocated to schools, particularly in urban areas, is spent on food, healthcare and other aspects of social welfare assistance. Schools also pay healthcare benefits for teachers. Unlike the United States, in most other developed countries school funding is mainly dedicated to educational purposes (Collier, 2011).

Recognising that the state of public schools in many areas of the United States is frightful, Darling-Hammond in her 2010 book *The Flat World and Education: How America's Commitment to Equity Will Determine Our Future* calls for quality and equality in genuine school reform. In doing so, she argues for a new model in educational policy formation, both nationally and in individual states. This new model should be driven by the dual assurances that it will '*support meaningful learning* on the part of students, teachers, and schools, and ... *equalize access to education opportunity*, making it possible for all students to profit from more productive schools' (Darling-Hammond, 2010: 279). From the premise of these two assurances, she explores her vision of the ideal educational policy. She states that the policy should contain five key elements:

1. *Meaningful learning goals*: These learning goals should equip students with the knowledge and skills for success, using new and inventive methods of learning, and also by giving responsibility to schools to manage the curriculum and assessment so they have control in monitoring and enhancing student and teacher progress.

2. *Intelligent, reciprocal accountability systems*: this includes creating systems which assure that students will experience good teaching and have a variety of learning opportunities. The systems will also involve processes for evaluating teaching, learning and the curriculum.

3. *Equitable and adequate resources*: Funding to enable all students to meet the learning standards and have the opportunities for success. This will also include a fair system for the availability of well-trained teachers through the setting up of an organisation for the recruitment and preparation of all teachers.

4. *Strong professional standards and support*: this will ensure that all teachers have access to excellent teacher education and mentoring during their career. It should also include the opportunity for teachers to develop their own education, both practical and academic.

5. *Schools organised for student and teacher learning*: Intended to allow greater freedom for groups of teachers to have a say in designing curriculum content, this element envisages a collaborative approach in creating innovative teaching methods and realistic assessments of students' performance.

(Darling-Hammond, 2010)

Further to these key elements of a new model of education policy, Darling-Hammond also argues that students' basic needs should also be provided for, such as food, health and housing, so that when they arrive at school, they can focus on learning rather than just existing. She contends that the US education system will continue to be neglected at a huge cost to society if policy is not revitalised to equalise access to high-quality schooling. 'The path to our mutual well-being is built on educational opportunity ... and an unquestionable entitlement [to] a rich and inalienable right to learn' (Darling-Hammond, 2010: 328).

It was Darling-Hammond's experiences with other policy-makers, her engagement with schools in New York City and her work with Teachers College at Columbia University that gave her the chance and stimulus to reflect on how to create robust structures to promote and sustain a strong base for teacher professionalism. Such structures would amalgamate teacher education, 'ongoing professional development in collegial settings and a system of professional accountability' (Lieberman, 2001: 288). According to Darling-Hammond, teacher professionalism needs to be embedded into new and reformed educational policies that clearly specify what teaching is and the manner in which schools are structured to enable teaching to take place. This, she argues, should contain three core categories:

(1) Policies governing entry and continuation in the profession; (2) policies and practices defining what teachers do in schools and classrooms; (3) policies governing how – and by whom – decisions about professional membership and teaching practices are made. (Darling-Hammond, 1990: 33)

Apart from the need to embed professionalism into new educational policy reform, she outlines her own definition of professionalism where

> members of an occupation share a common body of knowledge and shared standards of practice in exercising that knowledge on behalf of clients. It incorporates conditions of specialized knowledge, collective self-regulation, special attention to the unique needs of clients, autonomous performance and a large dose of responsibility. (Darling-Hammond, 1990: 32)

A large element of teacher professionalism for Darling-Hammond is teacher education. She has championed the cause of high-quality teacher education, arguing that well-trained teachers are vital to student success. She has also lamented the fact that the United States, unlike other high-attaining countries, has not yet formed a vigorous and widely accepted structure for teacher education which ensures that all new teachers are well prepared for the classroom. Moreover, the teacher education curriculum had changed little in decades. Many of the programmes appeared to be training for skills acquisition, rather than being an education in the sense of an induction into the teaching profession. What appears to be missing in these programmes are the notions of 'teachers as critical inquirers, of schools as centres of reflective practice, as educators as moral agents, and of schools as places for both equitable and excellent education' (Sirotnik, 1990: 318). Answering a series of questions regarding what makes effective teacher preparation practices, she reiterates a cliché to stress the importance of the link between theory and practice: 'there's nothing as practical as a good theory, and there is nothing as theoretical as good practice' (Darling-Hammond, 2001b). She also found that the states that lowered the teacher education training requirements, particularly for those entrants who were to teach in low-income and minority schools, had received:

> little training in areas such as child development and learning; how to construct curriculum and develop assessments; how to teach reading, mathematics, or other subjects; how to manage a classroom productively; and how to teach special education students or those learning English for the first time. (Darling-Hammond, 2010: 45)

Darling-Hammond has also been an advocate for a standardised and thorough form of student teacher recruitment, teacher induction, teacher tenure, meaningful and recognised teacher certification and ongoing professional development (Darling-Hammond, 2012).

The involvement of and collaboration with universities in teacher education is seen as crucial by Darling-Hammond in producing highly capable and professional teachers. She contests that, especially in today's complex and diverse society, teachers need an in-depth education, both practically and academically, to cope and succeed in classrooms. She maintains that teachers need to 'teach for understanding and to teach for diversity ... to understand subject matter in ways that allow them to organize it so that students can create useful cognitive maps of terrain' (Darling-Hammond, 1999: 13). Teachers also need to evaluate and reflect on their own practice, and consider and learn innovative pedagogies and forms of assessment. They also need to know how to motivate, research information, and keep up with new technologies and curriculum changes. All these aspects of becoming a professionally educated and competent teacher involve experiencing practice in the classroom which is underpinned by a theoretical framework in collaboration with universities (Darling-Hammond, 1999). A core element for all aspects of teacher professionalism is collaboration: collaboration between teachers, school mentors and with students in teaching and assessments.

Darling-Hammond considers collaboration between educators to be fundamental to the fostering of high-quality teaching and assessment practice which would benefit all students. Such collaboration is evident in the manner in which teaching and assessment is modelled and shared in **Professional Development Schools** (PDSs). The PDSs are small urban schools that become principal sites of best teaching practice and teacher education. Darling-Hammond was involved in implementing the PDSs and promoting their work. New teachers in the profession were partnered with accomplished practitioners where they learnt through rigorous supervision and reflection about advanced teaching and assessment methods. The whole setting of the PDS 'is organized around teacher learning as much as it's organized around student learning' (Darling-Hammond, 2001b). Within this environment accomplished teachers also acted as a nexus between PDSs and universities, which not only enabled close links to be made between practice and theory, but also offered opportunities for practitioner-based research, ideas that Darling-Hammond campaigned for (Hagger and McIntyre, 2006).

Darling-Hammond advocates the notion of equitable and democratic schools and the practice of child-centred teaching. For her, such schools are environments where students are encouraged to 'own their own learning, to become efficacious in pursuing their own goals by helping others to participate in building a healthier and more just society' (Darling-Hammond, 2013: xii). Her vision of these schools includes the notion that students take part in challenging and real-life learning activities that involve problem solving. Also, that these schools foster trusting relationships between teachers, students and the students' families, as well as with the local community. Rather than being overburdened with the preoccupation with test scores and school league tables, her idea of school is one where students experience support, encouragement, self-worth and an enthusiasm for learning. These schools are also places where students have opportunities to show their understanding and learning with the use of diverse and authentic methods of assessment (Darling-Hammond, 2013).

These authentic assessments are, for Darling-Hammond, a needed alternative to the standardised testing systems employed by many schools. Standardised testing, she argues, has hindered the learning opportunities for both lower and higher ability learners. The tests themselves have deterred teachers from trying to develop their students' deeper learning 'skills by having them conduct experiments, make oral presentations, write extensively, and do other sorts of intellectually challenging activities' that stimulate the curiosity for learning (Darling-Hammond, 2014: 6). She promotes the notion of **performance assessments**. This allows students to demonstrate the more developmental and higher-order intellectual levels of learning, rather than the regurgitation of facts or the recognition of possible right answers evident in much of the standardised testing. 'Performance assessment must construct an answer, produce a product, or perform an activity' (Darling-Hammond, 2013: 15). Bloom's taxonomy is the concept underpinning performance assessment. Students progress through the mastery levels of knowledge, understanding and application to the higher-order or developmental levels of analysis and synthesis to evaluation (Bloom, 1956). The use of performance assessment in schools, she argues, would also enable the United States to develop the required skills and knowledge to compete with other developing nations (Darling-Hammond, 2014).

Overall, her ideas are closely linked with other educational thinkers, particularly those whose concepts focus on democracy, equity, collaboration, teacher professionalism and teacher education.

LINKS WITH OTHER THEORISTS

Darling-Hammond's notion of an equitable and democratic education is very much in tune with John Dewey. He challenged the older traditional methods of teaching and learning in favour of a more child-centred approach to practice. Dewey also stressed the significance of schools as collaborative environments, which should structure the curriculum to meet the needs of students in preparing them for the real world. There is also a striking parallel between his Chicago Laboratory School and Darling-Hammond's involvement in the PDSs. Dewey used the Laboratory School 'as a force for changing our existing schools and school systems' (Sarason, 1990: 66). There are also close links between Lave and Wenger and their socially situated learning and communities of practice, and Darling-Hammond's notion of the importance of collaboration in the process of learning for students and teachers. For them, like Darling-Hammond and her championing of the PDSs, true learning involves a communal experience where people learn from their more experienced colleagues. Learning, therefore, becomes an active process where knowledge and skills are accomplished and refined, which is very fitting for practice-based professions such as teaching.

Darling-Hammond's views on innovative and challenging learning activities, which are embedded in the social and cultural background of the students, are associated with Freire's notion of problem-posing learning. The foundation of all Freire's work is also based on aspects of equity and social justice. In the same vein as Darling-Hammond fighting for equity for the students in urban schools, Freire also argued for meaningful educational opportunities for those he considered were the *oppressed* (Freire, 1970 [1996]). Another educationalist who has strong connections with the notions of Darling-Hammond is Lawrence Stenhouse and his ideas of professionalism, the active engagement of teachers in curriculum research and design, and the benefits of forming collaborative partnerships between schools and university departments of education. His model of extended teacher professionalism resonates with what Darling-Hammond advocates for practitioners working actively and collegiately to improve and develop their practices. His idea behind the Centre for Applied Research in Education (CARE) at the University of East Anglia is aligned with the PDSs, as both afforded opportunities for teachers to be active researchers of their own practice in classrooms and to become involved with collaborative projects between schools and universities (Stenhouse, 1975). Darling-Hammond's notion of performance assessment is based on the concept of Benjamin Bloom's taxonomy where learners pass through the mastery stages of knowledge, understanding and application, then on to the more developmental stages of analysis, synthesis and evaluation. Another contemporary kindred spirit was John Goodlad, a leading educator who had, like Darling-Hammond, an alternative concept of what education should be, based on notions of ethics, social justice and democracy. Goodlad (1984 [2004]) also strove to convince both teachers and policy-makers to adopt his progressive ideas in education and create schools as better places for students to learn. There are also similarities with Michael Apple, who, like Darling-Hammond, advanced the notion of equitable schooling and raising the profile of teacher professionalism. Even though Darling-Hammond's ideas are in tune with other educationalists who strive for social justice, some of her ideas have attracted levels of censure.

⊛ CRITIQUING HER IDEAS

There are two major themes of criticism regarding Darling-Hammond's work: the first is to do with the practical aspects of her policy ideas and practice, and the second relates to her socio-political stance. The practical aspects involve concerns about cost, matters of accountability and the sustainability of her ideas for school reform, and the enhancement of teacher professionalism. It is considered that these ideas would create 'expense, unclear lines of authority and confusion' (Darling-Hammond, 1990: 43). Her idea of schools being given more autonomy might lead to damaging educational decisions being made; also, collaborative decision-making may not be a practical option as 'ultimately, no one will be in charge, and chaos will reign' (Darling-Hammond, 1990: 45). Furthermore, the high staff ratio needed to support new entrants to the teaching profession in the PDSs is a somewhat idealistic concept that is neither cost-effective nor sustainable for all schools or even all urban schools (Sarason, 1990).

There is also some disquiet on the topic of performance assessment; this concerns matters of cost, technical issues, and the demands upon teachers and students.

Performance assessment has also attracted criticism because of anxiety about its trust-worthiness, in particular around aspects of the reliability and validity of what is being assessed. Many of those teachers who have been involved in performance assessment have voiced their concerns. These concerns relate to whether performance assessment actually assesses the learning that it is meant to, and to what extent consistency of assessment is achieved between schools, assessors, students and assessment activities (Darling-Hammond, 2014).

The second theme of criticism is associated with her socio-political viewpoint. It is suggested that despite her impassioned ideas for improving the public schooling system, she has failed to address and challenge the underlying causes at the root of the educational inequity in the United States. These are fundamental 'problems and struggles that are inextricably bound up with the intersection of cultural politics and political economy' (Saltman, 2012: 680). According to Saltman, Darling-Hammond should have adopted Giroux's critical pedagogical approach to her work, which would explore the deeper struggles of class and culture which are blighting the educational opportunities for students in urban schools. Furthermore, he suggests that Darling-Hammond

> accepts the neoliberal framing of public schooling as principally serving the ends of global economic competition ... education is for competition in a corporate-dominated capitalist economy; the goal of schools is to include more students into the existing social order, not to produce critical citizens who can challenge and transform that order. (Saltman, 2012: 681)

From this point of view, Darling-Hammond has not challenged the political and class injustices that are embedded in the public school system; rather, she has cooperated with the system. Regardless of these criticisms, there are aspects of her ideas that can be embraced in both the way we think about education and the manner in which professionals work in schools.

APPLYING DARLING-HAMMOND'S IDEAS IN PRACTICE

After briefly exploring Darling-Hammond's thoughts on successful schooling and teaching, this section will consider her ideas for collaboration, including how they can be applied in teacher evaluation and induction, engaging students in learning, and finally performance assessment. For Darling-Hammond, the best schools are those that create structures that empower teachers to get to know their children and the children's families. These schools are also places that build close relationships between students and teachers. In such schools, she argues, students not only attain higher grades, but they become more confident about themselves as people (Darling-Hammond, 1997). She contends that there is a clear correlation between successful schools and successful teaching. For this to happen, teachers must have both the knowledge about teaching and learning needed to manage the complex process of getting diverse students to learn well and the discretion to practice variability rather than routinely. Successful education can occur only if teachers are prepared to meet rigorous learning demands *and* the different needs of the students ... Teachers must be able to develop learning experiences that accommodate a variety of cognitive styles, with activities that broaden rather than reduce the range of possibilities for learning. They must understand child development and pedagogy as well as the structures of subject areas and a variety of alternatives for assessing learning. (Darling-Hammond, 1997: 335)

Successful teaching, she argues, is associated with the creation of collaborative and democratic opportunities where students can learn from each other in small group work activities. Darling-Hammond contested that many learners, even when working in groups, are still somewhat passive receivers of teaching. Harkin et al. (2001) argued that to ensure that classrooms are more participative they should be environments that model democracy. To create this model, teachers need to concede 'there is more that unites people than divides us and that the basis of this fundamental unity lies in communicative language use, as distinct from the language used for domination' (Harkin et al., 2001: 142). Collaboration is also at the heart of her thinking when she advances her notions of teacher development and professionalism.

She advocates the use of 'team teaching' where instead of one teacher being responsible for large groups of students, teachers share the task. This form of collaboration offers a number of possibilities, such as supervision opportunities, sharing ideas for lesson planning and teaching methods, and developing approaches for meeting the needs of individual students (Darling-Hammond, 1990). Such practice also allows teachers to work with other practitioners to help solve problems and develop skills together in supportive and progressive teaching communities. Successful schools which have robust teaching communities have a shared agreement concerning classroom practice and how to take practice further (Collier, 2011). By teachers working together in this manner, they are much better placed to share their knowledge of individual students with one another and, if appropriate, relay that knowledge to the student's family. In this way, 'the rewards of teacher communities go beyond individual teachers to benefit students, families, and society as a whole' (Collier, 2011: 14). Furthermore, by forming partnerships with university education departments, akin to the practice with the PDSs, teachers would broaden their collaboration network and develop their practitioner research skills.

Darling-Hammond extends her notion of collaboration for use in teacher induction and teacher evaluation. Induction of new entrants into the teaching profession usually means a series of lesson observations as a form of periodic evaluation of the inductee's skills in classroom practice. These evaluations are in the form of mechanistic checklists that record to what extent the teaching and learning standards were met, or not met, by the inductee. This process is then followed by a brief post-lesson feedback discussion between the inductee and the observer. This process, she argues, is not ideal and she offers an alternative practice. Her idea is that induction should be a process where inductees have mentoring by

> expert, experienced practitioners who have substantial time to provide continuous supervision to new practitioners, helping them learn to make the thousands of important decisions that a teacher must confront every day. This function can be best performed by mentor teachers providing expertise specific to the subject area, or grade level taught. (Darling-Hammond, 1990: 36)

This method of evaluation can also be employed for qualified teachers, and is very evident in highly successful collaborative settings. This takes the form of the evaluation of lessons through peer review. Teachers observe each other's teaching to highlight possible difficulties and share classroom practice. The openness of the process of peer review, she argues, enhances teaching practice 'by decreasing teacher isolation and providing directly relevant opportunities for professional growth' (Darling-Hammond, 1990: 42).

Although the focus of Darling-Hammond and Ifill-Lynch's 2006 article concerned encouraging secondary age students to engage in homework, it also provides a number of practical *and* stimulating ideas that can be applied to engaging students in the classroom as well. They found that many of the students who did not engage in set tasks were unsure of what was required of them. They set out a series of applied ideas that teachers could use to encourage students to engage with their school work. These include suggestions for how practitioners can facilitate engagement:

1. *Give students work that is worth the effort*: Allocate tasks which are based on real life, and topics which students are interested in. Long-term projects which students become deeply involved in are productive activities.
2. *Set work which is achievable*: Give clear directions as to the needs for completing tasks, including how the task relates to the learning outcomes. Ensure feedback from the task is timely, and developmental in nature.
3. *Discover what the students need*: Endeavour to create challenging and meaningful tasks which meet individual student's needs by finding out what their aspirations are, and how they are best motivated; then implement individual learning plans to enable learning to take place.
4. *Allocate the time and space*: Be flexible with creating learning opportunities by using spaces such as libraries and by the use of classrooms during break times; if appropriate allow time extensions for students to complete tasks.
5. *Disseminate students' work*: Display the work of students that meets the required standards to demonstrate to others that such tasks are achievable. This also enables students at differing levels to work together to encourage peer tutoring and social collaboration.

(Darling-Hammond and Ifill-Lynch, 2006)

This final suggestion of displaying and disseminating students' work can also be used as part of performance assessment. Students' projects can be exhibited and presented to a panel for assessment; this panel could include members of the local community, fellow students and teachers. Students who exhibit their work have the opportunity to talk, use multimedia or display products and portfolios that have been created as part of their projects. According to Darling-Hammond,

> As students repeatedly develop and revise projects and exhibitions evaluated according to rigorous standards, they internalize standards of quality and develop college- and career-ready skills of planning, resourcefulness, perseverance, a capacity to use feedback productively, a wide range of communication skills, and a growth mind-set for learning – all of which extend beyond the individual assignments themselves in shaping their ability to learn in new contexts. (2014: 29)

Apart from these methods, performance assessment uses a wide range of tools that include 'completing a sentence with a few words (short answer), to writing a thorough analysis (essay), to conducting and analyzing a laboratory investigation (hands-on)' (Darling-Hammond, 2014: 15). In summary, performance assessment can be used to appraise what students can achieve using what they know. Moreover, with the experience of conducting performance assessment teachers become better informed regarding their own teaching, as well as more familiar with the learning needs of their students (Darling-Hammond, 2014).

Darling-Hammond's ideas are very much related to schooling and teaching in the context of the US educational system. However, it is maintained that many of her ideas for teacher evaluation, collaborative practice, engaging children in learning and performance assessment can be adapted by practitioners outside the United States.

REFLECTIVE TASK

Darling-Hammond contends that 'effective schools ... are those that create structures for caring ... that enable close, sustained relationships among students and teachers' (Darling-Hammond, 1997: 333).

Reflecting on your own experiences of school, college or university:

1. List the structures or opportunities that were/are in place to enable and foster such close relationships.
2. What other structures or opportunities could be added to the above to strengthen these relationships?

SUMMARY

Darling-Hammond remains one of the most influential champions for educational reform in the United States. Her work spans a number of areas, but it is her quest for parity in the public school sector that stands out, particularly for children in urban areas. She has been involved in many persuasive and significant national educational policy initiatives as a social activist and policy-maker, where she sought to move away from the corporate model of schooling towards a more equitable model. Her prominence as a reformer and policy-maker was recognised when she was appointed to lead President Obama's education policy transition team. Within this drive for more equitable education, she advocated a much deeper notion of teacher professionalism, which included a more robust teacher education that combined both the practical and intellectual aspects of being a teacher. At the heart of the idea of teacher professionalism is collaboration – between teachers, between teachers and university staff, and between teachers and students. Darling-Hammond's view is that teaching should be interactive and involve project work, problem solving and be connected to the real world. She also advanced the idea of performance assessment as an alternative to standardised testing.

Darling-Hammond's ideas have similarities with other educationalists, especially those who have stood up for a democratic and equitable education, as well as those who supported the call for teacher professionalism and collaboration. These include Dewey's ideas of schools being democratic and collaborative environments; there are also close associations between his Chicago Laboratory School and Darling-Hammond's involvement with PDSs. There is further evidence of links with Lave and Wenger's socially situated learning and communities of practice, with her call for collaboration. Her idea that teaching should involve real-life problem solving is also associated with Freire's notion of problem-posing learning. Her interest in teacher professionalism and teacher education have resonance with Lawrence Stenhouse and John Goodlad. There are also similarities with Michael Apple who also called for more equitable schooling, and in raising teacher professionalism. Furthermore, her notion, and the process, of performance assessment is aligned with Bloom's taxonomy. There are criticisms of her works, which are based on practical and socio-political issues. The practical issues are around cost, accountability and that her ideas are not sustainable for all schools. The disquiet about socio-political issues relates to her not addressing the root causes of the inequity in schooling, such as struggles of class and culture which impair equal opportunities for all students.

Despite these criticisms, there are a number of her ideas that can be put into practice in schools and classrooms for the benefit of students, teachers' professional development and the community. These include seeking opportunities for collaborative practice, using more problem solving and group projects in teaching, and finally, by raising the profile of using alternative forms of assessment which are authentic and measure all-round performance in students' learning.

GLOSSARY OF TERMS

Collaboration   Darling-Hammond thought that collaboration between educators, school mentors, students, and extended to parents and the community, was vital in the fostering of meaningful and high-quality teaching, learning and assessment practice. Collaboration with university teacher education programmes she felt produced highly competent and professional teachers who would engage with theory to develop their classroom practice. Such collaboration involved sharing ideas and resources about teaching and assessment through teacher mentoring schemes, all of which she maintains will enable teachers to grow as practitioners and as academics. These forms and processes of sharing partnerships are very evident in Professional Development Schools.

Performance assessment   Unlike standardised assessment that relies on the mechanistic reiteration of facts and the identification of possible correct answers, Darling-Hammond promoted the use of performance assessment which lets students show development and a higher level of learning. Performance assessment is based on the concept of Bloom's taxonomy where learners pass through the mastery stages of knowledge, understanding and application, then move on to the more developmental stages of analysis, synthesis and evaluation (Bloom, 1956). She is quite explicit about the process of performance assessment in that it 'must construct an answer, produce a product, or perform an activity' (Darling-Hammond, 2013: 15).

Professional Development Schools   Professional Development Schools (PDSs) grow into major sites of best teaching and assessment practice, as well as teacher education. It is in these PDSs that collaboration thrives, and where teaching and assessment methods are modelled and shared for the benefit of the learner in the classroom, and the enhancement of teaching practice. New teachers are partnered and supervised by veteran and accomplished teachers to develop, with the aid of reflection, highly developed teaching and assessment strategies. These veteran teachers also act as a link between the universities which help connect theory with practice and encourage practitioner-based research.

Teacher preparation and teacher education   For Darling-Hammond, high-quality teacher preparation and teacher education were paramount in providing meaningful student learning in schools. She argued for a standardised and recognised teacher certification, as well as for more robust forms of student–teacher recruitment and selection processes, better teacher induction programmes, secure teacher tenure of employment and the provision of progressive professional development opportunities for teachers, all of which she contests are crucial for ensuring that new teachers are well prepared for the classroom, and also important in helping to improve teacher retention in the profession.

Teacher professionalism   Darling-Hammond promoted embedding teacher professionalism in education reform policies; these, she argued, should include policies regarding recruitment into the profession, policies about teachers' practice and policies relating to decisions made about professional membership. Her own notions of teacher professionalism included collaborating and sharing knowledge and standards of practice, gaining specialised subject and pedagogic understanding, demonstrating responsibility and autonomy, using self-regulation, and in particular paying attention to the needs of the learners. Furthermore, she calls for a more reflective research-informed profession where experience is reinforced by theoretical structures, in collaboration with universities (Darling-Hammond, 1999).

FURTHER READING

Darling-Hammond, L. (ed.) (2010) *Next Generation Assessment: Moving Beyond the Bubble Test to Support 21st Century Learning*. San Francisco, CA: Jossey Bass.
A comprehensive review of assessment in the United States which argues for the adoption of performance testing that measures the higher order cognitive skills, instead of large-scale standardised testing.

Goodwin, A. (ed.) (1997) *Assessment for Equity and Inclusion: Embracing All Our Children*. London: Routledge.
Very much aligned with Darling-Hammond's ideas, this text challenges the use of standardised testing and offers inclusive alternatives for a diverse range of students.

Osguthorpe, R., Harris, R., Fox Harris, M. and Black, S. (eds) (1995) *Partner Schools: Centers for Educational Renewal*. San Francisco, CA: Jossey Bass.
This book explores the positive opportunities for teacher education and development that arise when schools and universities become full partners in striving for educational renewal.

REFERENCES

Amrein-Beardsley, A. (2011) *Interview with Linda Darling-Hammond*. Available online at: http://insidetheacademy.asu.edu/linda-darling-hammond
Banks, J. (2010) 'Foreword'. In: Darling-Hammond, L. (ed.) *The Flat World and Education: How America's Commitment to Equity Will Determine Our Future*. New York: Teachers College Press.
Bloom, B. (ed.) (1956) *Taxonomy of Educational Objectives: Cognitive Domain*, Vol. 1. London: Longman.
Coffield, F. and Williamson, B. (2012) *From Exam Factories to Communities of Democracy: The Democratic Route*. London: Institute of Education, University of London.
Collier, L. (2011) 'The need for teacher communities: An interview with Linda Darling-Hammond'. *The Council Chronicle*, November: 12–14.
Darling-Hammond, L. (1990) 'Teacher professionalism: Why and how'. In: Lieberman, A. (ed.) *Schools as Collaborative Cultures: Creating the Future Now*. London: Falmer Press.
Darling-Hammond, L. (1997) 'Restructuring schools and student success'. In: Halsey, A., Lauder, H., Brown, P. and Stuart Wells, A. (eds) *Education: Culture, Economy, Society*. Oxford: Oxford University Press.

Darling-Hammond, L. (1999) 'The case for university-based teacher education'. In: Roth, R. (ed.) *The Role of the University in the Preparation of Teachers*. London: Falmer Press.

Darling-Hammond, L. (2001a) *The Right to Learn: A Blueprint for Creating Schools that Work*. San Francisco, CA: Jossey Bass.

Darling-Hammond, L. (2001b) *Linda Darling-Hammond's Thoughts on Teacher Preparation*. Available online at: http://edutopia.org/linda-darlinh-hammond-teacherpreparation

Darling-Hammond, L. (2006) *Powerful Teacher Education: Lessons from Exemplary Programs*. San Francisco, CA: Jossey Bass.

Darling-Hammond, L. (2010) *The Flat World and Education: How America's Commitment to Equity Will Determine Our Future*. New York: Teachers College Press.

Darling-Hammond, L. (2012) 'The right start: Creating a strong foundation for the teaching career'. *Phi Delta Kappan*, 94 (3): 8–13.

Darling-Hammond, L. (2013) 'Foreword'. In: Steele, D. and Cohn-Vargas, B. (eds) *Identity Safe Classrooms*. Thousand Oaks, CA: Corwin.

Darling-Hammond, L. (ed.) (2014) *Next Generation Assessment: Moving Beyond the Bubble Test to Support 21st Century Learning*. San Francisco, CA: Jossey Bass.

Darling-Hammond, L. and Ancess, J. (1994) *Authentic Assessment and School Development*. New York: National Center for Restructuring Education, Schools, and Teaching, Teachers College, Columbia University.

Darling-Hammond, L. and Bransford, J. (2005) *Preparing Teachers for a Changing World: What Teachers Should Learn and Be Able to Do*. San Francisco, CA: Jossey Bass.

Darling-Hammond, L. and Ifill-Lynch, O. (2006) 'If they'd only do their work!' *Educational Leadership*, 63 (5): 8–13.

Freire, P. (1970 [1996]) *Pedagogy of the Oppressed*. London: Penguin.

Goodlad, J. (1984 [2004]) *A Place Called School*. New York: McGraw-Hill.

Hagger, H. and McIntyre, D. (2006) *Learning Teaching from Teachers: Realizing the Potential of School-based Teacher Education*. Maidenhead: Open University Press.

Harkin, J., Turner, G. and Dawn, T. (2001) *Teaching Young Adults: A Handbook for Teachers in Post-Compulsory Education*. London: RoutledgeFalmer.

Liebermann, A. (2001) 'Linda Darling-Hammond, 1951–'. In: Palmer, J. (ed.) *Fifty Modern Thinkers on Education: From Piaget to the Present*. London: Routledge.

National Commission on Teaching and America's Future (NCTAF) (1996) *What Matters Most: Teaching for America's Future*. New York: NCTAF.

Sadovnik, A., Cookson, P. and Semel, S. (eds) (2013) *Exploring Education: An Introduction to the Foundations of Education* (4th edn). London: Routledge.

Saltman, K. (2012) 'Why Henry Giroux's democratic pedagogy is crucial for confronting failed corporate school reform and how liberals like Ravitch and Darling-Hammond are making things worse'. *Policy Futures in Education*, 10 (6): 674–87.

Sarason, S. (1990) 'What are schools of education for?' In: Lieberman, A. (ed.) *Schools as Collaborative Cultures: Creating the Future Now*. London: Falmer Press.

Sirotnik, K. (1990) 'Society, schooling, teaching, and preparing to teach'. In: Goodlad, J., Soder, R. and Sirotnik, K. (eds) *The Moral Dimensions of Teaching*. San Francisco, CA: Jossey-Bass.

Stenhouse, L. (1975) *An Introduction to Curriculum Research*. London: Heinemann.

INDEX

CPSIA information can be obtained
at www.ICGtesting.com
Printed in the USA
JSHW012351230822
29477JS00005B/20